FOUR THERAPEUTIC APPROACHES TO THE BORDERLINE PATIENT
Principles and Techniques of the Basic Dynamic Stances

Andrew B. Druck, Ph.D.

JASON ARONSON INC.
Northvale, New Jersey
London

Library of Congress Cataloging-in-Publication Data

Druck, Andrew B.
    Four therapeutic approaches to the borderline patient /
Andrew B. Druck.
        p.   cm.
    Bibliography: p.
    Includes index.
    ISBN 0-87668-963-2
    1. Borderline personality disorder—Treatment.   2. Psychoanalysis.
I. Title.
    [DNLM: 1. Personality Disorders.   2. Psychoanalytic Theory.
3. Psychoanalytic Therapy.   WM 460.5.P3 D794a]
RC569.5.B67D78   1989
616.89—dc 19
DNLM/DLC   88-37146
for Library of Congress   CIP

Manufactured in the United States of America. Jason Aronson Inc. offers books and cassettes. For information and catalog write to Jason Aronson Inc., 230 Livingston Street, Northvale, New Jersey 07647.

To Beverly, Danielle, Avigayil, and Tamar

Contents

Testing • Development of the Capacity for
Ambivalence • Structural Consequences of
Splitting • Splitting • Splitting and Repression • Examples of Splitting • Primitive Idealization and Devaluation • Denial and Projective Identification

Part Four

EXPANSION POSSIBILITIES
WITHIN CLASSICAL TECHNIQUE

Preface

This book is about the relationship between theory and technique in clinical work with the more seriously disturbed patient (primarily diagnosed borderline, narcissistic, and psychotic, but also severely character disordered). We explore the ways in which the therapist's underlying theoretical assumptions lead to particular clinical emphases and foreclose other options. Differences in basic assumptions result in major differences in clinical approach.

Despite the polemics among various psychoanalytic theorists, there is much to learn from all of them. The appropriate question is not, Which theory is right? but rather, To what clinical issues can the therapist become more sensitive by understanding a given model? Much of the polarization among psychotherapists is a result of an emphasis on one factor and a relative neglect of others. Since patients can be understood from a number of points of view, a discussion of differences in emphasis is more helpful to the clinician than a debate about ultimate truth.

As we can see in the following example, the therapist's assumptions greatly affect his response.

A therapist is in the last session with a patient, preceding a week-long vacation. The patient has been working on her tendency to forget everything that has been said in a session as soon as she leaves the therapist's office. She has reacted to previous separations from the therapist, some of them quite short, by missing subsequent sessions, binge-eating and vomiting, and developing suicidal thoughts. There is clear evidence of defenses organized around splitting. For example, the patient feels entirely self-sufficient outside the therapist's office, feels helpless and hungry in his office, and cannot affectively connect the two states. She also has difficulty maintaining an internal image of the therapist with which to soothe and regulate herself during the therapist's absence. At this last session, the patient asks the therapist if he thinks about his patients while he is away.

Therapists working with neurotic patients are taught to refrain from answering such a question directly; rather, they are advised to inquire into the patient's associations to the question, to interpret defenses, and then to interpret the underlying transference fantasy. The assumption is that the patient is able to tolerate the frustration inherent in such an approach. This frustration tolerance is one of the factors evaluated in determining whether a patient is analyzable.

Such an approach presents difficulties with this particular patient. If the therapist refrains from answering the patient's question, the inherent frustration in asking the patient to associate further may recapitulate, in the session itself, the therapist's actual absence. This could lead to derivatives in the session of the patient's symptoms of regression outside sessions, including dismissal, panic, tendency toward action, and cognitive difficulties—all of which will make interpretation of the patient's unconscious transference wishes more difficult. For the neurotic patient, answering the question makes interpretation more difficult because it restricts the field for fantasy. With the severely disturbed patient, not answering may threaten the structural preconditions essential for analysis of transference fantasy.

Does the therapist refrain from answering the question and instead ask for associations? Not if he feels that the patient cannot tolerate the delay and will react to his request for further associations with structural regression and acting out. Does the therapist respond first and then ask for associations? That may be preferable at this specific point with this particular patient, because the therapist will minimize frustration and maximize the possibility that the patient will feel willing and able to explore his question further.

How, then, does the therapist respond? Does he attempt to interpret the patient's possible unconscious wish to ruthlessly possess the therapist? He might, if he understands her question as a manifestation of a split-off primitive object relationship in the transference. Does he focus on her problem with libidinal object constancy? He might, if he understands the patient as wanting to attempt a connection with him, albeit in a projected form. In the first response, he would be interpreting latent and ego-alien content. In the second, he would be responding to predominantly manifest and ego-syntonic content on its own merits. For some patients, the former response would require an already-established working alliance in order to be effective. For others, it is the interpretation of unconscious transference fantasy itself that establishes the alliance and works against an insubstantial alliance based on primitive idealization.

Should the therapist answer the question without further comment? Many therapists would not. If the therapist does not think of the patient during his vacations, then he has to either say no or lie to the patient, both of which present obvious problems. But even if he does think about the patient, to simply answer without further elaboration does not advance the therapy at that point and skews the transference in a positive direction at a time when the patient may want to express conflicted negative feelings about the separation.

However, if the patient were evaluated as too disturbed to engage in further exploration, there are some who might simply answer the question without further exploration. By answering the question and even sharing some personal detail ("I'm going to Europe for a convention"), the therapist helps the patient keep him in mind by locating him in a particular space. He also helps the patient with merging fears and fantasies by implicitly emphasizing that he has a life of his own, apart from her. The patient cannot ruthlessly use the therapist or merge with him. The message is thus supportive on both the manifest and the latent level.

These clinical choices reflect the therapist's beliefs about the nature of the patient's strengths and primary difficulties, and about the corresponding therapeutic stance. The responses we have outlined touch on many issues, including issues of essential pathology in the borderline patient, of the proper psychoanalytic stance, of the meanings and purposes of abstinence and gratification, and of the various mutative roles of interpretation and experience. A cookbook approach to treatment does not help to resolve these issues. Neither rigid adherence to rules of technique nor wild analysis can guide therapists. They must combine knowledge of theory, of their patients, of their countertransference, and of their own intuitions in arriving at an appropriate response.

These issues are considered in greater depth throughout this book. In Chapter 1, four approaches to the borderline patient are contrasted, in a manner that highlights the connection between assumptions of basic pathology of the borderline patient and corresponding clinical approaches. In the second chapter, a case example is presented to illustrate the ways in which different conceptions of pathology lead to different clinical interventions. In Chapter 3, definitions of supportive and expressive psychotherapy are evaluated. The connection between these definitions and the four models is highlighted. In Chapters 4 and 5, modifications of the therapist's stance are evaluated. Criteria for use of a transitional object are presented and discussed in Chapter 4. This leads us to a discussion of parameters and the boundaries of the classical psychoanalytic stance, which is the topic of Chapter 5.

I have concentrated primarily on two models in the second half of the book: Kernberg's approach and what I have termed modifications of classical psychoanalytic technique.[1] I have focused on Kernberg in Chapters 6 and 7 because he is probably the single most important figure in the field of the borderline patient. Many analysts (myself included) disagree with many of his points, but he must be understood by anyone working with the borderline patient. His work is often difficult to understand, however, and since his books are compilations of his papers, chapters are often repetitive and important points are elaborated in bits and pieces, scattered through four volumes and assorted journal articles. Thus I felt it would be important to organize and systematically clarify his assumptions and the way in which he translates these assumptions into clinical recommendations. In Chapter 6, these assumptions are reviewed in a discussion of developmental factors in splitting defenses. In Chapter 7, Kernberg's approach to treatment is reviewed.

In the last three chapters, I examine the manner in which classical psychoanalytic theory and the classical psychoanalytic stance have within them the theoretical flexibility to accommodate to the demands of the borderline patient. Psychoanalytic theory includes within it the insights of other models, without some of their difficulties, and offers the potential for substantial improvement in very difficult treatment cases.

---

[1]The other models are presented quite well in other volumes. Adler (1985) has presented a model of work with the borderline patient that is influenced by aspects of the representational-deficit approach. Stolorow and his colleagues (1980, 1987) have applied the self psychology model to work with borderline patients. Those interested in the ego-deficit emphasis are urged to read the work of Blanck and Blanck (1974, 1979). Pine (1985), while not subscribing to these particular models, has written clearly, sensitively, and insightfully about developmental factors in psychoanalytic work. Thus the reader interested in further exploration of these approaches can consult these and other sources.

However, various analysts understand basic psychoanalytic concepts differently, in ways that lead to different emphases in clinical work. In Chapter 8, evolving conceptions of the psychoanalytic stance are reviewed. In Chapter 9, I focus on the relationship between metapsychological assumptions and conceptions of therapeutic stance. Differing emphases within psychoanalytic theory are outlined, and implications of these assumptions are discussed with regard to such issues as the working alliance, regression, reality, abstinence, and gratification. In Chapter 10, clinical implications of these views in work with the severely disturbed patient are presented. The central figure in these last three chapters is Loewald (1980), whose papers provide the framework for a major rethinking of psychoanalytic theory. The implications of his work for clinical practice have not been fully appreciated. Loewald's ideas provide a unifying framework for many analysts working with the borderline patient within classical psychoanalytic theory.

For reasons of confidentiality, none of the clinical illustrations is from my own practice. Furthermore, all of the examples (particularly the case in Chapter 2) have been disguised. Rather than exploring the dynamics of a specific patient, the examples demonstrate the role of theory in shaping clinical interventions.

I write of psychoanalysts' contributions to psychotherapy. I assume that readers of this book are either psychoanalysts conducting psychotherapy or therapists interested in the ways in which psychoanalytic thought can enhance their psychotherapeutic work. Thus I will use the words *therapist* and *analyst* interchangeably.

Andrew B. Druck
New York City

Acknowledgments

As a teacher and supervisor, Dr. Marvin Hurvich shaped my way of thinking about the borderline patient and spurred my interest in the different models of treatment. Portions of this book benefited directly from his comments; his influence, however, is fundamental and transcends specific comments. Ideas that he first suggested to me can be found throughout this book and I thank him as well for his contribution to my clinical work.

Dr. Richard Lasky was also invaluable. He read a long first draft and returned it with specific comments on almost every page. As I revised the book, I felt as if he and I were engaged in a continuing dialogue. Dr. Lasky is a man of erudition, scholarship, and great intelligence, and his comments were always learned, pointed, and helpful. Moreover, his enthusiasm was a great support as I went through the long rewriting process.

Steven Gross introduced me to the computer, and even bought one and installed it for me. He patiently answered my many questions, and I am grateful to him for all his help.

I would also like to thank: Dr. Joyce Aronson, for

originally suggesting this book; Nancy Andreola and Gloria Jordan for their editorial work; Dr. Walter Gadlin, for his comments on Chapter 5; Judy Grauman for the Wallerstein book; and Dr. Fred Wolkenfeld, for his comments and insights.

Much of my initial experience with borderline patients came during my years at the Psychiatric Day Treatment Center at St. Luke's Hospital in New York City. I have been enriched by working with the patients at the Day Center and by supervising psychology interns and psychiatric residents at the hospital. I thank them all. I also thank Dr. Robert Cutick and the late Dr. Adam Munz for their administrative support and their friendship. My early papers (1978, 1982) were based on my work in that hospital setting. I no longer work at the Day Center, but I miss grappling with issues in milieu treatment of the borderline patient, and I think fondly about the day treatment program we developed.

Writing this book has been a long, enriching task, extending over several years. I have been blessed with the support and encouragement of my wife, Beverly, and my daughters Danielle, Avigayil, and Tamar. I thank them for their love and apologize to them for the time stolen by my book work. I dedicate this book to them in return for all that they have given me.

The author gratefully acknowledges permission to reprint the following material:

The development of intrapsychic structures in the light of borderline personality organization, by O. F. Kernberg. In *The Course of Life*, vol. 3, ed. by S. I. Greenspan and G. H. Pollock, copyright © 1980 by Otto Kernberg, published by the National Institute of Mental Health, Washington, DC. Reprinted by permission of the author.

Recommendations to physicians practicing psychoanalysis, by S. Freud, in vol. 12 of the *Standard Edition of the Complete Works of Sigmund Freud*, trans. and ed. by James Strachey, copyright © 1964 by Sigmund Freud Copyrights Ltd. Reprinted by permission of Sigmund Freud Copyrights Ltd., the Institute of Psycho-Analysis, The Hogarth Press, and Basic Books.

Developmental Theory and Clinical Practice, by F. Pine, copyright © 1985 by Yale University Press, New Haven, CT. Reprinted by permission of the publisher.

Narcissistic States and the Therapeutic Process, by S. Bach, copyright © 1985 by Jason Aronson, Inc., New York. Reprinted by permission of the publisher.

Transference and Its Context, by L. Stone, copyright © 1984 by Jason Aronson, Inc., New York. Reprinted by permission of the publisher.

The Therapeutic Experience and Its Setting, by R. Langs and L. Stone, copyright © 1980 by Jason Aronson, Inc., New York. Reprinted by permission of the publisher.

Some pressures on the analyst for physical contact during the re-living of an early trauma, by P. J. Casement, in *International Review of Psycho-Analysis* 9:279–286, copyright © 1982 by Institute of Psycho-Analysis, London. Reprinted by permission of the publisher.

Part One

Four Models
and Their
Clinical Implications

1

Four Models of Therapy

In this chapter, we explore the connection between theoretical assumptions and clinical approaches with the borderline patient. While the psychotherapist's personal characteristics are one major determinant of his approach, his theoretical assumptions also play a large part. These often implicit theoretical beliefs determine how the therapist understands what the patient says, how he intervenes or does not intervene, and, more generally, how he defines his role as a therapist for that patient. The context within which the patient is understood may differ markedly from one set of assumptions to the next. This context becomes the intellectual aid to what Schafer (1983) has called the analyst's "stamina." Thus it seems worthwhile to highlight prominent theoretical models that provide such differing contexts.[1]

---

[1]Similar efforts to trace the connection between theory and technique have been made by Aronson (1977), with regard to the relationship between theories of psychosis and treatment approaches, and by a group of analysts (Lichtenberg, 1987) who discuss case material from differing theoretical perspectives. Schafer (1985) has also discussed this question, with reference to "wild analysis."

The four models to be contrasted—Kernberg's approach, the representational deficit/self deficit approach, the ego-deficit approach, and what will be called "modifications of classical psychoanalytic technique"—are attempts at synthesis of differing trends in the psychoanalytic theory of treatment of the borderline patient. They are constructed, in that I have taken central questions and addressed them from differing points of view. The models differ in the extent to which they can be identified with a single analyst. Kernberg has developed a comprehensive system and has taken explicit positions on each of the issues we will address. For the other approaches, a model is presented as if there were one approach when, in fact, no one analyst has specifically addressed all of the questions discussed. In these cases, I have attempted to fit together the contributions of several analysts to form a relatively consistent model. Thus, analysts may be grouped within a given model on the basis of their similarities with respect to some issues, even though they differ from one another on other issues.

The central characteristics of these models have been highlighted so that we can thoroughly examine the differences and similarities between them. Although the models are sharply contrasted for didactic purposes, the reader should keep in mind that differences between models are sometimes differences in emphasis rather than in kind. Differences are highlighted here in order to contrast models but are often not so clear in actual clinical work.

We will approach the four constructed approaches to treatment of the borderline patient by focusing on the following questions:

1. What is the primary etiology of the borderline patient's psychopathology?
2. What kind of patient is treated?
3. What is the role of interpretation and confrontation?
4. What is the stance of the therapist?

5. How is resistance understood?

6. What are important aspects of the course of treatment?

Kernberg's Model

THE PRIMARY ETIOLOGY OF THE
BORDERLINE PATIENT'S PSYCHOPATHOLOGY

Kernberg (1975, 1976, 1977, 1980a,b, 1984, 1985, 1986, 1987a,b) believes that the fundamental difficulty for the borderline patient is an excess of aggression. The aggression may be genetic in origin, or it may be the result of excessive childhood frustration. It must be defended against through the use of splitting and its related defenses (including primitive idealization, omnipotence, devaluation, denial, and projective identification). These splitting defenses protect the positive self and object representations from being overwhelmed by negative self and object representations. Defenses organized around splitting are inherently ego-weakening, since neutralization of aggression, which takes place through integration of positive and negative self and object representations, cannot occur when splitting predominates. Splitting both results from incomplete neutralization and interferes with the process of neutralization. Because major negative elements of the child's life are denied, they cannot be integrated. The central "good" core of the self remains weak. If neutralization is prevented because of excessive splitting, then the patient is left with primitive, nonmetabolized internal objects, major structural difficulties, and a sense of emptiness. The sense of emptiness is a *consequence* of the patient's primary internal conflict over excess aggression. Similarly, difficulties in libidinal object constancy are understood as consequences of intrapsychic conflict rather than as primary deficits.

Kernberg offers several related assumptions. The first is that a conflict model is necessary to understand borderline psychopathology. That is, splitting, which is initially developmentally appropriate, becomes an ego defense, protecting "good" self and object representations from destruction by "bad" self and object representations. The second assumption is that borderline pathology originates during the rapprochement crisis. Thus the origin is preoedipal, and issues that may appear to be oedipal in these patients turn out to be preoedipal in nature. Dependency issues, for example, are commonly sexualized and may then appear oedipal in nature.

Kernberg's third assumption is that splitting and its associated defenses are specific to the borderline and psychotic patient, in contrast with the neurotic patient, for whom defenses are organized around repression. Splitting defenses serve different functions for borderline and psychotic patients. In the borderline patient, the defenses protect weak positive self and object representations from threatening negative self and object representations. In the psychotic patient, self and object boundaries have not been securely established, and the defenses function to differentiate between self and object—that is, to defend against fears of merger. The psychotic patient using such defenses achieves a modicum of psychological separation but pays the price of feeling alone in a hostile world. The borderline patient, in contrast, has achieved self and object differentiation but is unable to integrate positive and negative self and object representations. For this patient, the defenses protect "good" from "bad" at the expense of continuity in intrapsychic and interpersonal experience.

Kernberg emphasizes the fantastic (that is, fantasy-dominated) element in the patient's defenses and object relationships. Primitive idealization, for example, is the "direct manifestation of a primitive, protective fantasy structure in which there is no real regard for the ideal object, but a simple need for it as a protection against a surrounding world of dangerous objects" (Kernberg 1975, p. 30). It is these fantasy-dominated elements of the borderline patient that become manifest in the transference and that must be worked out in psychotherapy. Indeed, one's knowledge of the degree to which the observed transference corresponds to the actuality of a patient's past family life is limited by the strength of the fantastic elements; it is only late in treatment that the therapist and patient discover the more realistic aspects of a patient's past.

TYPES OF PATIENTS

Kernberg focuses on patients whose anger is prominent, who devalue or overly idealize the therapist, and in whom dependency is generally ego-alien. Kernberg views what others call "dependence" on the therapist as a manifestation of primitive defenses and of the patient's incapacity to truly depend on the therapist and to take what he can actually give.[2] Kernberg's emphasis is not on the patient who has great difficulty tolerating time away from the therapist; instead, it is on how to control turmoil and transference psychosis within the therapy sessions.

THE ROLE OF INTERPRETATION
AND CONFRONTATION

Confrontation and interpretation are two forms of therapeutic intervention. Interpretation generally refers to the therapist's making conscious an aspect of the patient's mental state that had previously been unconscious. The therapist inter-

---

[2] A female therapist was sitting in the subway watching the following scene: A bag lady was berating a dignified-looking woman sitting across from her. She loudly repeated "Tell me to have a nice day, tell me to have a nice day, tell me to have a nice day. . . ." The dignified-looking woman looked very uncomfortable and got off at the next stop. The bag lady turned to the therapist and began anew: "Tell me to have a nice day, tell me to have a nice day, tell me to have a nice day. . . ." The therapist looked at the lady, and said to her, "Have a nice day." The lady looked back at the therapist and exclaimed, "You're ugly!" This is the dynamic of a Kernbergian patient.

prets aspects of id, ego, and superego. The patient gains insight into his unconscious wishes (id), how he has protected himself from acknowledging these wishes (ego), and the ways in which he may have punished himself for forbidden wishes (superego). All of these insights, difficult as they might be to hear and assimilate, are consciously (albeit conflictually) welcomed by the patient because they help him gain insight into a problem that is ego-alien. Since both therapist and patient are felt to be working on a mutually agreed-upon problem, interpretation reflects an atmosphere of therapeutic cooperation.

Interpretation certainly contains elements of confrontation, in that the patient is asked to look at something that he has attempted to avoid. However, the emphasis in confrontation is on the therapist's more forcefully drawing the patient's attention to an aspect of character or resistance that is ego-syntonic and that the therapist has not been able to make ego-alien through interpretation and other standard technical means (enumerated by Bibring 1954). Myerson (1973) writes that the therapist's forcefulness and persistence are one factor in defining an intervention as confrontation. Corwin (1973) distinguishes between "routine" confrontations, in which the patient is made aware of resistances in the usual technical manner, and "heroic" confrontations, in which standard technique has been ineffective and the therapist feels he must do something "extra-analytic" (Corwin, p. 82). In such a case, the therapist confronts the patient with her resistance in a manner implying that the patient must change in a certain way in order for the analysis to continue. Because the therapist is forcefully confronting the patient with something that she herself does not consider problematic, confrontation reflects difficulty in the working alliance. Interpretation aims to further insight within an assumed working alliance; the heroic confrontation, a parameter used in situations of therapeutic impasse, aims for resumption of the working alliance in its absence.

For Kernberg, both confrontation and interpretation are central to psychotherapy with the borderline patient. While

Kernberg emphasizes both techniques, his stress on initial confrontation of defenses assumes that the initial focus of treatment will be on making ego-syntonic and ego-weakening defenses ego-alien, a task which may lead to difficulties in the working alliance. Confrontation of splitting defenses is essential, because they are inherently ego-weakening. Without this confrontation, such concepts as ego building, building a positive therapeutic relationship, internalizing a good object, and providing a corrective emotional experience simply make no sense, since the patient, according to Kernberg, is interacting with a fantasy-dominated part object. Under such circumstances, the therapist is alternately idealized or devalued, and the patient does not perceive an integrated whole object with whom to identify. It is primarily through confrontation of the defenses and concurrent interpretation of transference that the borderline patient is able to integrate split positive and negative self and object images.

THE THERAPIST'S STANCE

The therapist is neutral and inteprets from this position. He is neutral with respect to the way in which he listens to the patient and in regard to his realistic position with the patient. Kernberg is careful to avoid placing himself in a position of managing the treatment. He insists, for example, that a potentially suicidal patient assume responsibility for himself outside of sessions as a condition of treatment. If the patient cannot take on such responsibility, he is treated in a hospital. Similarly, the patient who needs concrete services is seen by a social worker so that the therapist can remain neutral. Kernberg creates a sort of reality prosthesis to contain the patient. One may contrast this sort of holding the patient through external environmental means with the self psychologist's holding the patient through a self–object transference and with Grunes's (1984) "psychic prosthesis" (p. 127). For these analysts, it is the therapeutic relationship that holds the patient.

Kernberg is aware of the patient's potential splitting of therapist and social worker. He is not concerned, however, with the implicit split made by the therapist, who, on one hand, acknowledges that the patient has real (not neurotic) needs for something more than interpretation (otherwise the therapist would not make the referral to a social worker; he would just interpret the wish) but is at the same time acting as though the wish for assistance was primarily neurotic and to be dealt with interpretively and as though the concrete services from the social worker, a surrogate of the therapist, are coming from someone else.

Kernberg sees the therapist's role as primarily that of an interpreter of transference. He does not agree with the comparison of the therapist–patient dyad to the mother–child dyad—a comparison that is central to self psychology and to the ego-deficit model, and that has been used by British object relations theorists such as Winnicott (1975). For Kernberg, it is not the way in which the therapist holds the patient emotionally (analogous to the mother's holding the child) that is mutative. Rather, it is through the therapist's rational, interpretive holding, which he feels is different from the way in which the mother holds her child, that the treatment achieves its mutative effect.

RESISTANCE

Resistance, the central concern of Kernberg's work, is understood as a manifestation of defenses organized around splitting.[3] As such, resistance must be confronted and analyzed. Kernberg's overriding theme is that the "bad" within the patient threatens the "good" and needs to be confronted, and that the patient is unable, because of his excessive anger and consequent defenses, to take the good that is offered by

---

[3]Freud (1926) enumerated five forms of resistance. Kernberg focuses on resistances which primarily serve defensive purposes.

the therapist. Kernberg (see especially 1977) focuses on lack of improvement in treatment and on the negative therapeutic reaction. In contrast with every other model we discuss, Kernberg ignores the adaptive function of resistant-appearing behavior.[4]

IMPORTANT ASPECTS IN
THE COURSE OF TREATMENT

We have discussed Kernberg's focus on confrontation of defense and interpretation of transference. These transference reactions reflect

> the dissociation of contradictory, potentially severely conflictual and anxiety-raising object relations. These object relations are primitive, fantastic, and unrealistic in nature, and these characteristics become manifest as the internal object relations are reenacted with the therapist in the transference. [Kernberg 1977, p. 278]

Interpretation of these transference reactions leads to neutralization of excessive anger and integration of positive and negative self and object representations. Kernberg's treatment approach is noted for its stress on confrontation of primitive defenses and interpretation of part-object transference reactions.

Kernberg is concerned with preventing both transference psychosis and the vicious cycle wherein the therapist, under pressure from the patient because of projective identification, devaluation of the therapist's competence, empathy for the patient's aggression, and the pull from his own aggression, is provoked and then retaliates. Kernberg believes that allowing the patient to express primitive aggressive wishes in sessions by, for example, continually yelling at the

---

[4]Kernberg's approach to resistance is contrasted with the self psychologist's approach in greater detail in Chapter 7, pp. 251–255.

therapist, is a mistake because the catharsis provides more gratification for the patient than any insight could.

The enactment of primitive aggression can be contrasted with the patient's talking about anger or expressing it in some manner indicating a potential self-observing context for the anger. The patient who is enacting primitive aggression rapidly becomes furious at the therapist and may yell at him in session after session without any attempt to understand his feelings. The patient who is expressing anger, on the other hand, may eventually analyze his defenses against his anger and may then allow himself to become angry at his therapist in a way that makes contextual sense and that he eventually attempts to understand. The therapist can interpret such an expression of anger. The repetitive yelling, on the other hand, is dealt with by limiting the patient's expression of such anger. Thus Kernberg (1975) suggests firm limits on the patient's enactment of aggression in sessions. In general, the suggestion is consistent with Kernberg's belief that firm limits combined with empathy for the patient's aggression is the best way to deal with the borderline patient.

Kernberg's concern with disruption of sessions stems from his focus on the pathological effects of the patients' anger and defenses, especially projective identification. There are those, particularly Stolorow and Lachmann (1980), who feel that the disruptions observed by Kernberg can be understood differently, as the patient's iatrogenic reactions to the narcissistic insults of the therapist's confrontations. They believe that a therapeutic stance that acknowledges the patient's developmental deficits and encourages a self–object type of transference produces far less disruption. Although Gill (1984) does not share their belief, his point that the regression is shaped by the nature and timing of the therapist's interventions also raises the question of the therapist's role in facilitating or discouraging certain kinds of transference reactions.

The Representational-Deficit/
Self-Deficit Models

THE PRIMARY ETIOLOGY OF THE
BORDERLINE PATIENT'S PSYCHOPATHOLOGY

Buie and Adler (1982) describe the patient's experience of aloneness, which they term the "fundamental psychopathology of the borderline personality" (p. 59), as "the experience that accompanies the need for a real holding (self) object under circumstances of not having an adequately functioning holding introject" (p. 64). The cause of this feeling is the patient's inability to maintain a positive internal soothing image of the loving object—what they term a "holding introject" and which accompanies libidinal object constancy. The internal sense of aloneness is projected into the environment, so that the patient experiences her surroundings and her life as empty and without purpose.

Patients often express a variation of this aloneness in yearning for someone, with the concomitant feeling that their longing will never be gratified (here the focus is on their disappointment and anger) or that their yearning will go on forever (here the focus is less on others). In both cases, the patient believes that the latter (the feeling that it will go on forever) is a result of the former (the strong yearning). I believe, however, that it is one feeling, in which yearning brings with it an experience of timeless longing, rather than a bounded "missing someone" with the accompanying sense that, at some imagined future time, the yearning will end. In this distinction, of course, we see the difference between feeling alone and feeling lonely.

Patients who have achieved a holding introject reflect on their previous sense of aloneness as follows. One patient said, "I've never had the experience of missing someone I've respected," adding that he had devalued those who were significant to him when he felt a separation approaching.

Another patient, toward the end of treatment, when he was able to tolerate separation from his therapist and correspondingly saw him more realistically, said, "I've come to the conclusion that memories are better than fantasies. Of the many fantasies I've made up, I can't really remember one fully. Memories are harder to come by, but they have textures and feelings I never could have made up."

The patient with tenuous holding introjects relies on others for soothing. As a result, he is ever susceptible to intense separation anxiety. Such anxiety leads to panic, and when the patient is not held enough by the therapist—that is, when his "entitlement to survive" (Buie and Adler 1973) is not met—he goes into a rage. The rage further interferes with maintenance of a holding introject because, in his anger, the patient expels positive internal images from his mind. Under primary-process thinking, the wish becomes the psychic deed and the therapist is thus dead to the patient. Anger also interferes with the patient's cognitive capacity for recall of a tenuously held holding introject (Buie and Adler 1982). Thus a primary deficit in the patient's capacity for maintaining holding introjects leads to the use of others for such psychological holding and to inevitable disappointment, accompanied by panic, ego distortion, and rage—consequences which themselves contribute to a spiraling cycle of structural regression. Within this framework, excessive anger is seen as narcissistic rage (Kohut 1972) rather than as the primary cause of structural difficulty.

In this model, then, the analyst looks for the patient's *legitimate* needs for an object relationship that addresses structural deficits and developmental failures. Buie and Adler (1973) distinguish between the borderline patient's narcissistic entitlement and his entitlement to survive. Narcissistic entitlement refers to object-directed behavior reflecting pathological grandiosity. Entitlement to survive refers to behavior toward others that appears similar to narcissistic entitlement, but that reflects the patient's attempt to force others to serve as psychologically necessary holding objects. Both may lead to demandingness, rage, and withdrawal from the object, but they are psychodynamically different from each other. Buie and Adler (1973) note that "one is a wish, the other a need" (p. 131).

Therapy stresses developing and interpreting impediments to holding introjects and responding to legitimate structural needs, rather than interpreting manifestations of splitting and other ego-weakening defenses. This model is the mirror image of Kernberg's model. Where Kernberg sees the therapist who is being rejected and besieged by an overabundance of anger and pathological defenses in the patient, Buie and Adler see a patient who requires a holding self-object and whose anger is largely reactive. There is a corresponding emphasis on what is claimed to be the reality of the patient's needs, which Buie and Adler suggest are being objectively expressed in the therapeutic relationship, in contrast to Kernberg's emphasis on the fantastic elements of the patient's relationship with the therapist.

Adler and Buie's work, with its focus on a deficit in an internal holding introject, may be categorized within the "representational deficit" model. Adler's work draws from several sources, including classical psychoanalytic theory, ego psychology, object relations theory, and self psychology. In this chapter, Adler's similarities with self psychology are emphasized. To appreciate the similarities and differences between these two models, it is necessary to review the contributions of the self psychologists to treatment of the borderline patient.

For Kohut (Kohut 1971, 1984, Kohut and Wolf 1978), the borderline patient's self-deficits are paramount and quite serious. The borderline patient is viewed as similar to the psychotic patient, but with stronger defenses. Kohut and Wolf (1978) write that, in the borderline states, "the break-up, the enfeeblement, or the functional chaos of the nuclear self are also permanent or protracted, but, in contrast to the psychoses, the experiential and behavioral manifestations of the central defect are covered by complex defenses" (p. 415).[5]

The borderline patient fends off potential psychosis by using these complex defenses, which tend to be distancing ones, such as those found in schizoid or paranoid personalities. The true borderline patient is a "covered-over" psychotic (Kohut 1984, p. 71). Tolpin (1978) discusses another category of borderline patient, one with a more cohesive sense of self and defenses that are less avoidant. However, both categories of borderline patient are seen as more seriously disturbed than narcissistic patients. For the self psychologists, narcissistic patients are healthier because they have already established a self. The narcissistic patient's psychological difficulties are the result of temporary (rather than permanent) enfeeblements, distortions, or lacks of cohesiveness in the self. Kohut considers the borderline patient unanalyzable, in contrast with the narcissistic patient, who can be analyzed. Kohut reaches this conclusion because he believes that the narcissistic patient can tolerate a necessary transference regression, with working through of early needs, whereas the borderline patient cannot tolerate such a regression. For the borderline patient, the self is too vulnerable to deal with the frustration inherent in the psychoanalytic situation as narcissistic needs emerge. The period of fragmentation and depletion would be too prolonged for the patient to tolerate. In addition, the borderline patient's near-psychotic self-vulnerabilities and his distancing defenses make him less responsive to empathic analytic interventions. In contrast, the narcissistic patient is considered a candidate for analysis because of his possession of a self (albeit a vulnerable and weak one), his ability to respond to the analyst's empathic interpretations and merged transference

---

[5]These self-deficits are closely related to deficits in the capacity for holding introjects.

closeness, the temporary nature of regressions in his "self," and his capacity to emerge from regressive experiences. Most of Kohut's work has dealt with the narcissistic patient rather than the borderline patient.[6]

Self psychologists emphasize that they do not diagnose a patient based only on manifest behavior. Like all analysts, they make a diagnosis based on the nature of the patient's internal psychological structure. However, they emphasize that the patient cannot be diagnosed as if he had a psychological disorder that resided solely within himself, apart from the diagnostician evaluating him. That is, diagnosis is based both on the patient's transference and on the analyst's response to this transference. A patient who appears borderline or psychotic with one therapist may appear narcissistic with another therapist who is more able to handle the transference. Diagnosis is thus dependent on the therapist's and the patient's responses within an "intersubjective" field (Stolorow et al. 1987). Self psychologists contend that the patient's capacity for analysis depends upon the extent to which the analyst can understand and empathically convey to the patient the understanding that seemingly distorted and

---

[6]Kernberg and the self-psychologists differ dramatically in their conception of narcissism. For Kernberg, the more narcissistic the patient, the poorer the prognosis. For the self-psychologists, on the other hand, the more narcissistic the patient, the better the prognosis. For Kohut, the grandiose self, pathological though it may be, reflects a developmental step, one that the borderline patient has not yet made. The grandiose self aids in self-esteem regulation, self-coherence, and self-soothing. Thus the unstable fragile self indicates a developmental achievement that should be supported. In contrast, for Kernberg, the patient's narcissism is part of an essentially flawed psychological structure. It reflects a static and pathological mode of functioning, one which is ego-weakening, rather than an early and fragile step in a developmental line. The sustaining function of the pathological narcissism, along with the patient's devaluation of his need for others, makes the patient less responsive to the analyst and to treatment, and leads to a poorer prognosis. It is in middle age, when narcissistic triumphs are fewer, that the prognosis for these patients improves (Kernberg 1975, 1980a).

critical transference reactions are a psychologically valid attempt to remedy a parental trauma. In one of his last works, Kohut (1984) writes:

> Specifically, the question we must ask ourselves in arriving at a differential diagnosis is whether or not the patient is able to develop a self–object transference when the opportunity to reexperience the self–object of childhood is offered to him in the psychoanalytic situation. If the answer is yes, we will diagnose the patient as a "narcissistic personality disorder"; if the answer is no, we will diagnose him as "borderline." The line . . . is not an immovable one. It may depend, for example, on the skill and special gifts of the therapist or on the special psychological fit between a given patient and the personality of a given therapist. A psychosis or borderline state in one situation may be a severe narcissistic personality disorder in another. . . . I am a diagnostic relativist up to a point. I say "up to a point" because there are many instances when the confluence of severe early trauma and congenital vulnerability lead to such severe impairment of the ability to fit into a responsive self-object milieu that no therapist, at least with the psychotherapeutic tools that are currently at our disposal, would be able to provide a milieu in which the would-be-analysand could develop a self–object transference. [p. 219]

Stolorow and his co-workers (Stolorow and Lachmann 1980, Stolorow et al. 1987) have applied Kohut's ideas to the borderline patient (and to other diagnostic groups). They believe that the borderline patient's pathology is due to a developmental deficit in the self. Splitting, for example, reveals not pathological and inherently ego-weakening (and therapeutic alliance–weakening) defenses, but a developmental arrest, which impairs the borderline patient's "ability reliably to synthesize affective discrepant experiences of self and others" (Stolorow et al. 1987, p. 107). The therapist serves a holding function for the patient who splits. It is

through the therapist's empathic understanding and tolerance of these states that the patient is able to develop the
capacity to synthesize them. Similarly, projective identification does not reflect the patient's wish to destroy the therapist, but is the result of narcissistic rage. Stolorow and colleagues emphasize the patient–therapist combination in their
definition of borderline personality characteristics. They define these as "phenomena arising in an intersubjective field—
a field consisting of a precarious, vulnerable self in a failing,
archaic self–object bond" (Stolorow et al. 1987, p. 116).
They disagree with Kohut's early assessment of the borderline patient's relative incapacity to be analyzed, and they
stress the role of the analyst's empathy in allowing such a
patient to tolerate and benefit from analytic treatment.

Adler's work and Stolorow's work are considered here
within this "representational deficit/self deficit" grouping
because of many commonalities in approach. In both models,
the self is an essential structure of the psyche. Rather than
focusing on conflict and ego characteristics, the primary
deficit is related to difficulties in the self. Aggression is
generally understood as narcissistic rage. Internalization is
seen as a major mutative factor in treatment. Theoretical
terms used by Buie and Adler in their description of both
psychopathology and treatment do not include the structural
terms used by other schools, and attempts are not made to
extend conceptualizations to classical metapsychology. Such
attempts are more characteristic of the ego-deficit model
with regard to conceptions of psychopathology (as defects in
ego functions) and treatment (ego-building). (See, for example, Blanck and Blanck 1974, 1979.) In the representational-
deficit model, as in the self-psychology model, it is believed
that once the holding introject has been established, weakened ego functions will automatically become strengthened.
One sees this in Adler's (1980) discussion of the therapeutic
alliance, where he states that it is during the period when the
self–object transference is most established that the patient's
perceptions of the therapist are most accurate.

These analysts differ significantly in emphasis, however. For example, Stolorow and colleagues focus more on disturbances caused by the therapist's failure to respond to the patient's self–object transference than they do on the patient's own conflicts in maintaining closeness irrespective of the therapist's response. Adler and colleagues, in contrast, give significant attention to the patient's own conflicts in developing and maintaining a transference that would help develop a needed internal holding introject. Both Adler and Stolorow are influenced by Kohut's emphasis on deficits in the self as a primary cause of psychopathology, by his focus on rage as largely reactive, and by his ideas regarding an optimal therapeutic stance. However, Adler integrates Kohut's ideas with other ideas that are closer to the mainstream of psychoanalytic ego psychology and object relations theory. Stolorow, on the other hand, extends them in a manner that is a more explicit departure from traditional psychoanalytic theory.

TYPES OF PATIENTS

Stolorow and Lachmann (1980) distinguish between patients with structural conflict and those with developmental arrest.[7] They compare patients in each category, and suggest that aggression plays a different role for each of them. For developmentally arrested patients, dependency wishes are ego-syntonic and anger is defended against because it threatens a valued object relationship. For patients dealing with conflict-based psychopathology, dependency wishes are

---

[7]Despite Stolorow and Lachmann's valuable attempt to distinguish between patients with pathology of developmental arrest and those with pathology caused by conflict, the major thrust of Stolorow's work in the 1980 volume and in later work has been to focus almost exclusively on pathology due to developmental arrest and to define conflict within a framework different from that of more classical theorists (Stolorow et al. 1987).

ego-alien. The anger has produced a certain degree of self–object separation, and the patient prefers isolation to people. Patients with developmental arrest are emphasized in this model.

THE ROLE OF INTERPRETATION
AND CONFRONTATION

For Buie and Adler (1982), the major focus in the first phase of work with the borderline patient is to develop and sustain holding introjects and to interpret threats to such introjects caused by the patient's anger, fears of incorporation, guilt, and other dynamic factors. Interpretation is thus a tool to enable a reparative relationship to succeed. Such use of interpretation differs from that in the classical psychoanalytic model, in which interpretation is viewed as the primary instrument of cure, with the relationship second in importance.[8]

Confrontation is also understood quite differently by analysts working within this model. Whereas Kernberg confronts the primitive unconscious fantasy underlying the manifest reality of the analyst–patient relationship (that is, the primitive idealization underlying what may appear to be

---

[8]The "rules" of understanding and interpreting what the patient says also differ between the self-psychological and the classical psychoanalytic model, in a manner discussed by Reed (1987). According to Reed, the rules of interpretation in self psychology focus on discovery and exegesis of a predetermined theory of the self embedded in the latent content of patients' communications. The analyst asks what the words really mean, what aspect of self-psychological theory they represent. The classical analyst, in contrast, concentrates on interpreting the process through which multiple symbolic meanings of patients' words are disguised. The analyst's focus is on how unconscious elements are transformed and used in a process of intrapsychic conflict, as well as on their multiple (as opposed to singular) meanings. Reed believes that, because the classical analyst is more concerned with illuminating unconscious process than unconscious content, the classical analyst is less bound by general theory than is the self psychologist.

a positive transference), Buie and Adler confront the patient with the realistic dangers to which the patient is exposing himself because of actions based on unconscious fantasy.

For Buie and Adler (1973), anger and accompanying object loss lead to avoidant defenses, such as projection, denial, distortion, and avoidance through action. These defenses result in some loss of reality testing and in the potential for real harm to the patient, who may place himself in dangerous situations while denying feelings. Buie and Adler use confrontation both to remind the patient of safety in the actual patient–therapist situation (that is, to remind the patient that the reality of the therapeutic situation is different from the patient's fantasy of the situation, enflamed as it is by fears of abandonment and attack, projections and introjections of anger, and feelings of aloneness) and to emphasize to the patient the actual danger in the patient's expressing feelings in action and placing himself in realistically dangerous situations.[9]

Adler and Buie enumerate three such real dangers: (1) danger in relationships with others who suffer from borderline personality disorder, where merger and gratification of infantile wishes are the sole basis for the relationship; (2) danger in actions used for defensive purposes, such as running from the therapy session or displacing anger onto outside figures; and (3) danger in actions used to discharge impulses, such as self-destructive behavior, drug and alcohol use, and sexual promiscuity.

Buie and Adler add another situation for which confrontation is necessary: when a patient is using massive denial, often of murderous feelings toward the therapist. Such denial must be confronted because the defense is very brittle and can lead to sudden, uncontrollable, and often destructive

---

[9]Here therapists stress their view of reality rather than accepting the patient's reality. The situation is understood to be a dangerous one for the patient, however, and thus deviation from the ideal self-psychological therapeutic posture becomes justifiable.

expression through action, sometimes with overwhelming feelings and sometimes accompanied by absence of feeling. Confrontation, and sometimes hospitalization, is necessary to help the patient gain awareness, control, and abreactive relief.

Buie and Adler thus confront the dangerous consequences of a patient's transference fears, rather than confronting the fantasies themselves. In fact, for analysts working within this model, it is a misuse of confrontation to confront the validity of certain fantasies too early in treatment. They feel that confrontation must take into account the therapeutic alliance, which is built on the patient's belief that her therapist is sensitive to her, and particularly on the conviction that the therapist will not subject her to more stress than she can handle at a given moment. Thus Adler and Buie recommend the following: (1) that the therapist refrain from using confrontation at a time of stress in the patient's life outside of therapy; (2) that the therapist respect the patient's needed defenses; (3) that the therapist avoid overstimulating both the patient's wish for closeness and his rage; and (4) that the therapist recognize both the difference between narcissistic entitlement and entitlement to survive, as well as the sustaining and regulating aspect of the grandiose self, so that, accordingly, he is able to refrain from confronting narcissistic entitlement until late in treatment, after holding introjects have been securely established. If these principles are followed, Adler and Buie suggest, treatment will be less stormy, the working alliance will be strengthened because the therapist is realistically earning the patient's trust in his psychological titrating of stress in treatment, and the chances will be improved that a supportive atmosphere can be developed within which holding introjects can be more readily established and narcissistic rage can be understood. Stolorow and Lachmann (1980) make a similar point when they discuss the ways in which confrontation may produce iatrogenic anger in treatment.

Adler and Buie caution the therapist to be aware that confrontation may be an expression of countertransference. For example, the therapist may attempt to rescue the patient through excessive gratification, the patient may continue to regress, and the therapist, with his omnipotently-based wishes to cure frustrated, may, in a psychological turn-around, confront his patient with the unreality of his demand. Adler and Buie see this confrontation as a counter-transferential response which causes narcissistic injury to the patient rather than as a neutralized intervention that is made in order to help the patient understand an aspect of his psychological experience. They also see confrontation, at other times, as a devalued therapist's attempt to retaliate toward the patient or to diminish his own sense of isolation and abandonment. In all of these instances, confrontation serves the therapist's needs. (It is useful to recall that Kernberg [1975] cautions against this same therapeutic situation. In fact, many of Kernberg's recommendations are designed precisely for the purpose of protecting the therapist under these circumstances.)

THE THERAPIST'S STANCE

The therapist is not neutral, in the sense of adopting a perspective equidistant from id, ego, and superego. Rather, the therapist accepts as legitimate a desired affective state (such as a patient's wish to be fully understood by his therapist) and interprets conflicts that interfere with this desired state. The therapist interprets in order to help the patient preserve this desired state; he does not view the desired state as defending against other affects, wishes, and fantasies and then interpret the patient's wish from that more traditionally neutral perspective. The therapist working in the former mode might say to his patient, "When I didn't know exactly what you meant, I made you feel that I could never understand you in the way you would like." In contrast, the therapist working in the latter mode might say,

"You want me to understand you perfectly so that you can run away from how you hate me when I don't meet your expectations." Stolorow and Lachmann (1980) make this distinction as follows:

> [T]he essence of Kohut's technical suggestions is to focus empathically on the *state which the developmentally arrested patient needs to maintain or achieve*, whereas Kernberg strongly emphasizes interpreting *what* the defendint patient needs to ward off. [p. 99, their emphasis]

Buie and Adler (1982) stress the therapist's concrete gratifying behaviors with regard to formation of a stable holding introject for support during therapeutic separations, as a narcissistic self–object, and as a model for internalization. Thus ego and superego functions in the areas of self-esteem are aided

> through identification with the homologous functioning of the therapist as a self object. That is, the therapist, verbally but largely nonverbally, actually does provide the patient with a holding function, a function of loving in the affectionate mode of object love, a function of validating (enhancing the reality of valence of) the patient's competences, and a function of enjoying the exercise and fruits of the patient's competences. [p. 78]

For Stolorow and Lachman, the therapist seems to take greater responsibility for the patient's reactions than that proposed by other models. Stolorow and Lachman (1980) emphasize the *patient* in cases of structural conflict and emphasize the *analyst* in cases of developmental arrest. They write that, in cases where they assume the pathology to be the result of intrapsychic conflict, ". . . historical reconstructions alert the analyst to the infantile satisfactions and fantasies that the **patient** will *wish to repeat* in the transference." In contrast, where pathology is assumed to lie in developmental arrest, ". . . reconstructions of the patient's past alert the analyst to the pathogenic developmental traumata which the **analyst** will *strive not to repeat* with the patient" (Stolorow and Lachmann 1980, p. 99). (Italics reflect their emphasis; boldface is author's emphasis.)

Stolorow and Lachmann continue:

> With structural conflict, early experiences have been *repressed* or otherwise defended against. These are reanimated and analyzed in the transference. With a developmental arrest, experiences that the patient legitimately *needed but missed* or prematurely lost are understood within the transference in order to assist the patient in his belated development" [pp. 99–100; italics reflect their emphasis]

While both Stolorow and Adler emphasize pathology due to developmental arrest and the mutative effects of internalization, Stolorow seems to place more of the emphasis on the therapist's responsibility for the patient's reactions, and almost no emphasis on the patient's conflicts as motivating these reactions. Adler and Buie give interpretation of conflict a major role in their work, even though such interpretation supports the more primary mutative factor of internalization. Stolorow and Lachmann give much less emphasis to interpretation of conflict in cases in which they diagnose developmental arrest.

RESISTANCE

Because this model of borderline pathology deemphasizes aggression and wishes against the therapist, resistance is not a paramount concern. Resistance and anger can be understood as a reaction to narcissistic slights from the therapist (particularly by Stolorow and Lachmann [1980]) or as a defense against oral fears (Buie and Adler 1982). Implicit in

Stolorow and Lachmann's view is a conception of patient resistance as a response to a real event by a nontransferentially distorted therapist (for example, narcissistic rage; see Stolorow and Lachmann's [1980] example, pp. 167–168).

The self psychologists have been criticized by Kernberg for this characterization of anger and resistance. Kernberg (1987b) believes that, by viewing aggression as predominantly narcissistic rage, Kohut ignores "the *motivational* aspect of aggression, the unconscious functions of aggression in the transference" (pp. 8–9, emphasis his). Kernberg (1987b) writes as follows:

> Kohut also ignores the structural consequences of aggression. He only sees ideal internalized objects, what he calls self-objects. They are all good self-objects, a good thing to have, the more, the merrier. But there are no negative, hostile self-objects in Kohut's conceptions. Yet, clinically, we find the activation of bad internal objects in the transference as a most prevalent, almost obvious, pervasive observation. [p. 9]

We can understand this difference of opinion in several ways. It is first of all a reflection of these analysts' differing theoretical starting points regarding essential pathology in the borderline patient. This is why Kernberg sees the self psychologists ignoring the negative internalized objects, while the self psychologists accuse Kernberg of precipitating iatrogenic negative transferences in his patients because of his confrontational approach (Stolorow and Lachmann 1980).

One might also regard this difference of opinion as a question regarding the working alliance. That is, how can the therapist help the patient acknowledge and reflect upon those aspects of himself that are most troublesome for him? These areas often concern the negative introjects. One might then argue that the therapist should be more empathic at the beginning of treatment and then, as the therapist–patient relationship evolves, help the patient confront the more ego-alien aspects of himself. Such an approach is implicit in the work of Modell (1976, 1978) and is assumed by most classical analysts. However, therapists such as Stolorow do not write as if the empathy in the first part of the analytic work is later supplanted by interpretation of conflict. On the contrary, one gets the impression that their work with developmentally arrested patients remains focused on empathy and attunement throughout the treatment, as the therapist attempts to substitute a new experience with a caregiver who is better than the original, unattuned parent.

Kernberg (1987b) makes this kind of point when he writes:

> Clinically, the consequence of Kohut's approach is to grossly neglect the analysis of the unconscious meanings of the transference. Empathy with their patients' subjective experience is used as a rationalization for collusion with the patients' defense ego functions, and what the patient cannot tolerate consciously is not interpreted, because it is painful. [p. 8]

At the same time, however, Kernberg seems to indicate that no preparatory period is necessary before the patient is asked to examine some of the most ego-alien aspects of his character—namely, his own hatred and destructiveness. Kernberg assumes that the patient must confront these aspects at the very beginning of treatment, rather than later in the evolution of the therapeutic work, in order for the treatment to be meaningful. In this matter, too, Kernberg and the self psychologists have opposing points of view.

IMPORTANT ASPECTS IN
THE COURSE OF TREATMENT

In this model, the supportive, self-enhancing function of treatment is promoted and stressed. In the representational deficit model, the first phase of treatment is devoted to helping the patient establish holding introjects. The therapist accomplishes this task by facilitating internalization within the context of a holding environment (Modell 1976, 1978) and interpreting impediments to such internalization. These impediments result from conflicts around rage, fantasies of incorporation, and primitive guilt. As these conflicts are interpreted, the patient is able first to use the therapist as a holding introject and then to internalize him.

Because the therapist attempts to establish a supportive atmosphere within which internalization will be facilitated, he is less concerned with disruption of treatment within the session than he is with disruption of treatment outside the session, when the patient is away from him and cannot use him to mitigate the chronic feelings of aloneness. For this reason, Adler and Buie (Adler and Buie 1982, Buie and Adler 1982) recommend the use of transitional objects to help evoke the therapist's image during absences. In the next stage of treatment, a stage which echoes Kohut's (1971) description of treatment with the narcissistic patient, idealized internalizations of the therapist are gradually modified through discussion of what are considered optimal disappointments. Finally, Buie and Adler focus on attempts to establish benign superego functioning.

The Ego-Deficit Model

THE PRIMARY ETIOLOGY OF THE
BORDERLINE PATIENT'S PSYCHOPATHOLOGY

In the ego-deficit model, as in the self-deficit and representational-deficit models, a developmental deficit is considered the primary difficulty. The self-psychology model postulates the self as a psychic structure equal in stature to the id, ego, and superego, and then sees the deficit as reflecting a fragile self (Stolorow and Lachmann 1980). The representational-deficit model sees the deficit as indicating inadequate holding introjects (Adler and Buie 1979). The ego-deficit model, on the other hand, sees the deficit as one in ego functions, caused by the patient's inability to fully master the rapprochement crisis (Blanck and Blanck 1974, 1979, Mahler et al. 1975). The ego-deficit model attempts to remain rooted in classical psychoanalytic ego psychology (in contrast with the self-psychology model) and places the beginnings of borderline pathology in the preoedipal stage of development. While adherents of this model believe that the traditional analytic emphasis on interpretation of the transference is appropriate for neurotic patients, they feel that focus on ego deficits is most relevant for the borderline patient.

Blanck and Blanck (1974, 1979), whose theoretical formulations fit most closely into this model, see borderline pathology as rooted in the patient's failure to navigate the "developmental fulcrum" (Blanck and Blanck 1974). They stress the shifts in ego function that occur as the child moves toward libidinal object constancy. These include changes in psychosexual functioning, neutralization of drives, nature of defenses, quality of object relations, and the capacity for internal regulation of anxiety, soothing, and self-esteem. The changes also include a shift from annihilation anxiety (Hurvich 1985) to signal anxiety, and development of the capacity for a coherent identity, separate from the mother. The borderline patient, because she has not navigated the rapprochement crisis, is deficient in these ego functions.

In this model, the therapist does not view the patient's anger as a primary destructive force, inimical to the working alliance, to the therapy itself, or to the patient's capacities for adaptation. Blanck and Blanck distinguish between drive and conscious affect, and they stress that angry affect may accompany the aggressive drive which fuels separation, just as loving affect may accompany the libidinal drive which fuels movement toward objects. Confrontation of a patient's anger may mean confrontation of the aggressive drive necessary for the patient to separate, from his mother in "reality" and from the therapist in the transference. Thus, aggression, properly channeled and neutralized, is seen as essential to separation rather than as the dark force working against internalization.

TYPES OF PATIENTS

Theorists from this school focus on patients who are seen as exhibiting ego deficits. As previously noted, Blanck and Blanck (1974, 1979) discuss patients who have not navigated the developmental fulcrum. Wexler (1951, 1971) takes a similar approach with the schizophrenic patient, emphasizing basic structural problems as the primary cause of psychopathology. These analysts tend toward explanations based on structural difficulty, in contrast with analysts such as Abend and colleagues (1983), who emphasize conflict (rather than deficit) from both preoedipal and oedipal levels of development, and who argue that what might look like an ego deficit may also be understood from a dynamic point of view as, for example, identification with a disturbed patient.

THE ROLE OF INTERPRETATION
AND CONFRONTATION

Interpretation is deemphasized. There is little intrapsychic conflict to interpret because, according to this point of view, there has been minimal structure formation. The major emphasis of treatment is on ego building through neutralization and internalization. Interpretation, then, seems to acquire a secondary focus. Its main purpose is "the furthering of impeded development" (Blanck and Blanck 1974, p. 315). As such interventions as clarification, questioning, and confrontation are usually seen as intermediary steps on the road to the goal of an interpretive statement, for Blanck and Blanck, interpretation becomes, like these other interventions, an auxiliary statement, a means to the end of object tie and inner structure.

Confrontation is not used and is viewed as inappropriate for various reasons. Some are similar to those of the self psychologists (it represents an unnecessary narcissistic blow; it destroys inner holding images of the therapist), while some, such as the following, are specific to this school:

1. It is preferable to support the developmental thrust toward separation which is accompanied by the aggressive drive than to confront the angry affect and risk appearing to be against the patient's separation.
2. The patient's defense (that which could be confronted) is viewed as a manifestation of internal structure and autonomy in a patient for whom such structure is a tenuously held achievement. Confrontation of such a defense could lead to intensification of symbiotic concerns. If the therapist refrains from confronting the defense, the patient is reassured of having enough space, and he can then more easily move closer to the therapist.
3. Further, Blanck and Blanck believe that the patient may attempt outward behavioral changes in order to please, and to retain as a good object, the person who is doing the confronting, whether a family member, friend, or therapist. They believe that such behavioral change does not lead to internal structure and does not last.

Blanck and Blanck prefer what they call "confrontation from within," by which they seem to mean the process of an aspect of character becoming ego-dystonic. As the patient begins to examine her own behavior and motivation, she is more likely to accept the self-confrontation. The act of self-confrontation is also in itself ego-strengthening.

The deemphasis on interpretation in this model is superficially similar to the deemphasis on interpretation by Adler and Buie. However, the models differ in two important respects. First, Adler and Buie make extensive use of interpretation, even though they see the goal of therapy in the initial stage as the patient's establishing holding introjects. They interpret the patient's conflicts over establishing such introjects—that is, the impediments to optimal closeness, such as narcissistic rage, envy, fear of destroying or being destroyed by the therapist, and so on. In contrast, the ego-deficit model deemphasizes, in all stages, interpretation of conflict. Second, Adler and Buie focus primarily on internalization and on the holding introject. Therapists using the ego-deficit model focus less on internalization directly; instead, their focus is on ego deficits, which are the result of poor internalization. Adler and Buie seem to focus more on the transference, while the ego-deficit therapists focus less on the relationship and more on the ego functions. Both models see the internalization of the "reality" therapist as a primary vehicle for cure, however.

THE THERAPIST'S STANCE

If one believes that the origin of psychopathology is in a developmental deficit, then one naturally looks to the parent–child relationship as a model for the therapist–patient relationship. In the ego-deficit model, similarities between therapist and parent are stressed. The therapist's role is less to analyze intrapsychic structural conflict from a position of technical neutrality, and more to facilitate the developmental process.

Pine (1976), although a classical analyst, has written of similarities between parenting and doing psychotherapy. The therapist is a model for identification, essential for structure formation. He is steady, reliable, empathic, neither corrupted nor corrupting. He confirms the patient's inner reality and performs certain educative functions in the arena of the patient's subjective life. He models thought, reflection, anticipation, delay, introspection, and a host of ego functions. He is also a model for superego functioning, both in the appropriate expectations he has of the patient and in the manner in which he judges and evaluates the patient's libidinal and aggressive life; that is, he is not overly critical, nor does he "let it all hang out," which is a defense against an appropriate superego signal function. He is able to contain the patient's feelings. In general, the therapist is a model of secondary-process functioning. These nonspecific qualities that a therapist shares with a good parent exist along with specific functions, such as affirming the patient's self-love and exhibitionism, helping patients differentiate between emotional states, and helping patients develop the signal function of anxiety.

Myerson (1981) approaches the parallel between parent and therapist from a slightly different perspective. He notes that the transactions that occur in treatment include (1) statements in which the patient puts into words previously unarticulated feelings and (2) placement of such statements into context with other feelings. "I wish someone would die" is an example of the former statement, while an example of the latter statement is, "I am angry *because* someone does not reciprocate my love and I am afraid my anger will cause him to become alienated" (Myerson 1981, p. 675, emphasis his). The second, linking statements, help promote perspective and reality testing.

For a patient to be able to make these kinds of statements in therapy, he must have been helped as a child to make such statements. Thus a child needs his parents to encourage expression of feelings (Myerson emphasizes feelings of desire and anger) and differentiation between feelings, and to help in establishing contexts and perspectives for such feelings without using such contexts to negate the feelings. The child then learns that he is an active agent who is responsible for his feelings, in the sense that he can identify the feeling and knows that it is his feeling. And, because the child has experience in expressing his feelings, he learns that he can sometimes be hurtful to others but that the world doesn't come to an end at those times. Finally, when he uses repression, he will repress wishes and fantasies that, to him, lead to intrapsychic danger, but these will be repressed wishes and fantasies that have him as an active agent, owning the forbidden thoughts.

If parents do not acknowledge that a child has feelings and do not help him identify and differentiate these feelings, then the child will feel overwhelmed by inchoate feelings of desire and anger and will use primitive and passive defenses, such as projection, to deal with them. The child then fails to learn that he is an active, responsible agent, "owning" certain feelings. He will have difficulty differentiating between his constant fantasy/fear that expression of feeling will alienate others and occasions when he is, in fact, hurtful to others. Finally, rather than developing a sense of himself as an active agent with forbidden wishes, the child will repress a general sense of something traumatic, disastrous, and inarticulate. Myerson's description of such a process lends developmental perspective to Giovacchini's (1982) description of patients who act provocatively in order to elicit a response from the therapist so that, through the therapist's response, they can identify their own feelings.

Blanck and Blanck (1979) attempt to modify the therapist's stance to take into account ego functions that have been inadequately stimulated by parents. They attempt to carve out a place for the therapist that includes both the discipline of the classical analyst and the opportunity for appropriate and necessary gratification for patients deemed in need of it. Thus they see a role for the therapist in pointing out patients' distortions, but they also see a reparative, experiential, non-transferential role for the more disturbed patient:

In psychotherapy, there are diagnostic considerations for providing *measured* gratification in those instances in which there has been deprivation severe enough to have impeded ego growth. Never is so much gratification provided that it becomes a fixation in therapy itself. It must always be in symbolic form, usually in words and not in touching, feeding, and other real acts that will keep the patient from proceeding further in his development. [Blanck and Blanck 1974, p. 130]

They describe the therapist's role in terms that reflect their wish to be as precise as possible in responding to subphase inadequacies without intruding on the patient's autonomy. They assume, in their descriptions of the therapist as "catalyst" or "leader into the object world," that it is possible for the therapist to be involved with the patient in a manner that is both active and limited. This may not be possible, but it reflects their attempt to modify the traditional concepts of neutrality and abstinence without abandoning them.[10] They are aware that the patient's difficulty is with internal objects and that he needs help with latent ego functions and with distortions; any attempt at new mothering or at a global corrective emotional experience to address manifest external difficulties would simply miss the point. Yet they also feel that legitimate ego dysfunctions must be specifically addressed. Thus their attempts at compromise.

There are at least two such crafted definitions: The therapist as catalyst who is "a presence that does not participate in the action" (Blanck and Blanck 1979, p. 243), and the

---

[10]Blanck and Blanck attempt to sidestep the issue of the patient's internalizing aspects of the therapist. They speak of the patient's internalizing ego functions prior to (and without) more global internalizations of the therapist. I don't believe that this is possible. I think they take this position because of their emphasis on remnants of what I will be calling the right wing of classical psychoanalytic theory. They can be compared with Grunes (1984), who, along with an approach which contains within it a more dynamically oriented focus in an atmosphere permitting more of a controlled regression, is not afraid of dealing with the therapist's influence as a major aspect in treatment. One may also compare this to Stone's (1984) quoting Glover as saying that ultimately, in treatment of the severely disturbed patient, it is the therapist's personality that is crucial. Both of these points are elaborated further, primarily in Chapter 9, and in this chapter in "Modifications of Classical Technique."

therapist as "representative of the object world." In the latter case, "the analyst or therapist does become real to the patient but in a circumscribed way—not really himself, but as a representative of the object world, especially when the patient's connection with the real world is uncertain" (p. 115). The therapist performs these last functions in the working-through phase, which Blanck and Blanck (1979) define as "discovery and rediscovery, separating it from resistance analysis" (p. 117). Thus Blanck and Blanck work on the provision of an ego growth–facilitating climate in which psychological structure necessary for later interpretive work may be developed. They write:

> Where the patient lived, as a child, in a "climate" that failed to encourage ego apparatuses, the therapist provides or helps the patient provide a more favorable or conducive climate. Then the cognitive and emotional capacities combine to make interpretation usable. Most neurotic patients, being analyzed within a reasonably good therapeutic alliance, already have the capacity to use a correct and well-timed interpretation because interpretation connects with existing cognitive capacities and a high level of object relations. Object relations determine not only the quality of the therapeutic alliance but also transference and even transference neurosis. In most instances, borderline patients cannot be assumed to possess such capacities and so it becomes one of the very purposes of the therapy to promote them. [p. 118]

It is not simply that the therapist works in a benign atmosphere. Rather, Blanck and Blanck help the patient become aware of what was lacking in her past life by awakening certain ego functions and avoiding distortion (via transference frustrations) as an internalized bad object. The patient does this at her own pace, with the therapist neither thrusting awareness onto her through confrontation nor assuming a special role for the patient as a new object who will gratify her needs.

RESISTANCE

We can examine two intimately related forms of resistance: (1) the defenses themselves, as they are manifested in the patient's communication to the therapist, and (2) action taken against insight (that is, defenses manifested in action), including concrete demands on the therapist, threats to leave treatment, and the like. In general, defenses are viewed as evidence of beginning structure, and are thus not actively confronted. Actions against insight are understood (1) as attempts to achieve from the therapist in some form what the patient is unable to do for himself because of his ego deficits (Blanck and Blanck 1979) or narcissistic deficits (Stolorow and Lachmann 1980) or (2) as attempts by the patient to separate from the therapist or to protect himself, in an active and concrete manner, from merger with the therapist, or (3) as a concrete response to narcissistic injury (Stolorow and Lachmann 1980). In all of these instances, the adaptive aspect of resistance is stressed by the therapist, both theoretically and in his responses to the patient.

IMPORTANT ASPECTS IN
THE COURSE OF TREATMENT

This treatment is seen as ego-building, with a focus by the therapist on the specific and nonspecific developmental tasks provided by the parent. There is an emphasis on manifest content and a deemphasis on transference and interpretation because the patient is seen as not developmentally advanced enough to be capable of true transference or intrapsychic conflict. Treatment involves the therapist's detailed inquiry into aspects of the patient's ego functioning, with an attempt to focus the patient's interest on these ego functions. This kind of inquiry also tends to limit regression in sessions. Such a limitation has advantages and disadvantages. Since rapid and excessive structural regression is often a problem in treatment of the severely disturbed patient, an approach that tends to limit regression has obvious strong points. Patients treated in this model may do well as ego functions improve. In the long run, however, an approach that focuses primarily on ego functioning, with a marked deemphasis on dynamic issues, internal conflict, and transference in an environment that permits controlled regression, may limit the patient's ultimate achievements.

For Blanck and Blanck, ego-building takes place within the context of the patient's oscillation between closeness with the therapist (union), accompanied by the libidinal drive and positive affect, and movement away from the therapist (separation), accompanied by the aggressive drive and angry affect. This oscillation is central to their notion of the therapeutic process. It is viewed as paralleling the process of separation-individuation. Thus internalization takes place during times of closeness, and then anger accompanies the patient's attempt to become more independent of the therapist. Ideally, such independence does not lead to loss of internal holding because identifications have been established in the previous stage of closeness. As the oscillation of closeness and separation continues, the patient is able to relate to the therapist in more psychologically advanced ways, indicative of a higher level of ego functioning. "The analyst or therapist does not take on the role of a real object in this process, but acts as a catalyst of development by recognizing and encouraging each drive manifestation as it presents itself" (Blanck and Blanck 1979, p. 49).

Modifications of Classical Technique

The models of expressive psychotherapy described vary in the degree to which they may be associated with the work of a single analyst. The attempt has not been to fit analysts into models, but to see how certain, often implicit, assumptions lead to certain clinical implications. Even with Kernberg's model, there are other approaches that might "fit" with

Kernberg's assumptions about etiology, stance of the therapist, and so on. The other models discussed draw from the work of many analysts, and certain contributions from one analyst may be described in one model while other aspects of the same analyst's thought are described in another. Analysts who disagree on many issues may be grouped together because of their agreement on other issues as we have seen in discussion of the representational-deficit/self-deficit models. While the "fit" between a particular analyst and model is closest with Kernberg, it is weakest with this last school, which I have termed "modifications of classical psychoanalytic technique." This model, more than the others, attempts to fit various psychoanalytic contributions into a coherent model.

Kernberg's model can be viewed as concentrating on aggression, resistance, fantasy, and psychic reality (and as minimizing the influence of the child's continuing interactions with developmentally significant figures). The representational–deficit model can be seen as concentrating on aloneness and on the vicissitudes of attachment. The self–deficit model focuses on the fragile self. The ego-deficit model concentrates on ego deficit, separation–individuation, and adaptation. These latter three models deemphasize internal conflict and emphasize the influence of developmentally significant figures. In contrast to these models, one can view this last model as retaining assumptions of classical psychoanalysis while attempting to reformulate and apply core concepts such as interpretation, resistance, and the working alliance so that they can be used with the more disturbed patient.

These analysts attempt to maintain an analytic situation that will lead to insight through interpretation. They do not conclude that a patient is unanalyzable on the basis of diagnosis. Rather, they examine the implicit requirements of various components of analysis, and then they attempt to help the patient meet these implicit tasks and use the psychoanalytic process. For example, they ask what is required of the patient to hear and use an interpretation. They pose questions like, What psychological task does hearing an interpretation place on the patient with regard to balance of defenses? To stress? To object connection with the analyst? How, then, can the analyst make it easier for the patient to use an interpretation? By separating the task of hearing an interpretation into component tasks, they are more able to find ways to help the patient hear. They go through a similar process with other aspects of the psychoanalytic process, such as the working alliance and the patient's assumption of a shared reality with the analyst. Throughout this process, however, they maintain the centrality of insight through interpretation as a major factor for change. The attempt is not seen as doing psychoanalysis with parameters. Rather, it is understood as a modification of psychoanalysis, albeit a modification that attempts to retain the essence of traditional psychoanalytic technique.

THE PRIMARY ETIOLOGY OF THE BORDERLINE PATIENT'S PSYCHOPATHOLOGY

From the foregoing, it can be seen that this model does not necessarily focus on preoedipal factors as the major cause of borderline pathology, and there is even some question as to whether borderline personality is a valid diagnostic category. Abend and colleagues (1983) believe that the borderline diagnosis is a broad designation of character pathology rather than a specific diagnosis, and that preoedipal factors are not more important than oedipal factors in its genesis.

Abend and colleagues disagree with the major postulates of each of the preceding models. They disagree with Kernberg in their belief that one cannot diagnose borderline personality disorder on the basis of splitting defenses. They hold this belief for several reasons, including the fact that they observed repression and defenses under the rubric of repression in their borderline patients. They prefer, for theoretical reasons, not to postulate a unique grouping of defenses organized around splitting. They understand borderline phenomena using traditional defenses, such as identification with the aggressor. What Kernberg terms "projective identification," a unique defense, they call "projection and identification in a patient whose ego boundaries are more fluid than those of neurotic patients and whose reality testing is more impaired" (Abend et al. 1983, p. 166).

Abend and colleagues also disagree with Kernberg's hypothesis that preoedipal events, especially excessive anger leading to splitting, are crucial in pathogenesis. Finally, they disagree both with the way in which Kernberg conceptualizes unconscious fantasy and with his emphasis on the fantasy element in primitive self and object representations. They feel that Kernberg

> does not give sufficient weight in his discussions to the real experiences of the child in relation to the real objects in his early life. Instead, Kernberg focuses on the infantile "primitive," "fantastic" images of mixed self and object introjects in their earliest and most primitive form. . . . He hypothesizes that the critical conflicts which dominate the growing child's psychic development continue to be between these polarized "internalized objects," rather than between the child's changing self-representations and the ever-changing mental representations of the objects in his environment. [p. 162]

That is, Kernberg's is a theory of the interaction between primitive internal object representations, rather than a theory of object relationships.

Abend and colleagues make a similar point in their discussion of splitting. For Kernberg, as they interpret his position, the child "splits" the negative affect in order to protect the positive internal representation of the mother. For Abend and co-workers, the child protects the gratifying object rather than more abstract internal entities. For Kernberg, it is as if further developmental experiences exert little effect on psychic structure once the child has undergone initial developmental experiences that facilitate splitting. These external realities become so contaminated by the child's fantasy life that they exert little modifying effect in their own right. This concept is noted in Kernberg's discussions of superego development and the nature of borderline transference, as well as in his conception of psychotherapy, which deemphasizes the therapeutic effect of support and internalization of the therapist as long as the splitting defenses are still operative. In contrast, while Abend and colleagues certainly emphasize the major role of fantasy, they leave more room for the effect of the child's evolving experiences in their own right. Thus, they will focus on the child's identification with the aggressor as reflecting a certain reality of the child's development, over and above the distortions of anger and idealization.

Abend and co-workers differ more fundamentally with the ego-deficit and self-psychology schools in their strong emphasis on intrapsychic conflict and in their denial that preoedipal factors are the primary cause of psychopathology. When they discuss the demands by these patients for concrete gratification in treatment, they say that these are due, not to ego defects or limitations, but rather to

> a relative failure of reality testing. This pattern seems to result from the complex interplay of defenses against anxiety, guilt, and other unpleasurable affects, combined with attempts to obtain direct gratification of libidinal and aggressive drive derivatives, according to the principle of multiple function. [Abend et al. 1983, p. 235]

Similarly, with regard to the pronounced reactions to separation, Abend et al. consider these to result from severe conflicts with both parents throughout all developmental phases, rather than from early maternal failure. These two ideas—stress on causative factors from all psychosexual stages and the central role of intrapsychic conflict—differentiate the model advanced by Abend and co-workers from the deficit models.[11] It should be noted, however, that Abend's group emphasizes conflict and minimizes ego difficulties much more than do other analysts who have been included in this model.[12] These others, whom we will discuss in following sections, allow for the effect of structural difficulties in addition to conflict. They are less concerned with illustrating how preconceived theoretical assumptions about a patient (be it the role of splitting, ego deficit, or intrapsychic conflict) will manifest themselves in treatment and more concerned with how and why a patient is finding the classical situation difficult. Pine (1984) and Grunes (1984), for example, are descriptive in their listing of the difficulties these patients present in treatment, but they do not commit themselves to a specific diagnosis. There is less concern with having treatment follow the theory and more concern with molding the treatment to the individual patient.

---

[11]Abend, Porder, and Willick base their conclusions on their ability to analyze four higher-level borderline patients by classical methods, without resorting to parameters of technique. They go beyond their data in asserting that their findings also extend to other, lower functioning borderline patients; for example, that all borderline patients can be analyzed by traditional means alone, and that their psychological difficulties can be best understood through the same metapsychological assumptions that govern work with neurotic patients. These are partially questions of analyzability; different patients with a "borderline" diagnosis will have different capacities for classical psychoanalytic work and different prognoses (Meissner, 1984; Kernberg, 1975). They are also, perhaps more importantly, questions of metapsychological preference. Abend et al. present their data in order to support their metapsychological assumptions over competing assumptions, especially those of Kernberg and theorists with deficit models.

[12]Abend and colleagues work on the basis of assumptions from the "right wing" emphasis of classical psychoanalytic theory, whereas most of the other analysts mentioned here fit within the "left wing." These differing emphases within classical psychoanalytic theory are discussed and elaborated in Chapter 9.

TYPES OF PATIENTS

This model is concerned with the patient who has, as Eissler (1953) puts it, an ego which is less than "normal." Pine (1979) classifies this patient as showing pathology in relation to the undifferentiated other. Patients discussed here exhibit marked structural impairment. It is because these patients do not "take" well to psychoanalysis that analysts attempt to rethink traditional assumptions in order to work with them. However, this model does not decide, on an a priori basis, that there are specific difficulties that will need to be addressed. This is in contrast with the three preceding models, in which the analyst knows what his focus will be as soon as he learns the patient's diagnosis.

THE ROLE OF INTERPRETATION
AND CONFRONTATION

Confrontation is stressed only in Kernberg's model, since he believes that further therapeutic work is impossible unless the splitting defenses are addressed. If one does not share Kernberg's theoretical assumptions, however, then there is no compelling necessity for confrontation and it loses prominence as a technical recommendation.

Interpretation is a central mutative factor, as it is for Kernberg, but as it is not in the deficit approaches. *What* is interpreted are a wide range of intrapsychic conflicts from all developmental levels and defenses against these conflicts, especially when these defenses become apparent in the transference. These analysts differ from Kernberg in that they are not as focused on interpreting primitive defenses, negative transference, and fantastic, internal, primitive nonmetabolized objects. Rather, they interpret a broader range of material. Further, although they interpret unconscious fantasy, their understanding of fantasy differs from Kernberg's. For Kernberg, fantasy is primitive and id-like. For classical analysts, fantasy is less driving and urgent. It reflects a more highly developed compromise among the three structural components, serving multiple functions, and it is interpreted accordingly.

While all agree on interpretation as the mutative agent in psychotherapy, all also agree on the difficulty of using interpretation with this group of patients. Abend and colleagues, who studied the psychoanalysis of four relatively high-functioning borderline patients, said that the work was exceedingly difficult and discouraging, with the need to continually reinterpret defenses. In response to these difficulties, analysts have attempted greater sensitivity in *how* they interpret. For example, Grunes (1984) has written of "adjustments" made by the analyst to take into account the borderline patient's "deformations." Such adjustments include emphasizing object relationship and ego functions, rather than drive, or not interpreting as acting out behavior that the patient uses to regulate the treatment relationship. Pine (1984) has discussed ways in which the therapist can maximize his support during the "interpretive moment." By, for example, "striking while the iron is cold"—that is, interpreting at a moment when the patient is least likely to be panicked by the interpretation— the therapist can help the patient to use the interpretation. For both analysts, these modes of intervening are embedded in an expanded view of the analyst–patient relationship.

THE THERAPIST'S STANCE

The therapist's stance is particularly important with the borderline patient because of the patient's pressing, determined, angry demands for immediate, concrete gratification. The juxtaposition of the patient's difficulty with symbolic communication and the essential symbolic as-if nature of psychoanalytic psychotherapy raises complex issues regarding the relationship between interpretation and the therapeutic relationship. That is, what about the therapeutic relationship facilitates interpretation, and how does that change with the more disturbed patient?

All agree that the therapist's primary function is to interpret unconscious process. However, classical analysts disagree with one another regarding their *attitude* toward adjustments in interpreting, and regarding the degree to which
the analyst–patient relationship is valuable in its own right.
Analysts range from those who believe that this relationship
has no mutative effect and should not be given theoretical
and clinical consideration to those who assign it a major
mutative role, alongside insight through interpretation. Analysts differ both in *how* they mix relationship and interpretation and in the *attitude* they have toward these mixtures. It
should be evident that those who give greater mutative value
to *both* relationship and interpretation will have a potentially
more flexible stance with the borderline patient. These analysts will view adjustments and emphasis of object needs as
part of the treatment rather than as a preliminary phase of the
treatment.

In discussing this question, we must again look at the
relationship between theory and technique. We have been
discussing the relationship between assumptions about the
nature of pathology and corresponding clinical strategies.
Here, however, we must look at the relationship between
various emphases within classical psychoanalysis with regard to development, and corresponding emphases regarding
mutative factors and the analyst's role. There are two emphases within classical psychoanalytic theory. They are not
mutually exclusive, but they do lead to different ideas about
the therapist's stance. We will discuss these in detail in Chapters 8 and 9, but we will summarize them here.

The first emphasis may be termed the "right wing" of
psychoanalytic theory. In its metapsychological positions,
the child is seen as driven by instincts, with the object as
recipient of these instincts. The child is initially separated
from the object, and he becomes connected to it via instinctual gratification. The child's environment is essentially hostile to instinctual satisfaction, so he must grudgingly move
from the pleasure principle to the reality principle. The child

learns to live in a dangerous world by learning to satisfy derivatives of his original wishes. It is optimal frustration of instinctual wishes that helps the child accommodate to the world and develop secondary-process functioning. Defenses become paramount in psychoanalytic theory, because instinctual satisfaction places one in jeopardy, and the ego must protect itself from potentially threatening wishes.

The clinical implications of these metapsychological views are as follows: Pathology, the result of intrapsychic conflict, is ameliorated through interpretation, resulting in insight. Interpretation and insight, rather than a new experience with the analyst, are emphasized. Concepts stressing new experience are regarded with suspicion because they are viewed as threatening to the primacy of insight and as leading to the possibility of cure through suggestion.

Insight is most effectively gained through analysis of the transference. The analyst's function is to analyze the transference, which he does most effectively from a position of neutrality and abstinence. Technical concepts such as the analyst as blank screen, mirror, and surgeon are understood broadly and are seen as facilitating development and analysis of the transference neurosis. Analysts help the patient develop psychologically by calling up the patient's repressed instinctual wishes and then repeating the process of optimally frustrating these wishes so that the patient can see their infantile and unrealistic nature and modify them in accord with reality. Within this framework, gratification is understood as libidinal, and it is frowned upon because it makes analysis of the unconscious wishes, and their subsequent modification in light of the ego's adult understanding, more difficult, if not impossible.

We can contrast this position with that of other classical Freudian analysts, whom we will call the "left wing." This position has been advanced primarily by Loewald (1980).

From a metapsychological point of view, these analysts understand instincts as shaping and being shaped by object relations. They do not see an inevitable opposition between the child and the environment. Rather, they see the child's acceptance of the reality principle as occurring primarily through the child's attempt to retain, on an increasingly abstract level, his original symbiotic connection with the mother. Primary identification is emphasized, along with secondary identification with the aggressor.

Interpretation and insight remain the most important agents of change, but other factors are also understood to be operative, usually in conjunction with insight. These analysts also believe in the primacy of analysis of the transference neurosis. Here too, the patient must come to terms with reality. However, it is believed that the more severely disturbed patient sometimes needs help in creating a sense of reality that feels stable, alive, and self-discovered rather than something imposed that must be grudgingly accepted. It is through the relationship with the analyst that the patient is helped to gain such an experience of reality, an experience which is generally assumed to preexist for the neurotic patient. The analyst's role is therefore broadened considerably.

The analyst creates an environment within which the analyst–patient relationship serves an initially major mutative role. It is later in the analysis that the relationship itself is analyzed. Within this relationship, gratification, understood here as implicit gratification of object needs, may be necessary in helping to establish and maintain an analyzable transference. The concepts of neutrality and abstinence are understood within a broader framework, and concepts such as the analyst as mirror, blank screen, or surgeon are understood in a limited, technically restricted way. These analysts remain within the rubric of classical psychoanalysis because they view these patient–analyst experiences as facilitating the patient's capacity for developing a transference neurosis, which is eventually analyzed.

These broad differences affect understanding of basic clinical concepts, including the working alliance, abstinence, and modifications in the analytic stance. (These concepts will be discussed in Chapter 9.) Suffice it to say that therapists from the left wing have more theoretical rationale for flexibility in their response to a patient's difficulties in the treatment situation. They are less concerned that an intervention will become an unanalyzable parameter. This does not mean that "anything goes." Rather, it means that certain forms of implicit object gratification, internalization, and initially nonanalyzed relationship are seen as fostering the ultimate goal of insight rather than as foreclosing it.

RESISTANCE

Resistance is understood as it has always been by Freudian analysts—that is, not as an impediment that must be confronted and overcome in order for treatment to succeed, not as something that accompanies adaptation and separation and that must therefore be allowed and not analyzed, but as another aspect of psychological functioning, serving multiple purposes and worthy of analysis from all aspects at the patient's own pace. Schafer's (1983) description of an affirmative (in contrast with an adversarial) approach toward resisting expresses this tradition. Schafer echoes Freud's treatment of resistance as analogous to his treatment of manifest dream material—that is, as the starting point for analysis.

Resistance and defense analysis has been approached in a different context by Silverman (1984), who has discussed what he considers to be the beneficial aspects of imagery in psychoanalysis. For example, he might ask a patient to describe images that come to mind about a conflictual situation, in an effort to have the patient express the warded-off wishes. He notes that there are those who believe that such an emphasis bypasses defenses. However, he has commented that if one analyzes defenses after the wishes have been expressed, then the patient is more able to analyze the defenses without feeling criticized by the analyst, as so often occurs when the warded-off wish is out of the patient's awareness. Certainly such an approach might be helpful in work with the primitive, harsh superego precursors that are projected onto the analyst by the more severely disturbed patient. One should realize, however, that such an approach to resistance—that is, analysis of it after the fact—is antithetical to Schafer's approach, which is more traditional and which views it as an error to be interested in repressed content at the expense of defenses.

Still, Silverman's ideas about resistance, along with Fox's (1984) ideas about a certain amount of gratification as essential to the development of transference, are consistent with an emphasis, with the more disturbed patient, on stressing new object ties *prior* to focusing on object loss. This emphasis would encompass the technique of occasionally stressing that which has been repressed before stressing the defenses. Although the implicit ties to the analyst are enough to permit the neurotic patient to relinquish his original objects, these implicit ties may have to be made explicit with the more disturbed patient. For this patient, resistance analysis may be too close to an internalized and then projected harsh superego precursor for the patient to examine the defense together with the therapist. Analysis of warded-off imagery may, in addition to whatever work is done with the image, permit more collaboration between patient and therapist and allow a stronger alliance as they then examine together the ways in which the patient had previously "resisted" the analyst. In essence, this describes a situation in which the therapist may "strike while the iron is cold" (Pine 1984) in looking at resistance.

IMPORTANT ASPECTS IN
THE COURSE OF TREATMENT

There are no special qualities to the treatment within this model, such as there are in the other models. Treatment with the more disturbed patient is not presumed to focus on any specific content area. What characterizes this approach, however, is molding on the part of the analyst to those aspects of the patient that make it difficult for him to use interpretation. Through this molding, which may occur in any of the elements of treatment and which Grunes has called "a type of psychic prosthesis" (Grunes 1984, p. 127), the patient is helped to eventually gain insight through interpretation.

* * *

Is it possible to "diagnose" patients as being suitable for one or another of these models? Stolorow and Lachmann (1980) attempt to distinguish in theory between patients suffering from conflict and those suffering from developmental arrest; in practice, however, they seem to view most patients as suffering from developmental arrest. Pine (1979) attempts to distinguish between patients who have difficulty with separation from differentiated others and those who have difficulty with being psychologically separate from undifferentiated others. Surprisingly, with the exception of these theorists, there is little attempt to diagnose patients' suitability for treatment within a particular model.[13]

One rough diagnostic criterion, elaborated by Stolorow and Lachmann (1980), seems to be the degree of aggression. The more such aggression is manifest, and dependent feelings are denied, the more one might adopt an interpretive approach. If the patient's aggression is expressed openly and predominantly as devaluation of the therapist, one might interpret within Kernberg's model. If dependence is ego-syntonic and aggression is denied, and there is evidence of ego weakness, one might work within the framework of the deficit models.

A second rough diagnostic guide is the degree to which the patient has been able to achieve psychological separation

---

[13]Perhaps this is because, for the first three models especially, the predisposition to a theory of essential pathology determines the therapist's view of the data, which then calls for a particular approach.

from a differentiated other (Pine 1979), which determines the degree to which the therapist will have to provide necessary psychological functions for the patient (Adler and Buie 1979). This may be a difficult parameter to assess, and one therapist's diagnosis of ego weakness and lack of libidinal object constancy may be another therapist's diagnosis of identification with a helpless parent as a defense against separation. Still, the therapist must make this rough diagnostic guess because it will determine the treatment approach. Pine (1979) suggests that one can assume that the patient has been unable to separate from a differentiated other when one sees panic or ego-syntonic disturbed behavior (often psychotic identifications) accompanying statements about loss of self. That is, therapists must see signs of structural difficulty in order to diagnose pathology in regard to the undifferentiated other; they cannot rely on manifest content alone.

A second question is whether one can move from one model to another. This question may arise partially as an artifact of the way in which these models have been presented and contrasted. By emphasizing differences among models and deemphasizing areas of overlap, the areas of agreement among models and the large degree of flexibility within each model is minimized. There are changing focuses at different times of any treatment, and each of these models sees evolution within the course of therapy. To conclude that Buie and Adler never confront splitting, for example, or that Blanck and Blanck never interpret dynamics is to take emphases within schools and caricature them. There are large areas of overlap between the models and the clinical emphases that derive from them. And there are those, such as Silverman (1986), who have discussed movement between models.

Still, movement from model to model may be difficult and confusing for patients and therapist because of the models' fundamental incompatibilities. Despite some areas of overlapping agreement, therapeutic strategies employed by the various models may be quite different from one another at certain points. For the therapist to move from model to model in an attempt at eclecticism may confuse the patient. This line of demarcation—the point at which movement from model to model changes from making clinical sense to being clinically confusing—is never clear and must be defined anew in each clinical situation.

The four models lead to different ways of understanding patients and, consequently, to different kinds of interventions by the therapist. In Chapter 2, we will illustrate these differences in discussion of a case example.

2 ─────────────────

Different Understandings Lead to Different Clinical Interventions: A Case Presentation

I have contrasted four models with respect to several clinical issues in order to illustrate the close connection between theory and technique and to demonstrate the ways in which certain overall therapeutic strategies hang together. At this point, I will focus on just how these models lead to different clinical interventions.

The following material is adapted from a case presented at a seminar. The case illustrates difficulties commonly faced by therapists in treating borderline patients. It is presented in a way that permits the reader to second-guess the therapist as treatment proceeds. Throughout the case presentation, I will point out how different understandings of the patient lead to different clinical choices for the therapist.

I have tried to be as fair as possible to all of the models, for they all have something important to add to our understanding of our patients. However, my bias is toward the model I have termed "modifications of classical psychoanalytic technique." Because the models have areas of agreement, what I will describe as one model's emphasis may also be consistent with one of the other models. As with the other case material presented in this book, I have significantly altered identifying data.

The Initial Evaluation

The patient was a black male in his mid-30s who consulted a therapist, a young, black female psychiatric resident, at a hospital outpatient clinic. He wanted therapy because he was lonely, could not establish a steady relationship with a woman, had doubts about his vocational future, and had a history of alcoholism. He had seen four previous therapists for short periods of time (two to six months) but had terminated after finding fault with them. His last therapist, for example, was "nice" but "not smart enough." He had had two psychiatric hospitalizations.

The therapist inquired about his reasons for seeking treatment and took a brief history in the opening sessions.

The patient described his father as ordinary and superficial, noting that he was often out of the house. His mother was "exciting." He had no siblings, and his parents had divorced when he was 10 years old. He had vivid memories of seeing his mother with her many boyfriends throughout his adolescence, and feeling that she treated him like one of these boyfriends. He grew up in the suburbs of California and went to college in the Midwest, where he became a born-again Christian in his sophomore year. He spent his time fighting with teachers and trying to convert fellow students. He believed that in his Christianity he had found a consistent philosophy and that he was the representative of "holiness" in his college. He felt "pristine, pure, and isolated." He did not trust the environment. He felt that he was living in a bubble; it was a spiritual feeling, a feeling of being at one with Jesus. He felt secure and close to God. He would think about the Scriptures and sing religious hymns as he drove to school.

The patient did moderately well in school, immersed himself in intellectual pursuits, did not date or have many friends, and was peripherally associated with black organizations on campus. He found himself seeking only idealized men and women, ministers from campus religious organizations, and asking them question after question in order to learn the "truth." These ministers were mildly encouraging to him. He also found himself "falling in love" with his female church minister. He dated the onset of his difficulties to his senior year, when he took a psychology course. He had difficulty learning the material, argued with the instructor, and believed that he was representing the forces of religion against the values of a Freudian world. He became increasingly anxious: "I felt like I was walking on a tightrope. I started to believe that messages on the herbal tea boxes were meant for me. I would sit and shake. I thought that there was a war going on between Jesus and Freud, and that I was being tested. I'd look at people around me on campus and I'd mutter to myself 'unclean, unclean,' and I'd walk to church and pick up a prayer book." He began drinking heavily. One day he began to scream uncontrollably. He called the minister, who comforted him, but he was forced to drop out of college. He saw a therapist but discontinued treatment after six months. He moved back to California.

At the age of 23, he married a woman whom he had met through his church, but the marriage lasted only a month; he found, once they were married, that she was "disgusting." His mother died when he was 28, after which he had his first hospitalization for panic and "depression." He married a second time when he was 32. Soon after the marriage ("before I had a chance to really get to know my wife"), his father died. He grew depressed again and was hospitalized, at which time his wife left him. He became a heavy drinker. He seemed unconcerned about his drinking; he was much more anxious as he discussed feeling "alone." It turned out that he drank more heavily when he was alone.

During these years he had several jobs in business, but he did not enjoy his work. He was contemplating returning to college to complete his education and begin a new career. He had few friends, men or women, and nobody with whom he was close. He dated frequently, but felt that the women weren't "strong" enough for him. He lived alone. He thought often about a minister he had idealized in college, and he maintained contact with her. He said that he became attached to ministers and therapists, that he believed in them more than in his "own internal strength." When he was disconnected from them, he felt anxious and insecure.

He seemed quite anxious as he told the therapist about himself. He said that the therapist's office seemed cold, and he wished that she had holy books on her shelves. He had a way of saying something, smiling anxiously and seductively, and then saying something almost completely out of context, such as, "You're cute." He brushed off the therapist's initial attempts at encouraging self-reflection. At one point, for example, she said that he seemed to want to focus on settling external, practical matters, such as which subject to major in, as a way of quieting his internal, pervasive doubts. He looked at her and said, "How's that going to make me feel better?"

The therapist identified further diagnostic evaluation as her initial goal, particularly with regard to the nature of his reactions to separation, his experience of being alone, his defenses, and the nature of his object relations. She also wanted to assess how he would respond to interpretive statements, to what degree he could reflect about himself and think psychologically, how much frustration he could tolerate, and how he would respond initially in the transference. Her concern about a too-rapid regression in a patient whose ego capacities were in question led her to decide against three sessions a week and use of the couch. She decided that twice-weekly face-to-face sessions would offer time for evaluation, support, and some interpretive work.

Alternate Approach

It is helpful to formulate an initial diagnostic impression, particularly with regard to the patient's general level of ego functioning. This patient does not appear to be neurotic, based primarily on the initial interview. The immediacy and crudeness with which "you're cute" is expressed argues against a diagnosis of neurosis. The neurotic patient might think that his therapist is cute, but he would not express this at the first meeting. Considerations of appropriateness, which reflect ego capacities of judgment and general ego modulation of impulses, would keep "you're cute" at the level of thought. Similarly, his asking "How's that going to make me feel better?" with a smile reflects (1) difficulty with frustration tolerance (he wants immediate gratification), which indicates that (2) much of his functioning is based on the pleasure principle (I won't tolerate delay or anxiety), which indicates that (3) the therapist is experienced as a real object who must gratify him concretely, which means that (4) if she acts as therapist asking him to delay immediate gratification, she will be seen as withholding. In these and other areas, the patient is experiencing and expressing himself in a manner that evidences minimal ego modulation and major ego deficits; his statement that the office was cold is an example.

These hypotheses are supported by the available historical data, especially his difficulty with separation, his hospitalizations, his seeing four therapists for periods of two to six months (suggesting quick flight from the transference, or difficulty forming and maintaining relationships, or difficulty working out interpersonal conflict) without leaving his two brief marriages, his history of heavy drinking, and his general pattern of transitory, stormy, superficial object relations.

These characteristics seem to meet Kernberg's (1975) criteria for borderline personality organization. The patient's structural difficulties suggest Pine's (1979) description of pathology in relation to the undifferentiated other. The patient's history indicates that he relates to others through fighting, which may help him maintain his ego boundaries. He was not psychotic during the interview; there was no thought disorder, and reality testing was intact. For the moment, a preliminary diagnosis in the category of borderline personality disorder or narcissistic personality disorder seems appropriate, although one cannot completely rule out a diagnosis of chronic paranoid schizophrenia in remission.

The patient deals with his fears through reaction formation (he becomes holier than anyone) and identification with an idealized, pure, religious authority. These defenses could be neurotic, but their intensity, exaggerated quality, and tendency to dominate the patient's life and thought process suggest a more serious quality. We could call these defenses "primitive," as Kernberg might. Or, following Abend and colleagues' (1983) understanding of so-called primitive defenses, we might view them as "projection and identification in a patient whose ego boundaries are fragile and who exhibits serious difficulties in reality testing. Our choice would be somewhat theoretical, revealing our views on the nature of primitive defenses. But regardless of what we choose to call them, they are, in general, what are usually described as borderline defenses.

We also know that the patient's defenses are not effective. He lives in constant anxiety, has been hospitalized, is a heavy drinker, and is unconcerned about his drinking. His lack of concern is particularly important in this regard, and is consistent with defenses organized around splitting.

Thus far he looks like a patient who can easily be understood from a Kernbergian perspective. We have seen how his defenses seem to fit the category of defenses organized around splitting. In this context, his feeling "at one with Jesus" reflects the omnipotent, grandiose, "good" self, which defends against the "bad" self through projection. Other perspectives could also apply, however. His difficulty with separation could reflect the lack of holding introjects (Adler and Buie 1979), so that his attachment to idealized figures could be understood as his attempt to find someone who can concretely satisfy his legitimate need for soothing from an outside object. (We assume that the figures are idealized because he speaks of them unidimensionally and imme- diately assumes that the therapist has heard of them.) Those who follow the ego-deficit model might emphasize the pa- tient's many ego difficulties and might understand his fight- ing with others as his attempt to maintain psychological boundaries in the face of his wishes for merger.

These differences will determine the therapist's initial approach. Does she want to confront the borderline de- fenses? Does she want to permit a self–object transference that will hold the patient? Does she want to focus more on his daily difficulties, in a kind of ego-building? At this stage, it seems best for her to do what she hopes to do: learn more about him. A schedule of three sessions a week does seem excessive. The transference already shows signs of becom- ing enflamed, and the patient shows little tolerance for mod- ulation and introspection, so the therapist might find herself with a transference psychosis early in treatment. On the other hand, she needs to see the patient often enough to permit some degree of controlled regression. Twice-weekly seems to be a reasonable compromise at this stage.

Early Sessions

In early sessions, the patient spoke of how he often felt alone and lost. In order to avoid feeling anxious, he dated many women, but he felt that they were all inade- quate. When he spoke to them, he did not feel as good as he had felt when he spoke with his church minister, about whom he thought daily. However, he believed that even his minister avoided him and didn't fully respond to his questions. He also discussed his vocational problems. He wanted to complete his bachelor's degree and had to register by a certain date, but he was not sure whether he could manage school work or whether he could support himself if he took a leave from his job in order to return to school. He wanted the therapist to tell him what to do. He wanted very much for the therapist to speak.

The therapist did speak, but felt that the patient was humoring her in his responses. He would reply to a question, pause, and then ask, "So will you cure me now?" He assumed that the therapist knew his minister and was uninterested in exploring the reason for this assumption. When the therapist started to speak, he would interrupt to disagree with her. He was able to tell the therapist that when she was quiet, he felt like he had as a child, completely alone and cut off from others. He also stated that the therapist's gaze was similar to his mother's critical gaze. His ability to establish distance from these feelings in sessions was unclear. He continued to press the therapist for an immediate "cure."

In one session, he spoke of a brilliant minister who had taught a theology class. The patient would write pages of questions and then seek the minister out after class, asking his questions in an attempt to resolve his "philosophical" dilemmas about the nature of good and evil. The patient's associations were filled with allusions to Thomas Aquinas, Freud, and behavioral psychologists. He then reported that he was dating a woman who wanted to marry him. Although he did not love her, he believed that he should marry her because she was a "good catch." He thought that marriage would make him feel secure. He would no longer have to come home to an empty house. He had been feeling extremely anxious lately and had been binge eating to feel better. What should he do?

The therapist commented on his attempt to "figure things out" intellectually and said that it seemed to her that this way of approaching his problems missed the turmoil he was in, so he ended up unfulfilled and anxious, searching endlessly for an authority to tell him the right thing to do. He responded by saying that she was "acting like a therapist by looking for underlying meanings." The therapist, nonplussed and irritated, was quiet. He then said that she was too quiet and complained, "You still didn't figure out whether I should get married." The therapist believed that his major interest was in obtaining magical solutions from her, that this reflected his wish to defend himself from primitive levels of anxiety through attachment to an idealized (and then quickly devalued) authority, and that he was employing classically borderline defenses, especially primitive idealization and projective identification. She decided to confront these defenses.

Alternate Approach

What are the therapist's options? Her difficulty is that even though the patient gives her material for analysis, he speaks in the service of getting her to do something concrete, something other than interpretation, to "cure" him. He tries to mollify the therapist by talking, but he is not interested in what she says; his major interest is in getting something from her. There is no working alliance. The manner in which the therapist understands this difficulty strongly affects her intervention strategy.

The therapist has decided to adopt what she understands to be Kernberg's view, which is primarily dynamic. That is, the therapist understands the patient's presentation in treatment to be a manifestation of his primitive defenses, particularly primitive idealization and projective identification. Her focus is more on the destructive aspects of these defenses and on the patient's possible unconscious magical wishes for merger with an idealized figure. The focus is less on the patient's anxiety when he is alone. The therapist is made to feel like the critical denier of a "cure" to her imploring patient, or she is made to feel that she is imploring her patient to be a patient, and to make sense of what he is saying; he then becomes the critical one who denies her wish and her "cure." That is, if he becomes a patient, she is a therapist; to the extent that he is not a "patient" who reflects on his feelings, she becomes a "sick" analyst.

The therapist could understand the patient's associations about his mother's critical gaze, his looking to his minister for answers to questions about good and evil, and his questions about dating a woman who wanted to marry him and with whom he would feel secure, all within this transferential context, reflecting both a particular set of primitive wishes and defenses and a particular nonmetabolized internal object representation that is continually switched between patient and therapist in shifting projections and introjections. The therapist has made the decision to confront the defenses and to interpret the part-object transference which accompanies these defenses. While Kernberg repeatedly cautions the therapist not to confront the patient when he is angry at him, the therapist is otherwise on reasonably sound ground in adopting a Kernbergian perspective.

One may choose to view the initial difficulty from a perspective that is perhaps more classical. The therapist may view the patient's presentation as resistant and as containing an as yet undefined constellation of unconscious wishes, but may believe that there is still no reason to assume a particular set of primitive defenses or object relationships or a particular unconscious wish. Indeed, there is no clear evidence for the content of his unconscious wishes. Even if there were such evidence, the patient is not interested in interpretation. The therapist could content herself with drawing the patient's attention to what is going on in treatment—to the resistance—and encourage his interest in understanding it.

This approach differs from Kernberg's point of view in that no a priori assumptions are made about the nature of the defenses or the conflict. To make the early interpretations that this therapist plans runs the risk of wild analysis and of the patient's feeling that an omnipotent therapist can read his mind or will badger him to accept the truth. Further, the therapist will highlight the differences between therapist and patient by focusing on the irrational and unacceptable elements of his demands, thus further emphasizing the negative elements in the transference. The therapist will thereby repeat in the transference this patient's experience of ministers who know the truth and refuse to give it to him, give it to him in an unpalatable way, or require him to accept their truth.

The therapist might choose to address the patient's initial transference reaction more directly. There is a strong initial reaction, to which the patient refers, including his reference to a strong woman who wants to marry him. We can understand this as projection of his wishes to be cared for by the therapist through merging with her. These wishes are displaced outward so that he experiences a strong woman wanting to marry *him*, rather than his *own* wish to merge with a strong therapist. The defenses do not work well, and the patient remains in conflicted turmoil. Even the act of listening to the therapist becomes laden with unconscious meaning, as we see in the patient's initial insistence that his therapist speak to him and then stopping her from speaking. Listening to her is the psychological equivalent of merger, and the patient must then protect himself by fighting with the therapist to reestablish his own boundaries.

Some therapists might directly address this initial transference reaction and interpret both the unconscious wishes and the defenses against these wishes. However, this patient has shown little capacity for reflection, and it is probable that such interpretation would lead to further anxiety and greater defensiveness, including flight from treatment. The therapist might take these factors into account by interpreting upward. She could then review the patient's associations to earlier authority figures and suggest that the patient might be frustrated because his efforts at relationship with such figures had not been previously successful, and that he was searching for a way to relate to them successfully. Making such a comment both addresses the manifest content of the patient's communication in a way that touches on ego-syntonic concerns and hopefully should lead to the patient's feeling understood and responded to. The therapist could continue to focus on the patient's attempts at a safe mode of relationship and, in this way, do some productive therapeutic work without focusing directly on unconscious transference fantasies. When the transference does come up, in the form of the patient's frustrations with the therapist, it could be focused toward the way they might work together, productively, rather than on unconscious wishes which could not be gratified.

By initially focusing on matters of satisfactory communications and relationships outside the therapy, and by then focusing on these aspects of the therapist-patient relationship, the therapist works on developing an alliance that helps to manage possible merging fears. She implicitly sets a structured agenda for exploration. Such an agenda is reassuring for this patient, who cannot at this point deal more directly with transference or with an unstructured therapeutic situation which heightens transference concerns. For the therapist to directly interpret the patient's defenses against unconscious fears, may make the patient feel simultaneously drawn further into a feared transference relationship as well as rejected. In effect, the therapist tells him that she cannot give him what he wants, while offering him interpretations he cannot understand, tolerate, or utilize. When the therapist tells him that his attempts to speak philosophically really defend against unconscious feelings, she is *telling* him what he is running from, what he is defending against, rather than *joining* him in exploring the adaptive aspect of the issue— what it is attempting to do, albeit unsuccessfully. The latter approach might be more helpful at this point in treatment.

Such an approach, with its focus on adaptation, and in its recognizing, but not interpreting, early transference reactions, is also consistent with an ego-deficit approach. Such an approach takes cognizance of transference and of dynamic factors and attempts to support the patient's ego functions in a manner consistent with these areas.

Therapists who wish to focus more on ego building but who don't fully appreciate the complexity of this approach, might make didactic statements such as "We can try to understand your feelings together, and we can do it by looking at what it is that you say and feel. Your job is to try to talk about how you feel and how you make sense of your feelings, and I can help by saying how I make sense of what you say." These kinds of statements are used by many therapists early in treatment, but such statements don't move the therapy along unless they are used as a means toward reflection at a *specific moment in time* in the treatment. That is, the kind of statement just quoted ought to end with the therapist's pointing to something that has just transpired in treatment, perhaps reviewing his associations, and then asking the patient to do his "job" by reflecting on his associations. This kind of statement is nondynamic in nature, and if it is too often repeated, it keeps treatment at a surface, manifest-content level. It is the refuge of therapists who don't understand their patients. This kind of statement is presumed when therapists from any model make interventions. In this case, the therapist could precede her focus on resistance with a didactic statement indicating that such a focus is part of treatment.

The adaptive focus of the classical and self-deficit approaches would be shared by the representational-deficit and self-deficit approaches. However, while these approaches would look similar, they would have slightly different goals. In the classical model the analyst would have the goal of securing a working alliance through an interpretation of intrapsychic conflict appropriate to a weak ego. In the ego-deficit model, the focus would be on the ego itself. In the self-representational deficit models, emphasis would be placed on the therapist-patient relationship. The therapist would approach the patient by not thinking about the problem in treatment as involving resistance at all. That is, the therapist would not focus on the patient's desire for an irrational and impossible gratification from the therapist (her telling him whether or not to marry). Rather, the therapist would focus on how, from the patient's perspective, he is attempting to settle into a relationship with a therapist toward whom he has conflicting feelings and on how these conflicting feelings are expressed in his demands. Here the therapist would be primarily focusing on the patient's sense of aloneness, and the conflicted but legitimate need for relationship rather than on the primitive defenses. Not only would the therapist understand the patient's associations transferentially (all approaches would do this), but she would assume the legitimacy of his demands in her comments to him. She might make any of the following interpretations:

> "Perhaps you feel most comfortable in our getting to know each other through talking about intellectual topics."
>
> "Perhaps you feel the only way to approach these questions is through the mind."
>
> "I wonder if there's something about our talking about ideas or your plans that feels particularly comfortable, especially now, when we're just getting acquainted."
>
> "I think that, by your wanting me to solve your problems quickly and by your wanting me to make you feel good and not act like a therapist, you're telling me how much you'd like a special relationship with me, where I'll be there for you, but in a kind of intellectual way— almost like a dictionary of answers to the problems of life—a way that's safe because it's just in the mind."
>
> "Perhaps you feel that if we look at underlying meanings, then I'll be the therapist and you'll be the patient and there'll be this big gulf between us."

The foregoing statements assume the legitimacy of the patient's wish for a particular kind of connection with the therapist even as they explore the connection further. This last approach is closest to the self-deficit and representational deficit approaches, although it is not aimed at creating a self–object transference. It merely adopts the patient's perspective and does not explicitly or, even more important, implicitly challenge this perspective from the point of view of the therapist's "reality."

Confrontation of Defense

In the next session, the patient asked his therapist, "Did you figure out the cure yet?" She wondered what made him ask. He blandly replied that that was her job and he didn't feel like looking at it. He said that he felt alone when she didn't talk to him. The therapist pointed out that when she did speak, he interrupted her and disagreed with her. She wondered whether he was experiencing two aspects of his feelings: one side that wanted to be comforted by someone who knew all the answers, and another side that wanted to maintain his independence by opposing the authority. He agreed, commenting on how lonely he had been since he had begun to doubt Christianity. He knew he had to get married and have children, but he was not interested in the women he was dating and he knew that a wife and children would be too demanding of him. He asked whether he could call the therapist between sessions. The therapist asked why he would want to. He grew tearful and said that he was often lonely. The therapist said that he could call if he wanted to.

Alternate Approach

There are several difficulties with what the therapist said in this session. Most important, she did not confront the patient's defense against experiencing both aspects of himself, as seen, for example, in his expressing one aspect of himself without any recognition that the other aspect exists.

The patient shows no curiosity about what the therapist had wanted to, but did not really, confront, which is the alternation in the transference of conflicting self–object representations. It is insight into the process of splitting, not the elicitation of further material expressing an aspect of the split, that Kernberg sees as one goal of confrontation.

The therapist then abandons an interpretive role, concentrates on manifest content, and is seduced—or relieved—by the patient's switch from demanding anger to sadness. She does not follow up her focus on splitting, nor does she think of what he says symbolically; for example, he says that a wife and children would be too demanding and then asks if he can call her, and she does not wonder about the connection. Further, she pays lip service to exploring his request for telephone calls, just as he pays lip service to her request that he reflect on what he says. If she is asking, then she should really want to find out and to thereby teach the patient that therapy works through both patient and therapist looking seriously at the symbolic meaning of the patient's requests. She would thus be building the therapeutic alliance by example. As it is, she not only does not find out, but she implicitly goes along with his fantasy of her as the omnipotent therapist who will gratify him concretely (through the telephone call).

This is not at all meant as a position against telephone calls. Certainly many analysts, including but not limited to the deficit schools, believe in the use of telephone calls for the patient who needs to hear the therapist's voice to bolster an inadequate or unstable representation of the therapist. In this particular context at this particular time, however, the therapist agreed too quickly and did not remain consistent with what she had decided would be her treatment focus.

First Dream: Idealization and Devaluation

In subsequent sessions, the patient spoke of his loneliness as a child and his search for intellectual and religious systems to resolve his doubts, which he continued to view as philosophical. He pressed his therapist for concrete help with his vocational questions and brushed off her interpretations of displacement from internal questions to vocational questions. Despite his having asked whether he could call her between sessions, he did not do so.

One day he reported a dream in which the chief minister of his church, whom he saw as having powers of supreme holiness, was giving a sermon, but he was wearing street clothes. He looked different. The patient was disappointed in him.

The therapist suggested that both she and the minister were first idealized and then quickly devalued. The patient responded that she was better than his previous therapists, who were kind but stupid. Still, he did miss them. His current therapist didn't talk all that much, but what she said was new; actually, it wasn't so new, but he felt she had the potential to say something new. She at least knew the ballpark of his ideas, but she was still getting to know him and hadn't said anything helpful yet. He still did not know what to do about his career, and his drinking had grown more serious. He wanted her to talk more. He reported that he went out with students who were training to be ministers, and he was always able to find a flaw in their theological positions.

At one point, when he had meant to say that his therapist was "playing therapist," he said, "I'm playing patient." The therapist focused on how he made what he learned into a game, a role, as a way of minimizing its significance and mollifying his therapist so that she would give him the "real stuff." The patient agreed, and admitted that he did think briefly about what the therapist said, but he usually forgot it immediately. He then asked whether they would ever get to talk about "practical" things. The therapist responded by noting that he had just made what they had spoken about into something meaningless. The session ended.

Alternate Approach

The therapist continues to assume that the patient's primitive idealization and devaluation are the major treatment issues. The two go back and forth, with the therapist trying to encourage the patient to look at how he distances and devalues her and ignoring other aspects of the transference. Those who argue that the patient's associations convey accurate perceptions of the therapist would find much with which to support their position in this session. The therapist, a student presenting the case to a seminar, ignores the patient's references to playing therapist, vocational plans, students in training, and the like. The therapist instead focuses on *the patient's* playing a role and on *his* pathological defenses.

The therapist might get a bit further if she focused less on the patient's pathological tendency to put her on a pedestal and then put her into street clothes. He might find it more acceptable if she asked what it was like for him to be with someone who didn't meet his initial high hopes, who seemed to be ordinary and to be learning her trade, who was not the "chief" minister. She could ask this in a way that showed how she listened to him as a therapist by reviewing and interpreting his associations as unconscious associations to her, and by connecting his disappointment in her to his drinking.

One could argue that, by phrasing her interventions this way, the therapist treats the patient as a passive victim of his doubts, rather than as an active agent in creating his doubts. However, if the therapist is successful in conveying a picture to her patient of his activity, then he will get a sense of himself as a "bad" person, criticized by his therapist/mother. That is, if the patient wants to discharge his feelings of badness through projection, but the therapist responds by prematurely putting the feelings back into the patient, the patient might feel once again overwhelmed by the bad feelings and might then tend to act out by, in this case, drinking. If the therapist leaves open the question of who is "bad," the patient might feel more able to examine his badness at his own pace.

In general, the therapist is not doing as much as she could, even if we assume that she is working within Kernberg's overall orientation. I am not sure whether the constant confrontation will improve either the patient's reflective awareness or the therapeutic alliance. One option for the therapist, reflecting a recommendation by Kernberg, might have been to comment that the process that she was interpreting in the session—that is, that she and the minister were idealized and then devalued—might also have applied to his first marriage. By including his first wife, the therapist would have deflected the transference away from the therapeutic relationship, which might have been too much for the patient to handle now, to an outside relationship, which might have been easier for him to discuss. In this process, as Havens (1976) has pointed out, the therapist would be an implicit ally (as they both look at an outside relationship) rather than an implicit adversary (as he looks at his devaluation of her). The therapeutic alliance is fostered more easily in the former situation. Furthermore, the therapist is attempting to make ego-alien a defense—idealization and devaluation—that is ego-syntonic. She has a better chance to succeed at this if she focuses first on something about which the patient may have conscious distress than if she focuses on something that the patient is not only not troubled about, but that he consciously states saves him from unbearable loneliness.

Evolution of Transference Work

The patient came into the next session threatening to quit unless the therapist told him something he did not already know. After the last session he had felt so caught up in thought that he had to go to a movie to ease his mind. No, these were not new thoughts; they were things he already knew. The therapist spoke with him about the paradoxes she saw in his life: his urgency outside the hour, when he was alone and when he drank, juxtaposed with his seeming lack of concern about his problems inside sessions; his wanting her to talk, yet his interrupting when she spoke and his disagreeing with everything she said. She said that these contradictions reminded her of his seeking out religious authorities with his lists of questions and yet finding fault with their answers, and of his asking her for new insights and yet not thinking about what she had said when he went home. She suggested that there might be underlying explanations for these paradoxes. For example, he might feel that she had the right answers about his doubts and that if he seduced, cajoled, or threatened her enough, then he would force it out of her, and when this did not solve his problem by the end of a session, then this hope was dashed and he became angry and hopeless. Perhaps, she continued, even his initial wish—that she was a powerful authority with an answer for everything—was troublesome for him; perhaps it threatened something in him, so that when she even started to answer, he had to interrupt her. It was this conflict, about wanting and at the same time fearing the absolute truth from a powerful authority, that seemed to explain what appeared to be paradoxical.

The patient immediately replied that he knew all of this. All relationships were hard for him because people left; his therapist could leave; he often dreamt about people dying of cancer; even his parakeet had died when he was a child. He used to overprotect his dog, but it didn't save him. He had never had satisfying relationships. He had had one friend in high school that he always had to agree with, and then that friend left the church and was shunned by the church membership. The patient then paused and looked at the therapist.

The therapist commented that she felt he expected her to say something, and even though what she had said seemed to touch something in him which he had started to explore, he was now stopping his own exploration and looking to her to take over for him instead. He was again pushing aside his own feelings and looking for an authority to answer him and help him avoid where his feelings might lead him.

The patient sighed and nodded and spoke of how he compartmentalized everything in his life. He always felt hopeless, sad, depressed, alone; he always thought of calling her. But, he said, why go into it; if he went further, he'd only feel worse. He felt alone when he was with his girlfriend.

The therapist agreed that his compartmentalizing had helped him limit his sadness, but that his solution was also part of his problem. By cutting himself off from his feelings about himself and others, he also limited how much he could psychologically take in from them. He spontaneously spoke of his compulsive and excessive drinking. The therapist said that perhaps he was expressing these conflicts through his drinking, and that he kept his anxiety about the drinking at arm's length in order to keep his anxiety about what was expressed through the drinking in a separate compartment. He nodded and began to cry.

One session later, the patient wanted to know whether he should marry his girlfriend. Two sessions later, he called and asked for a referral to a dentist. The therapist asked whether he knew of other sources for such a referral and when he said that he did, she suggested that he ask them. He refused to discuss his request and her response at the next session. At that next session, which fell near Easter, he brought a cake with him, explaining that he hadn't had time to celebrate and assumed that the therapist had also been busy, so they could celebrate together. The therapist politely declined and wondered aloud about what his gesture told them about his feelings toward her.

Alternate Approach

The patient has made three consecutive requests for something concrete. In the last two instances, the therapist is in an awkward position. She can understand the patient's requests both as stimulated by the previous sessions and as reflecting his ego weakness. That is, perhaps feelings of closeness that arise after he has had an insightful session stimulate his wish for "more," which is expressed through his wish for something concrete from the therapist. One might even argue that the other side of his ambivalence is being expressed in his putting the therapist in a position that he must know would be awkward for her, and that he is thereby attempting to irritate her and drive her away. The ego weakness is expressed in the concrete way in which he needs evidence of closeness. The therapist's meeting his concrete request—that is, giving him a referral or having cake with him—might go along with his wish that the kind of giving she provides be concrete in nature, might arouse expectations of further concrete help, and might put the therapist in a position of functioning in the same concrete mode as her patient.

It would be preferable for the therapist to establish herself and the therapy as working more symbolically. The therapist is in an awkward position, however, because it is difficult to refuse the patient's requests without rebuffing his consciously experienced sincere need for a referral or his offer of cake. She needs to explain her refusal in a way that furthers the working alliance and that also does not require the patient, through identification with the aggressor, to adopt rules in which he does not really believe. The therapist seems to manage these requests well, but she should be alert for narcissistic rage.

I have assumed that the therapist ought to refuse his requests. Some might argue that the therapist should accede to the patient's requests because he does operate on a concrete level; because there is a tenuous working alliance; because it is impossible for her refusal to be experienced as something other than a narcissistic blow; and, ultimately, because the therapist can build a working alliance by starting on the patient's level of functioning. I do not agree. I believe that the therapist has a greater chance of doing insight-oriented work if she follows the former course. The latter alternative seems to offer too much opportunity for malignant regression and for demands by the patient that they focus on the manifest content of his material.

The patient responded by saying that therapy was like a date for him—but, he added quickly, he had not slept with his mother and did not have an Oedipus complex. He did dress up for his sessions and looked forward to them. He spoke of how confused he had felt as a child when his parents had divorced and his mother lived with a succession of young men. He had tried to push out his confused feelings because he had needed to connect with a strong woman. He felt good with his mother; she was strong and dynamic. He tried to feel connected with his therapist and with people at work, but these people weren't good for him. People were dangerous; he could get sucked into their problems. He had gone to a Christian college to escape the chaos in his family when his parents divorced. People were out of control; he wanted rules and certainty. So, the therapist said, he had looked for a clear, strong religious system that would help him feel safe from his chaotic feelings. He agreed, remembering that he had seen a poster saying "Jesus Saves" and had thought about Jesus as the answer for him. He had then decided to go to the Christian college.

Alternate Approach

The therapist would do better by emphasizing the patient's ambivalence—his wanting, on the one hand, to compete with his mother's boyfriends, and his fear, on the other hand, that he would be interested in his mother in what might feel to him like a sexual way. The therapist might connect this conflict to his fear of being "sucked in" to others or to the security in identifying with a nonsexual and powerful figure (Jesus). She might also tie this to his dressing up for the therapy sessions. How much of this to interpret is, again, a matter of judgment and tact. I think, though, that if the therapist refrains from interpreting the conflict against which the patient is defending, he will not become aware of it and will continue to act out aspects of it with the therapist. The therapist might lessen the probability of his acting out by helping him see the nature of the conflict along with his defense.

One might argue that the therapist's even mentioning the patient's competition with his mother's boyfriends or his sexualized wishes toward his mother would frighten him. He does, after all, hasten to tell his therapist that he has no Oedipus complex, and we know that he hears her interpretations as criticism. But if she phrases the interpretation in terms of his defenses against his own possible fears about competing for his mother or his own doubts and questions about his feelings about his mother, then she sides with his conscious defenses as she opens up the question of his unconscious wishes. Calling something a fear rather than a wish may make a considerable difference. Further, emphasizing that they are *his own* fears works against his tendency to project them onto the therapist.

> During the next session, the patient said that he was angry with the therapist because the appointments reminded him of appointments with his mother and the attention she paid to him—but he didn't want to get into that "oedipal thing"; he had learned all about that in school. He felt that the therapist criticized him and wasn't supportive. Her hair was the same color as his mother's.
>
> The patient then missed the next two sessions because he "forgot." He called on the telephone, and then threatened to quit because the therapist didn't spend enough time on the telephone with him. At about this time, the therapist announced a summer vacation. The patient became angrier, and a crisis developed around his current job. The therapist scheduled an extra session prior to her vacation and gave him her vacation telephone number for emergencies. The patient calmed down and spoke of missing her already.

Alternate Approach

The therapist might wish to address the denied "oedipal thing." The kinds of defenses the patient uses, including denial, projection, and flight indicate his panic. Thus, if the therapist interprets the "oedipal thing" directly, or interprets defenses against it directly, the patient is likely to become more frightened. The transference is sexualized and highly charged, however, and it needs to be addressed so that it can be altered to some analyzable form.

· Perhaps the therapist could interpret upward. She might say, for example, "It must have been hard for you, after your parents' divorce, to see your mother interested in men. You wanted your mother's support, and you might have started to think that the way to get her attention was through how you looked. Maybe you even started to confuse the support you wanted with sexual feelings that you really didn't want, and then you had to block the whole thing out. And now, in here, maybe you want my support and my attention, and you automatically start confusing that with sex, and then you get scared and forget the sessions." Such an intervention would place the situation on a more intellectual and controllable level, partially because it "interprets upward" to conflicts that are more socially acceptable and ego-syntonic. The therapist does give the patient her attention and her telephone number, and he calms down as these demands are met, but he has no insight into the way he sexualizes these needs and into the emerging transference and his defenses against it.

The patient called his therapist three times over her month-long vacation. Each call lasted for over a half hour. The two spent a good deal of time discussing his sense of emptiness and panic. All of his friends were away for the summer, and he had nobody. He was afraid to be alone in his apartment. He took long subway rides and picked up several women. They had mild sexual encounters which left him unsatisfied. He was drinking more heavily and had begun using barbiturates. The therapist listened to him, asked what his ideas were as to how he could get some control over himself, and supported his more practical suggestions. She also reminded him of when she would return, and she reassured him that they could then continue to look into what was so distressing to him.

Alternate Approach

Here it was more appropriate for the therapist to allow the patient to call. There is ample evidence of regression and dangerous behavior which is both a reaction to his sense of aloneness and a search for someone to fill him up. The therapist attempts to support his unstable holding introject through the telephone calls and supports his attempts to solve his practical problems while she is away.

Postvacation Sessions

In the first postvacation sessions, the patient reported that he felt more relaxed because he had a new girlfriend who had been paying attention to him. He denied feeling better because his therapist had returned. He eventually admitted that he felt good when he was singled out for special attention; it made him feel calm and forget how "gross" he felt. For the next two months, he seemed calmer.

The patient then took a job with a missionary organization for which he went from house to house handing out pamphlets, preaching Christian values, and attempting to recruit converts. The feelings evoked by the job were discussed in sessions. He had a sense of grandiosity (he felt like one of the original prophets, fighting against "secular decay" by his own people) and rationalized anger at "backstabbing Protestants who betray their own moral values."

Alternate Approach

Note that it is his "own" people and their "own" moral values against which the patient fights by attempting to convert those outside himself who possess the projected moral decay. As we see, this defense is not successful. Note also possible projected homosexual fears, which is one way of understanding what it is he is really fighting, as he rails against "secular decay" by "backstabbing" people who have betrayed their moral values.

He felt exhilarated, but seemed somewhat disorganized. He had difficulty sleeping and his weight began to drop, but he was unconcerned about his weight loss. He seemed a bit more scattered in sessions. He said that when he was not fighting with people, he felt "chaotic." He also seemed sexually stimulated by theological debates he was having with fellow missionaries and by those whom he was trying to convert. These emerging sexual feelings made him feel guilty.

The patient called after one session to report that he felt that everyone was laughing at him, but his friend had told him that it was just him laughing at himself. What did the therapist think? The therapist replied that she did not think people were laughing at him. He was glad that the therapist had said that. He said (for the first time) that he often felt that people were talking about him on the subway—didn't she know that? She said no, he hadn't told her. He replied, with annoyance, that he had thought she understood his problems, and he abruptly hung up.

In subsequent sessions, he spoke of his many girl-friends and his feeling that none of them equaled his ministers in appearance and intelligence. When the therapist suggested that perhaps his unfavorable comparisons of these women with his ministers had something to do with his dissatisfaction, he became irritated. He didn't want to hear interpretations; his goal was to feel good, and not to have his ideas punctured. He became more and more dissatisfied with treatment and several times threatened to quit. In one of these sessions, he said that he had to be "one up" on these women in order to maintain his individuality. He also spoke about his sense of guilt that others had been good to him but he did not reciprocate. He spoke of how he didn't want to be one of a crowd, so he reversed things and made sure he always had a string of women calling him.

These associations were always punctuated by insistence that his statements were meaningless and should not be analyzed. If the therapist suggested, for example, that his wanting a string of women chasing him was an attempt to reverse his feeling like one of a string of his mother's boyfriends chasing her after his parents' divorce, he said that she was too Freudian and, moreover, that she was wrong. He said he wanted her to make him feel good, to cheer him up; her comments were too critical. He would respond to the therapist's interventions by sarcastically asking, "Do you think that makes me feel good?" and to her silence by asking, "Do you think you're a better therapist because you're so quiet?" He complained that she didn't return his calls quickly enough and that she was short with him on the phone.

As the sessions continued, the therapist felt increasingly frustrated and irritated. As she understood the patient, he presented a combination of quick primitive idealization and then devaluation of his therapist, along with an acute experience of emptiness. When she attempted to be supportive by, for example, answering his questions whenever possible and permitting telephone calls, he told her that she wasn't at all supportive of him and that she hadn't ever said anything helpful or intelligent. At the same time, he dismissed whatever she did say to him and then asked for "support" because he felt so alone and panicked.

Throughout the stormy treatment, the therapist felt that she understood his intense conflict, yet she never quite felt comfortable as either analyst or source of support. One incident illustrates her feelings: The patient had called and left a message asking that she call him, that he wasn't feeling well. The therapist called several hours later, at her first opportunity, and was told by a calm-sounding patient that he felt much better, that he had spoken to several female friends and that everything was fine. There were several moments of silence. The therapist felt awkward at that point. She had just been told that she was not needed for whatever psychological emergency had prompted the call, and yet the patient showed no inclination to terminate the call. She had the feeling that he wanted to chat. The therapist said that she was glad he was feeling better and that they could discuss what had happened at their next scheduled appointment, the following day. He agreed and hung up, a bit abruptly. The next day, he was furious at the therapist for her "coldness," for her "rush" to end the telephone call, and for her lack of "support." He was totally uninterested in looking at what had happened.

The therapist again felt misunderstood and frustrated. She had returned the call as quickly as she could; she had been prepared to speak with the patient. He had seemed calm; he had implied in his tone and had said directly that there really was nothing he had to say at the moment. So she had, she felt, been following both his lead and conventional rules of courtesy when she had acknowledged that they had nothing to discuss on the telephone and would meet the following day. She even believed that she understood several of the issues: His rage, she felt, followed frustration of his unconscious wish that she chat with him and draw him out on the phone, like one of the girlfriends. Further, any woman was able to soothe him; women were interchangeable part-objects, and he was saying to her that while she was supremely important, she could also be, and had in fact been, replaced by several of his girlfriends. Yet the therapist felt frustrated in that the patient did not allow her to function as soother or analyst. When the therapist raised these issues, he would ignore her, feign interest and humor her, or dismiss any insight and ask how this would make him feel better.

The patient grew more and more convinced that the therapist wanted him to feel bad. She didn't like him, but he would get back at her by leaving treatment. He decided one day that the therapist's problem was that she was envious of, and rebellious toward, authorities in fields other than hers. He believed that this was particularly true for his field, theology. He believed that she wanted to convert him to her field, Freudian psychology. He expected that the therapist would claim that he was projecting, but he was certain that he was not.

Alternate Approach

The patient is rapidly moving into a psychotic transference. We can try to understand this from several points of view that highlight the therapist's stance.

The patient is torn over his conflict around his wish for merger through identification with his idealized therapist and his fear of such a wish. He is now working in a job in which he invites others to merge with him intellectually (one meaning of his attempting to convert them to his religion), yet he is probably often rejected; he even debates his fellow missionaries, with whom he is supposedly allied. He expects his therapist to know what he thinks without his telling her, and he is angry when she does not. He tells his therapist both that he wants to be singled out for special attention and that he will protect his boundaries by fighting with her and turning the tables on her. He can accomplish this only by rejecting everything she has to offer: support and interpretation. Thus, almost by definition, the therapy cannot work and the therapist cannot be important, for if she is successful and important, the patient will feel too drawn to merge with her. He fears that through merger he will lose something, perhaps his sense of identity. Of course, this is a simplified and global

view and neglects many other components of the transference, such as the patient's fear that his (sexualized) wish to
merge with the idealized therapist will touch on unconscious
sexualized wishes for his mother, whom he sees as strong yet
unstable. His wish and his maternal identification defend
him from his feelings toward and identification with his
"cold" father.

Within this broad outline of what may be going on in the
transference, the therapist's intervention alternatives depend
on how she understands (1) the nature of fantasy and (2) the
legitimacy or illegitimacy of the patient's demands.

First, a more classical perspective. From this point of
view, the conflict described is enflamed by fantasy. The patient may have the unconscious fantasy of being mommy's
special boy amidst all her boyfriends, which may cover the
unconscious oedipal fears that existed even before the
trauma of divorce. One might understand the patient's conflict around what seem to be issues of separation and individuation as really belonging to issues at the more advanced
oedipal level. On this level, he would fear closeness with his
therapist/mother because it would lead to retaliation by the
father, not because it would lead to a sense of merger and
loss of boundaries. His wishes toward his mother would be
sexual wishes disguised to some extent as wishes for closeness and dependence, because these would seem less oedi-
pally threatening.

The therapist would decide which level of interpretation
to emphasize by looking at the patient's structural level (Pine
1979). Whatever the level of interpretive emphasis, the fantasies are understood to have specific genetic referents, and it
is the defenses against these specific referents that are seen
as affecting the patient's current transference. These fantasies, like any other psychic act, have multiple functions; that
is, in addition to expressing a wish, they defend against other
wishes, serve an adaptive function, and reflect the various
psychological structures. These unconscious fantasies must
be interpreted in treatment.

The patient's demands, then, tend to be viewed as primarily (although not entirely) illegitimate; it is the unconscious conflict which is causing difficulty for the patient, and the therapist cannot do anything other than interpret this conflict. However, it is through her special sensitivity to the fragility of this patient's defenses and to his generally disturbed level of psychological functioning that the therapist will attempt to gear her interpretive efforts so that the patient will be more able to bear interpretations and benefit from the reparative object relationship that is inherent in this kind of therapy. The therapist would see her irritation as countertransference; if she kept her eye on the psychoanalytic ball, if she slowly and laboriously continued to point out the patient's conflicts, she would not be so irritated with him.

From a Kernbergian perspective, the fantasies reflect something over and above their genetic referents. They are inherent in the nature of primitive defenses and seem to exist almost independently of the patient's specific history. Thus, the patient's defense of primitive idealization comprises the primitive fantasy that an all-knowing, all-powerful "good" figure will protect him against all the "bad" that is around him. This defense supports an omnipotent, grandiose self-representation. We can see this defense operating in the patient's work, where he is identified with Jesus, and in the transference, where the therapist is alternately idealized and devalued.

Within the therapy, we see the primitive defense of projective identification. The patient puts into the therapist his own coldness and then attempts to control the coldness he has put into her; he treats her as if she were a cold person, thus finally evoking her coldness toward him, and thereby confirming the projective identification. There is reality in the projective identification, in that the therapist knows that there are cold aspects to her personality. But by the patient's treating her as if she were *only* cold, by ignoring the supportive aspects of her personality, by taking the "coldness" out of context and by completely denying the rest of her personality, the therapist is made to feel and to act like a cold person. The patient then attempts to manage and control the coldness, which is now located in the therapist instead of in himself. In this way, the projective identification is enacted.

Thus the therapist's feelings are not only what we would consider countertransference in the narrow sense—that is, inappropriate feelings from her past which she brings to the treatment situation—but can also be understood as countertransference in the broader sense—feelings that reflect her empathy for her patient and her immersion in the therapy. Here too, the therapist sees the patient's demands, as illegitimate, since they do not reflect the patient's dependency needs. Instead they reflect what Kernberg would describe as the patient's incapacity to depend on anyone because of splitting and related primitive defenses. Kernberg's technical recommendations are specifically geared toward dealing with the regression we are seeing. His focus would be on a combination of limit-setting and interpretation. Limits, such as prohibiting the telephone calls or, if necessary, forbidding discharge of unneutralized rage at the therapist, would be invoked both to give the therapist space within which to interpret (that is, to guard her technical neutrality) and to limit psychotic regression. Kernberg would set such limits early in treatment, based on his diagnostic assessment of the patient (Kernberg 1987b).

We can attempt to understand this patient from yet a third perspective. Here, unconscious fantasy is greatly deemphasized, and the legitimacy of the patient's demands is stressed. It is not only that his demands are understood to reflect legitimate psychological needs—perhaps the need for the therapist to act in some way to bolster an unstable internal representation (to act as a holding introject); it is also that the patient's perspective becomes of major importance. When the therapist attempts to decide what defenses are being used and what she will gratify or not gratify and what is legitimate and what is based on unconscious fantasy, she is establishing herself as an umpire of the patient's psychological life and of his reality. She may feel that she is neutral, but she is actually imposing her perspective on the patient. In contrast, the therapist may choose to try to understand the patient from his perspective as much as possible without deciding in advance what is or is not "realistic."

We would look for the therapist to implicitly or explicitly acknowledge the legitimacy of the patient's need for her as an idealized object, even as she interprets conflict around this wish. For example, in the therapist's account, he calls her, tells her that he feels that people are laughing at him on the subways, and asks her whether this is true. She then helps him reality test, occupying what might be called the umpire's point of view. He responds by being critical of her. Why not assume that she did, in fact, "not know" him at that moment and that there is some validity to his disappointment? He then says that none of his girlfriends equal his minister, and the therapist interprets to him that his unfavorable comparisons of his girlfriends to his ministers contribute to his disappointment with his girlfriends. Her interpretation is a statement about his behavior as seen from her outside perspective, and he responds, again, by saying that she doesn't make him feel good and that his ideas are "punctured."

The therapist continues in this vein, understanding his dissatisfaction as primarily defensive, and the situation continues to deteriorate, with his basic complaint being that she does not understand him or make him feel good. Again, I believe that the therapist's understanding is dynamically accurate, and I also agree with Kernberg's position that the therapist must be empathic with what the patient projects, especially the negative feelings, as well as with what the patient feels. Still, why could the therapist not accept the idea that his dissatisfaction comes from her repeatedly "puncturing" some unspoken wish and, from a perspective that accepts the legitimacy of his disappointment as his psychological truth, inquire and interpret his sense of specialness, strength, and power when he feels at center stage on the subway and when he feels connected with the minister? The therapist would not focus on what he does to destroy relationships with eligible women; rather, she would focus on how difficut it must be for him when the women he dates are so disappointing. Both approaches should eventually lead to his wish and conflict around union with an idealized female authority, but this approach might carry the patient along more effectively, since the issue would be approached from his perspective.

The therapist, again and again, is placed in the position of confronting a character defense that is ego-syntonic. The patient becomes "resistant," especially since he sees only disaster and loneliness as the "gain" in giving up his wish. In this third approach, it is the patient who will, at his own pace, decide to look at his wishes because he will see how, from his own perspective, he is left unfulfilled because of his own conflict. Further, he will become able to confront himself if he experiences the therapist as an ally in the process of making his defense ego-alien, not as an opponent who is "puncturing" his defenses.

Unfortunately, most of those who advocate this position state that they are facilitating a self–object transference at this stage. They then commit themselves to Kohut's theoretical position regarding the analysis of narcissistic patients. We are not necessarily talking about facilitating a self–object transference, and we don't need to adopt the assumptions of self psychology. We are discussing tact, pace of interpretation, technique of resistance analysis, and, perhaps, awareness of the working alliance and impediments to this alliance. All of these factors fall within the rubric of classical psychoanalytic psychotherapy, certainly as it is practiced and modified with the more disturbed patient.

Within this third point of emphasis, the therapist might make all of the interventions she has been making, but from a point of view that accepts as legitimate the patient's wish for a relationship with his therapist that is not threatened by her interpretive comments. The therapist would not, at this point, ask him to look at or focus on this wish. She might focus on his feeling that his special relationship won't last, and his tendency to "reverse things" with women or his need to ignore interpretations because he fears that they will destroy what he wants—a sense of union and perfect understanding with his therapist. In this way, the therapist interprets the patient's "resistance" as a fear that by looking at his motivations, he will discover feelings that will overwhelm his sense of closeness to the therapist.

This is not very different from Kernberg's theoretical understanding of the function of primitive idealization, but it is geared toward the patient's point of view: We're speaking of his *fear* that what he learns will be "bad" and will interfere with the special relationship that now makes him feel "good," rather than of his *wish* to create a special relationship in order to get rid of the badness he now feels. In the former case, he will feel good as he looks at his fear; in the latter case, he'll feel bad after the interpretation. The therapist might also focus on the other side: the patient's feeling guilty about his wishes because he sometimes feels anger at his therapist, or sometimes has to fight her to keep his own individuality. The therapist analyzes in all these instances, but here she implicitly respects his right to want this relationship instead of, at this point, analyzing and therefore calling into question his central wish. Perhaps this approach would lead to a less stormy treatment, and perhaps the patient would not call the therapist between sessions as much as he does because the cycle of his disappointment, then rage, then further seeking his therapist would be interrupted.

Finally, we can see the truth in the patient's final "paranoid" accusation; in fact, the therapist does want him to feel bad, to adopt her "Freudian" perspective. That is, she wants him to accept the loss of his infantile fantasies, modify his defenses, and accept reality. Note that the therapist never simply accepts his wish to "feel good"; she always interprets it or acknowledges it, only to dismiss it by saying that it gets him into trouble. It is true that one sometimes interprets a defense by showing the patient the price he pays for the defense. Again, we are talking about pace, timing, and tact. The therapist is impatient and wants the patient to grow up and listen to her, to her interpretations and her support. Meanwhile, she has no alliance with him and no agreement on what they are analyzing. She is trying to analyze defenses that are not only ego-syntonic but that are viewed by the patient as crucial to his own psychological survival.

The foregoing are three perspectives on the process of treatment of this very difficult patient. They all have a certain validity. My point has been to illustrate the ways in which these perspectives determine the therapist's treatment stance.

The Last Phase of Treatment

In subsequent sessions the patient alternated between criticizing the therapist and then telling her that, on a recent religious retreat, he had thought about her when he was anxious and that calmed him down. He spoke of feeling disorganized in his work. On inquiry, it turned out that he was unable to work when he was alone at home because he became too anxious. He felt that there was no God in his life. He went to church frequently but felt dissatisfied. His drinking had lessened for a while but had become more frequent again. Sessions before weekends were most difficult for him because he felt so alone and didn't want to leave the therapist. He called her one weekend and was angry when she didn't return his call that night. He complained that she didn't support him enough. In one session, he repeated that he forgot everything they had discussed when he left the session.

He told the therapist that when he had gone to a Christian summer camp, he had fallen in love with the director. In college, he fell in love with his minister. Since then, he had learned not to become involved. He accomplished this by forgetting things, especially his feelings. At school, he used to become so anxious that he couldn't concentrate and then he learned to get all his work done but he ignored everyone else, all of his social life. He left people out. He then began to cry and told his therapist that he was attracted to her and wished she would come home with him. The therapist replied that she could not do that, but that they could talk about how he could remember what they talked about when he was at home. The patient responded that that was not the same thing and that these were feelings he had never known he had. He said that he wanted to rest on a lap, "any lap."

The patient terminated treatment after five more sessions. Three of the sessions will be presented in some detail.

The Final Three Sessions

SESSION 1

The patient spoke rapidly throughout the session. His cousin had always shown a lot of bitterness to his parents, and he had an easy time with other relationships. He had no bitterness toward his parents but he had no feelings for others. He had started reading about humanistic psychology and he was neglecting his theological reading. Religion used to mean everything to him; now he walked around saying, "Prove it to me."

This reminded him of how he had become so depressed at school, when he felt his bubble burst. He believed that either he was right and everyone at school was wrong or they were right and he was completely wrong. He was totally consumed with Jesus and completely opposed to everyone else at school. He knew that something wasn't quite right with him. He wasn't "into the real world." He wasn't communicating with others; he believed that involvement with others would detract from his thinking about Jesus. He would talk only about Jesus, so he was alone most of the time. He would view fortunes on tea bags as major revelations. He would drive around and imagine his minister sitting in the car next to him.

He really believed that Jesus was born again and that he would meet him. He would see a man with long hair and a beard and think it was Jesus. He used to get excited reading the gospels. He would try to discuss scriptures with people. In psychology class, he perceived a war between secular values and religious values, and he was losing what he was given because he was choosing idolatry over Jesus. He failed his final exam in psychology. Everything around him was idolatry except for Jesus. When he spoke to his minister about the idolatrous secular values, the minister replied that maybe those values were inside himself; that response had hurt him.

The therapist commented that perhaps the patient felt that in his religious state he was missing something about himself and others, and that that was why he was at war.

Alternate Approach

The therapist's timing is off. She repeats the narcissistic blow delivered by the minister. The patient went to his minister with his problems; the minister interpreted them; and the patient felt bad. Now the therapist does the same thing. She should expect intensification of his defensive grandiosity in the transference. She might have done better by remaining silent or by talking about how the patient felt that the purity of his religious state was always threatened by what he was seeing and learning, and that he had no help in integrating his religious values with his college experiences; even his minister couldn't help.

The patient disagreed, insisting that he had actually been happier then than he had ever been before. He had believed that he was on a "high level." He was better than anyone else, but he didn't think that way. He saw himself as humble; he felt that he was fulfilling divine directives by not becoming involved with others. Now he was bothered by constant contradiction. Then he had felt no sense of pull; he always knew the answer. If he ever did anything "wrong," though, he felt terrible. Once he yelled at his roommate because his girlfriend had spent the night with him, and then he confessed to the minister how terrible he was.

He saw psychology as the epitome of everything secular. At school, he didn't do secular things, only Christian things. He went to church and read holy books. He didn't read trashy, cheap novels. He thought only about "higher things." He had been very closed minded, not in an intellectual way, but in that he could see only his own way. He had been very spiritual; now he wondered if there was anything spiritual in him. He used to "get high" on the Gospels; not it seemed ridiculous. Those he had seen as divine looked down-to-earth to him now. He was afraid. He feared that if he married, he would kill himself.

The therapist asked how he meant that.

The patient replied that he "couldn't do it." The thought of settling down, especially with a child, would be a terrible experience, so he would kill himself. He was very happy, but he had this tremendous fear, and he was getting to the stage at which he would have to marry and have children in order to be consistent with his religious values. He had believed that "truly Christian people," like the Amish, were better than he was, and now he viewed them as archaic. He saw no middle ground. He could not integrate loving Jesus and devoting his life to religious work with believing that those super-religious Christians had no understanding of Freud and reality.

He had always felt as though he were living in a bubble; he was totally pure. Later he realized how he hated himself. But the feeling of purity was real because he was pure; he was consistent with his ideals. Then the psychology class came along. They had ideas he had never thought about. A few years before, he would have taken the same class with the same ideas and he would have put them out of his mind. Now they shook him.

The therapist asked what it was that made him ready to hear those ideas at that point.

The patient replied that he realized that his problems had to surface before he graduated. He unconsciously knew that he had a problem and he had to take care of it before he graduated. He had to face it. But he had no idea what was going on; he had no conception of time or day. He had crazy dreams. But he was happy; he knew he had a problem, but he was happy. He was so happy and secure with Jesus and in that religious school that he was able to let his problems surface.

Alternate Approach

Here the patient momentarily relinquishes his externalization and says that he knew he had a problem. His statement that he was able to let his problems surface at school, where he was so happy and secure with Jesus, suggests something about the conditions necessary for him to speak about himself in therapy. What those conditions are is arguable. Self psychologists will point to the feeling of security in his identification with an idealized authority and will say that what is necessary for the patient is an idealizing transference. Others might focus on the "religious school" and emphasize a strong frame in treatment or interpretation of his sexualized transference along with, perhaps, a statement that such thoughts would not lead to actual behavior in treatment.

The therapist began, "So you were receptive. . . ."
The patient interrupted, insisting that he was not receptive. He had fought his professor all the time. But he knew the ideas enough that they shook him up.

Alternate Approach

The patient repeatedly plays out the content of his speech in the transference. He may also object to the symbolic meaning of "receptive." He may feel that the therapist is accusing him of being female, and he fears the homosexual aspect of his sexuality. This fear may also make it difficult for him to engage in joint therapeutic work with his therapist, and may make frequent defensive arguments necessary for him. To take on his therapist's perspective, to identify with her, to "take her in," may exacerbate passive, feminine fears. Thus, in addition to their historical meaning, the arguments protect against merging and against homosexual fears.

The therapist asked which ideas shook him up. The patient replied that there was a movie and a question on the final exam. A male character in the movie said that he was afraid that his mother didn't know him. On the exam, it was something about a mother who left her baby crying, something about spilt milk, and as soon as he got to that line, he began to tremble. He started to believe that he was receiving secret messages from his professor. He thought that he had a secret relationship with her, and what frightened him most was his belief that the final, which was standard, was geared specifically toward him. The patient ended by saying that he expected brilliant ideas from his therapist next session. His friend's doctor gave her new ideas all the time, but he never learned anything from his own doctor.

Alternate Approach

The therapist asks a question that elicits new, interpretable material. Further, the patient asks, in a challenging way, for an interpretation.

Several observations can be made at this point. The patient spoke rapidly throughout the session, and I believe that, as he spoke about his bubble bursting in school, he was simultaneously attempting to preserve the bubble in the session. One way to accomplish this task is to speak without thinking and to fight any comments by the therapist that might threaten the bubble, which is based on denial, externalization, and reaction formation. The bubble might be his need for a transference that would bolster his grandiosity, a shaky defense against his emptiness and low self-esteem; or "puncturing his bubble" might mean that he, as a female, is being penetrated by the therapist's interpretations. Regardless of which interpretation she chooses, the therapist might be most successful if she interprets from a point of view that accepts the patient in his bubble. The therapist needs to be interpretive, but in a way that is least narcissistically disruptive (least likely to "puncture" in the patient's term) and that is most likely to develop the working alliance.

The therapist could begin with the patient's defense: "You were telling me how you started to realize that even though you were happy in your bubble, you were also unhappy. But as you told me about this, I think you were trying, here with me, to keep the protection of your bubble a little while longer. You showed me that by interrupting me when I tried to speak and by denying your unhappiness and protesting about how good you felt, even while your point was how you had been protecting your unhappiness in your bubble. In fact, it sounds like you had decided to listen to ideas that disturbed you—in class then and in session with me now—even though you knew that you would fight them openly while you thought about them. So I think you do with me what you did in school: You start to face things about yourself here, in a place where you feel protected, but you have to fight me while you face them."

The therapist would at some point interpret that which the patient was defending against: the meaning of his failing his psychology exam. "I think what you were starting to realize was how special and loved by your parents you wanted to feel and how abandoned you did feel. Religion made you feel special for a while, but it wasn't enough anymore."

The therapist might try to break up the long interpretation, but she might alternatively consider just saying all of it in a soothing voice, with the idea that the "music" of her interpretation might be more helpful at this point than the words. That is, since the patient feels upset in a difficult-to-analyze way when he hears ideas which conflict with his own thoughts, the therapist could try emphasizing her soothing voice quality, which would make the patient feel less threatened by content and more enveloped in a joint bubble, a bubble of shared calm. Within this atmosphere, the patient would be threatened by closeness. The patient could then choose a part of the interpretation to deal with or argue against. Thus the therapist's voice and length of her remarks would provide an atmosphere balanced by the content of her words. The patient could then penetrate actively rather than being penetrated passively by short, succinct, content-oriented interventions.

The therapist can facilitate the working alliance by drawing the patient along with her as she interprets. If she helps him become aware of what he might perceive as a contradiction, then he will be looking, along with her, for the answer to the contradiction, which is her interpretation. In this way, the patient will perceive interpretation as help from a trusted figure rather than as another assault on ego-syntonic defenses.

SESSION 2

In the last session before a weekend, the patient began by saying that he felt very depressed. His supervisor at work called to change his schedule without asking him, and although he was furious at her, he couldn't tell her. Also, he was getting nothing from the therapist. This whole thing was one giant joke on him. He stopped, looked at her, and told her to say something brilliant.

The therapist began, "You know, I'm puzzled. . . ."
The patient interrupted, exclaiming that he sometimes

wished she wouldn't be so puzzled. He wondered what her medical degree was for!

Alternate Approach

It could be that the patient attacks her so quickly because her saying "I'm puzzled" breaks down the idealizing transference; Jesus is never puzzled. The patient also has not separated her mental representation from the representation of his supervisor, with whom he is enraged. Still, it is a quick attack.

> The therapist began again, "Actually . . ." and was again interrupted. The patient angrily asked why she didn't just say something to cheer him up; he was depressed. There were plenty of therapists that could make him feel good.
>
> The therapist replied by admitting that she was stuck. She wanted to say something to help him feel good, but it was hard to do that when he interrupted her and threatened her. It was all right for him to say those things, but it was hard for her, in that kind of emotional climate, to say something supportive to him, so she has to answer him this way: She thought he was depressed for many reasons, and the depression he usually felt at the last session before the weekend made it all feel worse.

Alternate Approach

The therapist is too angry to talk to the patient and should try to refrain from intervening until she regains her self-control. Kernberg repeatedly warns that the therapist should not confront a patient when he is angry. The patient demands a response from the therapist, however, even as he does not permit her to give one.

There are those who believe that therapists should share their feelings with the patient, as though the patient is responsible for the therapist's feelings. I do not agree with that position. What the therapist does is interesting, though, in that she starts out with her feelings ("I'm stuck") and attempts to express them in as neutral a manner as she can, by tying her reactions to the session ("I want to say something to help you feel good, but it's hard to do when you stop me, interrupt me, and threaten me"). Her superego intervenes at this point—"It's all right for you to say those things"—but she continues—"It's hard for me, in that kind of emotional climate, to say something supportive to you, so I have to answer you this way." By then she has regained her bearings, so she finishes with a rather bland comment. She needed to express some anger or frustration in order to get back to a position from which she could interpret. It is also not clear that the patient can in fact say whatever he likes; Kernberg might prohibit just this kind of statement in order to protect both patient and therapist from what might have happened here if the therapist had not been able to regain control of her anger.

> The patient asked why she thought he was so depressed.
> The therapist replied that it was because of what he had said last session, how underneath the bubble he felt that he didn't get a certain kind of milk from his mother and didn't have a special relationship with his father. When his supervisor forced him to change his hours, and when he thought that other patients get more insights from their doctors while he got nothing from her, she thought it reminded him of not getting those special things from his parents. So he became depressed and angry at her for not making up for those deficits.

Alternate Approach

By now the atmosphere seems to have changed and the therapist can make an interpretation.

> The patient sarcastically replied that that was what a therapist would say, but he seemed a bit more relaxed. He said that maybe he would call her that night to complain.

Alternate Approach

The patient still needs to oppose the therapist, but now he does it lovingly.

The patient did, in fact, call that night. The therapist answered, and he said he had expected her answering service. He had called to say that he felt all right. The therapist said that she was glad he felt better. There was a long pause. The therapist said that she would speak with him at their next session.

SESSION 3

The patient was furious with her. He was just filled with anger and frustration. He was going to leave therapy at the end of this year. She was no help to him; she didn't have an empathic bone in her body. He had called his friend to cheer him up and he gave him advice. When he called her, she should have realized that he was in pain and she should have reached out to him.

The therapist reminded him that he had said that he felt better, and that he hadn't even expected to reach her in person in the first place.

The patient replied that she was supposed to be a psychiatrist. She should have reached out to him. His other doctors would have. His last doctor was so out-reaching that she was probably divorced because she gave so much time to her patients. He then yawned and gave the therapist a broad smile.

The therapist pointed out the incongruity of his expressing his anger and then yawning and smiling.

The patient replied that he was yawning because he was tired. He didn't understand anything she said to him.

The therapist wondered whether the smile might give them a clue to something he was feeling that wasn't immediately obvious. What did he make of the smile?

The patient didn't make anything of it. There was a very long pause and then he asked abruptly, "What are you doing on Saturday night?" The therapist asked why he asked.

The patient explained that she obviously didn't have anything useful to say to him, and they had time to kill, so he figured he would ask. He couldn't understand anything she said to him, and whatever she said had no effect on his problems. After all, he was still drinking and he still felt depressed. Her insight approach didn't work. At that point, he smiled broadly.

The therapist pointed out the smile. It was almost triumphant.

Alternate Approach

The therapist is trying to get the patient to notice the smile as a way of encouraging his interest in his splitting.

So what, the patient said, so it was, so what if he was angry? What did that teach him about anything? He was less angry than other people in his family were. Now what could she tell him to help him with his problems? Everything she said was a criticism. She kept finding problems and insulting him instead of cheering him up. Like when she told him that he put down his girlfriends. That didn't make him feel cheerful. Didn't she have anything to say?

The therapist said that she thought that he got so angry with her that he wanted to totally annihilate her and make her feel as criticized and low as he often felt. He treated her like he felt she treated him. But the cost to him was that he felt alone after he had killed her off in his mind.

Alternate Approach

Here the therapist attempts to interpret projective identi-fication. The patient, in this session, provides clear examples of splitting and its related defenses, such as projective identification. His asking, "What are you doing on Saturday night?" for example, like his telling the therapist, "You're cute," are examples of unneutralized anger, even though the words are spoken calmly. It is not just that they are almost overtly hostile; it is that they seem to have no context other than that provided by the therapist as she attempts to understand his associations. The patient feels no need to attempt to provide such a context; he feels no need to provide a "because" to the anger, even though such a requirement is generally assumed by those working with secondary-process thinking. His smile, too, is dissociated from the content of his words. He says something hurtful, leans back, yawns, and smiles vaguely. We interpret that he smiles because he is triumphant over the therapist, but we categorize this behavior as splitting because of his lack of interest in the contradictory nature of his verbal and nonverbal communication.

The patient said that he knew he was angry with her. Couldn't she say something simple?

The therapist said that she thought he felt crushed by her, so he tried to crush her instead in order to feel powerful.

The patient replied that she wouldn't see him again.

CONCLUDING SESSIONS

In the next session, the patient said that he wanted to remain calm, that he didn't want to discuss anything that might upset him because he had important things to do at work. He wanted to leave therapy at the end of the month because she still depressed him. She was not cheerful, he said, although he did like her sweater. The therapist attempted to review what they had discussed and to offer an interpretation. The patient interrupted: He had already forgotten what she had said.

In the following session, he explained that he had decided to quit therapy because, he said, "You suck."

She was not helpful, and he was filled with anger at her. She concentrated too much on his problems, and he wanted to feel good. He had a referral from a friend for another doctor. The therapist suggested further discussion, but he declined: She wasn't helpful to him and that was that. He stood up and walked out the door.

3 _____

Supportive and Expressive Therapy

Psychoanalysts have long been concerned with defining psychoanalysis and differentiating it from psychotherapy. Psychotherapy itself has been further differentiated into categories, such as therapy with patients who diagnostically could work in psychoanalysis but who will not for a variety of external reasons, and therapy with patients who are too disturbed for psychoanalysis. Therapy with the former group has traditionally been called *expressive psychotherapy* or *psychoanalytic psychotherapy*, whereas therapy with the latter has been called *supportive psychotherapy* (Kernberg 1980a, Wallerstein and Robbins 1956). These distinctions have been the subject of considerable debate. The debate has had at least two unfortunate consequences. First, definitions of expressive psychotherapy and supportive psychotherapy have not sufficiently reflected recent advances in understanding of the severely disturbed patient. Moreover, supportive therapy has always been relegated to the bottom of the status scale (Schlesinger 1969).

Kernberg (1984) states that for "all nonpsychotic, non-organic psychopathology—supportive psychotherapy is rarely if ever the treatment modality of choice. In fact, I think that as a general rule the indication for supportive psychotherapy for these patients derives from the contra-indication for expressive psychotherapy" (p. 168). Pine writes that in the traditional contrast between insight-oriented psychotherapy and supportive psychotherapy, supportive therapy is considered "a mindless wasteland, not guided by a theory of human functioning" (p. 137), while insight-oriented therapy is seen as more influenced by psychoanalytic thought.

Little, therefore, has been written about technique in supportive therapy. Recent advances in our knowledge of the psychopathology of borderline patients clarify our understanding of the process of therapy and allow us to spell out the positive indications for, and the specific technique of, a psychoanalytically based supportive approach.

Traditional Definitions

Definitions of supportive and expressive therapy usually begin with a definition of psychoanalysis and then include similarities and differences between these two forms of psychotherapy and psychoanalysis itself. Gill (1954) defines psychoanalysis as "that technique which, employed by a neutral analyst, results in the development of a regressive transference neurosis and the ultimate resolution of this neurosis by techniques of interpretation alone" (p. 775). Gill (1954, 1984) then attempts to distinguish between psychoanalysis, on the one hand, and, on the other hand, psychoanalytic psychotherapy for patients who could benefit and those who could not benefit from psychoanalysis. As Wallerstein (1969) points out, however, this sharp distinction is controversial. Questions arise: What constitutes psychoanalysis? Is psychoanalytic psychotherapy an entity based on psychoanalytic theory that is more than suggestion? Should therapists sharpen or blur the distinction between psychoanalysis and psychoanalytic psychotherapy? Is there a distinction, within the rubric of psychoanalytic psychotherapy, between expressive and supportive approaches? It is this last question which concerns us most here.

There have been many attempts (Kernberg 1984, Schlesinger 1969) to distinguish between expressive psychotherapy (also termed psychoanalytic psychotherapy) and supportive psychotherapy. Most definitions follow those of Wallerstein and Robbins (1956) and Wallerstein (1986), who assert that supportive psychotherapy is devoted to strengthening defenses. They cite Gill (1951), who discussed methods of supporting defenses. Since the purpose of such therapy is to support defenses, then catharsis or insight, which are usually seen as characteristic of exploratory therapy, are permissible as long as their *use* is to support defenses, rather than to uncover conflict. For example, certain types of insight may strengthen defenses. Wallerstein and Robbins give the example of an intellectual, or "partial," insight, which functions to keep affective material in repression. Such partial insights, which bolster defenses, along with catharsis, identification with a benevolent authority, and some suggestion, have been considered hallmarks of supportive psychotherapeutic technique (Gill 1954, Kernberg 1980a, 1984, Wallerstein and Robbins 1956). Pine (1976) emphasizes the therapist's role in helping to maintain the patient's object tie thereby facilitating defense. Wallerstein and Robbins state that supportive psychotherapy is appropriate for healthy patients who are overwhelmed by panic in a crisis, and for chronically ill patients. Discussions of supportive therapy generally focus on work with the latter group.

Wallerstein and Robbins state that, diagnostically, supportive psychotherapy is appropriate for patients with "fragile egos," for whom uncovering techniques might increase anxiety in a manner that would overload the ego and lead to further regression. Supportive therapy seeks to stabilize a weakened ego, whether weakened through life stress or character pathology. The therapist stabilizes the ego by encouraging the patient to temporarily use his (the therapist's) ego.

This definition of supportive therapy is limited in its goals. Supportive therapy is viewed as a means of stabilizing a tenuous situation rather than as a first step toward more fundamental change. The definition omits the major hallmark of psychoanalytic work, which is classically seen as the route to fundamental and long-lasting change: analysis of transference. It is here that the demarcation between supportive and expressive psychotherapy is strongest. In contrast to supportive therapy, expressive therapy deals with interpretation of transference but without analyzing it back to genetic roots, which is within the province of psychoanalysis proper. Expressive therapy is thus the most inclusive category of psychotherapy, since *any* psychoanalytic psychotherapy that devotes any attention to analysis of transference (as opposed to recognition of or manipulation of transference) falls within this rubric. In psychoanalysis and expressive therapy, defenses are analyzed toward the goal of reintegration. Psychoanalysis and expressive therapy differ only in terms of the depth and breadth of the uncovering. Supportive therapy, on the other hand, works toward strengthening defenses in order to make repression more effective.

Difficulties with Traditional Definitions

Wallerstein (1986) notes that early definitions of expressive and supportive therapy sharpened the conceptual and technical differences between them. However, the distinctions between the two are quite difficult to maintain in clinical practice.

These distinctions have also been criticized on conceptual grounds. Schlesinger (1969) states that *supportive* and *expressive* are descriptive of *all* psychotherapy. Their use as category names confuses the clinician and obscures essential questions; for example, what in the patient needs to be supported or expressed? In what way can the therapist offer support or opportunity for expression? Schlesinger believes that we mistakenly write as if the terms are antithetical, that it is as if we do either supportive or expressive therapy. In practice, this is seldom the case, and the terms ought to be used more precisely to describe how each aspect is to be used within a given therapy. Wallerstein (1986) endorses this position in his analysis of the Menninger psychotherapy research study.

Pine (1985) has offered a similar criticism of the counterposition of *supportive* and *expressive* as category names. He proposes instead "two parallel terms: psychoanalytically oriented *insight* therapy and psychoanalytically oriented *supportive* therapy. . . . Supportive and insight therapies are not counter*posed* in some *opposition* to one another but counter*poised*, in some *balance* with one another" (p. 138).

Pine writes that the difference between supportive and insight-oriented therapy is not in emphasis on interpretation. Interpretation is seen as central in both forms. Rather, "the real dichotomy is in the *context* in which those interpretations are given. Interpretation can be given in the context of *abstinence* or in the context of *support*" (Pine 1985, p. 166, his emphasis). He later writes:

> Another way to look at support versus abstinence as the dichotomous contexts in which interpretations may be given is by asking which context will help elicit the content in *workable* ways (that will not flood the patient or cause him to flee) and which will allow the patient to *take in* and use the interpretation. [p. 167, his emphasis]

Although supportive psychotherapy and psychoanalysis are different forms of treatment, the therapist's underlying attitude toward the patient is the same in both. The way in which the therapist works toward the goal of cure through insight is different for each, however.

Another kind of criticism of these terms has been offered by analysts with as disparate points of view as Blanck and Blanck (1974, 1979) and Kernberg (1980a, 1984). These analysts argue that the concepts implied in the definitions used by Wallerstein and Robbins (1956) have been altered by new developments in psychoanalytic theory. Current analysts are more precise than Wallerstein and Robbins when discussing the fragile ego. They do not focus on the predominant conflict as between a strong id and a fragile ego. These analysts also emphasize internalization in treatment to a greater extent than did earlier analysts.

For Blanck and Blanck (1974), who feel that "in psychotherapy, structure building is the very purpose of treatment" (p. 122), the assumptions used by early theorists of supportive therapy have changed. Blanck and Blanck believe that a weak ego is not necessarily the result of inadequate repression, requiring supressive and supportive techniques.

> That view neglects psychoanalytic developmental theory altogether. It does not consider ego growth as a possibility; it regards suppression as competent to replace repression; it does not view support as ego support in the sense that ego building can, in many cases, follow support. We propose that the psychiatric "suppressive-supportive" techniques are now outdated. [p. 142]

Blanck and Blanck (1974, 1979) emphasize ego-building, with a focus on support and on the patient–therapist relationship. Wallerstein (1986), in analyzing the Menninger study, also sees these factors as crucial in work with disturbed patients, although he discusses them from his own theoretical point of view rather than from the approach advocated by Blanck and Blanck. In contrast, Kernberg disagrees with earlier conceptions of supportive and expressive therapy, but his criticisms lead him to focus on confrontation and interpretation rather than on support and relationship.[1]

Kernberg (1980a, 1984) also disagrees with the traditional assumptions regarding expressive and supportive therapy, but from a different theoretical vantage point. He amplifies the traditional ego-psychological conception underlying Wallerstein and Robbins's (1956) definitions of supportive and expressive therapy. According to Kernberg (1980a), the assumptions of ego psychology that underlie expressive therapy are that it

> . . . does not attempt to systematically resolve unconscious conflicts, and therefore, resistances, but rather to partially resolve some and reinforce other resistances, with a subsequent partial integration of previously repressed impulses with the adult ego. As a result, a partial increase of ego strength and flexibility may take place, which then permits a more effective repression of residual, dynamically unconscious, impulses and a modified impulse-defense configuration which increases the adaptive—in contrast to maladaptive—aspects of character formation. [p. 183]

Kernberg's difficulty with this conception of pathology is well known. He believes that expressive therapy is more effective for patients with strong egos than it is for borderline patients, and he offers several reasons. First, if one assumes that splitting defenses are inherently ego-weakening, then selective interpretation of some defenses does not help strengthen the fragile ego; instead, systematic confrontation of all these defenses is necessary. Second, material assumed to be repressed by traditional assumptions is, in fact, expressed consciously (in split-off self and object representa-

---

[1]Kernberg notes that he, too, bases his approach on findings of the Menninger study.

tions) and must therefore be addressed; the therapist simply cannot avoid it. Third, pathological defenses lead to paranoid distortions of the therapist, making it difficult for the patient to identify with him as a benign figure. Finally, the patient's demands do not reflect "realistic" dependency needs as much as they do defenses against aggression. Kernberg stresses the effect of pathological defenses both on ego functioning and on the patient–therapist relationship. For example, he writes: "Identification . . . instead of being with the benign aspects of the psychotherapist, are rather reconfirmations of highly idealized projected forerunners of the ego ideal" (Kernberg 1980a, p. 195).

Alternate Conceptions of Supportive and Expressive Psychotherapy

Kernberg offers a conception of expressive therapy in terms of three variables noted by Gill (1954) as essential elements of psychoanalysis proper: modifications of technical neutrality, use of interpretation, and analysis of transference. Insight through interpretation from a position of therapeutic neutrality is, according to Kernberg, the fundamental therapeutic agent. The patient's insight, rather than his relationship with the therapist, is ultimately mutative. In his conception of expressive therapy, Kernberg (1980a) focuses on interpretation of selected part-object transference manifestations and on "quite systematic" interpretation of defense. He writes that "[t]he interpretation of the constellation of primitive defensive operations centered around splitting . . . should be as consistent as their detection in the patient's transferences and his extratherapeutic relationships permits" (Kernberg 1980a, p. 197).

Kernberg uses the same technical tools as others do, but he sees their effect as different in patients with differing degrees of ego strength. In patients with good ego strength, interpretation of defenses allows repressed material to emerge and then become reintegrated on a higher level, thus further strengthening the ego; analysis of selected transference manifestations leads to a diminution of pathological transference displays via reality testing of the therapeutic situation; and technical neutrality creates the regressive conditions necessary for transference analysis. In patients with weak egos, interpretation of inherently ego-weakening defenses allows for increased ego strength through establishment of higher-level defenses; transference analysis is aimed toward unifying part-object fantasy-dominated transferences into more cohesive and less fantastic transferences; and technical neutrality protects the analyst in his role as interpreter (rather than gratifier).

Kernberg's theory of expressive therapy, based on his reconceptualization of the nature of pathology, extends to his reconceptualization of supportive therapy. Here too, he focuses on work with primitive defenses, albeit in a noninterpretive manner.

> The basic technique of supportive psychotherapy consists in exploring the patient's primitive defenses in the here-and-now, with the objective of helping him achieve control over their effects by nonanalytic means and fostering a better adaptation to reality by making him aware of the disorganizing effects of these defensive operations. In the process, manifest and suppressed (as opposed to unconscious or repressed) negative transference can be highlighted, reduced by means of consistent examination of the reality of the treatment situation, and utilized for clarification of related interpersonal problems in the patient's life. [Kernberg 1984, p. 155]

Thus Kernberg attempts insight into the nature of his patient's pathological defenses and their effect on reality-testing, judgment, and so on. This differs from advice-giving, which bypasses defenses. Kernberg assumes that insight into pathological defenses will allow the patient to make decisions. The therapist's stance is not neutral. Kernberg gives examples in which his goal for one patient is greater sexual freedom, and for another, adaptation to external reality. With these treatment goals in mind, he interprets defenses that make their realization difficult. Kernberg further supports impulse expression and adaptation by not interpreting the unconscious acting-out aspects of behavior which, while they may contain components of unconscious conflict, may also lead to the patient's achieving emotional gratification and new social learning in his social reality.

Kernberg is against general supportive statements and manipulations of reality. He believes that if the therapist must offer suggestions for psychotherapeutic adjuncts (such as medication or referral for a specific form of therapy, such as sex therapy), he should fully discuss his rationale for these recommendations. Such discussion (1) deemphasizes the patient's transference disposition to view his following the therapist's recommendations as taking orders from a pathologically idealized doctor, (2) emphasizes conscious goals of therapy and the patient's responsibility for his treatment, (3) reinforces secondary-process functioning, and (4) provides a reality base from which to interpret pathological defenses.

Kernberg's approach to transference interpretation differs in expressive and supportive therapy: The transference serves as the fulcrum for emphasis on reality and adaptation in supportive therapy, whereas the transference itself is the area of emphasis in expressive therapy. As Kernberg (1984) puts it:

> In all types of treatment, work with the transference starts with conscious and preconscious transference manifestations and is pursued until the patient's here-and-now fantasies about the therapist are fully explored and clarified. In supportive psychotherapy, however, this exploration is not connected interpretively with the patient's unconscious relation to the therapist or with his

unconscious past. It is, instead, used for confronting the patient with the reality of the treatment situation and with parallel distortions in his external life. The beginning of work with transference manifestations is the same in all three modalities of treatment, but the end point is very different. If a patient in supportive psychotherapy presents the therapist with very primitive regressive fantasy material, the communication is not neglected but is traced back to reality issues. In expressive psychotherapy, the direction is reversed: the usual path is from reality to exploration of the underlying fantasy. [pp. 163–164]

Further Difficulties with Traditional Definitions

From the question of how to define and differentiate supportive and expressive psychoanalytic therapies, there emerges another obvious question. What will we term Kernberg's form of expressive therapy in contrast with traditional notions to which the same term is applied? Should we call the former "expressive therapy based on Kernberg's theory of borderline psychopathology" and the latter "expressive therapy based on ego psychology"? If we do, then we are accepting the premise that the category name "expressive psychotherapy" must be used together with a theoretical context. Similarly, if we follow a distinction made both by Gill (1954, 1984) and, more explicitly, by Kernberg (1984) between expressive therapy for patients with good ego strength and expressive therapy for patients with weaker egos, then the category "expressive therapy" means little on its own, without reference to a particular patient group. The category name alone tells us little about the techniques employed or the patients seen (in contrast with psychoanalysis, a category that tells us something about both technique and patient).

A similar problem applies to the category "supportive therapy." First, Kernberg's supportive therapy differs from conceptions described by Knight (1953) or Wallerstein and Robbins (1956). Second, although one can conceptualize distinctions between expressive and supportive therapy, it is difficult to believe that these conceptual distinctions can be and are applied with such precision in actual clinical practice. Wallerstein (1986) states that, in the Menninger study which compared psychoanalysis, expressive therapy, and support-ive therapy, distinctions between psychoanalysis and expres-sive therapy were not only blurred, but "a similar blurring of the interface between the expressive and the supportive psy-chotherapeutic modes has also existed from the start in our observed data, and in our resulting conceptualizations about these treatment careers as well" (p. 687). This finding is not surprising given the conceptual confusion between the terms "expressive therapy for patients with weak egos" and "sup-portive therapy."

Third, as Schlesinger (1969) states, it makes for grave difficulty when elements such as uncovering, expression, and support, which are elements in *every* psychotherapy, are used as category names. Schlesinger's point is supported by the Menninger data and by Wallerstein, who uses the terms *supportive–expressive psychotherapy* or *expressive–supportive psychotherapy*, depending on which aspect he wants to em-phasize. He writes: "In this, I have been mindful (and some-times critical) of the clinical operating maxim that has guided so many of the actual choices in Menninger Foundation clinical practice—"be as expressive as you can be, and as supportive as you have to be" (Wallerstein 1986, p. 688).

Finally, while Kernberg defines psychotherapy in terms of techniques, even he states that the effects of these techniques vary according to the patient's diagnosis. Gill (1984) has also said that the therapist never knows the effect on the patient of any of his interventions. Pine (1984), similarly, has noted that a patient's reception of an interpretation is a psychological act serving multiple functions. Therefore, distinguishing between therapies on the basis of the goal of the therapist's clinical interventions may make more theoretical than clinical sense.

We are thus faced with models of psychoanalytic therapy that are not psychoanalysis, that may differ, depending on diagnostic category and theoretical orientation, and are defined by technique in ways that make conceptual sense but disregard the acknowledged uncertainty about the ways in which these interventions are affected by dynamic and structural factors for a particular patient.

We see in the work of Blanck and Blanck (1974, 1979) and Kernberg (1980a, 1984) that psychoanalytic theory, particularly regarding the "difficult" patient, has evolved dramatically, with an increased emphasis on the following elements: object relations (Mahler et al. 1975), the complexity of ego functions (Bellak et al. 1973), the role of internalization in ego development (Adler and Buie 1979, Pine 1974), the nature of the essential conflict (Adler and Buie 1979, Kernberg 1975), self-esteem issues (Kohut 1971), and characteristics in the patient that resist therapeutic help (Kernberg 1977). These emphases make the traditional goal of supportive or expressive therapy—that of strengthening a "fragile" ego against its impulses—seem overly simplistic. Our definition of the nature of conflict, of defense, of psychological development, and of what is ultimately mutative in psychoanalytic therapy has shifted, and these issues are the subject of heated debate. Therapeutic approaches based on these shifts simply cannot be classified accurately under prevailing nomenclature.

How, then, can shifts in our understanding of fragile patients, with consequent shifts in our clinical approach, be categorized? At what point does the term *expressive therapy* become so overused that it becomes meaningless? And at what point does what we term *supportive therapy* become so undervalued and ill-defined that no clinician wants to use that label to describe his work?

It seems impossible to find a category name that fulfills minimal labeling requirements—that is, a name that, when a therapist describes what he is doing as "expressive psychotherapy," tells something about what he is doing, with what kind of patient, how he is doing it, and why. It might be more useful to acknowledge the close relationship between method of psychotherapy and (1) dynamic and structural diagnosis of the patient, (2) theoretical assumptions as to the nature of the patient's essential pathology, and (3) consequent degree of emphasis on support and expression, with further explanation of what, how, and when something is supported or expressed (Schlesinger 1969). We will focus on the latter two issues in the next section.

What is Supportive and What is Expressive?

THE CONTEXTUAL NATURE OF THESE QUESTIONS

Chapter 1 discussed the relationship between various models of psychopathology and psychotherapy of the severely disturbed patient within the broad spectrum of current psychoanalytic thought. It is therefore difficult to use the terms *supportive therapy* or *expressive therapy* without reference to the relevant psychoanalytic model. Just as initial definitions of supportive and expressive therapy were dependent on a specific theoretical context (Kernberg [1980a] terms this the "ego psychological" model), so too do changes in this context suggest changes in definition of these terms. As Kernberg modifies the diagnosis of borderline personality disorder with a more specific character diagnosis,[2] so might one specify the context within which he recommends supportive or expressive therapy. Such an approach, which views these terms as rooted within theoretical models, is consistent with Schafer's (1985) point that one must understand the assumptions of a given

---

[2]Kernberg (1975) writes: "It is certainly not enough to diagnose a patient as presenting 'borderline personality organization.' The predominant constellation of character pathology should always be included in the descriptive diagnosis, together with the predominant neurotic symptomatology" (p. 113).

psychoanalytic model in order to determine which interventions would be considered by *that model* to be "wild analysis." Just as *wild analysis* is defined differently by those of differing theoretical persuasion, the meanings of the terms *expressive* and *supportive* depend on the context of a given theoretical system.

If we also accept Schlesinger's (1969) recommendation that we use *support* and *expression* to describe elements of a therapy, rather than viewing them as antithetical category terms, then we are left with the task of attempting to determine how Schlesinger's questions about therapy (What is supported or expressed? How is it supported or expressed? When is it supported or expressed?) are answered within the varying models. We may attempt the following answers for each of the models.

KERNBERG'S MODEL

Implicitly supported in Kernberg's model is the patient's tie to reality, both through the expectation that the patient will care for himself outside of sessions and by Kernberg's technical recommendations for preventing or managing the negative transference. Despite Kernberg's emphasis on interpretation of the fantasy-dominated part-object transference, the context within which this occurs assumes the patient's defined responsibility for self-control both in and out of sessions and the therapist's maintenance of a defined, neutral position.

Reality is further supported by Kernberg's overall attitude, which centers on diagnosis. The patient's categorization, not his subjective experience, is central. This approach contains an implicit bias toward the patient's "shaping up," which, if internalized rather than fought by the patient, can be quite supportive. Some patients feel comforted when they know their place, the analyst's place, and the expectations; their experience is that of being firmly held by an authority who is able to set defined limits.

Wallerstein believes that the supportive aspects of Kernberg's approach lie in Kernberg's provision of environmental support, provided through hospitalization. He sees Kernberg's criticisms of supportive psychotherapy as

> really the difference between *bad* (i.e., planless and conceptually unfocused) supportive psychotherapy and *good* (i.e., properly detailed and specified) supportive (or, better, supportive-expressive) psychotherapy—that is, a combining of specifically required, integrating, interpretive work with the equally specific structuring of a supporting and controlling environment (hospitalization *and* psychotherapy), within which the expressive interpretive work could be received and sustained. [Wallerstein 1986, p. 699]

Within Kernberg's approach, the patient's dependency needs are not supported or gratified, but are instead interpreted as manifestations of splitting and associated primitive defenses. *What* is expressed are part-object transference units, which are interpreted and ultimately integrated into a whole-object transference. What is *not* expressed is unneutralized affect, particularly anger. With regard to the question of *how* support is managed, it is through firm limits within and surrounding the therapeutic interaction. As for *when* support is particularly necessary, it is at times of increased negative transference, when reality is reaffirmed by the therapist. For example, the therapist will set firm limits on expression of unneutralized aggression within sessions particularly at times when a psychotic transference is imminent.

THE REPRESENTATIONAL
DEFICIT/SELF-DEFICIT MODELS

The patient's tie to the therapist is supported, in order to facilitate internalization of a holding introject.[3] The patient

---

[3]This model does not clearly distinguish among psychoanalysis, expressive therapy, and supportive therapy.

expresses his ambivalence and anxiety about closeness and his primarily narcissistic rage, which is interpreted within a warm context. The patient's dependency needs for assistance in keeping the therapist psychologically alive as a soothing internal object are seen as legitimate and are supported.

The therapist administers support by maintaining a warm, empathic alliance with the patient, by avoiding confrontation of the patient's defenses, and by carefully assessing the patient's capacity to handle therapeutic stress. For example, the therapist might give the patient a transitional object or encourage telephone contact during times of separation. The therapist also provides support by refraining from confronting the patient's narcissistic entitlement until later in treatment, after holding introjects have been firmly internalized.

The therapist's overall approach which focuses on the patient's experience, is in itself supportive. The therapist attributes a certain face validity to the patient's requests and then responds to them on that level. The therapist also helps the patient to maintain a desired state (such as one of affective union with the therapist) through disruptive affect, and listens to the patient's material from the patient's perspective (Schwaber 1983). For example, the therapist might go along with a patient's insistence that the therapist answer her questions before they attempt to understand why the questions are coming up at that particular point. The therapist thus accepts at manifest level the patient's difficulty in accepting a delayed answer (or no answer) and in tolerating treatment of her question as symbolic, rather than "real," communication. The therapist supports the patient's wish to avoid the object loss inherent in interpretation (Tarachow 1963) and in exploration. He thus defers (but does not abandon) his attempt to discuss what is warded off by the patient's question and by her insistence that it be answered. With regard to when support is offered, it is most important during those times that the patient feels psychologically alone, either because of excessive rage or because of actual separations from the therapist.

THE EGO-DEFICIT MODEL

According to the ego-deficit model, adaptive aspects of the patient's behavior are supported, whether they involve exercise of weakened ego functions or individual elements of resistance. The therapist avoids interpreting drive and instead points out specific areas of ego strength. For example, a patient's account of oppositional behavior is interpreted as the patient's having a mind of his own; a patient who is guilty about childhood sexual experiences is told that she was sexually curious and interested (Blanck and Blanck 1974). In these examples, areas of ego strength that the patient has not appreciated become the area of focus. Such an approach differs from interpreting upward or downward, which has to do with taking a patient's symptom or behavior and interpreting it at a more socially acceptable level (interpreting upward) or at a less socially acceptable level (interpreting downward). For example, a man's wish to be hugged by other men may be interpreted downward, as evidence of homosexual longings, or upward, as a sexualized wish to be comforted by fatherly figures. Therapists interpret upward when a particular problem is to be addressed, but they must not scare a frightened patient. Interpreting upward is a means of support, but it still involves addressing an unconscious fear, albeit in a way more acceptable to the ego. Ego support, on the other hand, does not address the conflict, but reframes the problem to help the patient become aware of neglected areas of strength.

With this model, as with all others, expression of unneutralized anger is seen as unproductive. This model is the least expressive of the four. Emphasis is more on modulation by the therapist (as parent) of the patient's manifest content. The therapeutic alliance is the method through which support is administered. The therapist's support of ego functions and psychological separation is consistent throughout treatment.

MODIFICATIONS OF CLASSICAL TECHNIQUE

The patient's capacity to do interpretive work is supported in this model. The attempt is to enable the patient to use interpretation, whether the therapist modulates the manner in which he interprets (Pine 1984), whether he uses the therapeutic relationship as a warm, "psychic prosthesis" (Grunes 1984, p. 127) through which new internalizations are acquired, or whether he titrates the amount of frustration and gratification delivered (Fox 1984). What is expressed is the patient's inner conflict. Support is administered in balanced doses according to careful assessment of the patient's stress level in any given session. Assessment depends on evidence of structural difficulty, rather than solely on the manifest content of the patient's statements.

The therapist–patient relationship is also important in itself (not only because of its use in balancing interpretive dosage). As Wallerstein (1986) notes:

> a major common operative mechanism (whether explicitly intended and fostered or not) was the evocation and the firm establishment of a positive dependent transference attachment (wholly or at least significantly uninterpreted and "unanalyzed"), within which varieties of conflicted transference needs and wishes achieved varying degrees of (conscious or unconscious) gratification. [p. 690]

Wallerstein discusses forms within which this relationship may be helpful. It is interesting that importance is attributed to the therapeutic relationship in every approach discussed here, with the exception of Kernberg's.

The patient's relationship with reality and his sense of reality (Frosch 1980) is also supported, as is the ego function of reality-testing, which was the primary focus in earlier forms of supportive therapy and, in another way, is the focus of Kernberg's approach. Bach (1985) particularly focuses on states of "self-constancy" and on the patient's difficulties integrating multiple perspectives of self and object.[4]

Support is not provided in a mannner that is designed to suppress conflict. Interpreting upward is an example of how the therapist can be supportive while addressing conflict; Pine's (1984) examples also apply here. Support is often implicit in the context of a therapist's interventions. For example, a patient was feeling panicky in the last session before the therapist's month-long vacation. The patient usually dealt with his panic by failing to come to sessions and by getting drunk. The therapist believed that if he focused solely on the patient's panic, or on the accompanying rage, he would increase the patient's affective load to an intolerable level. He would thus be adding to the patient's stress and increasing the odds that he would put himself in a harmful situation, using his customary defenses. On the other hand, the therapist had to address the patient's feelings; they were the central issue for the patient and could not be avoided. The therapist suggested that they should talk about how it felt to be in a session and to work on problems when all the patient wanted to do was to "get the hell out of there." The suggestion was phrased in such a way as to assume that the patient would stay and that he and the therpist would focus on the feelings from the ego's point of view. The therapist focused, not on the feelings themselves, but on how the patient managed to *tolerate* feelings of panic while continuing to work. Had he addressed the feelings directly ("You seem panicked. Tell me about it.") without emphasizing the patient's task of working in the face of those feelings, then he would have risked the patient's becoming disorganized.

---

[4]It should be made clear that Bach does not view himself as practicing supportive psychotherapy.

Therapeutic Potential

The roles of support and expression can be understood in a number of ways, depending on the theoretical frame of reference and on the conception of the patient's pathology. One might conclude that therapists would be excited by the intellectual challenges of supportive therapy. Within psychoanalytically oriented training programs, however, supportive therapy is accorded little status. Kernberg's dismissal of supportive therapy seems to be shared by much of the psychoanalytic community.

For those who practice this form of therapy, however, the goals of treatment have become ambitious, perhaps as ambitious as the goals of psychoanalysis. Helping the patient form psychological structure can lead to results as far-reaching as those brought about by resolution of neurotic conflict within established psychological structure. Even more important, in addition to our ability to theoretically conceptualize the goals more ambitiously, there is now evidence that support actually does have a major mutative effect.

Wallerstein, after reviewing the Menninger study of patients in psychotherapy and psychoanalysis, concludes not only that the conceptual distinctions between supportive therapy and expressive therapy were not clinically applicable but also, and perhaps even more important, that supportive therapy itself, and supportive elements in the other forms of therapy, produced unexpected, long-term results. Wallerstein (1986) states this repeatedly. He writes:

> [S]upportive psychotherapeutic approaches, mechanisms, and techniques . . . often achieved far more than what was expected of them. In fact they often reached the kinds and degrees of change expected to depend on more expressive and insightful conflict resolutions, and they often did so in ways that represented indistinguishably "structural" changes, in terms of the usual indicators of this state. . . . An important aspect of the

finding for supportive psychotherapy is that the changes predicted for the 20 patients in psychotherapy, though more often predicated to be based on the more expressive mechanisms and techniques, in fact were more often actually achieved on the basis of the more supportive mechanisms and techniques. [pp. 725, 726]

Although Wallerstein originally believed that the findings would show the strongest demarcation between psychoanalysis and expressive therapy on the one hand, and supportive therapy on the other hand, he found that this was not true. In every form of therapy studied, from supportive therapy to psychoanalysis proper, "the treatment carried more supportive elements than originally intended, and these supportive elements accounted for more of the changes achieved than had been originally anticipated" (Wallerstein 1986, p. 730).

On the basis of these findings, Wallerstein questions the hypothesis that links degree and kind of change with technique used (such as, the more expressive the therapy, the more "real" the change).

[A]n overall finding (almost an overriding one) has been the repeated demonstration that a substantial number and range of changes—in symptoms, in character traits, in personality functioning and in life styles rooted in life-long and repressed intrapsychic conflicts—have been brought about via the more supportive therapeutic modes and techniques, cutting across the gamut of supportive *and* expressive (even analytic) therapies. It is also clear that in terms of the usual criteria—slowness to change (i.e., stability, durability), capacity to withstand external or internal disruptive pressures, and the like—these changes have in many instances been quite indistinguishable from the changes brought about by typically expressive-analytic (interpretive, insight-producing) means. In other words, these changes have often been as much "real" changes or "structural" changes (in the ego, or, more broadly, in the total character organization) as those customarily defined as "real" or "structural." [Wallerstein 1986, p. 723]

These findings provide empirical evidence that support, based on some degree of internalization, is far more prevalent and mutative than had been predicted by traditional definitions of and distinctions between supportive therapy, expressive therapy, and psychoanalysis proper. In Chapters 8 through 10, we will see how these results can be understood theoretically and applied clinically.

Part Two

Variations in the Therapist's Stance

4

Use of Transitional Objects

Rationale

The thought of actually giving a patient a tangible object has always been anathema to the psychoanalyst. It has been regarded as evidence in itself of countertransference and as a violation of the essence of psychoanalytic work, which depends on verbalization, rather than enactment, of feelings and on a primarily symbolic and transferential, rather than actual and "real," role for the analyst in the patient's life. The degree to which an actual and new relationship, along with a transferential and symbolic relationship, forms a part of psychoanalysis and analytically oriented therapy is still discussed by many (Adler 1980, Gill 1984, Grunes 1984, among others). However, there has been little in the psychoanalytic literature, other than Sechehaye's (1951) account of her work with a schizophrenic patient and papers by Adler and Buie (Adler and Buie 1979, Buie and Adler 1982), that recommends actually giving the patient something concrete.

Nevertheless, this practice may be common, especially among therapists who are not psychoanalytically oriented.

131

For example, Torrey (1983) has written a 300-page book on schizophrenia which is antipsychotherapeutic in approach and which devotes just four pages to individual psychother- apy. He states that "[I]nsight-oriented psychotherapy, in which the therapist tries to make the patient aware of under- lying unconscious process, is now known to be not only useless in treating schizophrenia, but probably detrimental" (p. 124). He advocates a "supportive relationship," which, combined with drug therapy, reduces the rehospitalization rate for schizophrenic patients. Such treatment "is sometimes called 'supportive psychotherapy' but really consists primar- ily of friendship, advice, practical help in securing financial and supportive services, and caring" (p. 126).

As an example of such treatment, Torrey writes of a patient who receives a prescription for medication, rarely uses the medication, but carries the pills "continuously and is reassured by the rattle of the pills" (p. 126). When the pills turn to powder every year, the patient flies to his doctor's city for a medication refill. Torrey thus gives a clear example of the use of transitional objects in treatment but in a way that is not only unconnected with a conceptual base in psy- choanalytic theory but that is also actually against such a framework. Psychoanalysts reading this example would have little inclination to consider the use of such an interven- tion in their own work.

Yet, the problem of helping a patient tolerate time away from the therapist—vacations and intervals between ses- sions—is one often faced by the analyst who works with more disturbed patients, particularly those who may have difficulty evoking the therapist's image as a means of self- soothing and who panic and quickly regress. Buie and Adler (1982) have referred to this difficulty as the fundamental psychopathology of the borderline patient. They note that borderline patients have a developmental deficit—the inabil- ity to evoke the memory of a soothing person when they are apart from that person. The soothing internal representation of the object (the holding introject) is tenuous and easily lost, especially during periods of frustration and anger. The borderline patient feels alone because of this deficit and, during periods of intense aloneness, is apt to act out in order to mitigate this aloneness. A major goal of treatment is to help the patient use and eventually internalize the therapist as a holding introject. Toward that end, and as a means of helping the patient tolerate separations, Adler and Buie (Adler and Buie 1979, Buie and Adler 1982) suggest the use of transitional objects.

> This treatment must be conducted in an adequately supportive therapeutic setting, one that attempts insofar as possible to help maintain the tenuous holding introjects and internal objects, hence keeping annihilation anxiety within tolerable levels and maintaining cohesiveness of the self. The amount of support may considerably exceed that involved in most psychotherapies. To some extent the therapist in reality acts as a holding self-object. Transitional objects (e.g., vacation addresses and postcards), extra appointments, and telephone calls reaffirming that the therapist exists are required at various times and, for the more severely borderline personalities, brief hospitalizations, at least once or twice, might well be expected. [p. 67]

It is interesting, parenthetically, how one's conception of essential borderline psychopathology leads to an interest in certain technical problems. For Buie and Adler, who focus on the patient's difficulty with a holding introject, it is the time when the patient and therapist are *apart* that is most troublesome. They discuss the patient's difficulty within the session, but one gets the impression that if the therapist is sufficiently empathic and sensitive to the degree of stress that the patient can manage at any given time, then major difficulties should not occur *within* the therapy session. In contrast, for Kernberg (1975), who sees fundamental pathology in the borderline patient as essentially due to excessive aggression and primitive

defenses revolving around splitting, with the feeling of aloneness seen as a secondary problem, it is the time when patient
and therapist are *together* that is most difficult. Kernberg
spends considerable time discussing the effect on the therapy
of splitting, projective identification, and other primitive and
fantastic (fantasy-dominated) defenses. He is far more concerned about transference psychosis and decompensation
within the session than he is with regression outside the hour.
The latter problem is dealt with by definition; that is, as a
prerequisite for treatment, patients are expected to be able to
control themselves outside the session. Patients who cannot do
so are placed in a hospital, where they are under safe control
while the treatment begins and during difficult times in the
course of treatment. Thus what is a major problem for Buie
and Adler—how to maintain the patient outside of the session—is assumed as a given by Kernberg.

Buie and Adler do not elaborate on how, when, and
why transitional objects are used in treatment. In this chapter, we will examine just these questions, with the hope that
this difficult departure from traditional technique can be
integrated with our theory.

Role in Development

Winnicott (1951) describes the transitional object as that
which helps the child separate from the mother. At first, the
maternal breast seems to appear at the child's will and he feels
omnipotent. He has the illusion that he controls mother,
whom he needs for psychological survival. Through slight,
and usually relatively controlled, frustrations, the child becomes disillusioned. That is, he realizes that he is a separate
being from mother, that he is not omnipotent, and that he
must soothe himself. He does this in part through the development of libidinal object constancy (Pine 1974), and ultimately, greater internal structure. It is this process that Winnicott terms "weaning." The process is aided by the child's

use of a transitional object, an object that is simultaneously mother and not-mother, something both real and magical.

For Winnicott, the transitional object is an aid to the child as he navigates the process from subjective to objective reality. At first, the mother adapts to the child's needs, and the child develops the illusion that the world will adapt to his needs. This is a necessary step in development and a precursor to the second step, that of disillusion, or weaning. Because of the strain involved in this step, in both taking on external objective reality as "real" and keeping it affectively connected to inner subjective reality, the transitional object, at the boundary of internal and external reality, is helpful. It is an intermediate area of experience which can be enjoyed and used as a source of soothing without being subjected to claims of objectivity and reality-testing.

The child chooses the transitional object once he has achieved a modicum of psychological separation from his mother. It exists when there is a good affective relationship between mother and child. The transitional object reflects and keeps connected the positive external mother and the rudimentary positive internal representations of the mother. A bridge between external reality and the child's internal reality, it enables the child to make external reality into internal reality, to relinquish omnipotent control of a real mother for internal structure. It mitigates the loss of mother while the child develops an internal soothing representation of the mother. The transitional object, which the child chooses, owns, and treats as he wishes, helps the child both undo and master separation from the mother. It is the child's way of turning a passive experience into active mastery.

We have noted two essential characteristics of the transitional object: that the child chooses it once he has begun to separate from his mother, and that it is the child who selects the object. A third characteristic is that the child is, in some ways, more attached to the transitional object than to the mother. Why should this be? Winnicott distinguishes between use of the object as comforter and use of the object as soother. If the child still needs his mother as a soother, then the child has not begun psychological separation from his mother, which entails the development of internal self-soothing capacities. Thus the child will remain attached to the mother for soothing and will use the object as an adjunct to the mother, as a comforter. As the child moves away from his mother and begins to develop rudiments of psychological structure and self-soothing capacity, he will be more attached to his creation, the transitional object, which reflects his new stage of psychological development. The transitional object will be the soother, the primary substitute for mother, thus facilitating separation, rather than an adjunct to mother, which would delay separation.

The transitional object contains within it both mother and not-mother. It allows the child to partake of the mother's comfort without fear of maternal engulfment, while sampling reality, secondary process, and his own increasing ego capacities without fear that these are cold and without maternal comfort. The child may thus be more attached to the transitional object than to his mother because he will be less ambivalently involved with his own created object. By this stage of development, as Loewald (1951) and others have noted, the mother is feared as well as sought; she represents a loss of the fledgling individuality as well as a return to the bliss of symbiosis. For this reason, the transitional object, more than the mother, can both soothe the child and gratify his wishes for individuation.

When the concept of transitional object is discussed, the mind of the analyst inevitably turns to the fetish. The concepts are compared by Winnicott (1951), Greenacre (1969, 1970), Barkin (1978), and McDougall (1980). The concepts are linked for at least two reasons. First, there is a superficial similarity: In both there is a created object, something real that allows the individual to function. Second, more and more analysts see sexual fetishes and perversions as reflecting preoedipal concerns (Khan 1979, McDougall 1980). Issues of attachment to the mother and the use of others to maintain internal soothing and regulatory functions become very important in such cases. Thus the connection between the transitional object and the fetish becomes of interest.

The two are quite different, however. First, as Barkin (1978) notes, the fetish stimulates, while the transitional object soothes. Second, the transitional object, which gradually fades away when it is no longer needed, is an illusion that aids in greater ego mastery of the real world. The fetish does not fade away, and it is used because of defensive "delusion," which leads to restriction of the ego. Winnicott (1951) describes a fetish as an object "that is employed on account of a delusion of a maternal phallus" (p. 211). Greenacre (1971a) calls the transitional object a "temporary construction to aid the infant in the early stages of developing a sense of reality and establishing his own individual identity. It is of positive value in monitoring growth and expansion. . . . In contrast, the fetish serves as a patch for a flaw in the genital area of the body image" (p. 334).

Winnicott's work allows the therapist to appreciate the use of transitional objects in treatment from the object relations point of view, defined here as the way in which it aids the patient's connection with the therapist. Adler and Buie (Adler and Buie 1979, Buie and Adler 1982) understand the use of a "transitional object" from a different, perhaps more cognitively oriented, perspective. They relate the borderline patient's incapacity to maintain positive soothing images of others to two types of memory: recognition and evocation. The child with the capacity for evocative memory can summon a soothing image of his mother in her absence. He has achieved, in effect, libidinal object constancy. However, "for the infant with only recognition memory capacity, the presence of the transitional object is necessary in order to activate and maintain an affectively charged memory of the soothing mother" (Adler and Buie 1979, p. 87). From this perspective, the transitional object facilitates the fragile internal object representation, which is another way of making Winnicott's point.

For Adler and Buie, the goal of therapy with borderline patients is to help them establish and maintain an internal, affective, soothing memory of the therapist despite the vicissitudes of anger that disrupt such an internalization. They advocate the use of transitional objects to evoke through recognition the therapist's soothing quality. That is, the borderline patient's evocative memory has been weakened, and the therapist must work, sometimes with objects that stimulate recognition memory, to sustain the internal soothing memory of the therapist. Adler and Buie suggest as a transitional object, the therapist's telephone number on a piece of paper, the monthly bill, or a card with the therapist's vacation address and telephone number. A journal where the patient would record his thoughts for later discussion with the therapist also qualifies under the rubric of transitional object. Adler and Buie (1979) also suggest that a therapist covering for an absent colleague could act to help the patient remember the absent therapist through discussing details of the therapeutic work (pp. 92–93).

Adler and Buie's focus on the cognitive function of the transitional object—that is, on its role in helping sustain internal, affective memories and images of the absent object—should be considered in conjunction with Winnicott's insights. According to Winnicott, just any object will not suffice. The mother may have a beautiful blanket in mind for the child as a transitional object, but the child might instead choose an old teddy bear. The child's involvement in selecting the transitional object is vital. Thus, ideally, the patient would select an object from the therapist, rather than accepting the therapist's business card. Since few therapists will have a number of objects in their offices readily available for selection by their patients, they must tread a thin line between giving something to the patient and letting the patient choose something. Thus, Adler and Buie's discussion of the cognitive function served by the transitional object must be augmented by Winnicott's discussion of the origin of this object when applied to clinical practice.

Criteria for Use

The use of a transitional object in clinical practice is an unusual departure from traditional methods of supporting a patient. The following criteria for using a transitional object can be suggested based on the theoretical considerations discussed:

IT IS BEST NOT TO USE A TRANSITIONAL OBJECT

If feelings about separation can be discussed, they should be discussed, since verbal discussion reflects work on a higher level of organization. Speaking facilitates higher ego functioning, assuming that the speech is affectively connected to what the patient is feeling and thinking. Use of a transitional object indicates that the therapist has diagnosed the patient as both incapable of using interpretation to master feelings, usually regarding separation, and liable to malignant regression as a consequence of the separation. Since use of transitional objects often reflects countertransferential feelings on the part of the therapist—particularly fear of the patient's anger, a need to remain idealized and "depended on" by the patient, and the therapist's own fear of separation projected onto the patient—the therapist should be clear about the patient's diagnosis before using this technical tool.

In addition, therapists place themselves in a vulnerable position when they use this technique. Borderline and psychotic patients may stimulate a host of reactions in the therapist. They can engage in a variety of behaviors that continually test the therapist's judgment. For some, the issue of hospitalization is always present. One function of theory is to assist the therapist amid such turmoil. Following established procedures increases the therapist's "stamina" (Schafer 1983), which enables him to tolerate the patient's emotional reactions and projective identification without lashing back. The therapist who knows his limits, and whose sense of limits is aided by the security of a consistent treatment approach, is less likely to act out with the patient and more likely to allow the patient freedom of expression. One function of Kernberg's (1975) recommendations regarding limits with the borderline patient is to help protect the therapist from acting on the basis of the patient's projective identification.

The therapist who uses a transitional object is departing from established technique and working in a more intuitive manner. He may be doing brilliant and inspired work, choosing just the right transitional object, responding to the patient in action rather than in words. However, he may also be acting out with his patient, and brilliantly intuitive work with one patient may be totally off the mark with the next one. Thus, the therapist should think carefully before using the transitional object.

THE IDEA SHOULD COME FROM THE PATIENT

It is preferable for patients themselves to suggest the idea of a transitional object, and they should be as involved as possible in choosing it. This recommendation follows two of Winnicott's points about the transitional object: first, that it be something chosen or actually created by the child; and second, that it follows the developmental theme of building structure by taking an event that has been passively experienced and adaptively mastering it. Such activity strengthens ego functioning. Mastery by the patient can be aided by patient–therapist discussion of the transitional object. A journal in which the patient records his thoughts and then records the therapist's interventions is a joint creation that facilitates evocative memory. Patients leaving an inpatient milieu program may deal with their sense of loss by creating a scrapbook containing descriptions of accomplishments during their inpatient stay, and perhaps pictures of staff and patients. Such an object diminishes the likelihood that they will panic after discharge, lose sustaining memory of their experience, and regress to their prehospitalization state.

THE OBJECT SHOULD BE USED
TO FURTHER VERBAL WORK

Generally, the patient for whom the transitional object is necessary has difficulty speaking in sessions. Free association may be overwhelming to the patient, and its use therefore may be contraindicated (Blanck and Blanck 1974, Kernberg 1975). The patient may be blocked, have nothing to talk about, or be unable to describe, even minimally, affective turmoil outside sessions. The patient may feel that episodes of wrist cutting, drinking, binge eating and vomiting, and other such behaviors erupt suddenly, with no preceding feelings or thoughts. The use of a transitional object such as a journal that can be read and discussed in sessions both helps the patient with his holding introject and furthers reflective awareness and verbalization in therapy. Similarly, patients who forget the therapist as soon as they leave the session, either because they are unable to retain the image or as a defense against feelings associated with separation, will forget the content of the session along with the memory of the therapist. If these patients summarize the session soon after leaving, they will be helped to remember and to reflect on the therapist's interventions. Thus the transitional object should facilitate, rather than circumvent, the therapeutic process.[1]

This use of a transitional object is helpful on an inpatient unit, where acutely psychotic patients may benefit from having an appointment card with the therapist's name and their appointment times. They can also use the paper to jot down feelings they want to discuss in their sessions or to summarize sessions. Such use of a transitional object is help-

---

[1]It is preferable, in each instance in this paragraph, to attempt to analyze the unconscious conflict which leads to these symptoms. The therapist should consider a transitional object only after such analysis has been repeatedly attempted and when there is a clinical reason demanding further action.

ful with inpatients who, especially during an acute psychotic episode, rely on externalizing, denying, projecting, and acting-out defenses, and come to therapy with nothing to discuss or leave therapy with no memories of the session.

THE PATIENT MAY PRESENT THE THERAPIST WITH A GIFT

Some patients may give the therapist a gift in order to reassure themselves that the therapist will remember them. If they cannot take an aspect of the therapist or the therapist's office with them, then they will leave something of themselves in the therapist's office. One patient worked in treatment on his feelings about his father. In the course of treatment, he grew closer to his father, a carpenter. Together, the patient and his father made a miniature analytic couch as a gift to his therapist on termination. He felt that, through this gift, he could keep memories of himself and his therapy alive for the therapist.[2]

The transitional object may also facilitate the patient's use of therapy while in session. The patient may need to lie on the couch, for example, in order to feel, physically, a soft, holding, concrete representation of the therapist while not having to face the therapist directly. One psychotic patient brought a jar of candy to his therapist's office. He presented the candy to the therapist, placed it on the therapist's table, and proceeded to munch candy from the jar during the session, urging the therapist to join him. While the therapist did not join him, having the jar and candy present in the sessions helped the patient settle into treatment.

---

[2] In the treatment of a neurotic patient, this fantasy, and what it defends against, would be analyzed. Afterwards, the patient would not feel as compelled to give the gift and would not feel offended if the analyst did not accept it. This is also an optional way to approach gifts from borderline patients. However, for some patients, the gift, especially if it is handmade and filled with affective meaning, must be accepted even as the motives for the gift are analyzed.

THE OBJECT MAY HAVE MULTIPLE MEANINGS

The use of a transitional object is more than giving the patient something through which a memory may be facilitated. It is also a concrete form of nonverbal intervention that has multiple meanings (Waelder 1936). It will be understood by the patient on various levels (as seduction, dismissal, caring, and so on), all of which can be explored at the appropriate time.

The transitional object will also be a form of self-revelation by the therapist. Just as any intervention reveals something about the state of the therapist's mind, the particular transitional object he suggests will also reveal something about his own style of self-soothing and his preferred means of defense. Some therapists are more likely to suggest intellectual pursuits, such as writing journals; others are more likely to suggest activity-oriented pursuits, such as making things. However, what is more important for the purpose of this chapter, the transitional object can serve as a concrete interpretation. That is, the particular transitional object will have particular interpretive meaning. (Sechehaye [1951] has discussed this issue in detail.)

We can consider the various ways in which the giving of a particular object may have implicit interpretive meaning. It may mean, "I give to you, even though your parents never gave to you and you expect that I too will never give to you." If a therapist gives a patient his picture, he is telling the patient that the patient is in a panic because he cannot "hold" the therapist in mind. He also encourages symbiotic fears and fantasies, along with an image of therapeutic omnipotence. If the therapist gives the patient a notebook and encourages him to write down any thoughts he has before and after his panic attacks, stating that they will review the notebook at their next session, he is telling the patient that repression of such thoughts is involved in the panic attacks. He gives the patient an image to hold during separations, but it is an image connected with the therapeutic work. It is not just the therapist's image that is sustaining; rather, it is the patient's self-reflection, aided by the transitional object.

TRANSITIONAL OBJECTS CAN BE MISUSED

The most common misuse of the transitional object occurs when the therapist has gone overboard with a patient, usually for countertransferential reasons that are consciously rationalized as an attempt to respond to the patient's dependency needs and to provide a corrective emotional experience. At some point, the therapist realizes that he has gone too far, feels angry, questions his own behavior, and then abruptly decides to change his behavior, end certain gratifications, and reset limits. The therapist then tells the patient that these gratifications will cease and offers a transitional object as a substitute. This intervention seldom works. It represents an inappropriate use of the transitional object, and it usually results in the patient's becoming angry. The patient, who supposedly was unable to tolerate certain kinds of frustrations and was therefore being gratified, is being weaned suddenly, rather than at his own pace. Further, in response to this iatrogenic trauma, the patient is not creating a transitional object, but is being handed the equivalent of an imposed baby sitter. The transitional object becomes a reminder of the therapist's withdrawal rather than a reminder of the therapist's availability between sessions.

Clinical Use and Misuse

The foregoing criteria suggest when transitional objects may be used in therapy. It is not a complete list. They may be understood more fully through examination of clinical examples of the use and misuse of transitional objects. For purposes of confidentiality, the therapist and patient will always be described as male.

FAILURE TO USE A TRANSITIONAL OBJECT

In this first case, the therapist fails to use a transitional object where it might have been helpful.

> The patient complained of panic attacks, along with suicidal thoughts. He called his therapist repeatedly. The therapist did not discourage these calls, since he believed that they were attempts to obtain necessary soothing. However, they eventually began to try the therapist's patience. After several late-night and weekend calls, he was furious. He informed the patient that he could no longer call him between sessions. The patient at first said nothing, then made a mild complaint. After the session ended, he broke a chair in the therapist's waiting room.

This incident might have been avoided if the therapist had recognized his own limits. There is nothing inherently wrong with accepting late-night telephone calls. There are those like Blanck and Blanck (1974), who state that the therapist of a depressed patient must be prepared to be available 24 hours a day. However, the therapist must determine how much he can tolerate, and then communicate this to the patient. This determination is less a matter of theory than it is of personality style and the realities of the therapist's life. The therapist who is comfortable with frequent telephone calls allows them because he expects that, over a long period of time, the calls will diminish because of the patient's increased capacity for anxiety tolerance and self-soothing.

If the therapist needs to change the arrangement, there are ways to enlist the patient's involvement. Here a transitional object might be helpful. The therapist can begin by explaining the situation realistically—how he understands the importance of the phone calls, but how, for many reasons, he cannot be on call 24 hours a day. He can ask the patient how both of them can solve the problem of meeting the patient's needs in a way that is manageable for the therapist. The patient and therapist may jointly agree on a number of calls, on specific times, or on a schedule by which the number of calls will be reduced over a period of time. The patient and therapist may, as they examine the nature of the patient's need for the calls, decide that leaving a message on the answering machine may suffice, so that the patient can be sure that the therapist has a record of how he is feeling, and that on those occasions when the patient needs something more, he will let the therapist know and the therapist will then return the call.

The patient may decide to record his thoughts in a journal (which either the therapist or the patient may buy, each with different transferential implications). In that case, in addition to its use as a memory aid, the journal's first purpose will be to support impulse control ("Write down what you feel, and then if you need to, you should call me."). Later, it can be read to the therapist as an aid to the patient's ego function of reflective awareness ("Bring your journal in and we'll review it together and see how we can understand what you were feeling"). In each of these alternate interventions, it is the patient's active participation in solving the joint therapeutic problem and his assuming responsible control over certain kinds of gratification that make the transitional object acceptable and useful. If the journal were given to the patient without discussion, or without the patient's agreement on the need for a substitute for the therapist's constant availability, then the patient would react more negatively to the idea.

DETRIMENTAL USE OF A TRANSITIONAL OBJECT

In the following instance, the therapist uses a transitional object in a way that was detrimental to the treatment.

The therapist was seeing his patient on an inpatient unit. The patient had a history of multiple hospitalizations, with frequent wrist-cutting episodes and suicide attempts, along with psychotic episodes. The therapist, in an attempt to do supportive work, would discuss literature with his patient. On the eve of the therapist's vacation, the therapist gave the patient his copy of a book that they had discussed and his hospital identification badge as transitional objects. After the therapist left for vacation, the patient cut the therapist's initials on his chest. When the therapist returned from vacation, he realized that he had made a mistake. When the patient came in to his office between sessions and asked to speak with him, the therapist curtly refused. The patient responded typically: He became furious, threw a temper tantrum, and had to be placed in an isolation room.

The therapist's loss of therapeutic perspective is notable in this example. He is overinvolved in the concrete, action-oriented realm, through his giving the patient his identification badge and stimulating merging fantasies (one meaning to the initials). He is also too distant in the verbal and symbolic realm, as can be seen in the too-abrupt setting of too great a distance in the verbal sphere.

After supervisory consultation, the therapist realized that the patient had difficulty setting limits and boundaries, and that he himself had been overly close and then overly distant. He had been close to the patient through action (that is, by giving him the transitional objects), but he had been verbally insensitive to the patient and, in his attempt to build the patient's ego and to be supportive, he was too seductive. Instead, he might have dealt with his vacation by being empathic with the patient, so as to avoid frustrating him unnecessarily when such gratification was possible in the usual course of events on the unit; that is, he could have seen the patient for a moment when the patient requested that he do so. He also could have focused in therapy sessions on the ease with which boundaries are crossed, both in therapy and in community interactions. By defining the issue more precisely, the therapist would have helped the patient to define

boundaries both explicitly and implicitly (the act of discussing the problem in itself sets boundaries) and would have
supported the patient's observing ego.

The patient did not require a transitional object in order
to deal with the therapist's vacation. First, the patient was in
no danger of serious decompensation since he was protected
on the inpatient unit and had other staff and fellow patients
to "hold" him. Second, the particular transitional object
encouraged merger fantasies and behavior rather than
boundary setting and verbalization. There is a world of
difference between asking a patient to write his thoughts in a
journal that the therapist will review in the session after
vacation, and giving the patient an identification badge. The
former encourages impulse control (writing rather than cutting), thought, and reflective awareness; the latter implicitly
seduces the patient, encourages merger, and in no way helps
the therapy. It encourages a patient who already reacts by
action toward further action, since the therapist, instead of
acting as a model of thought and reflection, is acting as a
model for acting out. The therapist erred in responding to
one ego defect—difficulty in maintaining a holding introject,
with consequent panic and acting out—in isolation, out of
the context of the overall therapy. The identification badge
made the *therapist*, rather than the *therapy*, the patient's goal.

In another example of this distinction, the therapist
might give the patient a question to think about between
sessions, as a means of helping the patient to manage panic
attacks which come up between therapy hours. Two possible questions are: "What are you feeling before you start to
panic?" and "Can you think of what it feels like to be with
me, when you begin to panic?" If the therapist encourages
the patient to think about the therapist rather than the therapy (the latter question), then the therapist's image is seen,
by both patient and therapist, as the goal, the prize of treatment. If, on the other hand, the therapist asks the patient to
reflect on a question about himself (the patient) that came up
during the session (the former question), then the question

explicitly and implicitly makes the therapeutic work the goal of treatment, and the image of the therapist becomes a background aspect of the treatment. Both questions may be appropriate, at different times in treatment.

USE OF A TELEPHONE-ANSWERING MACHINE

Many patients discover the therapist's answering machine as a transitional object. They call the machine, especially during vacations, to hear the therapist's voice. There are others who will chastise the therapist on the machine, since the therapist can neither retaliate nor interrupt. Pine (1976) discusses his setting up a steady telephone appointment with a patient who needed the anchoring of a "home base" but couldn't attend sessions regularly. Providing her with such a base gave her control over access to her therapist, so that she could come closer or move away at her own will.

The answering machine can be approached by the patient, is always available, offers some of the therapist's soothing function, and yet may evoke less anxiety than the therapist's direct presence. However, it should be discovered by the patient who wants it, rather than offered by the therapist. It seems arrogant for the therapist to suggest a machine as his substitute. The patient will often let the therapist know about his use, and the psychological meaning of his use, of the machine, either directly, by telling the therapist (sometimes in a guilty way, sometimes defiantly) that he calls the machine when the therapist is away, or indirectly, by calling frequently but without leaving a return telephone number, or by ending a long message with "It's all right now."

WHEN THE PATIENT LEAVES ON VACATION

The patient who is leaving the therapist for a vacation may expect a major regression. This may occur around holiday times, for example, when the patient travels, often to a distant city, to visit family. The following three examples illustrate how transitional objects can be used to help hold a patient at such times. Each of the following patients had evidence of a thought disorder, along with a history of multiple hospitalizations and severe acting out, ranging from wrist cutting and suicide attempts to alcoholic binges with blackouts. These regressions had in the past been precipitated by visits to family, so the therapist had good reason to anticipate difficulty.

One patient, when asked what might help him, said that he would most miss the therapist's presence. He spoke of how he sometimes felt comforted when he imagined the therapist and his office and their talking together, but that as soon as he went home he forgot it all. The therapist suggested that the patient draw a picture of the office and the therapist, discuss it with the therapist, and then take the picture with him to help him remember their sessions.

Another patient frequently complained that he did not know what his problems were, that he had no idea what was the matter, and that he felt most pressured when family members confronted him about his lack of a good job and his need for continued treatment. The therapist suggested that the patient list all the questions he expected to face, so that they could review possible answers during their next session, before the trip. The patient could then record the answers and take the paper with him. The paper would assist both the patient's evocative memory of the therapist and the ego function of anticipation.

A third patient was attending a milieu treatment program, had progressed well, and held a position of leadership in the therapeutic community as attendance keeper. Nevertheless, he was sure that he would feel like a failure when he returned home. He wanted to feel competent while with his family. At first the therapist suggested that he take the attendance sheet home, as a

symbol of his role in the community. The patient declined, stating that he didn't need it, that thinking about
the therapist (which he could do without help) was
enough, and that talking about his accomplishments "to
anyone who will listen" made him feel good. Thus the
patient used words to evoke the therapist and the therapeutic community and, with those memories, a sense of
his accomplishments in that environment. The words did
not express a feeling but, instead, summoned evocative
images within which the patient felt competent. It is as if
the patient, by talking about his therapist, was uttering a
magical incantation by which he could summon up a
holding introject.

The use of transitional objects is not always effective. It
is assumed that the therapist is using this modification of
treatment after he has diagnosed the patient as insufficiently
responsive to just interpretation as a means of dealing with
severe regressive episodes, especially around separation.
Either the angry aspects of the patient's behavior are felt to
be secondary, or the therapist is assuming, as do Adler and
Buie (1979), that the patient's anger is a reaction to his
primary inability to maintain holding introjects. It is at that
point that the transitional object is used.

If the use of a transitional object fails, we can ask why it
failed. First, was it used correctly? Given that this is largely
an intuitive assessment, it may be difficult to answer such a
question. But there are times, as previously described, when
it is clearly a mistake. Second, perhaps there is too much of
what Adler and Buie (1979) call "diffuse primitive rage"
(p. 88). In such instances, the therapist will have to intervene
more actively, with additional sessions, telephone calls, and
often hospitalization. Third, is the dynamic aspect more
prominent than the therapist had previously considered?
The patient may need, for example, to intrude on the therapist's private life, or wish to defeat any successful work in
treatment, or enjoy rendering the therapist helpless and anxious with constant threats of suicide. Kernberg (1975) fo-

cuses on such dynamic issues in his treatment recommendations. When such dynamic factors are more prominent, interpretive focus is indicated and use of a transitional object is
less effective.

One way to determine the patient's capacity to benefit
from transitional objects is to assess the degree to which the
patient's need for the therapist is ego-syntonic. The patient
who openly seeks help from the therapist, even if he complains that he forgets the therapist after sessions are over, is
more apt to want a reminder of the therapist. The patient
who devalues the therapist and the treatment is less likely to
use a transitional object.

5

The Psychoanalytic Position: Contextual Aspects of the Therapist's Stance

In this chapter we will discuss alterations of the therapist's stance in response to patients' difficulties in the traditional psychoanalytic situation. These alterations may become necessary when the patient is unable to work within the therapist's usual framework and when interpretation alone is not sufficient in helping the patient deal with his difficulties. Any patient may have difficulty tolerating the relatively abstinent and symbolic nature of the psychoanalytic relationship, but such difficulties are more common in patients with major ego deficits.

Therapeutic alterations that may be effective with such patients have been termed *parameters* (Eissler 1953). Just as Eissler cautions us to evaluate a given symptom only within the context of the ego within which it is embedded, so too must we evaluate the therapist's alterations in context. In some treatment approaches, certain parameters are appropriate modifications in the psychoanalytic situation; in others, they violate it irreparably.

There is an inherent logic in the therapeutic process. That logic is expressed in the practical arrangements we establish for our sessions, as well as in the way we intervene with our patients. Changes that violate this internal consistency are more potentially damaging than those that are within the spirit (if not the external manifestation) of that consistency. For this reason, we need to be clear about the assumptions of a given psychotherapy. A therapist who has such clarity can more easily decide, when he is working at the boundary of his usual stance, which changes remain consistent within his system and which violate its internal logic.

Definition

The "psychoanalytic position" is a combination of the "analytic attitude" (Schafer 1983) and the treatment frame, which expresses the assumptions of the analytic attitude in concrete terms. The *frame* includes what the analyst *does*; it refers to the overt aspects of treatment, such as the type of intervention used (interpretations, questions) or the practical arrangements (use of the couch, arrangement of furniture, policy regarding payment for missed sessions). The *analytic attitude* refers to what the analyst *assumes* about the nature of psychopathology and the mutative factors in psychoanalysis. The psychoanalytic position connects these aspects to each other. The assumptions underlying one's analytic attitude distinguish permissible from impermissible alterations in the frame. Each aspect makes the other possible and meaningful. It is difficult to analyze in the way Schafer recommends unless the framework of analysis is established. It is also true that one can establish what seems to be a psychoanalytic framework and still conduct formal, mechanistic psychoanalysis. We are concerned both with how the therapist gives the arrangements meaning and vitality and with how the arrangements create a structured, controlled setting within which analysis can take place.

With the Neurotic Patient

There has always been a close relationship between the therapist's assumptions of what is mutative for the patient and the concrete arrangements of the frame.

In classical psychoanalysis, the patient attends sessions frequently, lies on the couch, and free-associates. The therapist listens neutrally for manifestations of unconscious wishes and defenses against these wishes, which are embedded in the content and pattern of the patient's speech and which emerge in the transference. This arrangement depends upon at least three assumptions. First, it assumes that the patient is neurotic, meaning that he has achieved a certain level of psychological development, resulting in difficulties that are due to unconscious intrapsychic conflict. This also means that the patient is able to regress in the service of the ego and can establish a predominantly illusional transference resolvable through interpretation. Second, interpretation of unconscious conflict and defense is seen as the primary mutative factor. Third, the analyst's stance is that of a neutral listener, a transference object, and an accurate interpreter (although, as we will see in Chapters 8 and 9, many classical analysts have a broader view).

The arrangements of psychoanalysis are the practical expressions of Freud's (1912a,b, 1913, 1914, 1915) technical recommendations, including neutrality, abstinence, and analysis of transference. These arrangements are designed to facilitate expression of data that are considered to be important. The therapist will hear from the patient about transference, fantasy, and the like only if they are promoted by such arrangements. Further, by assuming a concrete position (sitting behind the patient, who is lying on the office couch) and a certain listening attitude (designed to simultaneously gratify and frustrate the patient through interpretations of symbolism), the analyst facilitates a transference regression that may be unique to psychoanalysis (Stone 1961).

Aspects of the classical psychoanalytic stance have long been debated (see Brenner 1976, Friedman 1969, Greenson 1967, Langs and Stone 1980, Lipton 1977, and Stone 1961, 1984). These debates concern issues such as the meanings of neutrality and abstinence; the respective roles of interpretation, gratification, and new experience; and the function of the analyst in the analytic process. They are disputes about the analyst's stance and the way in which it is reflected in his analytic position; they ask what is allowable in an analysis that does not violate the letter and spirit of analysis and that facilitates insight into a dynamic unconscious through interpretation of transference. A permissible behavior is one that facilitates, and does not obviate, the goal of analysis. Analysts such as Brenner, Stone, and Greenson agree on the broad outline and concepts of the analytic stance but may differ over their clinical application. They may differ in their evaluations of the impact of any technical differences on the ultimate goal of analysis. That is, their differences involve issues of means rather than of ends. They might ask, for example, whether the analyst's answering certain questions facilitates or makes more difficult development of a transference neurosis and its resolution through interpretation.

The classical analytic position allows the analyst to be neutral. Such a position is difficult to maintain when treating an acutely suicidal patient. In such a case, the therapist is so concerned with the potential for suicide that he can neither remain neutral nor focus on analyzing the patient; rather, he must "manage" the patient. The ever-present risk prevents professional detachment, a detachment which enables the analyst to remain neutral, to analyze, to empathize, and to use the "second self" (Schafer 1983). Thus the real dangers with this patient make almost impossible the classical psychoanalytic position. It is for this reason that Kernberg advocates hospitalizing acutely suicidal patients. The short-term unconcern with the patient's everyday behavior, in the context of a long-term concern for the patient's inner life and autonomy, can now be reestablished, because the physical arrangement (the patient's being in the hospital) reestablishes the therapist's freedom to listen neutrally. Insight-oriented psychoanalytic therapy can take place because the therapist is no longer required to manage the patient.

For Winnicott, the practical arrangements take on symbolic meaning. He writes: "The analyst expressed love by the positive interest taken, and hate in the strict start and finish and in the matter of fees. Love and hate were honestly expressed, that is to say not denied by the analyst" (Winnicott 1954, p. 285). For example, a patient is asked to leave at the end of the hour because the session is over. He complains that he is being "kicked out." His elaboration of what it feels like to be told that the session is over (that is, to be "kicked out") is transferential, but in fact he *is* asked to leave at the end of the hour. He also *does* have to pay for the hour. These requirements are fundamental to the situation. Winnicott's point is that it is inherent in the arrangements of psychoanalysis that the patient come to terms with both loving and hating, or closeness to and separation from, the analyst. When the patient reaches that point, it means that the capacity for mature object relations has been reached. This is a goal of treatment. Thus the goal toward which the analyst works in verbal treatment is achieved partially because it is built into the practical arrangements. From this perspective, if the analyst changes the arrangements in a manner that portrays him as only loving or only hating, he will be establishing treatment arrangements which, in their inherent logic, work against his overt treatment goals.

With the More Severely Disturbed Patient:
The Concept of Parameters

We have considered classical analytic treatment with the neurotic patient. What of the more severely disturbed patient, who finds it difficult to work within the classical situation? Eissler (1953) deals with the problem by suggesting that, under certain circumstances, the therapist can modify the analytic frame through use of a parameter.

Eissler excludes consideration of the analyst's personality in his definition and discussion of parameters. Instead, he focuses on technique. Eissler (1953) defines a *parameter of technique* as follows:

> [T]he deviation, both quantitative and qualitative, from the basic model technique, that is to say, from a technique which requires interpretation as the exclusive tool. In the basic model technique the parameter is, of course, zero throughout the whole treatment. [p. 110]

Eissler advises that parameters be employed to the minimum extent possible, and only when interpretation is not enough. Moreover, they should be capable of self-elimination, and their effect on the transference must be interpreted. Parameters are employed for patients who occasionally and temporarily require something other than interpretation. Eissler introduces the concept of an alternative to interpretation, when it is clinically indicated, but he stresses the ultimate aim of abandoning and analyzing the temporary intervention.

Eissler's assumption of a basic analytic position is evident in his caution about the employment of parameters and in his care to distinguish them from modifications of technique that irreparably alter the analytic position and that make analysis impossible. Such modifications violate the internal logic of psychoanalysis, which depends on the analyst's interpreting transference and achieving results through this insight alone. For this reason, it is acceptable for the analyst to suggest that a patient with an elevator phobia go for an elevator ride, but it is unacceptable for the analyst to set an arbitrary termination date and to guarantee the patient complete recovery. In the first instance, the analyst still has an opportunity to interpret the transference meaning of his parameter. In the second example, the analyst no longer has the opportunity (because the analysis will have ended) and, further, has transformed his role from interpreter to magical guarantor of the future, with no opportunity to interpret that particular transference. Such a promise would violate the analytic position even if the analysis were not to end, because the analyst cannot both guarantee success and interpret the patient's wish to magically create him as such a guarantor.

Eissler (1953) affirms the classical analytic assumption that interpretation is the sole mutative agent and that any other (rare and limited) intervention must at some point be analyzed in order for the therapy to qualify as psychoanalysis. Although Eissler's paper was historically the most prominent initial attempt to discuss deviations with a disturbed patient within the context of a classical psychoanalysis, none of the parameters ultimately disturbs the assumptions of a classical analytic stance. Eissler's cautions regarding the limited nature, occasional use, and ultimate aim of eliminating and analyzing the parameter support the notion that insight is the primary mutative factor.

Eissler's position reflects deep commitment to structural change and suspicion of interventions that deprive the patient of opportunity for such change. As Eissler notes, a parameter may lead the patient to "falsify" the therapeutic process when the patient obeys the analyst instead of arriving at change through genuine insight; there is a great deal of difference between internalization and identification with the aggressor. Further, as Silverman (1984) notes, a parameter may steer the transference in a positive direction or help the patient cover important sources of anxiety. Finally, as Eissler notes, it may be easier for the therapist to introduce a parameter than to properly use an interpretive technique.

Eissler's term *parameter* and his paper as a whole are paradoxical. The word *parameter* connotes both a technical step designed to preserve an analysis (note the distinction between a parameter, which is ultimately analyzable, and a modification, which is not) and a technical step indicating that the analysis was not able to be carried out properly, using only interpretation as the technical tool (an analysis in which parameters were employed is often unacceptable as a training case in a psychoanalytic institute).

Eissler's paper is far-reaching in its ideas about the possibilities of technical modifications for the more disturbed patient. Eissler (1953) opens the door to wide changes in psychoanalytic technique. He writes:

> Freud's concepts—(1) the hypothetically normal ego as defined by the response in the situation of the basic model technique; (2) a scale leading by degrees to a state of absolute unresponsiveness to the analytic compact; and (3) the intervening variety of ego modifications to which a variety of techniques must be correlated—provide, in my estimation, a system which is ideally flexible and superbly adaptable to actual clinical work. [p. 125]

However, Eissler's assumption that interpretation is the primary mutative agent for patients with a certain ideal ego reflects a conservative theory of psychoanalysis. Within this framework, analysts ought not fundamentally alter their usual stance, and any intervention that cannot eventually be interpreted (that is, modifications that go beyond parameters) irretrievably breaches the analytic stance. The concept of parameters, while overtly concerned with expansion of psychoanalysis, also defines the boundaries of classical analysis; it reaffirms classical ideas about mutative factors.

With some patients, the therapist can have no realistic hope of ever being able to analyze the parameter. Blanck and Blanck (1974) seem to be referring to such patients when they suggest that, for patients with "unintact" egos, the strict criteria suggested by Eissler cannot be met. Blanck and Blanck deal with this difficulty by drawing a sharp division between psychoanalysis and psychotherapy. Psychoanalysis is for patients with intact egos, and, for treatment of these patients, Eissler's criteria for employment of parameters should be retained. For patients who lack intact egos, psychotherapy is employed, and for psychotherapy, the criteria for parameters are too restrictive. They state that interventions other than interpretation are necessary and that these interventions cannot eventually be eliminated by interpretation. They do not use the term *parameters* for such interventions. "[W]e might refer to them as departures from classical psychoanalytic technique in the less-than-neurotically organized personality" (Blanck and Blanck 1979, p. 115). Yet they insist on specificity in these interventions, based on the therapist's evaluation of particular ego defects. The interventions must "be addressed with as much precision as possible to the malformation in organization. We know of no better safeguard against wild psychotherapy then minute knowledge of subphase development" (p. 115). Thus Blanck and Blanck maintain Eissler's ideological assumptions about classical analysis, but they clearly distinguish it from psychotherapy, which becomes a different modality.

The Patient–Therapist Relationship

While Eissler attempts to define the limits of the psychoanalytic stance through technique (in his concept of a parameter as a deviation from standard technique), others attempt to examine the boundaries of the stance through the prism of the patient–therapist relationship. For example, Stone (1954) writes that parameters are acceptable when they are within the bounds of a therapist's role, "as opposed to good father, or solicitous friend, or magician," in which case they are unacceptable (pp. 576–577).

Jacobson (1954) also speaks of working psychoanalytically with severely depressed patients while modifying the patient–therapist relationship beyond that defined for classical work with neurotic patients. She stresses the analyst's need for flexibility in adjusting to the severely depressed patient's mood.

> There must be a continuous, subtle, empathic tie between the analyst and his depressive patients; we must be very careful not to let empty silences grow or not to talk too long, too rapidly, or too empathically; that is, never to give too much or too little." [p. 604]

Jacobson makes a similar point in her discussion of therapy with schizophrenic patients, in which she stresses allowing patients' use of the therapist to bolster their own structural difficulties. Jacobson (1967) writes that, at given times during the treatment's course,

> I permitted this patient to "use" me in the ways and roles he needed. I adapted my emotional attitudes and behavior to his wishes, either for warmth and closeness or for more distance. I let him "borrow" my superego and ego; regard and treat me as his bad id and his illness; project his guilt, his faults, and weaknesses onto me; or turn me into the ideal of saintliness he needed." [p. 57]

Jacobson waited until after periods of emotional stress for the patient had passed and was then able to interpret. She states that the interpretations were "surprisingly effective." She is careful to distinguish her approach from one that stresses the analyst's role-playing a given attitude in order to create a corrective emotional experience. Grunes (1984), Pine (1984), and Bach (1985), in work discussed in Chapters 9 and 10, take similar positions. These analysts speak of modulating the transference, of working with the therapeutic relationship in order to sustain the treatment. Their concern is with establishing the boundary for an analytic position through the relationship rather than through technique. It is the relationship that allows the technique to work; that is, it allows the patient to use interpretation. For these analysts, the relationship forms the foundation for interpretation rather than the threat to interpretation. For Eissler, the parameters are introduced after interpretation has failed, and his concern is that they not replace interpretation.

Tarachow (1962) also uses the therapist–patient relationship as a way of defining the boundaries of psychoanalysis. He writes that the therapist can treat the patient's verbalizations as symbolic communication and interpret them, or he can listen to them as manifest communication and react to them. To the extent that he does the former, he is engaging in psychoanalysis rather than psychotherapy. (His views are discussed more fully in Chapter 8.)

Although focus on the relationship rather than on technique to define the boundaries of psychoanalysis and psychotherapy may indicate differing ideas about the analyst's role (see Chapters 8 and 9) and about the natures of supportive and expressive therapy (see Chapter 3), all the analysts discussed agree that the major mutative factor in psychoanalytic work is insight through interpretation. That is the goal toward which the therapist must strive, knowing that, with the more severely disturbed patient, insight may be more limited to certain sectors of functioning than it would be for the neurotic patient.

The Locus of the Psychoanalytic Position

What is the locus of the analytic position? If one sees the analytic position as comprising a balance between the rigors of the frame and the analyst's judgment within the frame, then modifying the frame for clinical reasons becomes more acceptable. If the analytic position is seen as located only in the frame, then changes in the frame are seen as counterproductive and as a violation of the essence of psychoanalysis. It is precisely this issue that is debated by Langs and Stone (1980) in their joint publication.

For Langs, maintenance of a strict frame is essential. The frame "holds" the patient, and the maintenance of a secure frame is, in itself, productively gratifying. Langs also feels that a secure frame serves to prevent unproductive gratifications and "cures" that are brought about through discharge and action rather than through insight. The frame both provides a setting for insight and models verbal symbolic communication, delay of discharge, and other elements of more mature psychological functioning. The analyst is charged with maintaining a secure frame, containing the patient's impulses, and preventing misalliances and cures through collusive action by patient and analyst. If an analyst maintains a secure frame, he can interpret such wishes by the patient and help the patient reach cure through insight. Langs believes that the analyst's decision to modify the frame is invariably prompted by countertransference. Once the frame is modified, analysis of the wish prompting the modification is difficult at best and is impossible unless the modification is rectified. Any modification of the frame, including, for example, signing insurance forms for the patient, violates his conception of the analytic position. For Langs, the frame is equivalent to the analytic position.

Stone (1961) disagrees. Langs and Stone (1980) sees the analytic frame itself as more frustrating than gratifying. Stone believes that the psychoanalytic setting evokes

the repetitive phases of the state of relative *separation* from early objects . . . [The frame especially reproduces] that period of life where all the modalities of bodily intimacy and direct dependence on the mother are being relinquished or attenuated, *pari passu* with the rapid development of the great vehicle of communication by speech. [pp. 86–87, his emphasis]

While Langs focuses on the impulse-control aspects of the frame and the therapist-parental functions of control, Stone emphasizes the degree to which the analytic situation echoes the child's development from a psychologically merged state with the mother, with contact through concrete tactile modes, to a psychologically separated state, with contact through more symbolic and verbal means. Here too, as in Winnicott's example discussed earlier in this chapter, we see that for both Langs and Stone, the practical arrangements of the stance resonate with their emphasis in therapeutic work.

For Stone, it is the frustration inherent in the classical analytic frame that facilitates the transference neurosis and its interpretation. The analyst may find it useful to soften the inherent rigors of the frame, however. It becomes the analyst's responsibility to work within the frame in a manner that does not provoke unanalyzable regression and that enlists the patient's rational cooperation (rather than submission). Thus the analyst should use judgment when confronted with issues that threaten the frame. Stone believes that while "deviations" tend to evoke criticism, aspects of technique that are silent and do not reveal themselves in overt modifications may escape notice but may be more harmful. Thus the analytic position lies not only in the frame but in the analyst's creating and applying the frame. Stone contends that the patient will appreciate his analyst's use of judgment and rationality when modifications have been made and that fantasies about these modifications will be analyzable and accepted as reasonable exceptions to a general posture of abstinence.

At one point, Stone tells Langs:

There is, I think, an overestimation of the frame, important as it is. . . . The frame is important; the frame of a bed is important; the frame of a picture is important; the box in which one carries one's tools is important. It's not more important than the contents. It's there to serve the contents, to keep them usefully available. Now in your thinking . . . it attains a certain over-growth. You know, it's like the tail of a dog. The tail begins to be more important than all the rest of the animal. And the idea that there is always some neurotic purpose being served for the therapist if he finds it necessary or desirable to modify a rather overrigidly conceived frame is pure, unjustified assumption. [Langs and Stone 1980, p. 295]

It is clear that Langs and Stone have different conceptions of the frame's importance. Here too, however, as in our discussion of parameters, Stone and Langs substantially agree on the overall goals of analytic work and on the means by which this work is accomplished. Both feel that insight into unconscious conflict, communicated to the patient by interpretation of transference and resistance, is paramount.

Is Insight the Primary Mutative Factor?

As we have seen, the psychoanalytic position, in what we call "classical" technique, is based on the assumption that insight, achieved through interpretation of the transference neurosis, is ultimately mutative, and that such a transference neurosis is facilitated in a climate of abstinence and neutrality (Brenner 1976, Freud 1912a,b, 1913, 1914, 1915, Gill 1954, Stone 1961). This is true for both the neurotic and the more severely disturbed patient (Eissler 1953). Within this framework, the psychoanalytic position—reflected in arrangements such as use of the couch and in the analyst's unique way of listening and responding to the patient (Gray 1973, Tarachow 1962)—is designed to heighten the transference and to emphasize insight through interpretation as the prime mutative factor. This is the basis for the internal logic of the traditional psychoanalytic position.

What if the assumptions behind this internal logic are modified? One can modify this logic by examining the mutative factors or the patient variables. For example, the criteria that insight is the primary mutative factor and that the analytic position bolsters insight have grown more questionable as we have learned more about analysis and about the severely disturbed patient. Many analysts, including Balint (1968), Buie and Adler (1982), Grunes (1984), Loewald (1960), and Pine (1985), believe that factors in addition to interpretation have a mutative effect. Pine includes internalization, support in the context of interpretive work, and empathy as mutative factors. If these factors are taken into account, then the analytic position is broadened. Thus if the analyst modifies the frame in a manner that is not ultimately interpretable, it need not necessarily be seen as violating the essence of psychoanalytic work.

For example, Balint (1968) has questioned the emphasis on interpretation as the primary mutative agent for the more disturbed patient. For Balint, a new experience with the analyst is primary, not as a substitute for interpretation, but as a necessary response to a patient who is at a regressed stage in treatment, a stage where words are not communicative and, further, lead to a strain between patient and analyst. The analyst functions to provide an environment within which a controlled regression is possible. Aspects of this analytic function may be expressed through gratifications such as holding a patient's hand or providing extra sessions. One can readily see that for the therapist who believes in a therapeutic role broader than solely that of an interpreter of transference, the boundaries of the analytic position become enlarged.

Thus the analytic position is not fixed, but varies depending on what the analyst assumes is mutative for a given patient. An intervention appropriate within one context— such as using a transitional object or prohibiting a patient's yelling during the hour—is a violation of a psychoanalytic position within a different context. The question of whether a supportive therapy can be turned into an analysis hinges on these underlying assumptions; such a question has to do with comparative psychoanalytic theories. Perhaps Balint or Kohut would see a more classical treatment as evolving out of the earlier gratification; Brenner or Langs might consider the analytic position to have been irreparably violated by allowing a patient to hold the therapist's hand. In their view, such gratification obviates full analysis of the transference. They would expect a patient to move to a second analyst if he wanted a psychoanalysis after what would be seen as a preparatory psychotherapy.

If the analytic position is ultimately dependent on the particular analyst's theoretical emphasis, then the locus of the analytic position lies not in the analytic arrangements or frame, but in the analyst's mind. There are those who prefer to locate it in the practical arrangements. It is too simple to define an analytic treatment through external procedural details. It allows for ready criticism of colleagues who make an arrangement that the critic would not have. However, to locate the analytic position in the technical procedures rather than in the mind of the analyst is, to use Stone's expression, like the tail wagging the dog. It treats the technical arrangements as if they were immutable and asks that the analyst fit the procedure, rather than seeing the procedure as a tool of the analyst.

We have considered the analyst's theoretical emphases as crucial in determining his stance. Within any stance, the analyst's judgment will be a major factor in his decisions about implementation and modification of any particular position. There is a predilection toward classifying treatments by their external manifestations. Violations of these "rules" become debatable parameters and indications of countertransference rather than of clinical judgment. Stone (1961) writes:

> Whereas the term "parameter" arose from an interesting and specific metapsychological view of technique, one not seldom hears colleagues discussing the question of whether a given maneuver *was* a "parameter," as if that

were more important than whether or not it was a good
thing to do at the time! [p. 126]

Further, the assumption by the unknowledgeable therapist or by the therapist who uses technique defensively seems
to be that the more rigid the rule and the more ungiving the
therapist, the more analytic the treatment. Stone writes:

> I approve no more of people who adopt actively parental
> or coddling, not to speak of more obviously harmful
> positions in relation to patients, than I do of those who
> sit like graven images with their patients. It's just that I
> feel those errors have been understood from early on; in
> fact sometimes understood . . . to an exaggerated degree.
> That is, to be "tough" with a patient is regarded as all
> right. To be a little gentle with a patient is always
> suspect. To raise a fee is natural, good analytic work. To
> lower a fee is, a priori, dubious indulgence. To withhold
> information is, a priori, good. To give a little informa-
> tion because you think it, as a matter of judgment, desir-
> able at a time is, a priori, bad. [Langs and Stone 1980,
> p. 9]

Stone notes that analysts often prefer to make difficult
decisions by using rules. Rules alone are never enough to
guide the analyst through difficult times with patients, however, and they may be the analyst's means of evading responsibility, ambiguity, the need to exercise judgment, and the
human aspects of the analytic situation. (See Lipton 1977,
p. 262ff, for further discussion of this point.)

In case reports from experienced analysts working with
difficult patients, we see analysts who make exceptions to
their generally classical way of working because they have
internalized the essence of analytic work rather than relying
on external rules to define the work for them. For these
analysts, their deviations from the letter of the law—which
they generally follow and in which they believe—are within
the spirit of the law. In exceptional circumstances, they are

able to modify their manner of working to gratify patients or to work with genuine emergencies and threats to the treatment in a manner that keeps an analytic process going and that maintains an essential analytic posture, at least according to the assumptions within which they work. But the manner of deviation, the type of modification, cannot be specified in advance nor evaluated out of the context of their assumptions or the treatment as a whole. The responses will be based on the therapist's imagination, creativity, personality, and internalized knowledge about the basic principles of analytic work. It may be only retrospectively that we can evaluate to what extent a particular modification was necessary, and what the cost of the modification was in terms of missed opportunities for insight. This is why Stone writes that psychotherapy "often calls for greater skill than analysis. It should follow rather than precede analytic training" (Langs and Stone 1980, p. 94). (Wallerstein 1986, p. 697, makes a similar point.)

When we consider various therapeutic stances, we can often quickly tell whether a therapy is analytically oriented. In difficult situations, however, the analyst may be pressed to respond to the patient in ways that stretch to the limit the definition of psychoanalytically oriented treatment. For analysts who see insight through interpretation as the sole mutative factor in treatment and who rely on a strong frame as the context for interpretive work, almost any modification of the frame will move the treatment out of the psychoanalytic position (with the exception of a parameter, which must eventually be interpreted). Those who contend that noninterpretive factors work in conjunction with interpretation have a broader view of their role within the analytic situation and may then modify their stance and their technical arrangements in a more extended way than the first group of analysts.

There remains the task of differentiating this second group of analysts (those who adopt a broader view of analysis) from nonpsychoanalytic therapists. A concept such as the psychoanalytic position is not, at its boundaries, easily defined; there is enormous room for flexibility among psychoanalytically oriented theoretical viewpoints. Still, at a certain point, some stances become nonpsychoanalytic positions. A Gestalt therapist, for example, is consistent within his position, but it is not a psychoanalytic position.

One can use Pine's definition of psychoanalytic treatment to help clarify the distinction between those psychotherapies that are analytic and those that are not. Pine (1985) writes that a treatment is psychoanalytic if it focuses on two broad points of view:

> The first is the interconnected triad of *psychic determinism, unconscious mental functioning*, and . . . the *primary process*—or that aspect of thinking that works with symbol and metaphor, with "irrational" connections, and does not heed the rules of reality. I say these are interconnected because only through a recognition of the workings of the unconscious mind and the primary process can we see our way into the core concept of psychic determinism. . . . [The second] is a focus on *intrapsychic life*, especially as shaped by *early, bodily based*, and *object-related* experiences, and organized in *interrelated* (both *multiply functional* and *conflictual*) ways. [p. 71, his emphasis]

If these broad foci underlie certain technical modifications, then we may choose to consider that treatment psychoanalytically oriented. If they do not form the analyst's background focus, however, and if the treatment is instead based on only one out of the hierarchy of mutative factors (such as catharsis or nonspecific support), then we might consider that treatment to be outside of the analytic domain. Ultimately, then, the analyst's basic assumptions and goals, in conjunction with the manner in which they are implemented, are the basis of the analytic position. Thus it may be more appropriate to speak of *an* analytic position rather than *the* analytic position.

Modifications

It is with the more severely disturbed patient that the therapist becomes most aware of the close relationship between
underlying assumptions and therapeutic stance. When a patient cannot accept the rigors of a classical analytic position
and the therapist is confronted with a decision as to whether
to modify the position in some respect, it is important that he
be aware of his underlying assumptions and attempt, not so
much to derive an eclectic approach, but to ensure *consistency
within a given context.*

It is not that one position is inherently correct or incorrect. As was evident in our review of alternate models
(Chapter 1), there are several competing analytic positions.
However, shifts between incompatible positions can create
confusion for the patient. This is because the analyst's position—his practical arrangements, what he sees as permissible
and impermissible gratification, what he considers important
in interpretation, what he asks from the patient—creates a
certain atmosphere, an average expectable environment
(Winnicott 1951). Patients know what is expected of them
and what to expect from the analyst. They can internalize a
consistent analyst. They can fit into the environment and
express themselves in a manner suited to that environment.
This is one reason that patients of Freudian analysts dream
Freudian dreams, and patients of Jungian analysts have Jungian dreams, and patients of behavioral therapists behave
rather than dream: Patients "dress" their inner life in clothes
appropriate for their analyst and his environment.

Switching from position to position, then, perplexes the
patient. If one day he is asked to free–associate and his
communication is treated symbolically and not as "real"
(Tarachow 1962), and the next day he is asked to problem
solve cognitively and his verbalizations are treated on the
manifest level, then the patient has no expectable environment. To continue the clothing metaphor, if the patient
doesn't know whether he is attending a formal dinner party

or a picnic at the beach, he can never know what to wear and he can never feel comfortable. This is not, as Langs (Langs and Stone 1980) would have it, because the frame is not secure, but because the therapist is not secure. The problem is not necessarily in the frame; it is, more fundamentally, in the creator of the frame, the therapist himself and all his productions, which certainly include the frame but also include his entire Weltanschauung. Especially with the more disturbed patient, where internalization of the analyst is so important, consistency within a position is a virtue.

It should be stressed that we are discussing questions of relative emphasis as if they were clear-cut issues. Many therapists will shift their focus from interpretation to, for example, assisting patients with concrete needs when patients have pronounced ego problems and when these problems are not interpretable. Further, a therapist may shift from a supportive emphasis to a more interpretive one during the evolution of therapy. However, it is one thing to gradually shift emphasis during the course of treatment in response to changes in a patient, and quite another to alternate and shift emphasis throughout a treatment in a manner that may be abrupt and unconnected to shifts in the patient. Our overall discussion pertains to the latter situation, and the relevant considerations can best be understood through the kinds of sharp theoretical distinctions made here. However, this form of theoretical presentation runs the risk of appearing dogmatic in a way that is incompatible with the author's theoretical beliefs and clinical practice.

Clinical Use and Misuse

We may attempt to gain further insight into the boundaries of the analytic position by reviewing clinical cases. With the exception of the first case, these are not examples of patients in psychoanalysis. Rather, they have been chosen to illustrate the concept of the psychoanalytic position.

CASE 1: RESPONDING TO PATIENT DEMANDS
WITHIN THE PSYCHOANALYTIC POSITION

Balint (1968, pp. 170–172) describes a response to a patient's demands that does not violate the analytic position and that also furthers the working alliance.

> The patient, who has difficulty leaving his analyst on Friday, requested a weekend session. Although Balint had given the patient an extra session in the past, he believed that granting the request this time would add to the patient's sense of being weak and dependent on a powerful doctor. To give the extra session would be to act in consonance with the transference fantasy, as if the doctor were, in fact, an omnipotent object capable of satisfying his weak, dependent patients. It would reinforce and skew the transference despite any interpretation Balint might make of the request; the arrangements would work counter to the interpretation. On the other hand, to refuse and interpret the request would make the patient feel worse. If the patient agreed with the analyst's interpretation of his request as a form of neediness, he would feel guilty for demanding so much from such a kind analyst; if he disagreed with the interpretation, he would experience the analyst as cruel.
>
> Balint responded in a way that empathically clarified his dilemma. He told the patient that he recognized his discomfort, but that he felt that an extra session wouldn't give him enough of what he wanted and needed. Giving the session would make the patient feel weak and the analyst seem powerful, which would not help the treatment.

Balint explains that his decision was based on a desire to avoid encouraging, in the arrangements of the session, a situation of inequality between analyst and patient. We can also understand his action as demonstrating a connection with his patient—the same connection that the patient wanted to establish through the action of an extra session—through empathy for how the patient was feeling and, more important, for the conflict faced by the analyst and the patient. Balint acted to diminish what he terms an "ocnophilic" (clinging) relationship. This was accomplished not by refusing the extra session, since one can demonstrate power by denying a request as well as by granting one. Rather he demystified the rationale for his decision. By clarifying the dilemma, Balint became a rational authority rather than an arbitrary one. The patient could then not only feel understood by the analyst, which was the purpose behind his request, but he could experience himself as an adult partner in an understandable process. As Stone (1961) notes, it is this adult collaboration that underlies the analysis of the child in the patient. Balint artfully gratified his patient in a manner that facilitated the working alliance. However, it may also be that this gratification was in itself therapeutic (rather than being simply a means of furthering the process leading to a later therapeutic interpretation). It would be understood as therapeutic within the parent–child model elaborated by Loewald (1960), with the analyst organizing the patient's inchoate need, expressed concretely and through action discharge, into more verbal and symbolic form. It would not replace interpretive work, but it would have its own mutative value, alongside interpretation.

CASE 2: VIOLATION OF THE PSYCHOANALYTIC POSITION

> The patient is a severely underweight man who has had several hospitalizations and surgical procedures for serious medical problems associated with his anorexia. After some time in therapy, he has gained little weight, and the therapist, concerned about the patient's deteriorating medical condition, decides to weigh the patient before each session. She further decides that she will not see the patient for that session if his weight has dropped below the prescribed limit.

The therapist's rationale for these conditions is as follows: (1) She must take a position illustrating her opposition to his self-destructiveness outside the sessions, manifested in his refusal to eat. (2) The patient will identify with her as a setter of reasonable limits, and this identification will help him set his own reasonable limits. (3) Finally, the session will become a behavioral reward for his eating, and loss of the session will be punishment for his not eating.

One can appreciate the therapist's wish to do something about the patient's undereating. This needs to be addressed both for what it represents dynamically and because it presents the potential for life-threatening medical problems. However, one can question the therapist's decision on the grounds that it fundamentally alters the therapeutic situation in a way different from the use of a parameter. Why does the therapist withhold a session at a time when the patient seems most self-destructive? Is not the point of a session to help the patient understand and control his self-destructiveness? Why deprive him of the opportunity to do therapeutic work just when he is most distressed? The patient's capacity to benefit from therapy is not affected by his weight loss, as it might be if he were to come to sessions drunk, for example, and yet he is deprived of what is supposed to be his means of overcoming his self-destructiveness.

The therapist wants to be internalized as a firm limit setter, but her arrangement with the patient contradicts the conscious, overt message. Instead, she conveys the unconscious, covert message that she cannot deal with this form of self-destructiveness. She is internalized as the therapeutic version of a fair-weather friend.

With this eclectic mix of misunderstood psychoanalytic theory and behavioral therapy, the therapist acts to redefine her role in yet another manner inimical to the analytic position and to the patient's best interests. By taking away sessions when her patient continues to lose weight, the therapist defines herself not as someone who can help the patient understand his behavior, but as a reward that the patient will lose if he doesn't eat. Implicitly, through their arrangement, she defines their meetings as gratification and reward rather than as an opportunity for character change and insight. This position confounds interpretative work and leads to a fundamental and unanalyzable inconsistency.

Nevertheless, the therapist had to deal somehow with the patient's self-destructiveness. How could she have intervened without obviating interpretive work? Kernberg manages this situation by hospitalizing the patient and continuing treatment in the safety of the hospital. If hospitalization had not been possible for this patient, the therapist could have decided to hold the sessions regardless of the patient's weight loss. The focus would be both on the patient's self-destructiveness and on the manner in which the self-destructiveness prevents other gratification. The therapist would not respond to the patient's self-destructiveness and the consequent emptiness of his life by becoming his major object (that is, his reward for eating). Rather, she would use the therapy to call into question the way in which the patient makes his life empty. Thus the major focus would be the therapy, not the therapist.

There may be objection to an apparent inconsistency. In the discussion on transitional objects (Chapter 4), doesn't the therapist make himself the focus of treatment by giving the patient a transitional object? Yes and no. The therapist gives the patient something when he has decided that the patient has a deficit in holding introjects and, further, that there is a risk of serious acting out unless the patient can maintain the therapist as an internal holding introject. In some situations, perhaps early in treatment and with a more severely disturbed patient, emphasis may be on helping the patient retain the therapist's image during times of separation. A second step would be to emphasize use of the therapist as an internal object in a manner that keeps the therapy as the central focus. For example, the therapist might suggest that the patient use a transitional object to help him think of the therapist and of *how the therapist would have attempted to understand a given situation*. In this case, however, it is not at all clear that the patient's difficulties are due to a developmental deficit. It seems more likely that transference issues are central.

It is not clear what the patient's not eating represents in the transference. It might be that the patient's refusal to eat serves the purpose of defending against oral incorporative wishes toward the therapist. Or it might be that by creating a dangerous situation, he hopes to seduce the therapist into caring for him without his needing to acknowledge and express such wishes directly. There could be many other factors. By dealing with the symptom administratively rather than interpretively, however, the therapist has no chance of learning the symptom's meanings. If she had first inquired into the transferential meanings of the symptom, and if feelings toward the therapist had emerged more openly, and if such feelings would have been difficult for the patient to tolerate without resorting to serious acting out or regression, and if interpretation alone would not have helped the patient reverse the regression, *then* the therapist might have considered using a transitional object.

Utilization of a transitional object is more appropriate at a point in treatment when feelings about the therapist are more overt and when the patient is consciously yearning for the therapist rather than denying her importance, as was the case in this situation. The modification used in this case violates the analytic position and supplants interpretive work. In the cases that illustrated use of the transitional object, on the other hand, the modification was designed to support further insight and interpretive work.

CASE 3: A SECOND VIOLATION OF
THE PSYCHOANALYTIC POSITION

What might the therapist do when his patient, an actress who has been anxious and almost phobic about performing, asks him to attend the opening of her show? Most analytic therapists would not attend. From the perspective of the analytic position, to attend would be to abandon the role of interpreter of transference and to become, instead, a literal gratifier of transference wishes. If the therapist were to attend, he would be assuming that his patient's request expressed prestructural need rather than transferential desire. Should the therapist feel this way, he would address this issue within sessions rather than outside the therapeutic situation. By purposefully attending the opening, as opposed to accidentally meeting a patient at the theatre, by assuming in this way a real role in the patient's life, the therapist puts himself into a position which obviates eventual analysis of transference wishes.

Most analysts would not attend the opening for yet another reason. The demand does not arise intrinsically from the treatment situation. It is not a demand on the level of modifying the frame to deal with psychotic regression, a potential suicide attempt, or even a severe reaction to a therapist's vacation. Rather, it is an attempt at manipulation outside the situation to bolster a role that the analyst wishes to maintain within the session. Langs (who generally advises against modifications) writes:

> I believe that modifications should be confined, almost entirely, to those that are so to speak forced upon the therapist or therapeutic situation by the patient . . . [rather than being] invoked for many other more questionable reasons, such as strengthening the therapeutic alliance or being "real" for the patient. [Langs and Stone 1980, p. 98]

What if the patient does not ask the therapist to attend her show but instead wants to read her major speech in the office, to, in effect, do her act for the therapist? Assuming in both cases that the therapist first attempts to explore the issues with the patient, is this the same as the therapist's

attending the opening? I don't think so. Here the interaction
and gratification are taking place in the context of the analytic situation. The analyst has not moved out of the role of
therapist. The fact that the therapist could (although he
might not) make an interpretation about her speech in the
office means that the entire range of his role as therapist—
interpreter as well as gratifier—is available to him at that
time. At the theatre, in contrast, he can say virtually nothing
interpretive. He is outside the analytic position. Again, this
differs from retrospective analysis of accidental meetings
because both therapist and patient know that the therapist
did not deliberately arrange to meet the patient.

CASE 4: INTERVENTIONS WITHIN
THE PSYCHOANALYTIC POSITION

The analytic position reflects a therapist's overall and consistent idea of what is fundamentally wrong with the patient and of how the problem will be addressed therapeutically. Confusion here can produce an unexplained, conflicted
approach, often apparent in the practical arrangements of
treatment. Even when the therapist sets up an unimpeach-
ably correct frame, however, difficulties in the analytic
position may still be evident in interventions that are implicitly contradictory and that invite confusion on the patient's
part.

For example, a therapist was seeing a chronic
schizophrenic woman who began making seductive remarks and who said that she was not interested in therapy but wanted to know her therapist as a "real person."
The therapist might have responded to the possible unconscious wish to obliterate self–object boundaries, to
the patient's possible hostility, or to the sexual implications. The first response would have been best, since it is
most reflective of the patient's current level of function-

ing. However, the therapist decided to interpret the patient's manifest behavior—that is, her seductiveness. He erred in his assumption of a higher level of functioning. The patient was not expressing sexual wishes toward a psychologically perceived other. Rather, it was more a sexualized response to an indiscriminate and narcissistically cathected object. By focusing on the expressed sexual wishes, the therapist enflamed them in this regressed patient.

The patient became more extreme in her seductiveness, and the therapist began to feel engulfed, badgered, assaulted, and lost. The therapist then reminded the patient that they had a professional relationship and that they had to examine the meaning of her behavior. The patient became furious and refused to speak. We may understand her fury as narcissistic rage; it occurred because, in a subtle way, the therapist was switching treatment models midstream. To remind the patient of their professional relationship in the first session would have served to dampen the transference and to help the patient with boundary control. It would also have been consistent with the patient's concrete style. In other words, in order to use a transference interpretation, the patient must have a capacity for illusion, play, and self-reflection—all of which was missing in this patient. She could not operate in an "as-if" mode. She heard her therapist's focus on her seductiveness as an invitation. Given the therapist's decision to work interpretively, he could then have continued to work in this mode, assuming the capacity for insight into the part-object transference, even though it was a poor choice. Instead the therapist became frightened of the transference and backed off, adopting a more rational approach. Announcing to the patient that their relationship was professional, at that point, was tantamount to denying the transference that he had accepted in the previous session. Adler (1980) has commented, from a different vantage point, on therapists who mistakenly attempt to rationally clarify the working alliance in order to deal with their own empathic failure.

These are two ways of doing treatment, but to repeatedly switch from one to the next is to switch analytic positions. It is the equivalent of one day treating the patient's words as associations to be interpreted and the next day treating them as manifest content. Once again, these are issues of emphasis; they are seldom clear-cut. The analyst does not listen to words only as associations, but may respond to manifest content if it is clinically indicated. However, in this the therapist was not clear on his overall approach. Consequently, he ended up with a muddled analytic position and a confused, angry patient.

Part Three

Critical Inquiry into Kernberg's Technique

6

Borderline Defenses and Their Development

Kernberg postulates (1975) that the borderline patient's difficulties are due to an excess of aggression, which is defended against by splitting and by associated defenses organized under the rubric of splitting. The excess aggression may be genetic, or it may result from excessive frustration early in life (pp. 28, 34–35).

Although there are those who object to the idea of a genetic excess of aggressive drive, the fact is that aggression is a major problem for borderline patients. One need not accept Kernberg's postulate of genetic aggression in order to accept the broader, more fundamental proposition that aggression is the primary problem for the borderline patient, and that the other characteristics of the borderline personality, including a sense of emptiness, difficulty with libidinal object constancy, and associated structural difficulties, are the secondary consequences of primary aggression. Thus, while Kernberg's approach is not dependent upon his assumption regarding the possible genetic origin of aggression, it does depend on his assumption that excess aggression is the critical problem because it leads to two interrelated consequences: inadequate neutralization and excessive reliance on primitive defenses organized around splitting, with each of these affecting the other. We will discuss each in turn.

Neutralization

Neutralization is a concept related to the economic point of view in psychoanalytic metapsychology. Arlow and Brenner (1964) define neutralization as "deflection of energy from its original, instinctual, pleasure-seeking aims and utilization of it for ego functions which have no directly instinctual quality" (p. 36).

Neutralization has been defined both narrowly and broadly. Defined narrowly, neutralization is to aggression what sublimation is to sexuality; neutralization refers to the transformation of aggressive drive energy as sublimation refers to the transformation of libidinal drive energy. Defined broadly, sublimation is seen as occurring under the more general rubric of neutralization. As Hartmann (1964) explains:

> The term neutralization . . . is meant to cover, besides what Freud called sublimation (which he limited to one of the vicissitudes of the libidinal drives), the analogous change in mode of aggressive drives. If we assume the widest possible concept of neutralization (including sublimation), we may say that, though it may serve defense, it is of a far more general nature than other processes used for defensive purposes. Neutralization in this sense may well be a more or less constant process–if we are ready to assume that all the ego functions are continuously fed by it. [p. 171]

Neutralization provides the ego with energy for counter-cathexis, although this is not the only source of the ego's energy for defense. It is for this reason that difficulties in neutralization are understood to weaken the ego.

Neutralization is not an either–or process; there are degrees of neutralization. The concept helps to explain how aggression becomes more adaptive and drives become more postponable. The gradations of neutralization reflect the extent to which ego functions are invested with sexual or aggressive drives. The capacity to neutralize is an ego strength, and the incapacity for neutralization is a sign of ego weakness. Neutralization is seen clinically in the extent to which an act reflects modulation of drive (less direct and raw regarding aim; for example, the wish to defeat instead of kill) and increased ego control (the surgeon, for example, who channels his aggressive drive to cut with the aim of cure rather than the aim of harm). One evaluates the degree of neutralization in an aggressive act by asking, for example, whether there is a motive for the aggressive act: Does the person hit as hard as he can, or does he modulate the impact? To what extent is the act provoked?

Inability to neutralize interferes with interpersonal relationships since neutralization involves the capacity to put anger in context. We are not speaking of defensive, intellectual attempts to place angry feelings in context, to rationalize anger; rather, we are referring to the manner in which anger is actually experienced from the start. For example, a woman's husband arrives home late from work. To the extent that she is able to neutralize aggression, the angry wife will automatically place his lateness and her anger into the context of their broader relationship. She will recall that he usually arrives home promptly, or that he is often late but that he has other positive qualities. Her anger is juxtaposed with more loving and positive experiences of him and with him. This is not the same as the wife's denying or rationalizing her anger. She may experience and express anger, but the feeling is not overwhelming. It threatens neither the foundation of the marriage nor, more important, the wife's experience of herself and her husband as basically loving and lovable.

If the wife were unable to sufficiently neutralize aggression, her anger at her husband's lateness would become overpowering, pressing, and overwhelming. She would want to murder him or leave him. The anger would burst out uncontrolled, and she would be unable to keep in mind the context of their relationship. She would experience herself and her husband as hating and hateful, as if they never had, and never would have, loving experiences together. The wife might also have various symptoms of psychological weakness, including feelings of emptiness, self-destructiveness, and transient psychosis. It is due to inadequate neutralization that there is such an absolute, peremptory, demanding aspect to the borderline patient's expression of feeling and experience of self and of others.

Achievement of Reality-Testing

When aggression is insufficiently neutralized, splitting becomes the major mode of defense. Kernberg traces the developmental steps leading to excessive reliance on splitting as follows: Initially, the child has no psychological sense of himself as separate from others; there is no concept of self and object. Experience is organized around positive and negative affects. Each of these affects is associated with a nondifferentiated self–object image. The negative affects, along with their self–object images, are projected outward, in order to protect the fragile positive affect, with its self–object representations. These positive self–object representations become the nucleus of a positive sense of self.

As development proceeds, through experiences of gratification and frustration and through maturation of ego apparatuses such as perception, memory, vision, and so on, the child learns to differentiate between self and object. However, his initial differentiation is of self and object *within* the broader categories of positive and negative experiences. Thus he learns to differentiate between "good" self and "good" object within the positive affective realm, and between "bad" self and "bad" object within the negative realm.

At this juncture, which Kernberg believes to coincide with the rapprochement subphase of development (Mahler et al. 1975), because the child can differentiate between self and object, he is no longer considered to be in the psychotic range of development. The child's move out of the symbiotic phase and into the rapprochement subphase is clinically manifest in his capacity to reliably test reality, indicating his developed ability to know what is inside himself and what is outside of, and therefore not part of, himself. Reality-testing is the future borderline patient's positive developmental achievement. It is what he can (most of the time) do, in contrast to what he still cannot do.

Kernberg follows Frosch (1980) in his view of the capacity to test reality as the diagnostic criterion differentiating borderline and psychotic patients. For Kernberg, reality-testing is the ability to differentiate between internal and external perceptions. It is clinically evident in the patient's ability to accept the therapist's observations as relevant social reality. Kernberg tests the patient's capacity to question his own behavior, using the therapist's observations, as diagnostic of borderline (as opposed to psychotic) pathology (Kernberg 1975, 1977, 1980a). The social reality represented by the therapist becomes the referent to the therapist's confrontations; it is the context from which the therapist's remarks are taken seriously. It is in this sense that Kernberg (1975) states that the therapist

carries out a boundary function between the patient's intrapsychic life, which the interviewer tries to reach empathically, and the external reality represented by the social relationship between the patient and the therapist. . . . For example, if a patient presents a strange lack of affect in the face of an emotionally meaningful subject matter, this discrepancy may be pointed out to the patient and its implications explored. A borderline patient

will be able to recognize this discrepancy, while identifying with the reality implications of the interviewer's
question, and will become more realistic in this regard. In
contrast, the schizophrenic patient confronted with the
same discrepancy, may be unable to grasp the therapist's
point, or may interpret it as an attack, or may react by
further increasing the discrepancy between affect and
thought content. In other words, reality-testing increases
in borderline patients with such an approach, and de-
creases in schizophrenic patients. [p. 180]

The maintenance of reality-testing continues throughout treatment. Transference psychosis with the borderline
patient, for example, is usually limited to the therapy sessions, while transference psychosis with the psychotic patient leads to (or reflects) general decompensation and loss of
reality-testing through the whole gamut of the patient's life.
Transference itself differs in these patients, reflecting alter-
nating part-object transferences in the borderline patient and
merging transference, reflecting loss of ego boundaries, in
the psychotic patient.

Why should confrontation of splitting lead to improvement in the borderline patient and to further structural regression in the psychotic patient? The answer is unclear. Kernberg
understands this as occurring because the splitting defenses
serve different functions for these diagnostically different patients. The defenses protect good self and object representations from bad self and object representations in the borderline
patient, and they protect the psychotic patient from fusion,
with associated loss of ego boundaries (Kernberg 1986). Since
the defenses serve to establish boundaries for the psychotic
patient, interpretation of the defenses leads to loss of self, to
confusion, and to reduced reality-testing in the psychotic patient. In contrast, since self and object boundaries are relatively
firmly established for the borderline patient, and the defenses
serve to protect the patient from aggression in an inherently
ego-weakening way, interpretation of the defenses allows the

ego to momentarily gain strength and to contain its negative aspects. Interpretation thus leads to increased reality-testing.

There may be another way of understanding this difference, however. For the borderline patient to accept the therapist's referent and context as he interprets to his patient (Kernberg's definition of reality-testing) is perhaps to demonstrate the capacity for object relationship and to accept a certain inherent support in sharing a social context with the therapist. In contrast, the implicit object relationship offered by the therapist who uses the same interventions with the psychotic patient may be too close and threatening (rather than supportive) and may lead to regression as a defense against fears of engulfment.

When the therapist confronts the borderline patient from the standpoint of social consensus, the borderline patient is implicitly reminded of their shared social context. It is a form of implicit support for reality-testing through an increased level of social connection. The patient may then respond by integrating. If the patient does not already share this social context, however, he will experience the therapist's reminder of context, not as support, but as a demand for a higher level of psychological functioning by a therapist who is then experienced as intrusive and attacking. He is thus more likely to regress. If this way of understanding Kernberg's clinical findings is accurate, then we are speaking less of the effect of insight from confrontation of splitting and more of an underlying object relationship proffered by the therapist. This may be a function of the patient's fluctuating capacity to form a working alliance quickly, reflecting a modicum of capacity for object relationship.

Development of the Capacity for Ambivalence

Kernberg believes that, for the borderline patient, the difficulty does not lie in differentiation of self from non-self

(which is the psychotic patient's problem). Rather, the borderline patient's difficulty lies in a second developmental
task:

> The second task . . . of integrating self and object repre
> sentations built up under the influence of libidinal drive
> derivatives and their related affects with their corres
> ponding self and object representations built up under
> the influence of aggressive drive derivatives and their
> related affects, fails to a great extent in borderline pa
> tients, mainly because of the pathological predominance
> of pregenital aggression. The resulting lack of synthesis
> of contradictory self and object representations interferes
> with the integration of the self-concept and with estab
> lishment of object constancy or "total" object relations.
> [Kernberg 1980b, pp. 356–357]

It is this assumption that leads to Kernberg's clinical
emphasis on aggression and relative deemphasis of attachment and libidinal factors.

If the child has enough positive experiences with the
primary object, he builds up a basic positive "ego core"
(Kernberg 1976, p. 163) within which negative experiences
become assimilated and integrated. Thus, if the positive core
is strong enough, the negative experiences are not as threatening, and they can be placed into a positive context and
neutralized. If the positive core is tenuous, however, or if
constitutional aggression is too great, then negative experiences are more threatening and are warded off by splitting,
which acts to protect the positive from the negative. The
consequence of splitting is that the positive is never able to
assimilate the negative, and the ego remains weak. What
develops is reactive grandiosity and defensive projected
"badness," which leads to a basic paranoia and a world
populated by threatening objects (made threatening by the
projected anger).

In normal development, the child integrates positive and negative self and object representations as he passes through the rapprochement crisis (Mahler et al. 1975). The child's attachment to a loved figure aids in the process of integration. Attachment supplies a motive for integration (to keep the relationship) and an aid in integration (internalization of positive experiences with the loved figure). As he completes this developmental step, the child develops libidinal object constancy, which means that he will have a firmly established internal representation of a soothing "whole" object, that is, one in which both positive and negative affects are integrated, and that he will be able to use that internal representation for self-soothing in the absence of the soothing object. The establishment of libidinal object constancy is a major developmental step and indicates that the child has neutralized his aggression sufficiently so that he need not rely on splitting defenses. In other words, *in order to resolve splitting, the child needs to neutralize aggression, which he does by developing libidinal object constancy.*

The child is particularly vulnerable at the rapprochement stage because frustration by the mother and his own anger threaten to erode the newly established and still tenuous positive self and object representations. The child runs the risk of feeling completely alone and unprotected and at the mercy of his annihilating aggression. The child defends against these feelings by splitting—essentially denying not just the anger but the associated negative self and object representation. The negative self and object representation then no longer seems to belong to the child. According to Kernberg, such splitting is developmentally appropriate at an early stage of development, when the ego is weak; at a later stage, however, it is a pathological and inherently ego-weakening defense because it prevents neutralization and libidinal object constancy, and results in "pathology of internalized object relationships" (Kernberg 1975, p. 34)—that is, the presence of primitive, nonmetabolized, internal objects. Many other structural difficulties result.

Structural Consequences of Splitting

Structural difficulties result from the lack of interpenetration between positive and negative self and object representations, due to splitting and failure of neutralization. This condition leads to a lack of depth and to extreme, surface reactions in many areas, including feelings, internal structure, interpersonal relationships, acceptance of reality demands, and an integrated and stable sense of identity. The problems include (but are not limited to) the following:

DIFFICULTY IN AFFECT MODULATION

Nonextreme affects, such as affection and irritation, depend on neutralization and modulation of love and hate.

INADEQUATE SUPEREGO DEVELOPMENT

The superego has two broad components: the ego ideal (that to which the individual aspires) and the superego (which exercises evaluative functions). If self and object representations are extreme, distorted, and unidimensional, then the ego ideal will be based on grandiose self and object representations. Such an ego ideal, a problem in itself because of its unrealistic nature, will be difficult to integrate with the superego, which is based on an overly harsh, paranoid internalized object representation. These primitive self and object representations interfere with acceptance of parental demands and with overall internalization, since the child's experience of his parents and of their demands will be distorted by his paranoid projection and his inner grandiosity. The primitive and unintegrated superego precursors will be excessively harsh; the patient will aspire to grandiose and unreachable goals; the signal function of superego guilt will be disrupted; and superego values and standards will continue to be linked with part-object identifications (rather than being the more abstract and depersonified result of whole-object identifications).

POOR INTERPERSONAL RELATIONSHIPS

Kernberg focuses on the patient who is "shallow" and superficially socially adaptive, who tends to withdraw to protect himself against the activation of primitive conflicts in object relationships. The patient will tend to experience minimal guilt and little concern for others, since these feelings depend on the tension between integrated positive and negative self and object representations. The effect of splitting is apparent in these patients' depressive reactions, which "take primitive forms of impotent rage and feelings of defeat by external forces, rather than mourning over good, lost objects and regret over their aggression toward themselves and others" (Kernberg 1975, p. 35).

EMPTINESS

For Kernberg, the experience of internal emptiness reflects the pathology of internalized object relations resulting from splitting and its associated defenses. It indicates disturbance in the relationship of internal self and object representations—"that is, with the world of inner objects that fixates intrapsychically the significant experiences with others and constitutes a basic ingredient of ego identity" (Kernberg 1975, pp. 220–221).

IDENTITY DIFFUSION

A poorly integrated sense of self and others is the broadest consequence of structural pathology. Kernberg views it as diagnostically significant. In the same way that ability to test reality is the primary factor differentiating the borderline from the psychotic patient, the dimensions of (1) the predominant type of defensive organization of the ego (centering around splitting or around repression) and (2) ego identity (identity diffusion or identity integration) differentiate borderline personality organization from neurotic organization and normality. In fact, for practical purposes, it is the presence or absence of identity diffusion that most clearly differentiates borderline conditions from nonborderline symptomatic neurosis and character pathology. The evaluation of defensive organization, in contrast, reveals patients with various mixtures of defensive constellations and lends itself much less to a clear differential diagnosis of borderline conditions from neurotic pathology in the initial interviews. [Kernberg 1980b, p. 358]

Kernberg does not disregard the oedipal stage in his discussion of development. He believes that, because of excessive preoedipal aggression, the child enters the oedipal period both prematurely and defensively (as when, for example, the patient attempts to satisfy preoedipal oral longings through sexual activity) and he is therefore less well equipped to deal with oedipal issues on their own merits. Conflicts over preoedipal aggression "infiltrate all object relations" and "contaminate" object relations in the oedipal stage.

I am stressing that the consequences of severe preoedipal conflicts include pathological development of oedipal conflicts, but not an absence of them. I believe that the controversy regarding the predominance of oedipal versus preoedipal conflicts in borderline personality organization really obscures some of the significant issues. The question is not the presence or absence of oedipal conflicts but the degree to which preoedipal features have distorted the oedipal constellation and have left important imprints on character formation. [Kernberg 1980b, p. 363]

With the establishment of libidinal object constancy, the child is no longer potentially borderline. He can now both separate self from object and integrate positive and negative self representations and positive and negative object representations. He begins to use neurotic defenses—that is, defenses organized around repression rather than splitting. This development has important structural consequences, including the establishment of inner structure, the development of intrapsychic conflict (rather than conflict that is predominantly with the external environment), the capacity for self-regulation and self-soothing, the capacity for symbolization, and the development of signal anxiety rather than panic anxiety. In short, the child has psychologically separated from the parents.

From another perspective, neutralization of anger allows for gradual integration, depersonification, and abstraction of identifications, reflected in mature ego and superego development. Thus superego values and prohibitions becomes less tied to their specific original objects (for example, the mother who said no, or the father who emphasized success) and become generalized values. These structures persist during periods of regression, in contrast to psychological structure in the borderline patient, which more easily dissolves under stress to its constituent part-object building blocks. At such times, the organizing effect of structure fails and conflict is no longer between organized structures; instead, conflict is between contradictory self and object representations that are split off from each other. Since both are conscious at different times, we may speak of contradictory ego states or id-ego states. As Kernberg (1980a) notes:

[I]t is that contradictory ego states—or id-ego states—constitute the polarities of the conflict: both sides include primitive impulse derivatives embedded in a primitive unit of internalized object relation. Under these circumstances, defense and content can rapidly be interchanged in shifting equilibria of such activated part-object relations, and contradictory impulses are conscious and mutually dissociated or split off rather than unconscious—

that is, repressed. Here, the nature of consciousness and unconsciousness no longer coincides with what is on the surface and what is deep, what is defense and what is content. [p. 166]

Splitting

Splitting is a complex and imprecise concept. Because Kernberg sees splitting as an essential cause of ego weakness, and because of the controversial clinical recommendations he makes for its management, its very acceptance and importance have been the subject of continuing debate within the psychoanalytic community (Abend et al. 1983, Pruyser, 1975). In this section, we will examine the ways in which it is defined by those who believe in it, and we will see how it is manifested clinically.

Kernberg (1975) defines splitting in a "restricted and limited sense" as "the active process of keeping apart introjections and identifications of opposite quality" (p. 29). Like the defense of repression, splitting is both a specific defense and an aspect of a group of defenses that depend on and buttress splitting. Splitting occurs in combination with these other defenses.

Lichtenberg and Slap (1973) understand splitting to be an ego defense which is adaptive at an early age but which has become maladaptive with further development. Kernberg (1975) shares this developmental view:

[T]he integration, or synthesis, of introjections and identification of opposite qualities possibly provides the most important source of neutralization of aggression (in that libidinal and aggressive drive derivatives are fused and organized as part of that integration), and that therefore one consequence of pathological circumstances under which splitting is excessive is that this neutralization does not take place sufficiently, and an essential energy source for ego growth fails. Splitting, then, is a fundamental cause

of ego weakness, and as splitting also requires less countercathexis than repression, a weak ego falls back easily
on splitting, and a vicious cycle is created by which ego
weakness and splitting reinforce each other. [p. 29]

Splitting can develop as follows: A child feels good
about himself and his mother. She then says that she must go
out for a while and that the child will have to stay with a
baby sitter. The child is angry with his mother for leaving,
but to allow this anger into awareness threatens the memory
of his recent good experience with her. This memory is one
element in what will eventually become a positive ego core
comprising positive self and object representations. At this
stage, however, the memory is not firmly established and the
child fears its loss. If it is lost, he will lose the security offered
by the memory, a precursor of libidinal object constancy.

The child therefore protects the positive self and object
image by splitting off the positive self and object representation from the negative self and object representation. If he
splits off the positive side, he feels like a totally bad, unloved
boy abandoned by a totally bad and unloving mother. He
then feels angry, alone, and helpless. Thus he keeps in consciousness the negative self and object representations and
the linking affect, does not experience the positive, and thus
cannot feel the perspective and soothing offered by the neutralization which might have occurred if he had been able to
allow both positive and negative self and object representations into consciousness. If he splits off the bad and retains
the good, then he feels like an omnipotent, grandiose child
loved by an idealized mother. There is a brittleness to this
comfort, as the child fears an imminent end to this state,
caused by emergence of the split-off negative self and object
representations. Denial of the negative self and object representations also makes it difficult for the child to establish a
more rounded image of himself and his mother, based on
awareness not only of the loving aspects of both, but on the
limitations and aggressions of both. This rapidly becomes a

circular process. Splitting is a consequence of an incompletely internalized positive self and object representation; at the same time, splitting also interferes with development of such an internalized self and object representation, because as major elements of the child's experience are split off, they cannot be integrated and neutralized.

Splitting and Repression

Kernberg assumes that splitting and its associated defenses form a unique and primitive character structure, specific to the borderline patient. Both repression and splitting work to make the patient *less* anxious; confrontation of these defenses *increases* anxiety. However, while both "defend" against anxiety, the defenses are different in nature. In repression, drives and their derivatives are kept out of consciousness. Repression and its associated defenses (such as reaction formation, isolation, and intellectualization) depend on an ego strong enough to keep out uncomfortable affect—that is, strong enough for effective countercathexis. Through repression, the ego defends itself against wishes that are perceived as dangerous, or capable of arousing anxiety, by keeping out of consciousness the drive derivatives or aspects of these derivatives. Thus one may intellectually know that one is angry without experiencing anger; or one may experience the anger but displace it from the object toward whom it is directed to someone else.

In contrast, a splitting defense allows full emotional and ideational expression of certain drive derivatives but keeps them separate from other drive derivatives. Thus the borderline patient may experience murderous wishes (which the repressor might never allow), but he keeps them separate from loving wishes. Experience is sequential. When the patient experiences one group of feelings (technically, one constellation made up of a self representation and an object representation linked by an affective unit), it is as if the other never existed in the past and never will exist again. The patient either has no recollection of them or, if he has some recollection, it simply has no impact or relevance for him.

It is in this context that we can ask "Are borderline patients more in touch with their feelings than neurotic patients?" The answer is no, because the feelings overpower the borderline patient and are experienced out of the context provided to the neurotic patient by his defenses, which offer him regularity and stability of experience. The therapeutic goal for the neurotic patient is to allow into a highly developed defensive system greater awareness of unconscious conflicted wishes. The stability that constricts the neurotic patient also stabilizes his life and structures the nature and depth of his feelings. The feelings are the product of the patient's constructions and reflect the presence of psychological structure.

The borderline patient's feelings are less stabilized by existing structure. They are experienced as intense, raw, and unneutralized; the patient feels hatred and love more often than irritation and affection. Feelings may be expressed more easily and forcefully by the borderline patient than by the neurotic patient, but, in the intensity of their expression, they illustrate the borderline patient's primitive internal structure and contribute to further weakening of this structure. Further, to be "in touch" with one's feelings implies not only expression of affect but also integration of that affect; there must be an experiencer who is in touch with his experience. It is in this area, that of containing the experience, that the borderline patient has difficulty. It is partially for this reason—that expression of unneutralized aggression is not the same as expression of feelings—that Kernberg makes the technical recommendation to limit expression of anger in sessions under certain circumstances.

One major characteristic of splitting is the patient's lack of interest in the shifts and fluidity of his experience. The patient exhibits an attitude of *la belle indifference* when asked about feelings that were previously vivid to him. It is this lack of interest, along with the driven aspect of both sides of the split, which helps the clinician diagnose splitting. A neurotic patient may feel "split" between two aspects of himself and may have difficulty integrating these aspects. He may experience each side acutely. However, to the extent that he is curious and alarmed at this split, there is evidence of a functioning ego with attempts at synthesis and continuity of experience. The therapist must look at the ego within which the split takes place. A diagnosis of splitting is a statement about ego strength.

Examples of Splitting

SPLITTING OF TWO THERAPISTS

A patient was being seen on an inpatient unit following several suicide attempts with overdoses of prescribed medication. The treatment team elected not to medicate the patient, who did not have obvious psychotic symptomatology. Instead, they chose a verbal, insight-oriented treatment approach. Throughout the patient's stay, the staff had to contend with his acting-out around medication. The patient demanded a wide variety of medication, ranging from imipramine (with which he had attempted an overdose) to lithium. While out on a pass, he went to a pharmacy and bought imipramine (using an old prescription), which he brought back to the unit and hoarded.

The unit was geared toward short-term treatment, but under family pressure, the patient applied to a long-term unit in another hospital. He returned from his preadmission interview stating that the psychiatrist had told him that the approach would be predominantly psychopharmacological; they would first try imipramine, and lithium might be considered later. The patient did not tell the interviewer that he had been caught hoarding medication two weeks earlier. He later reported to his therapist that he had asked the interviewer about the medications he was recommending, saying that they had been previously administered; he told his therapist that the interviewer had replied, "They just read the book; we wrote the book here."

The therapist was understandably upset at this report, but the patient was calm. We see here the *la belle indifference* characteristic of splitting. After all, the patient had just been told by one doctor that his previous treatment approach was wrong. Most people would be somewhat concerned at this news and would question the doctors and themselves about the choice to be made between two different approaches. This patient felt none of this. Further, he had not given the interviewer relevant information for his treatment plan. Thus the patient participated in the interviewer's alleged contempt for his current therapist and allowed the interviewer to make a mockery of his current treatment. At the same time, he lied and made a mockery of the interviewer and his treatment prescription.

Although it is possible that the patient lied about the interviewer's remark, it is also likely that he did not lie but that he achieved the intended effect of splitting two treatment institutions by omitting contextual and qualifying remarks that might have altered the meaning of the alleged statement. Distortions usually take place not through direct lying (which has more serious prognostic implications), but through contextual omissions and variations in emphasis.

SPLITTING OF CONTRADICTORY FEELINGS
TOWARD THE THERAPIST

One of the more common examples of splitting occurs when a patient splits contradictory feelings toward one person. In one session, the patient referred to his therapist as his "life-line." The following day, he terminated a five-year treatment because he felt that he no longer needed help from a therapist who he experienced as ungiving. He felt no concern about how he might feel following the termination, although he had a history of severe reactions to separations in treatment. He felt no curiosity about his abrupt shift. He insisted that it was the therapist's problem that prompted him to want to discuss the decision. He denied any suggestion of acting out, hurt, or anger and seemed genuinely surprised that the therapist even questioned his decision.

This is an example of a rapid shift from viewing the therapist as a totally good part-object to seeing him as a totally bad part-object. The patient also shifted from a needy self-representation (supplicant from a therapist as lifeline) to a rejecting, independent self-representation (seen with the therapist as supplicant in wanting further discussion). The extreme shift, the sense of unconcern about it, the lack of perspective—all indicate splitting. Here, contradictory feelings toward the same object are split. At other times, the feelings are split between two persons. The patient may decide that his therapist is all good (or bad) and that someone else—another therapist, a friend, a teacher, a former therapist—is the opposite. The patient will then, sometimes in the same session or perhaps over time, reverse the characterizations. It is sometimes difficult to understand that these patients have no affective memory of their previous evaluations, and, further, have no concern about their shift in affective valuation, even after the shift is pointed out to them. It is this sort of splitting to which Kernberg refers when he speaks of the danger in supportive therapy with the borderline patient. Kernberg cautions that one may encounter a superficially friendly but bland and shallow relationship within the treatment, with angry feelings split off and acted out with figures outside of therapy.

In these examples, splitting is primarily manifested in patients' experience of others. There is a corresponding self-representation activated, but the patient's focus of attention and feeling is on the external object representation. Splitting may also affect patients' feelings about the world, their bodies, the continuity of their experience, and may become the focus of their attention.

SPLITTING AND ONE'S EXPERIENCE OF OTHERS

A patient frequently complained that her therapist was more attentive to her when she was in a panic. The therapist disagreed with this perception. He understood the patient's complaint as a manifestation of splitting. When the patient felt "good," not panicky, her experience was one of grandiosity, with an accompanying denial of self-doubt or a need for others. At these times, she would be contemptuous of her own needs and of the therapist. (Kernberg [1975, p. 38] has termed this "a kind of bland optimism based on denial, which represents the patient's identification with primitive 'all good' self and object images.") While in that state, she could not experience the therapist's attentiveness, since her wishes for help and attention and the therapist's attention to those wishes were split off.

As her experience shifted to the other side of the split, she felt herself in a "panic," and experienced her unmodulated desperate emptiness and need for others. Now she experienced the therapist as paying a maximum amount of attention to her because she was aware, in a magnified way, of her own dependency needs. She saw the therapist as an idealized provider of help, not as a devalued, contemptible person. Thus she inevitably experienced the therapist as more attentive in times of panic, regardless of the accuracy of this perception. In addition, the patient would often feel that what she was getting from the therapist was not good enough and that it would soon stop. Therefore, she would readily become angry at the therapist and engage in all sorts of acting-out and illegal behavior to both express the anger and to guarantee further help.

SPLITTING AND ONE'S SELF-EXPERIENCE

Some patients, especially those with eating disorders, are split between their "selves" and their bodies, which they experienced as alien, hostile forces. The body comprises impurity, need, and sex, and must be rigidly controlled. One patient experienced herself as the "ice queen" who was able to do without "dirty" needs such as eating and sex.

> Another patient's split between his "objective, work, reality" self and his "subjective, affective" sense of himself became apparent when he was unable to write his résumé in preparation for a job interview. For him, the written résumé meant that he had objectified himself, that his work experience comprised his totality, and that he had lost what he saw as his more affective, creative, "soft" self. Further, the "objective" résumé left him open to (his own, projected) "objective" criticism of how little he felt he had actually accomplished vocationally. It was as if the résumé, which was an expression of a partial truth about him, became the entire truth about him, forcing him to repudiate his subjective sense of himself and expose himself to objective criticism and attack. Objectivity and subjectivity could not be experienced as existing in the same person at the same time. He also couldn't understand that someone reading his résumé might take into account his various psychological difficulties and their impact on his career. Because he had not developed an integrated superego, judgment was based on a harsh superego precursor. He judged himself only coldly and "objectively," without affective empathy and understanding. It was judgment without mercy. Because he judged himself this way, he was certain that others would judge him in the same manner. The superego precursor, underlying his difficulty in self-evaluation, resulted from excessive reliance on splitting.[1]

Many borderline patients have similar vocational difficulties, for similar reasons. They must be cold and perfec-

---

[1]Bach (1985) would see this as an example of difficulty in integrating perspectives on self as subject and self as object, and would approach this from a very different theoretical framework.

tionistic at work because any mistake will reveal what they believe is their total inadequacy and will lead to sadistic criticism from their supervisors. Further, joking at work or allowing any affective expression is prohibited because it touches on dangerous dependency needs and wishes to be cared for. Work represents autonomy and separation. These issues are tenuous and conflicted. Affect opens the door to dependency longings and resentments about needing to work and "grow up." If these patients are able to work successfully, they work in a virtual experiential prison.

SPLITTING AND THE CONTINUITY OF ONE'S EXPERIENCE

Splitting dramatically affects the continuity of one's experience. Borderline patients may show sudden and dramatic breaks in their feelings, thoughts, memories, and behaviors. Planning is difficult because they do not know how they will feel or "be" at the appointed time.

In a day-hospital program geared toward treatment of borderline patients, the Friday community meeting was devoted to discussions of weekend plans. The Monday meeting included discussion of how these plans had fared. It was striking that consistently large numbers of patients had great difficulty making social plans for the weekend because they could not predict their emotional state a day or two in advance. Further, it was remarkable how many patients canceled their plans, often without calling the person with whom they had made the plans, because they did not feel up to carrying out the plan. At that moment they were too "anxious" or "depressed."

Neurotic patients also do not know how they will feel days in advance. However, the structure of the plan, the context of their enduring relationship with the person with whom they have plans, their ability to test reality, which helps them anticipate with relative certainty a steady mood rather than a potentially disruptive psychotic state, and their superego sense of obligation to follow through on their plans—all these are taken for granted by neurotic patients and stabilize their experiences and their interpersonal lives. By the same token, their feelings at that moment do not take over their experience to the extent that they dominate borderline patients' experience. Neurotic patients can put the feelings in context and can use their full range of internal resources and the elements of the external structure as well (meeting their friends, talking to them and, immersing themselves in the activity) to feel better. For neurotic patients, external structure is stabilizing; for borderline patients, the same structure is confining and must be fought.

One patient could not maintain the continuity of his experience from his therapy sessions to his life outside treatment. Upon leaving the therapist's office, he would forget the content of the sessions. In sessions, he was filled with anger and tears. Elsewhere, he was cold, grandiose, and self-sufficient. He had split his self and object representations in the sessions (self as hungry, needy, potentially devouring; object as giving, idealized, and omnipotent, with a positive affective tie) and his self and object representations outside the sessions (self as self-sufficient and grandiose; object as withholding, devalued, and absent, with a contemptuous affective tie) in order to defend against intolerable feelings of loss and abandonment when he had to leave. The psychological cost of this defense was a break in the continuity of his experience and the unavailability of internal sustaining images of the therapist for soothing between sessions. This resulted in panic attacks, drug abuse, and sexual promiscuity in attempts to fill himself up and soothe himself.

Manifestations of this kind of splitting are common among patients in day hospitals who are nearing discharge. They begin to do part-time work or attend school and attend the day program on a part-time basis. A month before the setting of a discharge date, they had seen the hospital as a warm, supportive, safe place, and the outside "work" world as cold and frightening. Once the discharge date is set, however, these patients begin to devalue the day program's tendency to "coddle" people. They miss days at the program and demand an earlier discharge in order to focus on the "real" world. They have difficulty with a paced, planned, transition because they have difficulty integrating their affective life and their performance-oriented external life. Since they cannot allow both simultaneously, in a manner that would allow one polarity to temper the other, they devalue one and idealize the other. It is not unusual for patients who leave under such circumstances to decompensate soon after discharge. Their split-off dependency needs return to haunt them. In addition, leaving with major aspects of their experience out of awareness leads to impaired judgment, anticipation, and reality-testing in the "real" decisions involved in vocational choice.

Primitive Idealization and Devaluation

The split between the patient's devalued dependency needs and his overidealized, "perfect," grandiose self may be projected onto the therapist. It underlies processes of primitive idealization and devaluation, two borderline defenses under the rubric of splitting. One therapist was forced to cancel several sessions, one at a time over a three-month period, due to personal family emergencies. The patient knew why the therapist had canceled. After each absence, the patient experienced a regression marked by feelings of emptiness and self-destructive behavior, and then by indignant fury at the therapist for being "unprofessional" for missing the sessions. While the patient's response can easily be understood as narcissistic rage or difficulty with libidinal object constancy, it can also be understood as projection onto the therapist of expectations based on the patient's internal conflict.

This patient either had to be a "robot" at his own demanding job, devoid of human frailties, or feel overcome by weakness and unable to go to work. He felt closely connected to his therapist and ashamed and guilty about these needs, which he likened to family connections about which he was highly conflicted. These sides of the conflict were split off from each other. One side or the other was projected onto the therapist, with the patient experiencing the opposing side. When the therapist held sessions regularly, this proved that the therapist was omnipotent, perfect, and a "robot" (primitive idealization). The therapist's absence, for family-connected emergencies, was evidence that the therapist had the same contemptible human frailties that plagued the patient. Under such circumstances, the patient devalued the therapist as he devalued himself. When the patient no longer had the experience of an idealized therapist with whom to identify, however, he lost his means of inner control and regressed. His difficulty in internal self-regulation was not due only to a deficit, but particularly to a marked and defensive shift from idealization to devaluation. This shift protected the patient from acknowledging his own conflicts about family needs and his envy that the therapist had others that he cared for more than he cared for him.

Kernberg (1975) defines primitive idealization as follows:

> This refers to the tendency to see external objects as totally good, in order to make sure that they can protect one against the "bad" objects, that they cannot be contaminated, spoiled, or destroyed by one's own aggression or by that projected onto other objects. [p. 30]

Primitive idealization is not a reaction formation against guilt over aggression, as is common in mourning reactions after the death of an ambivalently loved object. It is also not projection of idealized aspects of the superego onto others, as when one loves someone who stands for one's own values and ideals (a form of narcissistic object choice). Primitive idealization is not love for another, since love depends on depth of concern for the other based on awareness of the interplay of positive and negative feelings toward the loved person, and concern for the wants of the other, distinct from one's own wants. Rather, primitive idealization

> is the direct manifestation of a primitive, protective fantasy structure in which there is no real regard for the ideal object, but a simple need for it as a protection against a surrounding world of dangerous objects. One other function of such an ideal object is to serve as a recipient for omnipotent identification, for sharing in the greatness of the idealized object as a protection against aggression, and as a direct gratification of narcissistic needs. Idealization thus used reflects the underlying omnipotence. . . . [Kernberg 1975, p. 30][2]

In Kernberg's definition, the concept of fantasy is different from that held by classical analytic theorists. While all classical analysts emphasize the motivational qualities of unconscious fantasy, Kernberg, reflecting Kleinian influence, stresses unconscious fantasy that seems id-like. It is primitive, driving, and relatively unaffected by external stimuli or by the ego and superego. For others, fantasy is influenced by reality just as a dream is influenced by its day residue. The fantasy itself is a product of the interplay of ego, id, and superego (Arlow 1969a,b). Fantasy is more a wish than a

---

[2]The phenomenon where the patient may feel psychologically held because of the perceived omnipotence of the therapist is of primary importance for all models discussed in Chapter 1. Kernberg emphasizes the driving, fantasy-dominated, and irrational aspect of the patient's wish. For others, such as Adler, the irrational fantasies are not integral to the wish itself, which is seen as developmentally based. Rather, the fantasies to be interpreted accompany the wish and are interpreted in order to allow the more realistic aspects of the wish to be gratified in therapy sessions.

drive. It is the product of psychological structure rather than a basic determinant of such structure. It is thus more of a dependent variable than an independent variable.

For example, Schafer (1985) referring to Melanie Klein, writes:

> In Klein's system, the ego is presented as a set of primitive self-fantasies, for essentially hers is a theory of fantasy and not of psychic structure *and* fantasy. . . . What ego functioning she described is primarily desperate recourse to the mechanisms of introjection, projection, and splitting. . . . But the Freudian analyst would view fantasy content itself as a highly elaborated, hierarchically arranged, well-buttressed system that corresponds to the ontogenesis of the structured ego. . . . The Freudian cannot believe in structure-free fantasy and direct access to its various levels; the theory does not allow it.[Schafer, 1985, pp. 288–289, emphasis his]

This point could also be applied to Kernberg's conception of fantasy.[3]

The more primitive the idealization, the more useless is any role-modeling in the therapeutic relationship, because role-modeling involves one person with the psychological capacity to see himself as separate and distinct from the whole-object role model, and wanting to change aspects of himself in consonance with qualities of the role model. Role-modeling is not an analytic concept, but its meaning is somewhat expressed in a more psychologically sophisticated manner by concepts such as the therapist's allowing himself to be internalized, or to be used for soothing or for meeting narcissistic needs in a self–object transference, or to do ego-building.

---

[3]It is also possible that these analysts differ in their views of fantasy because Arlow and Schafer speak of fantasy within already-formed and developed psychological structure, while Kernberg is speaking about less structured states.

None of these are effective when primitive idealization predominates, since, under these conditions, the patient is ruthlessly using the therapist in a brittle and fantasy-dominated fashion. The therapist is certainly not experienced as a loved and valued separate, whole object. There is no real dependence on the therapist, partially because the therapist is not even allowed an independent thought. As Kernberg (1975) states in his discussion of omnipotence and devaluation, two defenses intimately connected with primitive idealization:

> [E]ven during the time of apparent submission to an idealized external object, the deep underlying omnipotent fantasies of the patient can be detected. The need to *control* the idealized objects, to use them in attempts to manipulate and exploit the environment and to "destroy potential enemies" is linked with inordinate pride in the "possession" of these perfect objects totally dedicated to the patient. . . . The devaluation of external objects is in part a corollary of the omnipotence; if an external object can provide no further gratification or protection, it is dropped and dismissed because there was no capacity for love of this object in the first place. [p. 33, Kernberg's emphasis]

The object is also devalued for other reasons, including revenge for having frustrated the patient's needs (Kernberg focuses on the patient's oral greed) and devaluation so that the object cannot become the patient's powerful persecutor.

It is difficult for the beginning therapist to appreciate the fantasy element in primitive idealization, especially when it is muted and subtle. The therapist is likely to see it as positive transference, or as a working alliance, or as realistic appreciation by the patient for his helpful qualities. This is even more likely when the patient comes to the therapist after one or more experiences in treatment with others who the patient feels have not been helpful. In such an atmosphere, it is easy for the therapist to bask in the patient's glow, to feel needed, valued, and appreciated, and to have his own omnipotence and grandiosity stimulated. When this situation is predominantly the product of primitive idealization, however, the positive feelings are shallow, brittle, and readily turned to anger, devaluation, and contempt. It is only when the idealization turns to devaluation, and when the therapist can do nothing right and is vilified both in the session and to others, that the therapist can begin to appreciate the extent of the fantasy element in the previous primitive idealization. He can now affectively appreciate that idealization is not love. It is from this perspective that Kernberg advocates confronting the primitive idealization as it occurs.

Idealization and devaluation may protect the patient from accurate, realistic perceptions of the therapist (or other figures), the implications of which the patient fears to confront. For example, a man who emphasized the great power of his feared boss proved to have an accurate sense of his boss's strengths and weaknesses. He feared acknowledging his accurate perceptions both because he would then be forced to confront his own competitive feelings toward the boss and because the world seemed safer when he was surrounded by powerful, albeit feared, authority figures. He idealized and devalued his wife in order to protect himself from facing her limitations (she was larger than life in both the idealized and devalued states) and his real choices (to remain married or not). To relinquish this defense would be to come to terms with himself as a person with strengths and weaknesses who had to make decisions when choices were unclear and involved compromise.

Kernberg does not stress this side of the defensive aspect of primitive idealization and devaluation, but it is implied in his observation that as the fantastic (that is, fantasy-dominated) elements of the transference are worked through in the course of treatment, they are replaced by more realistic parental perceptions, which must then be integrated and accepted by the patient. It is then that the patient discovers that some of the most influential aspects of his parents—both deprivations and gifts—were obscured and defended against in the intensity of the borderline defenses. It is also true that, as the more primitive aspects of conflict are worked through in treatment and as structuralization becomes more developed, the unconscious wishes and defenses become more defined and elaborated. The patient will work on unconscious fears of his own competition with a paternal authority rather than on fears of (projected) annihilation by a combination maternal-paternal mythic imago.

It is in discussion of primitive idealization and its effects on treatment that there is the occasion for a major criticism of Kernberg. He draws sharp distinctions and does not discuss gradations of change.[4] Theoretically, it makes sense that one cannot internalize as a whole object a therapist who is primitively idealized. But does this mean that *no* internalization takes place? Is the relationship composed *only* of fantasy? Does this fantasy relationship change absolutely after it is interpreted, so that internalization of a whole object then takes place fully? How does the therapist understand and

---

[4]This criticism can be made of other aspects of Kernberg's theory. For example, he contends that splitting interferes with neutralization because negative self and object representations must be split off and are therefore not integrated. But there must be some negative self and object representations that are not split off. Does that not lead to partial neutralization? What is the effect of such neutralization on ego development? What is the effect of partial neutralization on the overall prognosis? This is not only a theoretical issue about development; it bears directly on the process through which positive and negative self and object representations are brought together during the course of therapy. To the extent that this occurs over time, we must hypothesize some elements of internalization of a nonfantasy-dominated therapist. To the extent that patients differ in the degree to which splitting predominates, we can hypothesize a certain amount of repression along with splitting defenses. Under those circumstances, Kernberg's treatment recommendations become less logically compelling for certain borderline patients, and traditional methods of supportive and expressive therapy become more viable.

modify treatment as shifts occur in the degree to which a relationship is dominated by fantasy?[5]

Kernberg does not focus on these questions, but they are theoretically and clinically central. Pruyser (1975) contends that the concept of splitting, in addition to being too imprecise, asks the wrong question. Pruyser believes that the question is not how the ego splits, but how the ego is able to unify disparate sensations into coherent self and object representations. His critique that the concept is too broad and "radicalizes" a complex process is understandable. Kernberg's view omits a host of more precise process variables, such as "distributing, apportioning, allocating, assigning, reflecting, differentiating, sorting out, emphasizing, focusing, and a host of other terms implying some process of discernment" (p. 36).

The transformation of primitive idealization into realistic appreciation and love is illustrated in the ending of the classic story *The Wizard of Oz*. Dorothy and her friends—the cowardly lion, the tin man, and the scarecrow—travel to the Emerald City, fighting off wicked witches, in order to meet the idealized wizard who can give them what they are searching for—courage for the lion, a heart for the tin man, a brain for the scarecrow, and return to her loving home for Dorothy. They are finally granted an audience with the wizard. They believe that they are in the presence of an omnipotent figure until Dorothy's dog, Toto, pulls away the curtain, revealing an unimpressive human. They are initially disappointed, but they do not devalue the wizard. Two points become clear. The human wizard, as opposed to an omnipotent idealized wizard, is helpful as a human figure. Further, he shows them that they already have what they're looking for—courage, a heart, a brain, and for Dorothy, the

---

[5]Certain critics of Kernberg from the ego-deficit and self-deficit models assume *no* degree of motivating fantasy in the therapeutic relationship; rather, they focus primarily on manifest content. They make a similar error, but in the opposite direction.

capacity to return home (or perhaps to summon within herself internal soothing images of loved parental figures). The searchers are able to accept help from this real figure and to feel gratitude.

A patient who had idealized her therapist, who had enjoyed just looking at her (while covertly devaluing her) went through such a process toward termination of her therapy. As she began to find that just looking at her therapist no longer provided great satisfaction, she also began to feel good about her own increasing accomplishments. She started to see her therapist as human. She could feel gratitude toward a psychologically experienced separate person.

Denial and Projective Identification

Two additional defenses—denial and projective identification—fall under the rubric of splitting. Denial acts to reinforce splitting. The patient denies the emotion or the emotional relevance of something he has experienced in the past and is likely to experience again. The patient, under the sway of one side of the split, denies the emotional implications (not the actual perceptions) of the other side. Kernberg (1975) notes that, here, "denial simply reinforces splitting" (p. 31). The patient may, at a later date, acknowledge the other side, but he cannot emotionally link the two.

Kernberg contrasts denial with negation, a higher-level neurotic defense under the rubric of repression. In negation, the patient denies a thought that he feels the therapist "might think," but that the patient has never affectively experienced in his consciousness. Because the thought has never been emotionally experienced, negation is seen as a defense related to repression. For denial, on the other hand:

> It has to be stressed that that which is denied now is something that in other areas of his consciousness the patient is aware of; that is, *emotions* are denied which he

has experienced (and remembers having experienced)
and awareness of the emotional relevance of a certain
situation in reality is denied, of which the patient has
been consciously aware or can again be made consciously aware. [Kernberg 1975, p. 32, his emphasis]

One may contrast denial in borderline patients with
psychotic denial; the latter, because it occurs in a weaker ego
structure, involves a greater distortion in perception.

Projective identification is the most complex, misunderstood, controversial, and overused of the splitting defenses
(Kernberg 1975, 1987a, Ogden 1979). Kernberg's (1975)
definition of projective identification emphasizes the irrational, fantasy-dominated, and ego-weakened aspect of the
defense:

The main purpose of projection here is to externalize the
all-bad, aggressive self and object images, and the main
consequence of this need is the development of dangerous, retaliatory objects against which the patient has to
defend himself. The projection of aggression is rather
unsuccessful. While these patients do have sufficient development of ego boundaries to be able to differentiate
self and objects in most areas of their lives, the very
intensity of the projective needs, plus the general ego
weakness characterizing these patients, weakens ego
boundaries in the particular area of the projection of
aggression. This leads such patients to feel that they can
still identify themselves with the object onto whom aggression has been projected, and their ongoing "empathy" with the now threatening object maintains and
increases the fear of their own projected aggression.
Therefore, they have to control the object in order to
protect it from attacking them under the influence of the
(projected) aggressive impulses; they have to attack and
control the object before (as they fear) they themselves
are attacked and destroyed. [pp. 30–31]

In projection, as opposed to projective identification, the patient is not empathically connected with what has been projected. Projection takes place in a stronger ego than does projective identification; it is primarily a neurotic defense. Projective identification is more prevalent in borderline and psychotic patients. The intactness of reality-testing, rather than merely the use of the defense, determines whether a patient using projective identification is borderline or psychotic.

One can elaborate the components of projective identification as follows:

1. The patient attributes to the therapist something—it can be an affect or a self representation or an object representation—that he can not tolerate in himself.

2. The patient continues to feel empathically connected with that which he has projected, in contrast with projection proper, where the patient feels no emotional connection with either the projected idea or the person onto whom the idea has been projected. Projective identification is an incomplete projection because the patient continues to maintain contact with that which is projected.

3. Because of the empathy, he must act to control that which he has projected and which he now experiences as emanating from the other. He rationalizes that he must act in order to protect himself.

4. The patient will then provoke the other to act in a manner consistent with what is projected. He does this through real interpersonal pressure on the therapist to experience himself and behave in a manner congruent with that which has been projected. Ogden (1979) has emphasized this aspect of projective identification. The patient seems to be saying, "If you don't act in the way I expect you to, I'll treat you as nonexistent." The patient easily rationalizes his provocation, and the therapist's

having eventually acted in congruence with that which has been projected, by saying that he is simply responding to the reality of the other.

5. The therapist feels absolutely controlled, as though he can feel or say only what the patient wants him to feel or say; anything else feels enormously and sadistically hurtful to the patient, or irrelevant, or just stupid.

The therapist may feel seized by something outside himself, pressured to behave in an unaccustomed manner. The patient seizes on a real aspect of the therapist—sadism, coldness, intellectual defensiveness, aloofness, sentimentality, softness, sensuality, or any *aspect* of the therapist's many facets—and takes this aspect out of the context of the therapist's total personality as though it were in itself the sum total of the therapist. The therapist is treated as if he had *only* that one quality. The element of reality in the projection works to further unsettle and confuse the therapist and to undermine his functioning.

Kernberg stresses the way in which projective identification represents the patient's nonverbal communication. Projective identification is "diagnosable through the analyst's alertness to the interpersonal implications of the patient's behavior and to the activation in himself of powerful affective dispositions reflecting what the patient is projecting" (Kernberg 1987a, p. 801). Projective identification, then, is diagnosed when the therapist becomes aware of feelings in himself that are unusual and unexpected. That is, projective identification, by definition, will always elicit some form of countertransference (broadly defined) in the therapist. Such countertransference may be mild or severe, but it will always be present. Countertransference used as an initial step in diagnosis and treatment is apparent in Kernberg's clinical examples of projective identification (1987a), as well as in the clinical example by Porder (1987), who discusses projective identification from a perspective quite different from Kernberg's.

The therapist's function is to turn the nonverbal communication, expressed through induction of feeling in himself, into verbal communication. Ogden (1979) suggests that awareness of that which is projected onto the therapist is in itself therapeutic, assuming that the therapist can first contain the projected fantasy, assimilate it into his own personality, and not act to disavow it. If the therapist can metabolize that which is projected—that is, integrate it into the complexity of his own personality—then the patient, for whom projection and introjection are major defenses, will introject the newly digested and reworked projection. This process is more easily described than carried out, however. As Kernberg (1975, 1987a) notes, interpretation of projective identification is difficult because of the patient's regressed state, because of the disruptive affect stimulated in the therapist, and because of the often persecutory nature of the projection. Interpretation of the latter is likely to be taken as criticism by the patient. The therapist must deal with this by refraining from interpreting when he is angry and by maintaining his accustomed therapeutic frame. He must also realize that sometimes all he can do is delineate his and the patient's perspectives, deferring exploration of these perspectives for a later point in the treatment.

The countertransference would be seen as disruptive if the therapist reacted quickly and inappropriately to the patient's projective identification on the basis of a counteridentification, rather than processing the induced feeling in the context of his higher level of ego functioning and then interpreting to the patient. Disruptive countertransference would also be evident if the therapist was so distant from his patient that no feeling was induced. Some degree of "signal" induction is necessary for proper diagnosis and interpretation of projective identification.

7

Kernberg's Treatment Approach

Rationale for a Modified Approach

Kernberg contends that the borderline patient's fundamental difficulty is an excess of aggression, which must be defended against through the use of splitting and its related defenses, including primitive idealization, omnipotence, devaluation, denial, and projective identification. These defenses are inherently ego-weakening, because they interfere with neutralization of aggression. Neutralization, which occurs through integration of libidinal and aggressive self and object representations, is necessary for development of mature psychological structure and its accompaniments, including differentiation of affect, mature object relations, and a stable sense of identity. If neutralization is prevented because of excessive splitting, then the patient is left with rudimentary psychological structure and resultant difficulty with affect regulation and object relations, difficulty with libidinal object constancy (with a consequent sense of emptiness), identity diffusion, and primitive nonmetabolized internal objects.

The borderline patient's sense of emptiness and difficulty with self-soothing (two major signs of inadequate libidinal object constancy) are viewed by Kernberg as *consequences* of the primary conflict around excessive aggression (which leads to splitting and incomplete neutralization), rather than as primary causes of excessive aggression, splitting, and incomplete neutralization. In the latter formulation, difficulty in holding introjects (Adler 1985) is viewed as a primary deficit, and the anger is understood as a form of narcissistic rage, rather than as unneutralized aggressive drive.

Kernberg rejects a supportive treatment approach—an approach emphasizing strengthening ego defenses, limiting dynamic interpretations, and promoting identification with the therapist. Such an approach is ineffective because one cannot strengthen defenses that are themselves inherently ego-weakening. Kernberg reaches this conclusion because he sees defenses organized under the rubric of splitting as primitive and qualitatively different from defenses organized under the rubric of repression. To strengthen neurotic defenses promotes a stronger (if more rigid) ego; to strengthen borderline defenses perpetuates processes which lead to ego weakness. Borderline defenses must therefore be confronted. Thus an approach that, on the surface, seems harsh and nonsupportive in the moment is actually meant to promote neutralization and structure formation over a period of time.

Similarly, because of the interpersonal consequences of borderline defenses, these patients cannot use the therapist as an object of identification. Their anger is split off and acted out outside of therapy sessions, so that there is superficial blandness within the hour but no real process of internalization; alternatively, the analyst is seen through the prism of borderline defenses within the session as, for example, an idealized, omnipotent figure or a devalued, worthless figure.

Under such circumstances, again, identification with a benign supportive therapist cannot occur and confrontation of the borderline defenses becomes necessary in order for therapy to proceed.

Kernberg also rejects unmodified psychoanalysis for borderline patients because he believes that such an approach too easily leads to treatment-disruptive psychotic transference. Further, he feels that analysis could foster conditions in which the patient obtains gratification of primitive needs in a manner that may appear therapeutic but that actually works against insight. For example, the patient might spend several sessions yelling at the therapist in a manner resistant to interpretation, because he is gratifying primitive, split-off aggressive drives. Thus, what seems to be expression of affect turns out to be gratification of drive. This gratification is better than anything the patient may obtain outside of therapy, so the patient will not be as interested in examining it as part of the reflective aspect of treatment. The reduced motivation for reflection interferes with treatment because it hinders development of a working alliance and increases the potential for a psychotic transference. It also contributes to the patient's difficulty because reflective awareness would work against splitting and would indicate rudimentary attempts by the patient at neutralization and ego mastery; the absence of reflective awareness, therefore, represents continuation of primitive ego functioning. Kernberg therefore suggests a modified approach which revolves around confrontation and interpretation of borderline defenses and limit-setting in the session when aggressive drives become too prominent and are not accessible to interpretation.

Part–Object Transference Manifestations in Treatment

Because the neurotic patient has integrated positive and negative self and object representations, he is structurally capable of ambivalent wishes, expressed symbolically and verbally, toward a psychologically experienced separate whole object. These wishes gradually become conscious in analysis through interpretation of defenses organized around repression, especially as these defenses, along with the wishes against which they defend, become manifest and alive in the gradual unfolding of the transference neurosis.

Thus a neurotic patient may initially insist that he never becomes angry. As neurotic defenses (such as reaction formation, undoing, and isolation of affect) are interpreted, the patient slowly begins to see how he keeps himself from experiencing anger. He also becomes aware of the psychological dangers he avoids by repressing anger (for example, castration fears). Through this interpretive process, focused in the transference, he begins to experience anger.

For such a patient, it is a mark of progress in treatment for him to become angry at his therapist. This development is the result of a gradual process of interpretation. The gradualness reflects the patient's defenses, which, while neurotic, also indicate a certain level of structural development and help the patient maintain a stable sense of context and identity. These ego and superego strengths are manifested in various ways throughout treatment. For example, transference development is gradual and modulated. The patient is usually capable of moving from experiencing feelings to reflecting on these feelings. The patient is able to understand the analyst's role in its paradoxical symbolic and real aspects. Expression of anger never threatens the treatment or the patient's psychological equilibrium. Because of the neurotic patient's inherent structural stability, transference psychosis and psychotic regression are not risks. In this context, neurosis is a sign of strength. It is the developmental achievement in neurosis, the developed psychological structure that neurosis indicates, which supports regression and transference analysis while the difficulties of neurosis are analyzed.

Transference development is not only more gradual with the neurotic patient, it is also more rounded and steady. In contrast, the borderline patient's initial presentation in treatment is stormy, because he or she has difficulty with ambivalence and with psychological separation. Wishes are felt and expressed as immediate compelling needs and demands, which must be satisfied quickly and concretely. The therapist is not seen as a working professional who is there to analyze the way in which he becomes experienced by the patient as a stand-in for a past figure. In such a situation, the therapist's interpretations are ultimately gratifying in their own right; they are the therapist's unique way of giving. For the borderline patient, the therapist is experienced as the *actual* figure who ought to gratify him as he has not been gratified in the past. In this case, the therapist's interpretations are seen as depriving.

The patient's wishes and demands, and their associated primitive defenses, are manifestations of part-object transferences. As Kernberg (1975) puts it, the early stages of treatment are characterized by

> the premature activation in the transference of very early, conflict-laden object relationships in the context of ego states that are dissociated from each other. It is as if each of these ego states represents a full-fledged transference paradigm, a highly developed, regressive transference reaction within which a specific internalized object relationship is activated in the transference. [p. 77]

These nonmetabolized self and object relationships may be plentiful and chaotic at first, but they later develop into a limited number of part-object transferences. Certain states may be expressed nonverbally, and one important reason for Kernberg's choosing to have the borderline patient sit in a chair (rather than lie on the couch) is that, in the face-to-face mode, he is better able to observe and bring into the verbal sphere the nonverbal and dissociated aspects of the patient's behavior.

The concept of projection and introjection of split-off self and object representations between patient and therapist is important in understanding both the borderline diagnosis and the course of treatment. Unlike the neurotic patient, the borderline patient does not "transfer" a wish toward an integrated object in the transference. Instead, he transfers self or object representations. Although wishes are inextricably linked to these self and object representations, they are treated as "affect states" (Kernberg 1980a, p. 166). The affect states are virtually the direct equivalent of the representations with which they are associated, and which are expressed or defended against in the transference. In Kernberg's conceptions, one finds global and nonspecific pleasurable and unpleasurable affect states, rather than more specifically defined wishes. In contrast, Kernberg is quite specific about the self and object representations that are enacted in the transference. Thus with a borderline patient, one may not find an articulated unconscious wish, reflecting the influence of id, ego, and superego and serving multiple functions, as one would expect to find with a neurotic patient. As one reads Kernberg's presented cases (for instance, the one discussed on p. 230) it is often unclear just what specific unconscious wish the patient is gratifying or defending against.

Kernberg may understand wishes in this manner because he discusses primitive mental states in more severely disturbed patients. In these cases, where internal structure is not fully developed and self–object boundaries are relatively fragile, one would not expect to find fully articulated products of structure, such as formed, albeit unconscious, wishes and fantasies reflecting the influence of ego, id, and superego. Wishes would be more global, broad, and undifferentiated urges, closely linked to drive states and to self and object representations. All elements of mental functioning, including wishes, become more differentiated and articulated with psychological development. For this reason, we can understand Kernberg's treatment of wishes as urges, drives, and mental states of pleasure and unpleasure. Further, because of his Kleinian roots, Kernberg's treatment of fantasy differs from the more classical Freudian viewpoint. As we saw in our discussion of fantasy in Chapter 6, he tends to view fantasy more as a basic drive state than as a product of psychological structure.

Kernberg (1975) focuses on the vicissitudes of split-off self and object representations in treatment. These are part-object transferences. One aspect of the object representation (the totally sadistic mother, for example) may be projected onto the therapist, and the patient may experience a connected self representation (the persecuted child) with an affective tie between the two representations (fear). These self and object units are unidimensional caricatures because, as a result of reliance on splitting, the self and object representations have remained extreme and superficial. The connecting affective ties are also extreme (fury rather than irritation), for the same reason. The self and object representations are easily reversible. Thus therapy is characterized by the alternation of these self–object units, split off from each other.

> Rapidly alternating projection of self-images and object-images representing early pathological internalized object relationships produces a confusion of what is "inside" and "outside" the patent's experience of his interactions with the therapist. It is as if the patient maintained a sense of being different from the therapist at all times, but concurrently he and the therapist were interchanging their personalities. [pp. 83–84]

The therapist confronts and interprets both the splitting and the split-off self–object units.

Kernberg (1975) gives the following example of such therapeutic work. His patient is speaking about something in a bland tone—something about which she had previously spoken with much emotion. Kernberg encourages her to attend to her blandness, works hard at it, is unsuccessful, and finds himself distracted. He gives up. The patient then begins to insistently ask him for help with a reality situation that he feels is essentially trivial on its own merits. As she increases the intensity of her demands, he becomes impatient and distant. Kernberg then realizes that there has been a role reversal:

> The patient at first enacted an image of her own mother as a distant, aloof, indifferent person who had to be forced by the patient's plea for love and understanding to become interested; I represented the self-image of the patient as a frustrated, demanding child who was looking for a meaningful relationship. In the second part of the interaction, I had been put in the position of the indifferent and rejecting mother, while the patient was enacting her self-image of the frustrated, demanding, insistent child. Interpretation of this total situation led immediately to a sharper focus on the patient's conflicts with her mother and, eventually, to her understanding her own participation in these conflicts by acting at times like a demanding, greedy child (her self-image from the past), and at other times, like a disdainful, arrogant, rejecting mother (the reciprocal object image). [pp. 199–200][1]

---

[1]Note the specificity and focus on self and object representations, and the lesser emphasis on the particular wish. The patient wants her mother to become "interested" and is looking for a "meaningful relationship." The lack of specificity regarding the specific wishes is striking when compared with Kernberg's discussion of self and object representations.

Another example of rapidly shifting self and object representations comes from a therapy group in which two bulimic patients participated.

> Diane has just revealed that she has resumed binge-eating and vomiting. Carol is at first visibly upset and urges several practical suggestions for controlling the bulimia. She also presses Diane for her feelings. Immediately thereafter, she becomes furious, berating Diane for her "backsliding" and "irresponsibility." Carol then begins to sob inconsolably. She demands that Diane do something to make up for those weeks when she had lied to Carol, insisting that her eating was under control.
>
> The therapist and Carol later worked to understand this sequence. At first, it was as if Carol's self-representation as a bulimic child was projected onto Diane, and Carol took on her mother's part (that is, the corresponding object representation). Thus Carol became her own mother, trying to save the aspect of herself that had been projected onto Diane; this explained Carol's urgent suggestions. Carol's anger at Diane was similar to Carol's mother's anger at Carol, as were the words Carol used in berating Diane. The self and object representations were then reversed. Carol became the loving daughter crying in sympathy for her sick mother, who, she had recently discovered, had been hiding her own habit of compulsive gambling. Diane now "owned" the projected object representation. Finally, Carol became the abused child who had suffered at her mother's hands and who was, in the group, demanding concrete reparations from Diane, who, like her mother, had pretended to be healthy but was acting out her own difficulties and was neglectful of Carol.

It should be emphasized that these self and object representations shifted rapidly, were accompanied by intense affect, and were split off from each other; that is, the patient could not simultaneously experience both the self and object representations, with their associated affect. Such a capacity would have indicated that the patient was capable of ambivalence, a developmental achievement.

Difficulties in Forming an Initial Working Alliance

In the course of treatment, part-object units are readily activated, along with primitive defenses organized around splitting. Treatment is quickly filled with turmoil, with idealization and then rapid devaluation of the therapist, with strong (usually angry, sometimes extremely needy) feelings, and with great psychological stress for both patient and therapist. The therapist may now be the most important person in the patient's life. Some patients demand extra sessions, telephone contacts, and other forms of gratification. Kernberg takes it for granted that treatment will be stormy, for both dynamic and structural reasons.

From a dynamic point of view, Kernberg views as central the borderline patient's excessive anger and oral greed, projected outward onto the mother, who is then perceived as an angry, engulfing figure. The rage is generalized to both parents, and the patient becomes paranoid, defending himself from these bad objects through splitting defenses. The patient also defensively attempts to ascend the developmental ladder, sexualizing both his needs and his relationships. However, the early oral conflicts remain central and apparent. We can thus understand the promiscuous patient who, unsuccessfully, attempts to gratify pregenital needs through sexual means.

Dynamically, then, the initial transference is to an angry, demanding, withholding therapist, and the patient feels both ungratified and threatened. The patient's concrete demands, such as wanting to be able to call the therapist at all hours of the night, simultaneously serve a number of functions. First, they express anger. The patient pressures the therapist to abandon what the patient knows is the therapist's usual way of working. Moreover, the patient demands that the therapist accept unpredictable intrusions on his life. Second, the demands defend against the patient's anger. It is as if the patient is saying, "If I can call you or if you give me extra support, then I can reassure myself that I haven't killed you and that you don't hate me." Third, the patient's demands symbolically express more basic, more conflicted, and less readily verbalized pregenital demands.

Along with this rapid development of transference demands, the borderline patient's structural weakness interferes with his capacity to establish a stable working alliance. Several factors contribute. First, the borderline defenses are themselves ego-weakening. Second, the superego, which aids in personality cohesion and stability, is also weakened. Third, the manifestations of nonspecific ego weakness—difficulty with impulse control, poor anxiety tolerance, and limited sublimatory capacity—make a stable alliance much more difficult. And fourth, because the therapist, through projective identification, is seen as the enemy, participation in the working alliance is experienced by the patient as submission to a dangerous adversary. The combination of strong transference demands and weakened capacity for reflection often produces a breakdown in treatment and occasionally results in a full-blown psychotic transference.

Kernberg (1975) emphasizes the role of projective identification in this process. He sees it as the patient's primitive defense against rage, which leads him to perceive the therapist as a feared, attacking object and to simultaneously attempt to attack and control the therapist as he himself feels attacked and controlled.

> The patient may be partially aware of his own hostility but feel that he is simply responding to the therapist's aggression, and that he is justified in being angry and aggressive. It is as if the patient's life depended on his keeping the therapist under control. The patient's ag-

gressive behavior, at the same time, tends to provoke from the therapist counteraggressive feelings and attitudes. It is as if the patient were pushing the aggressive part of his self onto the therapist and as if the countertransference represented the emergence of this part of the patient from within the therapist. [p. 80]

Treatment Recommendations

The combination of rapidly developed primitive transference reactions and the diminished capacity to reflect on these reactions, with the resultant stalemate in treatment or development of psychotic transference, leads Kernberg (1975) to arrive at his treatment modifications. Kernberg's recommendations focus on confronting the negative transference and limiting expression of anger in sessions.

Kernberg makes these recommendations for three reasons. First, as Kernberg sees it, the problem is not that the patient needs a good object whom he can internalize. Rather, it is that the patient, because of his basic mistrust of the therapist, acts to destroy the help that is given him—to bite the hand that would feed him, so to speak. Thus the patient's destruction of potential help is the critical issue and central focus of treatment. Therefore, the therapist's first task is to confront the negative transference. Second, because his observing ego is weak, the patient is not able to use interpretation to understand his transference reactions, particularly under the influence of projective identification. Third,

such unrelenting transference acting out is highly resistant to interpretation because it also gratifies the instinctual needs of these patients, especially those linked with the severe, preoedipal aggressive drive-derivatives so characteristic of them. It is this gratification of instinctual needs which represents the major transference resistance. [pp. 85–86]

The patient may act out the transference by repetitively yelling, by devaluing the therapist, or by expressing contempt. This acting out must be differentiated from the patient's becoming angry after the therapist interprets his defenses against anger, or from the patient's expressing anger in a manner indicating a potential self-observing context for the anger. Such expression of anger can be responded to interpretively. The repetitive devaluation and contempt, on the other hand, is dealt with by limiting the patient's expression of such anger. The limitation accomplishes several goals. First, it modifies a situation in which the patient is filled with fury within the hour and is calm and controlled outside the hour. Following the limitation, the treatment hour becomes more conflictual, with more potential for self-reflection. Thus, Kernberg sees this as a situation in which an action by the therapist, in addition to interpretation, is necessary to facilitate treatment.

Second, the therapist, who is being undermined in his therapeutic role through projective identification, has a means of establishing himself as someone who can set limits. By taking a firm stand, the therapist helps his patient to test reality. The therapist becomes less susceptible to the self–object shifts caused by projective identification both because of the firmness of his stand and because the structure created by his prohibition facilitates secondary-process exploration rather than primary-process transference.

Third, the therapist creates a structure that protects him from lashing back at the patient. Kernberg suggests that the therapist not confront a patient when the therapist is angry. Kernberg is concerned about transference–countertransference interactions that repeat the original parental trauma, and his limit-setting may function as much to aid the therapist in keeping his moorings as to help the patient control himself.

Kernberg supplements his recommendation of setting limits with two other technical recommendations. First, he does not make genetic reconstructions. If the patient is aware of past events that have affected him, Kernberg will bring these into treatment as a way of gaining perspective and distance. However, to suggest to the patient what things might have been like—that is, to open up events that are not already accessible to the patient—encourages further regression in a patient whose reality-testing is already weak. Thus Kernberg interprets experience, which is based on transference, in the here and now. He might say, "You talk as if I were a vengeful man who wants to engulf you, and as if you were a persecuted woman who can only escape by silence," rather than suggesting, on genetic and reconstructive lines, "As a child, you must have felt like your mother would take you over if you told her how you felt." The determinant here is the extent to which the past event is available as a conscious memory. If such material is available, then reminding the patient of similarities between the present and the past is a useful and indicated way to help the patient gain reflective awareness in the session.

Kernberg's second recommendation is that confrontation and interpretation of the primitive defenses in the session be balanced with outward deflection and demonstration to the patient of how these defenses, which are evidenced within the session through the negative transference, are also operative outside the session and hinder his relationships with others. Deflection, which, as just mentioned, may also be to conscious genetic material, defuses stress in the transference and allows the therapist to be implicitly supportive of the patient as the two of them, together, on the same side, discuss what goes wrong outside of treatment. This is different from looking at what goes on within the treatment, where the therapist may be seen as opposing the patient. This point has been extensively elaborated by Havens (1976).

The pivots of Kernberg's approach to the borderline patient are therefore (1) confrontation of defenses organized around splitting as they become manifest in the transference, (2) limits on expression of anger in sessions, and (3) interpretation of part-object transference units in a manner designed to aid in integration of positive and negative part-objects, with the goals of (1) neutralization of anger, (2) greater tolerance of ambivalence, and (3) ego and superego development and elaboration.

Transference as Elaboration of Fantasy

Kernberg emphasizes the fantastic, or the fantasy-dominated, element in transference. As we have seen, he has a specific, Kleinian-influenced view of fantasy, and he repeatedly focuses on its motivating role in conflict. He views the patient's transference as filled with fantasy-dominated unconscious images. Such unconscious self and object representations may develop as follows.

When the event that serves as the stimulus for memory initially occurs, the child forms an image of himself, of the object connected to the event, and of an affective state connecting the self and object representations. This self-object-affect unit, along with many other such units, forms the building block of internal structure. The units are neutralized and depersonified over time. When excessive aggression prevents neutralization, splitting is used, and there ensues a vicious circle in which splitting leads to further ego weakness, leading to less neutralization, leading to greater reliance on splitting, and so on. Memories that are not neutralized and integrated, that remain laden with split-off self and object representations, and that are saturated with primitive affect components, are less likely to be modified over time and to be placed in context. Thus they remain fantastic (fantasy-dominated) not only because their origin is laden with fantasy elements, but also because they become more fantastic as they remain outside of an integrating context. This aspect of memory and fantasy—the fantasy-dominated elaboration of childhood experience in a split-off state—is Kernberg's focus.

It is because of his focus on this element of fantasy that Kernberg cautions against understanding transference as di-

rectly reflecting early development and early object relations. He believes that transference reflects a "condensation"
of the patient's early relationships, his fantasy distortions of
these relationships, and his primitive defenses against the
threats posed by these fantasy elaborations.

> Generally speaking, the sicker the patient, the more indi-
> rect and complex is the road from current transference
> developments to the genetic or intrapsychic history. . . .
> The underlying reason for this indirect relation between
> current transference—reflecting the predominant struc-
> turalization of the patient's internalized object rela-
> tions—and antecedent developmental features resides, I
> think, in the vicissitudes of fixated part-object relations.
> Patients dominated by part-object relations tend to
> maintain fantastic (in the sense of primitive, early, and
> diffuse), highly unrealistic affect states reflecting such
> relations, and to distort later, real interactions with exter-
> nal objects in the light of such earlier split-off internal-
> ized object relations. These patients create vicious cycles
> of projective mechanisms and reinternalization of highly
> distorted object relations which reconfirm and further
> distort their antecedent primitive part-object relations.
> [Kernberg 1980b, p. 362]

Thus, because we are dealing with part-object relationships—more subject to distortion than whole-object relationships because, by their very nature, they are unintegrated
and unneutralized—and because of the fantasy-dominated
dynamic vicissitudes of these internalized nonmetabolized
part-objects, we cannot draw accurate correlations between
current transference and the patient's development. It is only
later, after these transference fantasies have been analyzed,
that more accurate accounts of childhood traumata are available to both patient and analyst. It is then, Kernberg states,
that the patient often discovers that the most significant
traumata formed the background fabric of the patient's life,

taken for granted and relatively unnoticed behind the Sturm und Drang of the borderline fantasies.

Since fantasy is so prominent a factor in transference, Kernberg believes that one cannot understand the patient's behavior and manifest wishes as developmentally revealing, and that one therefore ought not attempt to undo perceived developmental traumata. He does not believe in the parent–child model as a valuable guide to the therapist. Rather, he contends, the therapist ought to confine himself to interpretation of the fantastic self and object representations as they are revealed in the transference. (This recommendation will be discussed later, in a review of Kernberg's conception of the proper therapeutic stance and of his approach to resistance.) It is Kernberg's belief in fantasy as an essential element in the transference and in self and object representations which leads him to suggest that the only proper role for the therapist is an interpretive one.

Kernberg's focus on the fantasy element is often misunderstood. When Kernberg speaks of fantasy, he is not suggesting that the patient is incorrect about the facts of his life. Patients who describe being beaten or sexually abused by their parents may be reporting reality experiences. Kernberg is referring to the patient's elaborations of the events, to the wishes that formed their context, and to their varied dynamic sequelae.

Interpretation of Transference

Kernberg emphasizes work with the borderline patient in the patient–therapist relationship as it is distorted by transference. He notes that this is unlike work with neurotic patients, for whom the therapist can more readily identify dynamic issues through historical material, but with whom transference manifestations are more subtle. With the borderline patient, because of excessive identity diffusion and other pathology, it is more difficult to obtain a coherent sense of their history and social circumstances and easier to observe transference manifestations.

> Here we find an immediate activation of primitive defensive operations and primitive object relations in the therapeutic interaction and, by the same token, the possibility of rapidly diagnosing early, predominant transference patterns and their current dynamic implications. Here, in other words, intrapsychic conflicts are not repressed or unconscious but are largely conscious and dissociated, and expressed in contradictory transference dispositions and defenses against them. [Kernberg 1980b, p. 361]

Kernberg's notion of transference reflects his views of the development of internal structure. Structure is built through internalization, depersonification, and abstraction of inner object representations. Since this process has not occurred with the borderline patient, it is the nonmetabolized and contradictory internalized self and object representations which are immediately activated in the transference. The therapist is confronted with the precipitants of an insufficiently dissolved personality mixture. Reflected in these part-object transferences are a meld of oedipal and preoedipal conflicts.

Kernberg emphasizes the necessity for transference interpretation. Interpretation with the borderline patient differs from interpretive work with the neurotic patient, for whom the conflict is intrapsychic and underlying wishes are repressed. In work with neurotic conflict, the analyst interprets from surface to depth, from conscious to unconscious, from defense and resistance to underlying wish. Such topographic distinctions do not apply with the borderline patient, since all elements of the conflict are conscious and unconscious at times, and the conflict is between prestructural elements—that is, part-object units that have not been integrated to form ego and superego. It is not only dynamic content which needs to be interpreted; it is the patient's inability to contain the conflict in internal structures and its consequent expression in the transference activation of contradictory self–object–affect units.

The therapist thus focuses his attention on these units.

> The analysis . . . of the nature of the immediate object relation in the transference and the defensive operations connected with its dissociation from other, contradictory object relations helps the analyst to clarify the meaning of the transference, the defensive aspects of the object relation activated, its motivation in protecting the patient against a contradictory or opposite object relation, and the implicit conflict between primitive ego structures . . . . If . . . the analyst first interprets the part-object relation activated and its affect state, and later, its defensive function against other, contradictory, parallel, or previously conscious affect states linked to other part-object relations, dramatic change and new understanding may be gained while the patient's reality testing returns to normal. [Kernberg 1980a, p. 166]

Confrontation of primitive defense is a major step in treatment, but interpretation of split-off part-object units, as they are manifested in the transference, is the ultimately mutative factor. Kernberg suggests that the transference may be manifested in what looks like a weak ego. He cautions that manifestations of deficient ego functioning in sessions may shift the therapist's attention to the deficient ego functions and away from the self–object transference that is being expressed.

> For example, the therapist may focus, in an isolated fashion, on the patient's difficulty in experiencing or expressing his feelings, on his difficulties in overcoming silence, his tendency toward impulsive actions, or his temporary loss of logical clarity, instead of on the total primitive human interaction (or the defenses against it)

activated in the transference. This is the danger of a simplistic ego-psychological approach which neglects the full analysis of the total human interaction. [Kernberg 1976, p. 177]

Kernberg notes that the weakness of the ego defenses is in itself the manifestation of a split-off self and object relationship, just as it is the result of such a relationship; that is, the weak ego reflects a conflict as well as a deficit. Therefore, he recommends against focusing on the weakened ego unless the therapist also interprets and identifies the self–object unit that is being expressed through the weakened ego functions.

Kernberg does consider the patient's ego functions as he interprets, but he responds to ego difficulties differently than do more "supportive" therapists. Therapists utilizing the ego-deficit model tend to focus on the various specific ego functions. They seldom interpret the dynamic function of these specific ego difficulties, but view them as ego deficits which require support.

When Kernberg writes of attending to ego difficulties, he refers to a dynamically motivated transference reaction. It is not that he is unaware of difficulties in the patient's specific or nonspecific ego functions (the latter include impulse control, anxiety tolerance, and sublimation capacity). But, in a comment specifically addressed to the issue of ego functions, he first points out the ego-deficit model's neglect of dynamic factors and then points to a transference distortion that he considers an ego-functioning difficulty.

[A] mistake . . . would be to interpret the object relation in depth, without sufficient attention to the patient's ego-functions—his capacity, for example, to understand and elaborate that interpretation or to become aware of his tendencies to use the interpretation magically rather than as a communication within a shared work relationship with the therapist. When the patient eagerly wants to comply with the therapist's "intentions"—or oppose them at any cost—this *relationship to the interpretations* needs to be interpreted; and when the patient insists on seeing as real what to the therapist appears as a transference distortion, this discrepancy needs to be worked through fully before interpretation of that transference reaction can proceed. [Kernberg 1976, pp. 177–178, my emphasis]

It seems that even in cautioning us to be aware of the patient's ego functions, Kernberg is showing us how he views ego functions as inextricably part of a transference reaction, such as the patient's wish to primitively idealize an omnipotent authority.

The Therapist's Stance

As his view of borderline pathology might lead one to expect, Kernberg sees the therapist working from a neutral position, using confrontation and interpretation. Kernberg deemphasizes the working alliance and the role of empathy. He stresses early and vigorous confrontation of resistance, acting out, and the negative transference, viewed as manifestations of psychopathology.

The therapist is primarily an interpreter of transference. He is not a new and better parent, a "catalyst of reorganization" (Blanck and Blanck 1979, p. 242), or the maintainer of a holding environment (Modell 1976). Kernberg is clear on the ways in which treatment of the borderline patient differs from classical psychoanalysis, primarily in the need for parameters to control the negative and psychotic transference. He believes, however, that the therapist's stance is similar in classical analysis and in therapy with the borderline patient. In each case the therapist interprets transference from a position of technical neutrality. Kernberg refers to A. Freud's (1946) definition of neutrality when he defines it as "equidistant from external reality, the patient's superego, his instinctual needs, and his acting (in contrast to observing) ego" (Kernberg 1975, p. 188).

Kernberg takes as a given the patient's capacity to tolerate such an approach—the therapist as solely analyst—and the patient's ability to function without making demands that would force the therapist out of a neutral position. The patient is expected to be able to control impulses such as wrist-cutting, suicidal behavior, and life-threatening medical conditions that can be managed by taking prescribed medication. The therapist cannot be neutral and primarily interpretive if he has to worry about the patient attempting suicide after the session or if the patient has lost his job, has no money, or is homeless. Kernberg attempts to maintain a neutral position by essentially creating a social prosthesis within which the patient can function. To accomplish this, he will use a social worker to help the patient with necessary concrete services, and he will use the hospital to keep the patient in a safe, controlled environment either during initial stages of treatment or during difficult periods in the course of treatment.

The Patient's Dependence on the Therapist

Borderline patients make demands on their therapists. These may include, as previously mentioned, demands for frequent telephone calls, extra sessions, contact during vacations, and concrete gratification during sessions (such as requests for hand-holding or for hugs); the patient may even refuse to leave the office at the end of sessions (Giovacchini 1982). The therapist must decide how to respond to these requests. To the extent that the therapist views them as appropriate manifestations of structural difficulty in the patient's capacity to function on his own, he will meet these requests if possible. Such conceptions of the source of the patient's demands, and differing treatment recommendations, are discussed by Buie and Adler (1982), Blanck and Blanck (1974, 1979), Stolorow and Lachmann (1980), and others.

For Kernberg, however, these demands are not the expression of dependency wishes, but the expression of pathological defenses, especially primitive idealization, omnipotence, and projective identification. In order to need or depend on another, one must have achieved a certain degree of psychological separation and structure. Dependence requires tolerance for ambivalent feelings toward another, trust in another as fundamentally "good," and the capacity to see another's wishes and needs as potentially separate from one's own. These qualities allow for dependence on a real person in the context of a close relationship, with its many gratifications and disappointments. The capacity for true dependence is a developmental achievement, similar to the capacity for love.

Kernberg (1975) contends that the structural development necessary for dependence is missing in the borderline patient.

What has been called the excessive "dependency needs" of these patients actually reflects their incapacity really to depend upon anyone, because of the severe distrust and hatred of themselves and of their past internalized object images that are reactivated in the transference. The working through of the negative transference, the confrontation of the patients with their distrust and hatred, and with the ways in which that distrust and hatred destroys their capacity to depend on what the psychotherapist can realistically provide, better fulfills their needs. [p. 91]

Kernberg is against the therapist's stepping out of the traditional role and meeting these needs, particularly becoming a "real" person and engaging in self-revelation. Granting extra sessions is suspect, since the patient's request may be an expression of his guilt over aggression toward the therapist.

Kernberg's decision to evaluate the borderline patient in terms of how he does *not* meet the criteria for mature dependency is important in determining his technical approach to expressions of dependency by the patient. He decides that what is experienced as dependence by the patient is a *symptom* of underlying conflict rather than an expression of feeling from the patient requiring responsiveness by the analyst on its own merits. By assuming that the patient's demands are the symptomatic and psychopathological *effect* of these underlying *conflicts*, the therapist refrains from responding to manifestations of psychopathology and maintains neutrality. From the neutral stance, the therapist interprets the underlying conflict and helps the patient gain ego strength. Kernberg's approach is based on a conflict-defense model and on viewing, diagnosing, and evaluating the patient from the *outside*. This implies defining, from the therapist's point of view, what is appropriate.

The following question might be posed to Kernberg: If dependence requires whole-object relationship, including tolerance for ambivalence, how do we describe what many view as the paradigm for dependence, the dependence of an infant on its mother? Certainly the infant has no notion of whole-object relationship. Kernberg is certainly entitled to posit a developmental progression in the capacity to depend, and to consider this immature rather than mature dependence. He might argue that there are vast differences between the borderline patient's relationships and the infant's relationship to the mother. However, to focus on the borderline patient's demands *solely* as pathological expressions, and to view dependence in terms of what it is *not* rather than in terms of whatever components of structural inadequacy it *does* represent (in addition to, not instead of, what it tells us about the effect of primitive defenses), seems to lead to theoretical and technical difficulty. Kernberg leaves little theoretical room for the therapist to appreciate and empathize with the patient's demands, and none for any sort of gratification of these demands, even symbolically. The patient's dependence is always a symptom to be interpreted rather than a need to be met.

For therapists who advocate a more supportive approach (Buie and Adler 1982, Blanck and Blanck 1974, 1979), and even for classical analysts working with the borderline patient (Bach 1985, Grunes 1984, Pine 1985), the borderline patient's demands are accorded greater legitimacy. The patient's difficulty with dependency is considered by Adler and Buie (1979) to be the result of a developmental deficit in holding introjects and by Blanck and Blanck (1974, 1979) to be the product of incomplete psychological differentiation. While these analysts differ from one another in their understanding and response to the dependency needs and demands, the demands are not understood solely as the expression of underlying primitive conflict. They are seen as legitimate from the *patient's* point of view. The patient is not diagnosed solely with regard to what he *cannot* do. Rather, the therapist assesses the patient's total functioning (where he *is* developmentally as well as where he is not). The therapist attempts to understand and to clarify for the patient what he is attempting to achieve, as well as what he is attempting to avoid. The therapist brings a more adaptive and developmental perspective, in addition to recognizing the effects of dynamic conflict.

It is from this perspective that Kernberg expects greater self-control from his patients as a precondition for treatment than do these other analysts. The patient's difficulty maintaining himself outside the session is not addressed directly by Kernberg. It is assumed by definition; those patients who decompensate between sessions are regarded as unsuitable for expressive psychotherapy or they are hospitalized if, during such psychotherapy, they cannot control themselves. In contrast, Adler and Buie (1979) assume that their patients will have difficulty maintaining themselves between sessions, and they offer suggestions as to how patients can be "held" between sessions.

The Working Alliance

References to the working alliance are found throughout Kernberg's work, and many of his recommendations are considered from the standpoint of the working alliance. He emphasizes that the therapist must take care to note and interpret the way in which the patient uses the therapist's comments. Kernberg believes that the therapist's focus on clarification of the patient's perception and use of the therapist's comments involves the patient in treatment, stimulating the working alliance. He also believes that interpretation of the negative transference strengthens the working alliance. He comes to this position because his focus is on the patient's motivated destruction of the positive aspects of treatment. "Supportive" therapists approach the issue from the opposite perspective, focusing on positive feelings toward the therapist, and on the way in which negative feelings such as narcissistic rage destroy the holding and internalizing aspects of treatment. From Kernberg's perspective, interpreting the negative will strengthen the positive, explicitly in that it removes impediments to the working alliance through interpretation, and implicitly in that, as they work together on impediments to treatment, therapist and patient are actually working in alliance with each other (Havens 1976).

Kernberg's technical recommendations—including limiting expression of unneutralized anger, not attempting genetic reconstructions, using conscious genetic information to help the patient gain perspective, and deflecting negative transference outward—are intended to help the patient gain perspective and develop the ability to test reality. These strengths maintain the working alliance and control transference regression, especially psychotic transference. Kernberg has patients sit in a chair, rather than lie on a couch, partially for the purpose of reducing uncontrolled regression. He interprets primitive idealization and the associated defenses, which appear positive but are actually pathological. He does not interpret the more modulated and appropriate aspects of the positive transference, again in order to facilitate the working alliance.

It is curious that Kernberg is often oblique about the ways in which these recommendations function to strengthen the working alliance. He does make the connection, but his lack of emphasis is striking. In any response to the patient, his concern is with the totality of the part-object transference. To focus on ego functioning alone, without considering the self-object-affect unit that is expressed in the poor ego functioning, is anathema to Kernberg, as we have seen. This implies that, *in the properly diagnosed* borderline patient, by definition, interpretation of the transference will improve ego functioning. For Kernberg, to advocate specific work on developing and maintaining the working alliance apart from interpretation of impediments to such an alliance would open a Pandora's box to consideration of other ego factors apart from their dynamic use by the patient. It is, therefore, in accord with Kernberg's emphasis on analysis of transference rather than on repair of deficit that he does not explicitly focus on the working alliance in itself in treatment of the borderline patient.

Empathy

Empathy is not considered to play a major mutative role in Kernberg's treatment of the borderline patient. In his discussion of empathy and the therapist's holding function, he makes several points. First, he contends that empathy is a prerequisite to interpretation, not a replacement for it. It is understood that a therapist is in empathic contact with the patient in order to be able to interpret. He subscribes to the traditional use of the word *empathy* as referring primarily to a mode of observation rather than a mode of interaction (Levy 1985). Second, Kernberg posits that the therapist must be empathic with aspects of personality that the patient has split off or projected onto the therapist, in addition to aspects of personality in the patient's consciousness. Thus the therapist ought to be empathic to ego-alien aspects of the patient.

Third, the therapist has empathy for the patient in common with the mother, but what differentiates the therapist from the mother and holds the patient is the therapist's intellectual understanding, "a totally rational, cognitive, almost ascetic aspect to the therapist's work" (Kernberg 1977, p. 303). This rational understanding of dissociated aspects of the patient, interpreted to the patient as they become manifest in the transference, is mutative. It is insight, not internalization or empathy or a new experience, which leads to ego strength and to therapeutic success.

In discussion of the holding environment, Kernberg (1984) describes his basic view of the therapist's task with borderline patients:

> The principal problem with these patients is their failure to achieve a satisfactory loving relation with an object that can be trusted and relied upon in the face of their aggression toward it, despite their awareness of the shortcomings of and frustrations stemming from that object, and in the context of tolerating painful guilt, concern, and gratitude toward that loved object. [p. 251]

Establishment of a close and truly dependent relationship with the therapist thus involves patients accepting their own aggression and realizing that their aggression will neither destroy the therapist nor destroy their positive feelings for the therapist. The therapist, correspondingly, must acknowledge his patients' aggression. Holding the patient involves

> accepting the reality of the patient's aggression without being overwhelmed by it, trusting in the patient's potential for loving despite his current difficulties in expressing love, and believing in the possibility that life has something to offer . . . notwithstanding his limitations. [p. 251)

According to Kernberg, therapists must accept their own aggression and be realistic about the therapeutic relationship; they cannot insist on a "naive, Pollyannaish neglect of the ambivalence of all human relations" (Kernberg 1977, p. 302).[2]

Resistance and Acting Out

According to Kernberg, resistance and acting out are manifestations of pathological defenses, and they must therefore be confronted and interpreted. He considers various manifestations of resistance, such as lying to the therapist, conscious or unconscious devaluation of the therapist, paranoid control over the therapist in sessions, suicide threats and attempts, self-mutilation, and expressions of resistance through refusal to eat or to take essential medications. These manifestations must be seriously evaluated in order to determine whether the patient can be responsible for himself over the course of treatment.

It is illuminating to note Kernberg's consistent focus on the dynamic, rather than the structural, aspect of resistance (by this is meant his focus on the dynamic relationships between internal part-objects and between nascent internal structures, as opposed to a focus on the effects of structural deficits and vulnerabilities). For example, when Kernberg (1975) discusses the patient's lying to the therapist, he writes as follows:

> In the immediate context, for example, the patient may lie because he wants to assert his superiority over the

---

[2]Parenthetically, Kernberg feels that it is because of the borderline patient's aggression that more traditional psychoanalytic therapy works poorly with borderline patients and, paradoxically, works best with patients who have greater ego strength. The neurotic patient does not seek to defeat the therapist and is able to identify with him.

therapist and defeat his efforts, exert control over him, protect himself from dangerous retaliation that he fears from the therapist should the therapist know about matters the patient wishes to hide, or consciously exploit the psychotherapeutic relationship for ends other than receiving help. From a longer-range perspective, lying implies a basic distortion of the human nature of the patient–therapist relationship, and an indication that the patient has at least temporarily abandoned any hope or conviction of the possibility that honest discussion of his problems might be of any help. Lying also implies that, in the patient's mind, the psychotherapist is either incompetent, a fool, or dishonest in lending himself to such a parody of treatment; again, this indicates a basic hopelessness in or unavailability for any authentic human relationship. [pp. 201–202]

Note the wide range of dynamic factors that Kernberg enumerates; any structural deficits are implied and are viewed through the prism of the dynamic point of view.

It is worth while, for the sake of contrast, to note Stolorow and Lachmann's (1980) view of a similar issue. In "The Analytic Approach to Acting Out," a section of their book, they consider a patient who insists on taking a three-month vacation from treatment following what the analyst considered a narcissistic rebuff to the patient. The rebuff was the analyst's exploration of the patient's "superior smile," a technical approach recommended by Kernberg. The therapist goes along with the vacation, understanding its significance as "a potentially constructive step." The therapist believes that by not interpreting the vacation as resistance or acting out and by not then inquiring into the unconscious motives behind this act, he was able to maintain a therapeutic environment which allowed the patient to return to treatment after his vacation, "with the budding narcissistic transference unharmed."

The therapist feels that the patient's vacation was in reaction to his intervention; it was "provoked unwittingly" when the therapist focused on the patient's smile in the early stage of treatment, when "a therapeutic alliance was not present." The therapist ought to have concentrated more on the patient's "continual need for mirroring and admiration of his grandiose self," which left little patient tolerance for joint reflection or self-observation. The therapist further understands the vacation to be "partly a test," which would determine whether he would allow the patient "to separate" or whether, alternatively, he would "hold on to him for his own personal needs, as his mother had." The therapist believes further that the patient took the vacation because he needed "this concrete act"; . . . "verbalization and fantasy alone would not have sufficed to provide the requisite narcissistic restoration." Finally, the therapist believes that his "nonjudgmental acceptance" of the patient's action allowed the patient to take a "developmental step" to accept the therapist as a "separate object." It was only after the therapist had accepted this vacation and the patient had returned that joint exploration became more possible. (All quotes are from Stolorow and Lachmann 1980, pp. 167–168.)

It is striking to note these analysts' differing theoretical perspectives. Stolorow and Lachmann (1) mention only implicitly a dynamic issue—the patient's fear that he will be trapped by the analyst; and (2) focus on a structural deficit—that is, the patient's narcissistic vulnerability, which is associated with yet another structural deficit, the patient's ego weakness in the area of symbolization. That is, the patient, because of structural difficulties, needs to enact something concretely and is unable to tolerate feelings and express them symbolically (that is, verbally). Because of difficulties in separation-individuation (these analysts would also stress narcissistic deficits), the analyst is not perceived as a separate object and is used as a self-object in the transference. This *structural* difficulty, rather than any *dynamic* issue, is the major focus.

We see further, again in contrast to Kernberg, (3) a focus

on the manifest content. The transferentially perceived therapist is equated with the patient's mother, and the vacation is considered an almost direct replay of difficulties in separation from the mother. We also note (4) a focus on the adaptive, rather than resistant, aspect of the patient's vacation. Furthermore, (5) the patient's action is reactive. It comes as a response to what is understood to be the therapist's technical error rather than being based on internal, unconscious motives. In addition, (6) the therapeutic alliance is seen as something apart from the treatment, something that was not present at the beginning of treatment but might be established later, once the analyst has permitted a developmental step. The therapeutic alliance becomes the goal of treatment rather than an assumed aspect of treatment, and technical steps such as permitting a vacation or allowing oneself to be used as a self-object are necessary prerequisites to formation of such an alliance.

Kernberg differs fundamentally with Stolorow and Lachmann on each of these issues. In Kernberg's (1975) discussion of why the patient might lie, he focuses on dynamic factors and does not give even one possible explanation that would understand the lying from a structural or adaptive point of view. He relies on interpretation of unconscious material (rather than on manifest content) and attempts to decide, in an initial diagnostic assessment, whether an adequate working alliance can be established from the start of treatment. He often cautions against assuming a direct correspondence between the patient's behavior toward the therapist and the patient's relationship with his parents.

While Kernberg does not usually focus on the adaptive aspects of the patient's behavior, there is one instance in which he considers acting-out as possibly adaptive.[3] He

---

[3] A second instance occurs in his model of supprotive therapy (1984), where he advocates looking at the adaptive aspects of the patient's action. Here, however, we are discussing his view of expressive therapy.

makes the point that prohibiting a patient's sexual activity as "inappropriate" and showing "lack of impulse control" made clarification and interpretation of her masochistic fantasies and her primitive sadistic superego more difficult. When her sexual activity was analyzed, rather than prohibited, she was able to work through her difficulties. Kernberg (1975) writes:

> To dissociate the normal, progressive trends within pathological sexual behavior from its pregenital aims is easier said than done. This must be a continuous concern of the psychotherapist working with such patients. [p. 104]

However, we should note that not only is his concern with the possible adaptive aspect of such behaviors unusual, but also that such behavior was not dangerous, did not express primitive defenses in a manner that was unanalyzable, and did not pose a major transference resistance. Thus there was no particular reason to prohibit such behavior. It is only this *prohibition*, based on ego deficits isolated from dynamic factors, against which Kernberg argues. Despite Kernberg's caution to the therapist, the main thrust of his argument is against a technical error rather than for consideration of a patient's behavior from the adaptive mode. Even this possible exception remains within Kernberg's general orientation of emphasizing the pathological rather than the adaptive aspects of the patient's behavior.

Criticisms

Many analysts have criticized Kernberg's views regarding the borderline patient. Here we will review only criticism of his technical recommendations. Perhaps the most central criticism has been of Kernberg's emphasis on confrontation of the latent negative transference (the anger and control underlying primitive idealization, for example).

EARLY CONFRONTATION MAY REPEAT PARENTAL TRAUMA

The therapist's confrontation of the patient can easily be taken by the patient as an invitation to battle, particularly when the therapist confronts ego-syntonic material and particularly under the influence of primitive defenses, which, as Kernberg notes, lead to the patient's viewing the therapist in a paranoid manner. If the therapist is vigorous in his confrontation, he may repeat parental trauma. He may also get the patient to agree with him as a form of masochistic submission to superior force. A narcissistically vulnerable patient will certainly find it more difficult to engage in painful self-exploration when there is the possibility of narcissistic rebuff.

The therapist may believe that his job is only to confront and interpret aspects of unconscious process. Actually, this is a misunderstanding of the therapist's role, which is to help the patient gain insight into his unconscious and learn about aspects of himself with which he may be uncomfortable. Interpretation is a means to this end, not the end in itself. Even brilliant, accurate interpretations will lead nowhere if the patient cannot listen. If the confrontation does not result in the patient's increased insight, it is not useful even if it is accurate. Kernberg is sensitive to this question when he emphasizes the need for the therapist to be alert to the way in which a patient uses interpretation; however, he does not consider the effect of a therapeutic atmosphere dominated by confrontation on the patient's willingness to take on for himself the self-observation and self-confrontation necessary for analytic work.

PREMATURE DEALING WITH AGGRESSION MAY PROVOKE
MALIGNANT REGRESSION

If the therapist works with the patient's aggression too early in the treatment, the patient may feel that all the good has been destroyed. In this situation, interpretion of the anger that the patient is projecting in order to save his nonprojected good internal objects will lead to return of the patient's experience of himself as bad. The same good objects will once again be in jeopardy. The therapist will be prematurely attacking a necessary defense before the patient is able to use the therapeutic alliance for support. Early confrontation can then provoke malignant regression, a frequent occurrence with the borderline patient. Stolorow and Lachmann (1980) argue that this regression may be an iatrogenic reaction to the form of treatment advocated by Kernberg.

There is another way to approach aggression early in treatment. The therapist can refrain from confronting or interpreting prematurely. The therapist can focus on how the patient feels the therapist is hateful and stay with the usual inquiring approach. This approach increases reflective awareness and does not give the patient the feeling that the therapist is smarter than he is. One needs to be careful with the classical Kernbergian interpretation, which is that the patient bites the hand that would feed him. Let us consider, for example, a patient who has been feeling out of control, alone, and in need of support, and who is told that if he wouldn't be so angry and push the therapist away, then he might be more likely to get what he wants. The patient is *prematurely* told that he is responsible for his suffering; he does not arrive at this insight at his own pace. He infers that his needs will not be met by the therapist. He feels humiliated, rejected, criticized, and abandoned. This outcome is also likely if the treatment atmosphere includes overtones of aggression and projected harsh superego precursors.

The therapist would do well to be accepting and giving to the patient even as he points out the patient's rejection of what the therapist can reasonably supply. This is inherent in the notion that the therapist metabolizes the patient's projective identifications. It is only after the projection is filtered through the therapist's more developed mode of functioning that it is interpreted to the patient. The therapist helps the patient achieve the regulation he needs through accepting the patient's needs and meeting them where possible within the psychoanalytic setting and in a modulated and appropriate manner, even as he works toward interpreting the irrational aspects of the patient's wishes and their unconscious roots. Both aspects of treatment work in tandem.

To phrase this differently, the patient's contempt is a form of connection as well as of devaluation. Kernberg does not refer to the patient's attempt at self-regulation through this form of relationship, although we know that many patients relate to others through provocation, fighting, and sadomasochism, depending on the level of character development. The therapist must accept and allow for that level of connection, *even as* it is interpreted.

Consider, for example, the case of a patient who complains during a session of feeling anxious and "racing." She states that therapy is useless because it is too slow, and that nothing will be accomplished through analysis. The therapist notes that she is devaluing him even as she implores him to help her. The patient, offended, becomes silent. One can argue that such an interpretation was given from the "outside." The patient concluded that the therapist would not meet her need and would maintain distance from her through interpretation. The therapist could have instead agreed that analysis is slow, not because he wants it to be that way, but because some things take time. He might have continued by inquiring about which particular interaction made her feel hopeless and offering her the opportunity to work on that. Note that here the therapist allies himself with the patient and emphasizes what they can do together rather than what they cannot do together.

While there are many contraindications to confrontation, there are also indications for confrontation. For example, while Kernberg confronts the defenses themselves, Buie and Adler (Buie and Adler 1973, Adler and Buie 1973) confront the patient when the consequences of his primitive defenses endanger him. Confrontation carried out for this purpose is illustrated in the following example.

> A patient discovered that her former therapist was getting married, and she had decided to disrupt the ceremony because the therapist "belonged" to her. She was willing to go to jail. The current therapist focused on how the patient, in order to protect her feelings of loss with a fantasy that she knew was not real, was willing to risk destroying what was real and valuable—her positive past relationship, new therapeutic relationship, and her job. The point was not to focus on splitting and anger, but to begin to enlist the patient's willingness to look at her actions and the unconscious fantasies they reflected. The therapist first pointed out the potential danger and then led her to ask herself about her motivations. The therapist remained on the patient's side. He was not questioning the pathology of the act as much as he was protecting the patient from the consequences of the act. Thus the establishment of a paranoid transference was thwarted.

KERNBERG'S FOCUS ON THE PATIENT'S ASSUMPTION OF OBJECTIVE REALITY

Another criticism is of Kernberg's stress on the patient's assumption of objective reality. He expects the patient to assume all the responsibilities of reality (including reality testing and secondary process functioning) when this may be, in itself, the basic treatment issue. Kernberg's expectation is apparent in many ways, including his insistence that the patient be capable of caring for himself during treatment, his assumption of a working alliance from the outset of treatment, his concept of dependency as reflecting what the patient has not achieved, and his interpretations, which approach the patient from the "outside." Kernberg's focus does not take seriously certain kinds of feelings and experiences.

Although these feelings might seem childish and inappropriate from an observer's vantage point, they are appropriate for an earlier developmental stage. They may need to be acknowledged and allowed to be modified at their own pace and from internal sources. Narcissistic wishes and demands for the therapist to act as an external holding object are examples of such needs.

Interpretation of such wishes as the result of intrapsychic conflict is appropriate once a tripartite structure has been established. In this context, interpretation is experienced by the patient as helpful, an aid to an ego that uses it for greater intrapsychic freedom. The therapist is not needed to gratify needs that are experienced as wishes rather than as demands, because the ego is able to perform narcissistic and holding tasks on its own. To interpret such feelings as the product of conflict in a patient who has not achieved full psychological development may reflect the therapist's demand that he assume an adult's perspective before he is ready to do so.

While such criticism has been made by analysts of the deficit models, a similar objection has been made by classical analysts. Calef and Weinshel (1979) write that Kernberg departs from basic psychoanalytic principles of technique such as the patient's free association and the analyst's corresponding freely suspended attention. Instead, the patient is

> viewed through a prism of prefabricated ideas, and his treatment is predicated on *what* is believed contained within a given diagnostic label and preformed ideas about *how* that diagnostic label should be approached. . . . this departure . . . entails the danger of a kind of activity which is based not so much on the analyst's responsibility to maintain the analytic process but on his preconceived notion of what the patient *must* be like and by a greater tendency to permit the analyst's own value judgments to intrude on the analytic work and the analytic process. [p. 489, their emphasis]

NEUTRAL LISTENING WITHIN A COMPROMISED
PSYCHOANALYTIC POSITION

One final criticism of Kernberg deals with his preservation
of a neutral stance from which he can interpret. When the
patient needs concrete help, Kernberg attempts to preserve
neutrality by enlisting a third party to provide that help. He
seems to deny the implications of his actually needing to help
his patient, since this help can be supplied by another professional. Kernberg seems to believe that he can preserve neutrality and his interpretive role by having someone else provide the actual help.

Traditionally, the concern in this kind of situation is that
the patient will split feelings between the therapist and the
third party. Kernberg deals with this possibility by communicating with the third party to obtain information that he
can bring into treatment without divulging nonpertinent
information about the treatment to this third party. However, there is another split here. The therapist arranges for
and prescribes certain concrete assistance from a third party
that the therapist determines is actually needed. Because the
third party is supplying the assistance, Kernberg then acts as
if it is not coming from the therapist. Thus the appearance is
maintained of treatment with a neutral therapist and a patient
who is being helped solely through interpretation. In actuality, the assistance provided by the third party must be understood as coming from the therapist, who has diagnosed that
the patient needs more than just interpretation. This assistance is an aspect of the therapist's help in a noninterpretive
and non-neutral mode, and the mutative possibilities (in
addition to the pathological potentials) of this help should be
openly considered. An overemphasis by the therapist on
third parties (including on hospitalization as a way to contain the patient during stressful periods) without concomitant discussion of the value of this help, which has been
arranged by the therapist, may protect both patient and
therapist from necessary and realistic acknowledgment of the

patient's genuine needs and of the steps that the therapist is taking, albeit through others, to meet these needs.

Strengths

Some aspects of Kernberg's approach seem insufficiently appreciated. Some analysts (Stolorow and Lachmann 1980) criticize his confrontive approach and state that the anger and acting out that he emphasizes is actually iatrogenic—that is, caused by the therapist, who is interpreting defenses as if the patient were functioning on a higher developmental level. This interpretation, according to Stolorow and Lachmann, may be

> the result of a failure to recognize the arrested developmental aspects of the patient's psychopathology so that vital developmental requirements revived in relation to the analyst have once again met with traumatically unempathic responses. [p. 191]

The patient reacts to such repeated trauma by decompensating and acting out.

Although there is much to be said about this criticism of Kernberg, it is in some ways unjust. Stolorow and Lachmann assume that empathy is a clearly defined concept that leads to interventions approaching the patient's raw experience. Actually, empathy is a poorly defined, complex concept (Levy 1985), dependent on the analyst's theoretical system (Schafer 1983). Empathy can be misused by *both* classical and self psychologists as a means of confirming and perpetuating a given theoretical system (Schwaber 1983).

Empathic listening has unfortunately become a code phrase for doing psychotherapy within a self-psychological framework. This implies that the therapist who is not a self psychologist is unempathic. In this light, Kernberg's comment that the analyst must be empathic to that which the patient has split off, dissociated, and projected is relevant. There are certain patients for whom Kernberg's confrontive approach may be more supportive and even empathic than it appears at first glance. Through confrontation, Kernberg acknowledges and is empathic to the patient's angry, orally hungry self. If this approach is correct with a given patient, the patient will respond to confrontation and interpretation by feeling understood and held. He will feel that his rage will not destroy the therapist, that his badness is accepted, and that he is not "putting something over" on the therapist. If, on the other hand, the therapist is wrong, as Stolorow and Lachmann point out, then the patient will feel misunderstood. A differential diagnosis is necessary here, as Stolorow and Lachmann acknowledge. It cannot be assumed that self psychologists have the corner on empathy and that Kernberg's method is, by definition, unnecessarily harsh and the cause of iatrogenic acting out.

Further, Kernberg's approach falls under the rubric of defense analysis, and one may assume that Kernberg carries out this *goal* of defense analysis through the traditional *means* of psychoanalytic technique. That is, one should assume that Kernberg does not do wild defense analysis, in the same way that one would assume he does not do wild id or superego analysis. Kernberg's entire approach is geared toward rigor, specificity, and control in technique. Thus confrontation may be carried out in a tactful and sensitive manner, so that the patient is not unnecessarily wounded.

Part Four

Expansion Possibilities within Classical Technique

8 _____

The Changing Conception
of the Therapist's Role

Freud

It is axiomatic that the mutative factor in psychoanalysis is insight into the unconscious, via interpretation of the transference, which is irrational, symbolic, and displaced. In his papers on technique, Freud emphasized insight and was suspicious of the mutative effect of other aspects of the analyst–patient relationship. For example, Freud (1912b) was always cautious of the degree of the therapist's warmth because he was concerned that (1) it would lead to cure by suggestion rather than cure through insight, (2) that the therapist's wish to cure could interfere with his capacity to listen with "evenly suspended attention," (3) that it might leave the therapist vulnerable to certain transference constellations revolving around the negative therapeutic reaction, and (4) that certain transference gratifications might interfere with the patient's motivation for further analytic work.

Although Freud was suspicious of other factors as mutative agents, he acknowledged and employed them as part of the overall relationship. Many analysts have remarked upon the manner in which gratification of derivatives of libidinal wishes was discouraged while other, more global and object-relational, gratifications were assumed. Stone (1961) has discussed Freud's pattern of first stating broad principles, such as that of abstinence or the analyst as surgeon, and then modifying and qualifying these principles with parenthetical reservations. Friedman (1969) has reviewed the complexity of Freud's thoughts about the patient's attachment to the analyst and the degree to which it is a necessary aspect of psychoanalysis. Lipton (1977) believes that Freud's recommendations were understood to be *technical* recommendations but that the whole of the analyst–patient relationship was understood by Freud to encompass more than the technical. Many analysts have noted that Freud did not follow his own recommendations in treating his patients, in that he was more giving than are today's classical analysts. We can see some of the basis for these remarks in Freud's own writings, where he seems to assume a wide sphere of interaction in the realm of object relationship even as he cautions against gratification in the realm of libidinal derivatives.

For example, Freud writes (1912b) that the analyst should be like the surgeon. In that recommendation alone there is much support for one who advocates an aloof analytic stance. He says that the analyst, like the surgeon, "puts aside all his feelings, even his human sympathy" in order to perform his task. "Therapeutic ambition" is another feeling to be avoided. He gives two reasons:

> [Therapeutic ambition] will not only put him [the analyst] into a state of mind which is unfavourable for his work, but will make him helpless against certain resistances of the patient, whose recovery, as we know, primarily depends upon the interplay of forces in him. The justification for requiring this emotional coldness in the analyst is that it creates the most advantageous conditions for both parties; for the doctor a desirable protec-

tion for his own emotional life and for the patient the largest amount of help that we can give him today. A surgeon of earlier times took as his motto the words: *Je le pansai, Dieu le gue'rit* (I dressed his wounds, God cured him). The analyst should be content with something similar. [p. 115]

We see Freud's overt "justification" for "emotional coldness" as protecting the analyst and allowing focus on the "interplay of forces" in the patient—that is, the intrapsychic conflict. The metaphor of the surgeon seems also to caution against grandiosity, against enmeshment in certain transferences (Freud writes of the patient's negative therapeutic reaction as one of these transferences in other papers), and for an emotional stance that will allow the analyst to listen neutrally.

In the same paper, Freud cautions against self-revelation by the analyst as an inducement for the patient to reveal more about himself; he writes that although the analyst's self-revelation may lead to the patient's further revelations, it "verges upon treatment by suggestion" (p. 118) and does not allow the patient to learn about his resistances. In today's terms, it focuses too much on id rather than ego. Further, it encourages potentially insatiable demands by the patient and might lead to a focus on the doctor rather than the patient. Finally, it makes more difficult the eventual analysis of the transference. Thus, Freud concludes:

I have no hesitation, therefore, in condemning this kind of technique as incorrect. The doctor should be opaque to his patients and, like a mirror, should show them nothing but what is shown to him. [p. 118]

Here too, Freud uses another well-known metaphor of the analyst as "mirror," and cautions against the analyst's moving out of a neutral position. Yet, again, just as in the case of the analyst as surgeon, the remark must be understood in the context of Freud's specific point: that the analyst should refrain from self-revelation as a means of encouraging patient revelation. He is making a technical point: that the analyst must maintain enough distance to allow development and analysis of the transference, and that these may become impossible if the analyst moves away from that setting.

But does this mean that, for Freud, there is no emotional relationship between the patient and analyst? No. In that same paper, sandwiched between metaphors of analyst as surgeon and mirror, Freud, in recommending that analysts undergo training analyses, writes "we must not underestimate the advantage to be derived from the lasting mental contact that is as a rule established between the student and his guide" (p. 117). Even as Freud emphasizes analysis of transference and the surgeon and mirror models, he seems to believe that there also is "lasting mental contact" (the mutative effect of internalization) between patient and analyst, who are seen through yet another model—that of "the student and his guide."

We see the interplay of models and mutative factors in another paper (1919), where Freud echoes his earlier (1915) recommendation for abstinence. He writes: "Analytic treatment should be carried through, as far as it is possible, under privation—in a state of abstinence" (p. 162). Freud emphasizes this statement, calling it a "fundamental principle which will probably dominate our work in this field" (p. 162). Abstinence is necessary so that the patient will not be prematurely satisfied and leave treatment.

> You will remember that it was a *frustration* that made the patient ill, and that his symptoms serve him as substitutive satisfactions. It is possible to observe during the treatment that every improvement in his condition reduces the rate at which he recovers and diminishes the instinctual force impelling him towards recovery. But this instinctual force is indispensible; reduction of it endangers our aim—the patient's restoration to health.

What, then, is the conclusion that forces itself inevitably upon us? Cruel though it may sound, we must see to it that the patient's suffering, to a degree that is in some way or other effective, does not come to an end prematurely. If, owing to the symptoms having been taken apart and having lost their value, his suffering becomes mitigated, we must re-instate it elsewhere in the form of some appreciable privation; otherwise we run the danger of never achieving any improvements except quite insignificant and transitory ones. [Freud 1919, p. 163, his emphasis]

Abstinence is not an absolute attitude, however. Freud (1919) writes: "By abstinence . . . is not to be understood doing without any and every satisfaction—that would of course not be practicable" (p. 162). The concept is based on Freud's belief that libidinal wishes, somewhat liberated in the analytic situation, will become satisfied with a new resolution, one which predominantly serves resistant functions. Once this occurs, there will be less motivation for treatment and less pressing and unrequited need to verbalize transference wishes. One only wishes for something when it is missing. The danger lies in the patient becoming satisfied with a solution that does not allow his fullest possible development. Here, the better becomes the enemy of the best. Thus, through abstinence, the analyst guards against this partial and incomplete resolution, specifically when it may become manifest in the transference, and the patient will seek uninterpreted transference gratification rather than analytic resolution of the transference. In this context, abstinence refers to a balance between analyst and patient, a balance which must be evaluated with each patient at various points in the analysis. The balance is evident as he writes:

The patient looks for his substitutive satisfactions above all in the treatment itself, in his transference-relationship with the physician; and he may even strive to compensate himself by this means for all the other privations laid upon him. Some concessions must of course be made to him, greater or less, according to the nature of the case and the patient's individuality. But it is not good to let them become too great. Any analyst who out of the fullness of his heart, perhaps, and his readiness to help, extends to the patient all that one human being may hope to receive from another, commits the same economic error as that of which our non-analytic institutions for nervous patients are guilty. Their one aim is to make everything as pleasant as possible for the patient, so that he may feel well there and be glad to take refuge there again from the trials of life. In so doing they make no attempt to give him more strength for facing life and more capacity for carrying out his actual tasks in it. In analytic treatment all such spoiling must be avoided. As far as his relations with the physician are concerned, the patient must be left with unfulfilled wishes in abundance. It is expedient to deny him precisely those satisfactions which he desires most intensely and expresses most importunately. [p. 164]

Of course, the reverse of Freud's analogy is not true— that one ought to provide a bare, nongratifying environment in psychiatric hospitals so that patients will be encouraged to focus on their intrapsychic conflicts and on meeting the challenges of life outside the hospital. Freud, while careful to safeguard abstinence and frustration, never overlooked providing his patients with a livable environment, including the rich stimulation of his office. Such a therapeutic environment was always assumed, just as the diagnosis of neurosis always assumed certain developmental prerequisites. Once these were met—developmentally and in the analyst's office—the focus could be on analysis of internal instinctual wishes. But, when a patient was hungry, Freud fed him (Freud 1909, p. 303).

In another statement, Freud (1919) discusses the judgment necessary in applying the principle of abstinence:

> We cannot avoid taking some patients for treatment who are so helpless and incapable of ordinary life that for them one has to combine analytic with educative influence; and even with the majority, occasions now and then arise in which the physician is bound to take up the position of teacher and mentor. But it must always be done with great caution, and the patient should be educated to liberate and fulfill his own nature, not to resemble ourselves. [p. 165]

Thus Freud consistently writes of abstinence in the context of a balance in the relationship between frustration and gratification. Abstinence is desirable for certain aims, but it is a relative rather than absolute principle, and it must be sensitively applied. Abstinence is also introduced to balance respect for the patient's autonomy with the analyst's function as "teacher and mentor." Freud (1919) writes:

> We refused most emphatically to turn a patient who put himself into our hands in search of help into our own private property, to decide his fate for him, to force our own ideals upon him, and with the pride of a Creator to form him in our own image and see that it is good. [p. 164]

In other papers, Freud refers to the analyst's functions as other than object and interpreter of transference. One would not expect to see such references if the analyst's role was solely to be understood as that of a blank screen or mirror. Yet Freud (1937a) writes:

> [N]ot every good relation between an analyst and his subject, during and after analysis was to be regarded as a transference; there were also friendly relations which were based in reality and which proved to be viable.

[p. 222] . . . [The analyst] must possess some kind of superiority, so that in certain analytic situations he can act as a model for his patient and in others as a teacher. [p. 248]

Brenner

The basis of what we might term the "right" wing of classical psychoanalysis has been formed by emphasis on that aspect of Freud's recommendations that stresses abstinence; the model of the analyst as blank screen, mirror, and surgeon; the focus on interpretation of intrapsychic conflict; and the generally frustrating stance. This view is predominant in psychoanalytic publications and is most clearly articulated by Brenner (1976, 1979).

Brenner's focus is on structural theory and its applications. He argues that any aspect of psychological functioning can be understood as a compromise formation, reflecting the contributions of id, ego, and superego. A patient's anxiety, then, is the result of this constellation of unconscious forces and is not due to his conscious reason for feeling anxious. Thus Brenner calls our attention to the latent content of the patient's material. It is an error, he believes, for the analyst to focus on the patient's manifest content, even if the patient is psychotic or, at the other end of the continuum, if the analyst can easily understand a "realistic" basis for the patient's anxiety. Brenner argues that all material must be regarded as manifest, with latent meanings to be derived through the analysis. This view leads to an important technical consequence: For patients at all diagnostic levels, analysts must not be diverted into thinking that the patient's anxiety, depression, or guilt is the result of the consciously perceived symptom. They should instead consistently analyze all of what the patient says so that they can determine the unconscious conflict that underlies both the symptom and the affects associated with it.

Brenner is against the notion of a working alliance because it seems to suggest that there is an aspect of the analyst–patient relationship that is not based on transference and that does not need to be analyzed. The concept of a working alliance also suggests that the analyst might have to do something to build this alliance—that is, do something other than consistently analyze the patient's material. Brenner rejects both of these ideas, believing that everything in the analyst–patient relationship is based on a sufficient degree of transference fantasy to require analysis, and that analysts should confine themselves to interpretation of the patient's associations and of the transference. It is assumed that patients diagnosed as "analyzable" will be able to work in this way. A consistent focus on interpretation may appear callous but is actually the best way for the analyst to be helpful to the patient in the long run.

Brenner's focus on the intrapsychic determinants of a patient's reactions leads him to deemphasize not only manifest content but also the "reality" of the analyst's behavior or of the analytic frame as a precipitant. He disagrees with Stone's belief that the frame is inherently frustrating, and he believes that the patient's transference is not affected by the analyst's unwillingness to move out of a classically abstinent posture. Brenner (1979) writes:

> Provided his analyst is competent (= adequately trained and himself sufficiently well analyzed), it is a patient's own illness that determines whether he experiences the analytic situation in and of itself as a source of pain, as essentially neutral, as a welcome anodyne, or as a positive source of pleasure. [p. 153]

Tarachow

Tarachow (1962) has used this model of the analyst's role as the basis for distinguishing between psychoanalysis and psychotherapy. For Tarachow, development and analysis of a transference neurosis, which is the defining criterion of psychoanalysis, takes place when the therapist imposes what Tarachow terms "the therapeutic barrier" (p. 379). In this situation, the therapist chooses to treat everything the patient says as symbolic: "The *real* situation is transformed into an *as if* situation demanding attention and comprehension" (p. 379, Tarachow's emphasis). It is this therapeutic attitude that differentiates psychoanalysis from psychotherapy.

> The difference is that in psychotherapy the real events are treated as *a reality*, while in analysis they are treated as expressions of the patient's fantasies and as determined by the inevitable needs of his solutions of his unconscious conflicts. . . . The critical concern is the status and function of the relationship between therapist and patient. If it is taken as real, then the symptoms and life events are also taken as real, and both therapist and patient turn their backs on the unconscious fantasies and anxieties. If the real relationship is set aside, then both therapist and patient turn toward an understanding and working through of the unconscious fantasies. [Tarachow 1962, p. 378, his emphasis]

To the extent that the therapist allows himself to take the patient–therapist relationship at face value, the treatment becomes more psychotherapy than psychoanalysis. Thus conducting analysis imposes an enormous burden of loneliness on the analyst. Tarachow writes that "Loneliness is not to be regarded in a naive sense. A casual remark about the weather breaks the loneliness and establishes real object relationship" (p. 381).

The conceptions of treatment presented by Brenner and Tarachow have a tight theoretical elegance. However, both assume an ego that can tolerate a therapeutic relationship which is solely an as-if, symbolic one. For Tarachow, therapy begins with the patient mourning the therapist as a real object. The mourning process begins with the first interpretation, which, by establishing the analyst as a symbolic figure and frustrating real object relationship, is in itself a deprivation. The patient must be able to use this situation for analytic gain rather than becoming overwhelmed by frustration and object loss. When Brenner chooses not to comment on a patient's life tragedy because he wants to limit his remarks to interpretations, he is assuming that the patient will not become enraged or narcissistically wounded in an unanalyzable manner, but will understand that this analytic posture is necessary and will accept it on that basis. As we have noted, the balance between gratification and abstinence was discussed by Freud. Brenner chooses to emphasize the analyst's abstinence, along with the implied belief that, in the properly chosen analyzable patient, correct interpretations will prove gratifying enough to sustain the patient through the abstinence. Eissler (1953) makes this same assumption when he speaks of the "normal ego" and when he decides that interventions other than interpretation are to be considered parameters, or departures from standard technique.

Tarachow also shares this assumption. However, after he defines the analyst's stance as based solely on interpretation of an as-if, symbolic, and transferential relationship, he seems to reverse his position. He opens the door to other aspects of the analyst's role and other mutative factors that were not included in his original schema. He writes as follows:

I have presented a rather rigorous conception of the ideal therapeutic relationship. The concept, i.e. the concept of the conditions of analytic work, must be grasped firmly, but none of this can be experienced as sharply as I put it here. For example: in addition to the strictly controlled "as if" relationship there is also the real relationship. The patient gets to learn real things about the therapist both in and out of the office and the therapist behaves in a real and human way toward the patient. . . . In fact, the reality of the therapist is a factor which keeps the treatment going. The real relationship leads to identification which also supplies motivation for the analytic work, for the ego splitting. The oscillation between the real and the "as if" relationship can actually facilitate analysis and, if considered in terms of oscillation between gratification and deprivation, can serve as a useful model for identification processes to take place. Seeing the therapist as he really is also assists the patient in correcting his transference distortions. In fact, it would probably be impossible to find any analyst who could rigorously maintain the detachment necessary not to use the patient as object at all. He would be bound to be real and treat the patient as real. Paradoxical as it may seem, the very human imperfections of the analyst make analysis possible in reality. Furthermore, it is the analyst's function to introduce reality to correct the patient's fantasies and distortions. The real relationship supplies the motivation to face the pain of the transference deprivations. In effect, there are two concurrent relationships, the real and the "as if." The very act of interpretation may have a double significance. What I have emphasized has been the function of interpretation in separating the patient and the therapist. But in another sense the interpretation brings the two together. [Tarachow 1962, p. 383]

This extraordinary paragraph adds a dimension to the analyst's position that is not included in Tarachow's original presentation. After a rigorously strict definition of the analyst's stance and of the essence of psychoanalysis, Tarachow states that there is both an as-if *and* a real relationship. It is this "reality" relationship that supplies a motive force for the treatment (not, as Freud and others write, solely frustration by the analyst). Tarachow also introduces another mutative factor, identification, which operates alongside the strict "therapeutic barrier." Identification, which is not fully considered in his initial description of the analyst's posture, facilitates interpretation. Thus while Tarachow initially defines analysis and the analytic stance as sparingly as does

Brenner, he then includes, as essential factors in the analysis of neurotic patients, other factors that are in the background in Freud's writings and that other analysts move to the foreground of the analytic stance.

One might argue that Tarachow is not being inconsistent and that there is nothing extraordinary about the cited paragraph. Noninterpretive mutative factors are assumed by all analysts. In order for interpretation to be mutative, other nonspecific and assumed background factors must be operative, and Tarachow is simply spelling out some of these factors. This argument would state that Tarachow, Brenner, and Eissler know that these other factors operate in the background of the analytic stance, and that the issue is whether or not to place them in the foreground. That is, these analysts are focusing on abstinence and interpretation because these are the most crucial factors in psychoanalytic work. However, this does not mean that these are the only factors. There is also the issue of the difference between what happens outside the analyst's active choice and what the analyst actively chooses. The implication here is that the real relationship is in the background and is assumed by the analyst (in the same way that he assumes the patient's capacity for continued autonomous ego functioning during transference regression); it is something that the analyst does not actively foster. The as-if relationship, on the other hand, is fostered by the analyst as he creates the conditions for an analyzable transference. If these background factors must be moved to the foreground of the analytic work, then the patient is not analyzable and the analyst is doing psychotherapy.

I do not agree with this argument. First, these distinctions deemphasize, in theory and practice, the close relationship, or interpenetration, among all aspects of the analyst's stance (Grunes 1984). Second, the argument implies that, if it were possible, the analyst would choose not to have even unavoidable reality factors operate. In other words, reality factors complicate rather than support the analytic work. Finally, theoretical emphases do make a difference. Theory lends itself to caricature. While it may be true that experienced analysts such as Brenner, Tarachow, and Eissler are aware of background factors and simply choose to emphasize only abstinence and interpretation, others may come to believe that the assumed background factors are nonexistent, trivial, or dangerous to psychoanalytic work. Shapiro (1984) cites the woodenness of first-year psychiatric residents, attempting to emulate an analytic stance they do not understand. The exclusion of certain factors from theoretical consideration, even though they may be assumed in clinical work, leads to poor theory and to restricted clinical options. The argument that clinical practice (and perhaps theory) always assumes the effect of other mutative factors is plausible, but it runs into difficulty because these other factors are not only missing from theoretical consideration but are actively excluded and dismissed by these analysts.

Lipton

Freud's relationship with his patients often transcended what is today considered appropriate for classical technique. For example, Freud (1909) reports giving the Rat Man a meal. Modern classical analysts say that Freud changed his technique in later years and that he would not have gratified his patients in this manner later in the evolution of his work. Lipton (1977) challenges this view in a way that bears on our discussion of the analyst's role.

Lipton, focusing on the Rat Man case, disagrees for several reasons with the belief that Freud changed his technique. First, there is no evidence in any of Freud's writings in the thirty years after publication of the Rat Man case that he had changed his views. Because Freud did indicate changes in his views on other aspects of theory and technique, Lipton argues that Freud never changed his opinion that the Rat Man's analysis was a successful example of analytic work. Further, while Freud was alive, no one questioned his technique in this case. Thus Lipton concludes that they must also have agreed that it illustrated a valid application of technique in a successful analysis or that, at least, it was an accurate example of Freud's work.

Finally, all Freud's case examples, and those reported by his patients through the years, are consistent with this mode of interaction with his patients. Lipton cites several examples: One of Freud's patients told him he was saving up to buy a set of his works. The following day, Freud gave the patient a set of his collected papers. Another patient reports that Freud interpreted a dream, then reached for a cigar, saying, "Such insights need celebrating." The patient said that she wanted to explore the dream further, and Freud responded by saying, "Don't be greedy. That's enough insight for a week" (Lipton 1977). Lipton believes that the reason Freud never discussed these interactions in his technical papers is that he did not view this aspect of the patient–analyst relationship as falling under the rubric of "technique." In this last argument lies Lipton's central point: The concept of technique has grown beyond its original meaning and is now considered to govern the totality of the analyst–patient relationship in a way never intended by Freud.

Lipton offers two corollaries to his main thesis. First, he believes that modern analysts evaluate the validity of a technical intervention based on criteria applied to an intervention at the moment of the intervention. That is, they believe that one can know immediately whether an intervention is "correct" without needing to observe its long-term effect on the analysis. Since the focus is now on the interventions themselves, rather than on the effect of these interventions, attention shifts to what Lipton terms "trivial matters," regarding the analyst–patient interaction rather than to the overall session or result of the work. Lipton writes that the analyst's focus becomes a conservative one, devoted as much toward minimizing interventions which could be technical errors skewing the future transference as toward understanding the patient's current transference. In Lipton's words, analytic technique acquires "a prospective or prophylactic approach rather than a retrospective one" (Lipton 1977, p. 262). The time spent by the analyst in avoiding potential technical error detracts from his focus on understanding the patient's associations.

In making the entire relationship a technical matter and avoiding interactions for fear that they might gratify unconscious fantasies and thus render them unanalyzable, modern technique tends to exclude any intervention except interpretation. Silence becomes idealized because it seems safest. This is Lipton's second corollary: The absence of an intervention is not evaluated according to the criteria used for evaluating an intervention itself. While an intervention may be seen as inappropriate, the absence of an intervention is not seen this way. Silence thus becomes the basis of correct technique. It is the safest technique for the analyst, and its detrimental effects escape scrutiny.[1] For Lipton, the major detrimental effect is "the danger of fostering iatrogenic narcissistic disorders by establishing an ambience in which the patient has little opportunity to establish an object relationship" (Lipton 1977, p. 272).

Lipton believes that modern technique is a reaction to Alexander's emphasis on a "corrective emotional experience," a term that stressed manipulating the transference relationship and emphasized experience rather than insight. These ideas caused a severe counterreaction in the analytic community and led to the modern deemphasis of the analyst's personality and relationship with the patient. Lipton compares his own understanding of Freud's technical views with Alexander's and with that of the modern analysts in his discussion of Freud's serving the Rat Man a meal. He notes that all agree that Freud's serving the meal became important

---

[1]This reason for silence—fear of intervening—would refer to a countertransference reaction. Most analysts are silent not out of fear, but rather to permit free associations.

to the patient. They disagree on how to regard serving the meal from a technical point of view.

Alexander would have attempted to use such a gratification systematically to advance the analytic work. Modern technique argues that such gratification should be avoided because it gratifies fantasy and thus obviates analysis of that fantasy. The analyst guards against this danger by limiting contact with the patient to interpretations. In this way, his realistic impact on the patient is more controllable, and he can focus on the transference as irrational. Lipton believes that Freud would argue (against Alexander's point), that serving the meal was a spontaneous and personal gesture and that to systematize it would make it artificial. With regard to the modern analysts' critique, Lipton feels that Freud might have said that failure to respond would make the analyst appear discourteous and could also lead to establishment of an unanalyzable transference. All views, Lipton adds, agree that the analyst must analyze the effects of any response he makes.

Lipton believes that Freud's original conception of technique was more restricted than it is in the modern view and that it allowed for a concurrent personal relationship between analyst and patient in addition to a transference relationship. This personal relationship, which was always understood to exist, is not easily defined. Lipton (1977) writes that "its essence is its purpose" (p. 269). That purpose is limited to continuation of the analysis. It is this restriction which defines abstinence; that is, the analyst allows a personal relationship as long as it leads to furthering the analysis. Any gratification that exceeds this restricted goal is prohibited under the principle of abstinence.

The personal relationship provides the context for Freud's technical recommendations. To Freud, these recommendations were tools to be employed within the larger relationship. For example:

> [H]is recommendations that the analyst be like a mirror, like a blank screen, and similar comparisons can be un-

derstood as purely technical recommendations. They were meant to emphasize the attitude of neutrality with which the analyst was to comprehend the patient's associations, an attitude which the patient understood and collaborated with. They were not meant to encompass the analyst's entire personality. The recommendation of neutrality is like that of aseptic technique for the surgeon. That necessity is confined to the operation itself and not, of course, to any other contacts with the patient which are necessary. [Lipton 1977, p. 272]

This relationship (which, Lipton believes, needed to be "reinvented" in the concept of a therapeutic alliance once it was prohibited by an extension of the concept of technique) both exists alongside the technique and forms the basis for technique; that is, the patient is able to tolerate abstinence because of the quiet gratification from the positive transference. Moreover, it is also the basis for the rules of technique. That is, there is a personal relationship between analyst and patient, and it, rather than a technical rule, is the basis for clinical decisions. The analyst's personal security, rather than a rule or a concept such as the therapeutic alliance, makes an analyst decide that he is able to work with a difficult patient and determines the way in which he works with him. In this realm, we see how competent analysts vary in their willingness and capacities to tolerate severe regressions and to work with the various problems that arise in the treatment of difficult patients.

Stone

Stone writes about the "psychoanalytic situation" and the analyst's role within it from a perspective congruent with Lipton's, although with reservations (Stone 1961, 1981).[2]

---

[2]For discussion and critique of Lipton's position, with clinical material, see Lipton and Kanzer (1983).

To understand Stone's contributions to the analyst's role, we must begin with his conception of the psychoanalytic situation. He uses the parent–child model in a way that is similar to Loewald's (1960) conception. For Stone, the developing child must achieve psychological separation from his mother and must substitute speech for touch as a mode of connection. This process involves the child's developing higher-order levels of psychological functioning and is mediated by the mother's verbally naming the child's feelings and sensations, thus organizing them and helping the child deal with them on a more symbolic level. Similarly, the patient in analysis must confront his wishes for union with the analyst, expressed through the various libidinal phases. These wishes are expressed in what Stone (1981) calls the "primordial transference" (p. 160). While the analytic situation certainly contains gratifying aspects, for Stone it is primarily frustrating because of the patient's experience of "deprivation in intimacy" (p. 161). The wishes for union provide the driving force for the transference, are organized at psychologically higher levels through the analyst's interpretations, and cannot be gratified.

The analyst has several functions in this context. Stone is firmly rooted in the classical analytic tradition. He believes in abstinence, neutrality, and the analytic frame, although he contends that these tools must be used on a level that can be understood and appreciated by the patient. While we tend to focus on the way in which Stone differs from analysts such as Brenner and Langs, it should be emphasized that these differences revolve around what Stone sees as extremes in application of these traditional concepts; there are almost no differences between these analysts in their views of the centrality of these concepts. So Stone, first and foremost, sees the analyst's role as that of analyzing the transference.

At the same time, Stone believes that the analyst ought to titrate the effects of the inherent frustration of the frame. It is true that transference requires a gap between what the patient wants from the analyst and what the analyst provides. It is also true, Stone says, that such a gap may be best developed, in an analyzable form, if there is some relationship between analyst and patient that helps the patient tolerate the frustrating elements of the frame. This view of the analyst underlies the positions that place Stone at odds with what he terms "neoclassical" technique. Like Lipton (who wrote sixteen years after Stone's book appeared), Stone argues that Freud's metaphors of the analyst as surgeon, mirror, and the like were specific recommendations referring to specific situations and were not meant to characterize the totality of the analyst–patient relationship.

Stone (1954) seems to take this position partially because of his experience with more disturbed patients. He is quite sensitive to the possibility of excessive and unanalyzable patient regression in response to a too-anonymous analyst. He returns to this possibility time and again in his writings, and he sees the analyst's activity in making the abstinence and frustration understandable as helping the patient tolerate the frame. However, it seems that the image of the analyst as modifying the frustration of the frame is part of Stone's theoretical conception regardless of the clinical problem of regression. We see this in Stone's (1961) statement, referring to the nonspecific gratification required in traditional analysis with the neurotic patient, that "he too legitimately requires something more than has hitherto been regarded as sufficient" (p. 54).

In further support of this view, one notes that, in his original and classic description of the "psychoanalytic situation," Stone (1961) first describes the overall formal analytic situation as inherently frustrating and then adds:

I must state my conviction that a nuance of the analyst's attitude can determine the difference between a lonely vacuum and a controlled but warm human situation. . . . The rigors of the analytic situation are subtle and cumulative, importantly operative, *whether evident or not*. . . . the intrinsic formal stringencies of the situation are sufficient to contraindicate superfluous deprivations in the analyst's personal attitude. [pp. 21–22, 69, Stone's emphasis]

Stone believes that the analyst must provide some kind of personal "peg" for the patient's transference. (We will see echoes of this position in Fox's [1984] paper, discussed in Chapter 9.) It is part of Stone's belief that the blank-screen model is impossible to carry out and may stimulate too severe a regression. Stone states that "for the person to have some outline picture of the analyst as a person in relatively neutral reference, especially noninstinctual and nonconflictual references, I thought provided a better basis for the development of the transference than the (presumably) bald, effortfully bald picture" (Langs and Stone, p. 113). This is not meant as an argument for excessive self-revelation. Rather, it is an argument for the idea that it is not necessarily destructive for the patient to learn certain things about the analyst. Indeed, some such knowledge could be helpful.

Stone argues against the belief that the transference unfolds only through its own internal dynamism, and that the analyst plays little part in this process. Competent analysts are not interchangeable. Stone (1961) writes:

> The enthusiastic and engaging assertion of an older colleague . . . that his patient would have developed the same vivid transference love toward him [even] if he had been a brass monkey is alas (or perhaps, fortunately!) just not true. [p. 41, Stone's emphasis]

Stone believes that the analyst as a person is important to the analysis. The analyst is not *only* the recipient of transference distortions. Stone, referring to a statement by Glover, states that "somewhere the patient is reacting to what we are in the very depths of our personalities, and that this can't be excluded. . . . I believe it is true . . ." (Langs and Stone 1980, p. 348). In a later publication he quotes Glover directly as writing: "This would suggest that in the deeper pathological states, a prerequisite of the efficiency of interpretation is the *attitude*, the true unconscious attitude of the analyst to his patients" (Glover, quoted by Stone 1981, p. 173 his emphasis).

Stone's belief about the nontransference aspect of the analyst–patient relationship accounts for some of the difference between his and Brenner's conception of the analyst's role. The reader will recall Brenner's remark that it is the patient's transference, rather than the analyst's actual behavior, which is the primary determinant of the patient's response. In his wish to emphasize the idiosyncratic manner in which the patient understands an external event, Brenner assumes an optimal analyst and deemphasizes the possibility that the patient may be responding, in a largely appropriate manner, to actual failures of a less-than-optimal analyst. Referring to this view, Stone (1981) writes:

> [I]t is overlooked that a real grievance, even though germane to individual personality structure (as are all responses), cannot be equated with a pure transference response and similarly reduced. The admission and correction of the analyst's error or of his failure of prior adequate explanation of a deprivation might, in some instances, render such an interpretation effective or at least restore such a possibility for the future. How a patient listens to interpretations, how he utilizes them, indeed the entire complex matter of his will to recover, are influenced by such considerations, as they are by the state of transference with which the adult attitudes are in constant, if fluctuating, interaction. But it must not be ignored that it is between the two adults that it all begins and ends. "What sort of person is this to whom I am entrusting my entire mental and emotional being?" [p. 169]

Ultimately there is embedded in the analytic situation, along with the transference, a new object relationship. This is why Stone, throughout his writings, states that a human error is far worse for the analysis than a technical error.

The Roles of Insight and Experience

We may ask at this point why the nontransference aspect of the analyst–patient relationship has not been accorded more theoretical recognition within the classical theory of analytic technique. Even a concept such as the working alliance—which, according to Lipton, is an attempt to bring the personal relationship (thrown out the front door in reaction to Alexander) back in through the rear door—remains controversial (Brenner 1979). Several reasons are suggested. Lipton, in his discussion of Eissler's paper on parameters, notes that Eissler explicitly excluded the analyst's personality from consideration. Lipton (1977) writes that "the effect of Eissler's attempt to exclude the personality of the analyst from his *discussion* of a model technique has been the exclusion of the personality of the analyst in *fact* from a model technique" (p. 265).

Friedman (1978) touches on this issue in his discussion of analysts' resistance at the Edinburgh conference to consideration of mutative factors other than insight. Friedman suggests that this resistance was related to competition from competing theories of psychotherapy. For one, interpretation and insight were what made analysis unique, and analysts wanted to emphasize what was unique about their mode of treatment rather than what was common to all therapies. Further, to speak of the therapist-patient relationship as having its own mutative effect might verge on acceptance of competing theories, ranging from object relations theory (at that time and now) and interpersonal approaches to analysis (in today's times).

Friedman also writes of analysts' concerns that opening the door to the mutative potential of the analyst–patient relationship would lead to role-playing which would both bind the analyst in the patient's transference web and restrict the patient's freedom to explore varying transference predispositions. Analysts wanted distance from their patient's affective predispositions and preferred to rely on objective truth to give their interpretations healing power. Friedman indicates that these objections were logically questionable and that the objections related to a somewhat illogical fear that to open the door to factors other than insight would be theoretically questionable and would be more difficult to control.

We have seen that, for one group of analysts who emphasize particular aspects of Freud's work, the focus in psychoanalysis is on interpretation as the sole mutative factor, and the analyst's role is that of interpreter of intrapsychic conflict as it emerges in the transference. The experience between patient and analyst is seen as transferential; it is not emphasized as helpful in supporting interpretation, nor is it understood as mutative in its own right, as part of a new object relationship. For these analysts, to posit that such experience is useful in its own right is to open Pandora's box to a host of difficulties, as Friedman (1978) has hypothesized and as we see in Brenner's (1979) criticism of the working alliance. How can one have experience that is understood as nontransferential? If such experience exists, then an aspect of the relationship is not analyzed, and this is both theoretically and clinically impossible. If, on the other hand, all experience is thought to be transferential, then it must be analyzed, and the real person of the analyst becomes irrelevant. These questions are the basis for the views of this group of analysts.

Lipton and Stone enlarge the picture of the analyst's role. They bring in the experience between analyst and patient, not as a mutative factor in its own right, but as something that supports the analytic process and facilitates insight through interpretation of transference. Experience supports interpretation, but neither supplants interpretation nor achieves a mutative role of its own. The role of the analyst is thus broadened, since experience occurs with a person who is more than a sum total of transference. The relationship exists openly and is not brought in through the back door.

While the relationship exists, and the analyst's role is broadened, the theoretical mechanism for this expanded role is not fully elaborated, although Stone does several times refer to the parent–child model, especially in his conception of the analytic situation and its frustration of "deprivation in intimacy." It is Loewald (1960) who brings the analyst–patient relationship into a theoretically central position. As he does so, he expands on the analyst's function and he makes prominent the mutative role of experience. Experience between patient and analyst is now important not only as support to interpretation, but also as a mutative factor in its own right. Interpretation remains the central feature of analysis, but it is understood to work in tandem with new experience. We will discuss Loewald's contributions in Chapter 9.

9

The Right and Left Wings
of Classical Technique:
The Influence of Hans Loewald

Loewald's conception of the analyst's stance is a logical outgrowth of his ideas about the nature of instincts, defenses, and psychological development. Loewald's views differ from the ideas advanced by those who represent what is often considered to be the "classical" psychoanalytic stance. Stone (1981) has described the classical technique as actually "neoclassical" and Lipton (1977) has termed it "standard" technique. We will refer to the classical emphasis as the right wing of psychoanalytic theory, and to Loewald's views as the left wing. It should be emphasized that these categorizations are broad and tend to overlap. We will examine and stress their differences and assume their substantial areas of agreement. In our discussion of these different emphases, we will stress how various conceptions of the psychoanalytic stance are an outgrowth of initial metapsychological assumptions.

293

The Right Wing of Classical Thought

METAPSYCHOLOGICAL ASSUMPTIONS

1. Instincts are biologically driving forces that impinge on what will become a psychological system, and that seek any object for satisfaction. The psychic apparatus is a closed system, and instincts work on a reflex-arc model. Objects are so termed because they are interchangeable vehicles for instinctual satisfaction. The child is initially separated from his objects, and the separation is overcome as the instinct cathects an object. The object relationship itself is secondary to instinctual satisfaction.

2. The environment (civilization and reality, along with the child's parents and later authority figures) is opposed to such satisfaction, and so the child internalizes controls through fear. That is, because the child fears that attempts to satisfy his wishes might lead to a developmentally evolving sequence of psychological dangers (loss of object, loss of object's love, castration anxiety, fear of the superego), he learns to modify and control his wishes through formation of internal structures (the ego and superego). Defense is emphasized in this model since a strong ego can protect the organism from disruptive instinctual wishes and their consequences.

3. While Freud acknowledges the role of primary identifications, he emphasizes the role of secondary identifications; thus Freud's emphasis on identification with the aggressor (the castrating father) as important in superego formation.

4. Frustration is crucial in the child's relinquishing his original instinctual wishes and accepting the demands of reality. The infant initially reacts to instinctual demands with hallucination, reflecting primary-process functioning. Optimal frustration of hallucination leads to secondary-process functioning, reality testing, and satisfaction of instinctual derivatives.

THE PSYCHOANALYST'S STANCE

These metapsychological assumptions lead to the following assumptions about clinical psychoanalytic work:

1. Pathology is the result of intrapsychic conflict, or conflict between formed internal structures (id, ego, and superego). This emphasis on conflict is maintained for patients of all diagnostic categories. In comparing neurotic and borderline conditions, Arlow writes that "The interplay of forces . . . is the same . . . except for the importance of prephallic drives, aggression, and the ease with which ego functions, ordinarily outside the realm of conflict, are brought into the nexus of conflict and are reinstinctualized or regressively altered during the defensive struggle" (Arlow 1964, p. 169).

2. This conflict is ameliorated through interpretation, resulting in insight. The emphasis is on interpretation and insight, rather than on a new experience with the analyst. Concepts stressing new experience are suspect because they are seen as threatening the primacy of insight and leading to the possibility of cure through suggestion.

3. Insight is most effectively gained through analysis of the transference.[1]

4. The analyst is outside the patient's closed psychic system. What defines psychoanalysis is the analyst's choosing to treat all of what the patient says as symbolic, as an expression of unconscious conflict rather than as "realistic" manifest-content communication. The analyst accomplishes this through what Tarachow calls the

---

[1]There is some disagreement about the comparative efficacy of interpreting transference only versus interpreting matters that are not transferential as well (Gray 1973, Leites 1977). The stress on insight through interpretation remains central, regardless of the area of interpretive focus.

"therapeutic barrier." Within this barrier, "the *real* situation is transformed into an as-if situation demanding attention and comprehension" (Tarachow 1962, p. 379, his emphasis). The analyst is essentially a mirror, a blank screen, the patient's creation. These concepts are understood broadly, as pertaining to the total analyst–patient relationship. The mutative factor in analysis is interpretation of intrapsychic conflict—that is, conflict within that closed system. The relationship between patient and analyst, unaccompanied by interpretation, is not mutative in its own right.

5. The analyst is neutral. He is an accurate reflector of the patient's projections, and he avoids reacting to the patient as the patient would transferentially wish. In other words, the analyst reacts the same way regardless of the transference. Neutrality allows him to maintain scientific objectivity and to be a tabula rasa.[2]

6. The analyst stands for "reality" in that he is the representative of secondary-process functioning and the source of the working alliance, through which irrational wishes are analyzed in the light of rationality. Further, since the analyst is seen as existing outside the patient's closed system, the process by which he or she ultimately (at the end of analysis) comes to know the analyst as a non-transference figure and to accept that initial transference wishes cannot be satisfied and must be modified, replicates the developmental process through which the child must succumb to the demands of reality through optimal frustration of object-directed drives. By coming to terms with the analyst as a representative of reality, the patient is able to come to terms with reality itself.

---

[2]The analyst may be scientific, objective, neutral, a surgeon, a blank screen, etc. without necessarily being cold to the patient. I have discussed elsewhere (1988) how aim-inhibited love is part of the psychoanalytic stance, even for "right-wing" analysts.

7. It is assumed that competent analysts are interchangeable—that is, that the specific character of the competent, analyzed analyst will not significantly alter the treatment. This is because the patient's feelings are assumed to be primarily transferential in nature, and thus superimposed upon the already-analyzed analyst who, by definition, does not bring his conflicts into the analysis. If the analyst's own feelings do become too strongly activated, it is understood as countertransference—seen as the analyst's problem and not related to the analyst–patient interaction. Scientific research is a model for psychoanalysis, where the researcher (analyst) is outside the object of study (patient), and where the object of research is not affected by the person studying it.

8. Gratification is understood within the sphere of drive theory—that is, as gratification of libidinal derivatives, which ought to be analyzed rather than gratified. Gratification of transference demands is unnecessary; it is based on misunderstanding of technique or on countertransference, and it is always frowned upon. It is optimal *frustration* of instinctual wishes which leads to their appearance as analyzable transference wishes and to the patient's eventually dealing with these wishes through analysis, reality-testing, and increased secondary-process functioning.

The Left Wing of Classical Thought

We can contrast this position with that of left-wing classical Freudian analysts. Although many analysts have made some of these points, it is Loewald who has most systematically extended aspects of Freud's thought. The body of this work challenges the assumptions of the right-wing group in the following ways. We begin with the metapsychological assumptions.

METAPSYCHOLOGICAL ASSUMPTIONS

1. Loewald believes that Freud modified his view of instincts from the reflex-arc model, where the aim is satisfaction and the object is variable, to a conception of the id, along with the ego, as pursuing synthesis. The id relates to its environment and is organized *by* its environment, although on a lower level of organization than the ego. Instincts are not forces pressing on the mind (defined as instrument) from the outside; rather, they are drives that are organized and represented by the mind (defined as organism) from its inception.[3] Like the parent and the child, the analyst and the patient, through interpretation, organize and integrate inchoate instinct at higher levels. This process occurs, for example, when the mother recognizes and names a need and fulfills it until the child can recognize and fulfill it on his own. As a need is satisfied, the environment is simultaneously reshaping the need at a higher level of psychological organization.

   In this view of instinct, there is no initial separation of child and mother; rather, the child and the mother form a unified system, from which the child gradually separates. It is the object relationship and its effect on the structuring of drives which is emphasized, rather than the drives and their effect on the child's finding of objects.

2. While Loewald has written important papers on the Oedipus complex, he also focuses on the child's preoedipal environment.

3. Loewald emphasizes the role of primary identifications, which take place in the child's early psychological unity

---

[3]For Loewald (1971) an instrument, such as a tool or camera, is used by people for certain definable purposes. An organism is the center of its own activity. It has its own purpose, and it influences the environment even as it is influenced by the environment.

with the mother, as well as of secondary identifications, which take place after differentiation from the mother. For Loewald, identification is not the consolation prize the child receives as he gives up instinctual satisfaction or the lost object; rather, it is a major developmental achievement in its own right, because it allows the child to form an enduring psychological world of his own. Loewald views internalization, in addition to defense, as what is unique and "healthy" about the ego. Loewald emphasizes that internalization is a continuing process, and that internalizations may become part of the ego. Thus, at its highest level, an identification may become so well-integrated into one's personality that the origin of the identification will no longer be noticeable. An ego relying on defense must keep unchanged instinctual wishes repressed, whereas an ego that has allowed various internalizations has accepted these wishes into its structure and has become enriched in the process.

4. Frustration is not central in the child's acceptance of reality. Loewald's focus is on how the child learns to retain its original mother–child psychological field at higher levels of abstraction, rather than on how the child learns to accept frustration of its instinctual wishes. Although the child must relinquish the original concrete form of its connection, it develops psychological structure as a vehicle for connection on an internal, and more abstract, plane. Thus structure is developed as a means of maintaining the original mother–child connection rather than as a means for the child to safely cope with a threatening reality. The child not only *submits* to reality, he *embraces* it; he makes it *his* reality in a manner that gives it zest and meaning, because by accepting reality, the child is accepting a world that contains within it remnants of the original mother–child bond. Since one version of the child's reality originally meant the experience of oneness with mother, the child learns to accept

reality in many of its other versions as well. This is very different from seeing reality as opposed to the experience contained in instinctual gratification. In the latter view, acceptance of reality requires coming to terms with frustration and with a cold, stark world of compromise and second-best.[4]

These metapsychological assumptions lead to the following assumptions about clinical psychoanalytic work:

1. The neurotic patient, by definition, has attained a relatively well-developed internal psychological structure, and neurosis is understood as the result of intrapsychic conflict. However, the left-wing analysts are quite sensitive both to more seriously disturbed patients, who have not yet adequately achieved internal structure (patients traditionally understood to be inappropriate for unmodified psychoanalysis), and to the processes through which structure becomes established.

   The developmental context within which intrapsychic conflict occurs, a context that is either assumed or not fully considered by Arlow (1964), becomes the focus of attention in treatment of the borderline patient. It does not replace focus on conflict, but it accompanies such a focus. Even with regard to neurosis, left-wing analysts focus on the *developmental strengths and achievements* of childhood which make neurosis (as opposed to more serious disturbance) possible. Analysts in the right

---

[4]Loewald's emphasis on adaptation is similar to Hartmann's (1958) stress on the ego's adaptive efforts. There are, however, major differences, which do not fall within the present discussion. Hartmann's view finds an incompatibility between ego and id, and speaks of the ego's strength in adapting to reality. For Loewald, there is also strength to be gained from the permeability between ego and id. Such permeability is thought to strengthen the ego in its overall adaptive efforts.

wing emphasize the *conflicts* of childhood which persist as fixations and form the nucleus of adult neurotic difficulty. Analysts of both wings emphasize conflict. However, for analysts of the left wing, conflict (found at any diagnostic level) is not, in itself, the defining trait of neurosis. Rather, it is adequate development of internal tripartite structure which defines neurosis.

2. Loewald agrees that interpretation is crucial, not only because it allows the ego power over the id, in a closed psychological system, but also because it allows the ego to organize id material at a higher level of development within the patient–analyst object relationship. Insight may also function as a marker of change within an object relationship that has mutative properties of its own. That is, some internalization of the analyst occurs in analysis, and this is also a mutative factor.

3. Loewald agrees that analysis of transference is primary.

4. The analyst's role is broadened considerably, however. The analyst creates an environment within which transference and its analysis are possible.

> The transference neurosis, in the sense of reactivation of the childhood neurosis, is set in motion not simply by the technical skill of the analyst, but by the fact that the analyst makes himself available for the development of a new object relationship between the patient and the analyst. [Loewald 1960, p. 234]

In this context we can see why, for Grunes, it is "therapeutic permeability" which makes possible establishment and analysis of transference, while for Tarachow it is the opposite, the "therapeutic barrier," which enables transference and its analysis.

The new object relationship between patient and analyst is based on the patient's rediscovery of the way in which he has developed his usual manner of object relations, which leads to "new discovery of objects" rather than "discovery of new objects" (Loewald 1960, pp. 225, 229). In the former case, the focus is on the patient's insight into how he has distorted objects because of unconscious transference wishes. As these distortions are analyzed, the patient newly discovers objects. In the latter case, the goal is to replace old objects with new ones, in the person of the analyst. In specifying the former over the latter conception, Loewald avoids corrective emotional experience, focusing instead on the analysis of transference.

Analysis includes periods of ego disorganization and organization, with the former taking place because the analyst offers the patient the opportunity for a new object relationship. This opportunity, which the patient attempts to turn into a repetition of old object relationships, is what gives the patient courage for the regressive transference neurosis; it is one meaning of the "positive transference." The analyst, as new object, "has to possess certain qualifications in order to promote the process" (Loewald 1960, p. 225). Loewald's understanding of the analyst's dual role in facilitating regression and interpreting it within the context of a new relationship has also been echoed by Stone (1961), Fox (1984), and Freedman (1985).

5. Concepts such as the analyst as mirror, blank screen, or surgeon are understood in a limited, technically restricted way. Neutrality is understood as pertaining to the analyst–patient object relationship, in addition to its implications for analytic listening. Neutrality has a "positive nature" (p. 230) that enables the analyst to help the patient become what is inherent *in* him, rather than what the analyst wishes *for* him. Loewald gives the example of the parents who see and deal with their child as he or she is now, but also project in their minds what the child might become years later, attempting to guide the child from where he is now to where he could be in the future. Loewald (1960) writes:

Through all the transference distortions the patient reveals rudiments at least of the core of himself and "objects" that has been distorted. It is this core, rudimentary and vague as it may be, to which the analyst has reference when he interprets transference and defenses, and not some abstract concept of reality or normality, if he is to reach the patient. If the analyst keeps his central focus on this emerging core he avoids moulding the patient in the analyst's own image or imposing on the patient his own concept of what the patient should become. It requires an objectivity and neutrality the essence of which is love and respect for the individual and for individual development. . . . [p. 229]

6. The analyst stands for reality in that, through the relationship with the analyst, the patient is helped to want to take on the demands of reality. The analyst is not only the external representative of reality; he is also the object through which reality comes to have affective meaning for the patient. Reality becomes suffused with the patient's transferential experience with the analyst, just as, for the child, reality is the medium of increasingly sophisticated means of connection with early objects. Here, the analyst–patient interaction is similar to the developmental process whereby secondary-process functioning emerges out of initial object relationships.

7. The analyst's personality makes a difference. Analysts are not interchangeable. Analyses with different analysts, even if they are equivalently experienced and analyzed, are different, even though the analyses may deal with similar issues. The scientific model, with its separation of subject and object, presents difficulties, both in its emphasis on science as the highest form of knowledge and in its assumption of the detached scientist. Given that the analysis succeeds because the patient forms a working alliance with the analyst (the analyst allies himself with the patient's observing ego), then this observ-

ing ego depends on the patient's identifying with the analyst. Thus, rather than the analysis depending only on the analyst's scientific *distance*, it also depends on his *involvement* (Loewald 1960, p. 227).

8. Gratification is unnecessary with the neurotic patient, but with the more disturbed patient it is useful and sometimes necessary. Here, however, gratification is understood as satisfying an object relationship that is developmentally necessary. Without such gratification, which is usually implicit and in the background of the analysis, analysis of transference is seen as impossible.

These differing emphases within classical analytic theory lead to differing research interests, differing conceptions of the therapeutic possibilities in supportive and expressive therapy, and differing attitudes toward the degree of flexibility in the analytic stance.

Within the left wing, analysts' research interests lie in issues that are central to treatment of the borderline patient. These include transitional relatedness (Bach 1985, Modell 1976, 1978), annihilation anxiety (Hurvich 1985), the process of psychological transformation in analysis (Freedman 1985), the interpretive moment (Pine 1984), the patient's finding his personal sense of reality and meaning (Bach 1985, Loewald 1951, Steingart 1983), and the role of the therapeutic object relationship in analysis (Grunes 1984).

These issues reflect a focus on developmental processes as they affect structure formation and analytic work, rather than concern with describing the interaction of formed psychological structures in conflict, which is the leading research interest of the right wing. While left-wing analysts certainly focus on analysis of intrapsychic conflict in their clinical work, they also pay particular attention to issues such as the patient's movement from reliance on discharge to increased capacity for symbolization (Freedman 1985), and the patient's accepting the demands of reality as belonging to him rather than as something to which he must submit (Bach 1985, Loewald 1951).

The differing valuations that analysts in these two groups place on the mutative roles of insight and internalization also lead to different valuations of supportive and expressive therapies. For the right wing, these therapies are limited in scope. This is because they do not lead to complete analysis of transference and therefore to the most lasting resolution of intrapsychic conflict. Instead, the mutative factors are seen as lying in variations of internalization, which are understood as transference cure (Kernberg 1984, Tarachow 1962, Wallerstein and Robbins 1956), based on suppression of certain conflicts.

In contrast, for the left wing, expressive and supportive therapies are viewed more ambitiously. Such therapeutic ambition is possible because this group places greater emphasis on how the therapist–patient object tie assists in the establishment of more fully developed internal structure. The therapeutic process is seen as facilitating eventual interpretation of conflict rather than as obviating such interpretation. What is transference cure for the right wing becomes structure building for the left wing.

The differing emphases between right and left wings also lead to different attitudes toward the degree of flexibility inherent within the analytic stance. While analysts from both wings see insight through interpretation of transference as the primary goal in analytic work, they disagree on the means of achieving this goal. The clinical differences revolve around the degree to which modification of the classical analytic stance is thought to be necessary in order to work with the more disturbed patient, and the degree to which such modification is seen either as violating central tenets of analytic work or as extending such tenets to patients who are not considered analyzable within the traditional framework. They may be said to revolve around different ways of understanding Freud's (1919) idea that

[t]he patient looks for his substitutive satisfactions above all in the treatment itself, in his transference-relationship with the physician; and he may even strive to compensate himself by this means for all the other privations laid upon him. Some concessions must of course be made to him, greater or less, according to the nature of the case and the patient's individuality. But it is not good to let them become too great. [p. 164]

Borderline, narcissistic, psychotic, and other severely disturbed patients are often considered unanalyzable. Patient characteristics that are assumed in discussions of the classical analytic stance cannot be assumed for these more severely disturbed patients. These characteristics include sufficiently autonomous ego functioning so that a working alliance is maintained throughout a transference regression; capacity for controlled regression in the service of the ego; capacity to use words that adequately convey internal states; capacity to maintain, with the therapist, a joint state of reality; and willingness to accept the inherent frustrations of reality and secondary-process functioning (such as having to speak in order to be understood). These and other factors are not present in the severely disturbed patient for a multitude of reasons, including interactions of conflict and deficit.

The right-wing emphasis has led to limited options in analytic work with more severely disturbed patients. They are generally considered unanalyzable and, effectively, ruled out of consideration within psychoanalysis proper. Abend et al. (1983) write that, for higher-level borderline patients, no alterations in the classical stance are necessary. Others, such as Eissler (1953), have felt that limited alterations in the stance were sometimes indicated, and have developed the concept of parameters of technique to deal with such changes that do not violate the classical stance. However, the concept of parameters is an ambiguous and limited one, as we saw in Chapter 5, and many patients require alterations in the therapeutic stance that go well beyond parameters. Theories of supportive and expressive therapies have been developed to deal with these patients' difficulties, but, as we saw in Chapter 3, these therapies have been devalued within the analytic community and they have been thought to be of limited success. As we noted in Chapter 1, other models have been developed to deal with problems posed by the severely disturbed patient, each with its own strengths and weaknesses.

An emphasis based on Loewald's work (the left wing) allows therapists to work analytically with this kind of patient in a way which allows them to remain within the rubric of psychoanalytic theory, and yet be more flexible in their stance. These analysts emphasize the manner in which certain developmental tasks must be accomplished in order for the patient to experience and analyze object-directed wishes toward a transferentially experienced other. They focus on this process in their work, particularly on the role of the therapeutic object relationship in developing the capacity for an analyzable transference neurosis. The increased emphasis on the analyst's adaptation to the patient within a broad analytic framework leads to greater emphasis on the importance of the patient's experience with the analyst in facilitating the development of a transference neurosis and its analysis through interpretation. It is from this perspective that issues such as the working alliance, the patient's experience of reality, regression, abstinence, and gratification become central.

Analysts in this group do not view their work on early developmental difficulties as preparation for later analysis. They do not consider their experience with the patient to have led to unanalyzable transference fantasies which require referral to a new analyst for resolution. On the contrary, they see the treatment as an integral whole. Regarding such early work in analysis with a patient, Bach (1985) writes: "I do not consider this a preparatory phase before the analysis begins; this *is* the analysis, conducted in another way" (p. 224).

The right- and left-wing theoretical emphases lead to differing conceptions of the working alliance, reality, regression, abstinence, and gratification. We will begin with the concept of the working alliance.

The Working Alliance

For right-wing analysts, the concept of a working alliance presents major theoretical problems. Analysts have long argued about whether the therapeutic relationship can usefully be thought of as having different components, most broadly a regressive, transferential component and a more reflective, rational component. Adler (1980) differentiates these aspects as follows: "The alliance aspects support looking, reflecting, examining, and insight. The transference supports attachment and emotional involvement" (p. 549). Although prominent analysts have emphasized the difference between these aspects (see Zetzel's 1970 concept of the therapeutic alliance and Greenson's [1967] concept of the working alliance), most analysts today emphasize the unitary nature of the patient–therapist relationship. That is, while they may discuss different emphases or aspects of the relationship by focusing on the transference or on the alliance because such distinctions are clinically useful, they understand these components as stemming from a unitary factor (see, for example, Friedman 1969).

Adler (1980) has argued that a self–object transference is operative in all treatment; it is less prominent with the neurotic patient, more prominent with the narcissistic patient. This self-object transference is the basis for the therapeutic alliance. Adler stresses that an autonomous therapeutic alliance is the *result* of an analysis, and that heavy-handed didactic statements about the alliance to patients at the start of treatment "can be used to obscure the fact that the analyst is not empathically in touch with his patient and is appealing to reason when he does not understand the patient" (p. 555).

Adler suggests that there are times when the analyst may err by responding to a patient's demands for concrete gratification by didactically reminding him of the working alliance or by sharing more about himself. Such information is only helpful if, by chance, it reestablishes the self–object transference, the rupture of which, Adler hypothesizes, is the motive for the patient's demands on the therapist. Self-revelation by the analyst or cognitive information about the working relationship could be seen by the patient as a second breach of empathy, however, and might lead to further disappointment followed by an escalation of demands. Thus, for Adler, the working alliance is sustained by an irrational transference. The analyst's empathy for his patient's narcissistic needs supports a climate within which interpretive work is possible.

Brenner (1979) has also argued that separation into alliance and transference is not useful, although his theoretical point of reference is quite different from Adler's. For Brenner, the patient is motivated by irrational, unconscious, and conflicted wishes which must be analyzed in a climate of neutrality and abstinence. Interpretation and the working alliance are not supported by these irrational transference wishes but, in fact, are threatened by them. The analyst, therefore, must focus on analysis of these wishes rather than on their empathic acknowledgment. A working alliance is understood from the start of treatment, and it need not be addressed specifically by the analyst during the treatment's course.

Brenner argues that the analyst's function is to analyze the patient, and that to separate certain elements of the patient's behavior as "real" and that of the analyst's behavior as "building the working alliance" means that one does not correctly analyze elements of the patient's behavior and that one substitutes changes in the analyst's behavior for interpretive comments. The analyst does not have to make comments that are not interpretive in order to build an alliance. Thus Brenner and Adler agree that the totality of the patient's relationship with the analyst rests on an emotional factor, but they disagree on the definition of this factor. Brenner emphasizes irrational transferential wishes, which are the product of intrapsychic conflict, while Adler emphasizes the sustaining foundation provided by a form of self–object transference that stems from prestructural phases. For both, the cognitive aspect of the relationship—the working alliance—arises from these roots. For Brenner, however, these roots represent irrational wishes which threaten the tenuous alliance; insight is wrested from these roots through interpretation. For Adler, the irrational wishes are more sustaining than threatening; insight is supported by the transference.

We can understand Brenner's position as reflecting the metapsychological assumptions of the right wing analysts. If we understand the alliance to reflect the patient's assumption of reality in the analysis—that is, his hold on the observing and analyzing aspect of the analysis—we can see that Brenner views the patient's assumption of that alliance as inherently suspect. Reality (the alliance) must be guarded by analyst abstinence. Since the patient ultimately does not want reality, but prefers transference gratification, the analyst's gratification (that is, violation of abstinence) jeopardizes the alliance and therefore the entire analysis.

If we make these assumptions, it becomes difficult to understand the therapist's efforts to modify the therapeutic relationship for a disturbed patient. Such interventions are designed to create a particular atmosphere or ambiance and are not, in themselves, interpretive. Those who believe that the analyst should confine himself to interpreting seem trapped in a conceptual dilemma. They are theoretically against the concept of a separate alliance, but they have no other way to understand the many subtle ways in which they modify their interventions for the more disturbed patient. Thus they practice what they do not preach and view their own interventions with suspicion.

Curtis (1979), for example, who deplores an overemphasis on the therapeutic alliance, discusses "special interventions to shore up the capacity to work analytically" (p. 174). Such interventions include letting the patient use the couch at his own pace, speaking frequently, answering questions, stressing that the patient's feelings are understandable, and so forth. He gears interventions to his disturbed patient's level of functioning, yet he sees these interventions as a separate aspect of the therapeutic relationship. He seems suspicious theoretically of what he values clinically. Curtis writes:

> Because it is clear that the real relationship does play a significant part in the total analytic process, it is important to define its place in such a way that it does not pre-empt the central role traditionally assigned to the analytic resolution of intrapsychic conflict by interpretation of transference and resistance. [p. 187]

In contrast, left-wing analysts do not necessarily believe that the patient only accepts reality (in this case, the working alliance) reluctantly. While it is certainly true that these analysts would focus much of the analysis on the patient's attempts to obtain transference gratification rather than insight, they would not necessarily view the patient's assumption of reality, as manifest in the working alliance, as a grudging acceptance of reality through frustration, an acceptance which is constantly threatened by gratification. They might see that, for certain disturbed patients, some forms of background gratification *increase* their willingness to assume the demands of reality and to analyze (rather than act), whereas frustration of certain object needs increases their propensity toward action rather than analysis.

This view is supported by Adler's (1980) belief that the patient's reflective awareness is at its best when the self-object transference is at its peak. The idea is expressed within a more classical perspective by Grunes (1984), who sees the entire range of therapist interventions as a unitary "therapeutic object relationship" in which both relationship and interpretation play central roles. Grunes does not believe that certain forms of implicit gratification of object needs are opposed to insight. Instead, he advocates unification of the real and transference relationship, with this relationship facilitating the capacity for insight and being, in itself, the "primary matrix of change."

In Grunes's concept of the therapeutic object relationship, we see a view of the connection between the working alliance and the transference that differs from Brenner's. For Brenner, the transferential dimension is the focus of treatment. The working alliance is assumed, not built through extrainterpretive means. It is one of the criteria for analyzability, and it is sustained by the patient's capacity for autonomous ego functioning. The working alliance is based on the patient's belief that he has a job to accomplish, rather than on his relationship with the therapist. The patient works analytically because he accepts the analyst's working plan rather than because he wants the analyst's love (see Friedman 1969). The latter would be seen as a form of transference, not working alliance. The analyst, then, does not have to focus explicitly on the alliance. Instead, the analyst's rational ego, in collaboration with the patient's rational ego, seeks out the manner in which transference has seeped into what are seemingly the most innocuous patient–therapist interactions. It is a constant struggle, and it depends on the therapist's steadfast determination to avoid seduction by the patient's insistence on the "reality" of an interaction. The therapist must remain abstinent, neutral, and nongratifying in the service of the higher goal of analysis. This follows a metapsychological position that sees the ego as mediating between reality demands and id and superego demands.

Grunes writes in the metapsychological tradition of Loewald (1980). For Grunes, the underpinnings of the working alliance rest on more than the patient's inherent assumption of reality, independent of the analyst (that is, the patient's autonomous ego functions). Rather, the alliance (and development of these ego functions) is nourished and sustained by the analyst–patient relationship. The therapeutic relationship is what makes the therapeutic work possible and meaningful. As Grunes (1984) describes it, with reference to the treatment situation:

> In my view, the therapeutic alliance is constituted and motivated by the primal intimacy of the empathic therapeutic relationship; and is therefore integral to the treatment, rather than detached from, or imposed upon it. The ego of reality and adaptation requires nourishment from retained levels of earlier ego modes of relatedness. In this framework there is also less need to take explicit notice of the treatment alliance to consciously appeal to it, for it will operate more automatically because of the depth of its motivational roots. . . . When the analysis of pathological transference, which cannot be therapeutically gratified, is excessively divided from the real relationship, the problem of what does the analyst gratify is significantly increased. The analyst of the treatment proper is overly associated with frustration, and the analyst of gratification is overly associated with the suspension of the analysis proper and the provision of a reality relationship—a relationship I have already described as overly rational. Within the therapeutic object relationship it is possible to meet symbolically defined needs for affiliation, empathic and communicative needs as well as nondefensive aspects of primal and childhood transference. Such forms of need satisfaction do not appear to interfere with the maintenance of the therapeutic tension level needed for free association and fantasy formation. [p. 139]

Grunes's conception of the analyst's role is broader than that of the right wing. He emphasizes Loewald's (1980) view of the analyst over Brenner's (1976). The relationship between patient and analyst—composed of transferential and nontransferential elements—facilitates insight and interpretation rather than threatening it. Such a conception allows us to understand more clearly the noninterpretive steps taken by Curtis and others. As we have seen, both left- and right-wing analysts advocate adaptation to the patient. However, if we compare Curtis's (1979) paper on the therapeutic alliance or Eissler's (1953) paper on parameters with Grunes's (1984) paper on the therapeutic object relationship, Bach's (1985) paper on "Classical technique and the unclassical patient," or Pine's (1984) paper on the interpretive moment, we immediately see that, for the right wing, these efforts at adaptation to the patient's level of functioning are regarded with suspicion and with the fear that they will become unanalyzable deviations from an optimal psychoanalytic position. From the left wing's perspective, these attempts to mold to the patient's level of functioning are not only an integral part of the analytic stance; they support the overall analytic process.

The Patient and Reality

Psychoanalytic theory has generally assumed that the patient and the analyst share a common reality. The classical emphasis has been on the patient's capacity for reality testing, an ego function assumed for the nonpsychotic analytic patient. The patient's own *experience* of reality was rarely studied in its own right. Loewald (1951) has examined the individual's evolving reality experience. He describes a continuum from "subjective" to "objective" reality. The capacity to experience objective reality is a developmental achievement, mediated through object relationship. Different states of reality, and the process through which patient and analyst come to share objective reality, may themselves assume analytic focus.

Loewald (1951) discusses the process whereby the child comes to accept reality and the objective external world. He reviews two different emphases in Freud's work. In both, external reality is first experienced as the child's primary narcissism is broken. The child then becomes aware of the outside, and a tension system is set up whereby the child seeks to reestablish the original unity between himself and his mother. It is through satisfaction of tension that the child attempts to maintain this unity. That is, by making the mother a "libidinal object," the child maintains a certain form of object connection.

Freud's main emphasis is on the manner through which the Oedipus complex leads to the child's final acceptance of reality. Here the focus is on the libidinal aspects of the object relationship. The father represents a hostile reality that prohibits gratification of sexual wishes. The child must submit to and identify with the aggressor. Internal modification (internalization, superego formation) results from this coerced submission. For Freud, the concept of reality is closely linked with a formulation of the father as a hostile figure whom the child must fight or to whom he must submit. Loewald (1951) writes:

> Reality, then, is represented by the father who as an alien, hostile, jealous force interferes with the intimate ties between mother and child, forces the child into submission, so that he seeks the father's protection. The threat of hostile reality is met by unavoidable, if temporary, submission to its demands, namely to renounce the mother as a libidinal object, and to acknowledge and submit to paternal authority. [p. 7]

The father interferes with the child in a way that ensures

> that the ego essentially is on the defensive, and in fact becomes the defensive agency within the psychic apparatus. The interference is directed against the strivings for gratification of the libidinal urges toward the mother, and under the assault of reality (father) the psychic apparatus undergoes a series of modifications, repressions, deflections of its original tendencies, the structural representative of which is the ego. [p. 8]

For Freud, however, reality was also connected with the beginnings of ego—that is, with primary identifications. Here the focus is on the total object relationship rather than on its drive components. Loewald believes that Freud's second conception of the way in which the child comes to know and accept reality did not achieve the theoretical emphasis of the first. In this second conception, the child's acceptance of reality has to do with the ego's attempt to recapture primary narcissism, but on successively higher levels of organization. Thus Loewald sees an initial unity between mother and child (rather than an initial separation, as in the former view). Reality emerges as the child perceives a difference between himself and his mother. It becomes the medium through which the child continues to maintain an affective connection with the mother. Now, however, the connection is made through verbal means and through sharing in a joint experience, rather than through concrete satisfaction of libidinal wishes. For Loewald, the primary purpose of ego is not defense, but synthesis and integration. The prototype of reality is not castration anxiety, but the aliveness of a permeability between inside and outside, between mother and child, and, later, between unconscious and conscious.

Loewald states that each parent is both a support and a threat for the child. Since reality is based on these initial object relationships, both parents play a part. The father is a castration threat, but the early preoedipal identification with the father helps the child separate from the mother. The mother represents the early omnipotence and primary narcissism, but she later becomes a threat to the child, who fears loss of his identity in merger with her. The father helps the child to defend against the dreaded mother of merger. The ambivalence of relationships with both parents leads to the beginnings of the child's experience of reality.

The child uses positive identifications with both objects (early narcissism with the mother and early identification with the father) as well as anxieties (fear of merger and fear of castration) to differentiate, move to a higher level of organization, and maintain an affective connection in reality. The capacity to accept external reality evolves in tandem with the evolution of object relationship. The child accepts reality as much out of love as out of fear. Connection with reality is valued because loss of this connection means return to earlier and more primitive levels of psychological organization. Loewald (1951) notes that "what the ego defends itself, or the psychic apparatus, against is not reality but the loss of reality . . ." (p. 12).

Loewald provides an understanding of how the child's experience of reality is tied to object relationships, and how the child's experience of external reality and of objects may change as psychological development progresses. Many analysts, from Jacobson (1967) within the classical analytic tradition to Kohut (1971) and others within the self-psychological tradition, have noted that some patients require a certain form of relationship with an external figure in order to maintain both reality-testing and a sense of aliveness in the experience of self, object, and reality itself. Bach (1985) has studied the patient's capacity for "state constancy," which he defines as

the capacity to move freely along a continuum of alternate states and yet, when necessary, to locate ourselves on this continuum with respect to consensual reality. It involves a capacity to give in to our subjective experience while at the same time retaining the capacity to observe and orient ourselves in reality. . . . [It is] a kind of superordinate reflective awareness that permits multiple perspectives on the self. While reality testing has always been considered a developmental achievement, it is sometimes achieved at the expense of an inner world, a fantasy life, the ability to love, or the ability to lend oneself to a transference experience. In such cases . . . we would view this as a conflicted achievement; the more complete achievement would be the capacity to conceive of oneself as the *same* self throughout a multitude of ego states. [p. 179]

State constancy, and the entire topic of the patient's subjective world, has rarely been studied within classical analytic theory. It reflects the influence of Loewald's theoretical contributions. In classical theory, the patient's associations are considered part of an object-related transference, implying the existence of relatively firm self–object boundaries, and a reality that is objective, consensual, and meaningful. The patient's capacity to test reality in itself indicates that these factors have been achieved. Difficulties in patients' experience of reality are seen as the result of dynamic factors (such as fear of projected rage), and analysis of these factors is assumed to lead to a more optimal experience of reality.

It is primarily Bach, within the classical tradition, and the self psychologists, within their own model, who focus on the patient's experience of the world and its relationship to experience of objects as worthy of investigation in its own right. It is not solely dependent on other dynamic factors. Reality testing may be adequate within a certain state of consciousness but inadequate in other states. Further, the capacity for alternation between states becomes an indicator of analyzability—one that is as important as the capacity to maintain reality-testing or other ego functions. Difficulty in state constancy, and fear of regression from a tenuously maintained state of consciousness, may keep a patient reality-bound and fearful of the transference, whereas a patient without such fears might be better able to tolerate regression in the transference even if the regression involved temporary loss of reality-testing.

The therapist working with patients who form an object-oriented transference neurosis has an external, objective perspective. The therapist working with a narcissistic patient, one who has not consolidated a firm sense of self and object, maintains a more subjective and experience-oriented viewpoint. The issues are different for the different patients.

[T]he transference neurotic . . . is trying to find out *what* his ego *wants*, whereas the narcissistic neurotic . . . is trying to find out *who* his self *is*. The transference neurosis speaks an objective language of desire, action, contiguity, and causality; the narcissistic neurosis, a subjective language of being, playing, continuity, and seeking. Whereas in the transference neurosis thought is trial action, in the narcissistic neurosis thought is trial identity. . . . The paradigmatic narcissistic transference may be seen as variations on the metaphor of "who": I am like you; you are like me. The paradigmatic object transference may be seen as variations on the metonymy of "what": What are you doing to me; what am I doing to you or to myself? [Bach 1985, pp. 172–173, his emphasis]

In treatment, Bach focuses on the patient's inner world, which is the patient's "voluntary, spontaneous creation" with a "cathectic attachment" (p. 211) and its own internally consistent form of thought organization. The analyst learns the rules of the patient's world and helps him navigate between his inner world and the world of external reality. In this way, the patient is helped to achieve greater permeability between states, which is an element of state constancy.

The analyst attempts to adopt the patient's perspective as closely as he can, rather than asking the patient to adopt his own perspective. It is hoped that, through self-reflection, the patient will eventually choose to enter the analyst–patient's joint world rather feeling forced to submit to it. Such reflection is facilitated through the analyst's mediation and his observations regarding the patient. That is, self-reflection depends on a degree of internalization. In order for the analyst's observations to be useful in facilitating such reflection by the patient, the observations must be made from within the patient's conceptual framework. This involves the analyst's allowing the treatment to "belong" to the patient as much as possible, and attempting to see things from the patient's point of view, without necessarily accepting it as the only valid point of view.

These beliefs differ from those of right-wing analysts, who, while they do modify their work to adjust for the patient's difficulties, do so reluctantly and attempt to use their modifications to make the patient join *their* perspective on reality. They do so implicitly, by considering the patient's associations solely from the viewpoint of conflict theory. The analyst's task is to point out to the patient the ways in which he is essentially disguising transference wishes. The patient is told that what he desires is unreasonable. It cannot be satisfied because it is conflicted, displaced from the past, and unrealistic. It is in this sense that Tarachow's remark that an interpretation is a deprivation is valid. However, one may also (*also* does not mean *instead*) think of the patient's associations as communication about his private world and attempt to learn from the patient the rules for that world. An intervention that acknowledges that world without implicitly judging it as unreasonable helps the patient to further define who he is rather than what he unreasonably wants. Bach examines the patient's experience and attempts to enter the patient's private world so that the patient can more fully accept the consensual world. His approach is not an active one. Bach does not *do* something different; rather he *is* a certain way. His approach is one of focused listening, along with tolerance for considerable ambiguity and multiple perspectives without an attempt to prematurely resolve them through interpretation. A similar conception of the analyst's stance, albeit one with much more activity by the analyst, has been described by Balint, writing from a differing theoretical perspective. We turn to this now, in a discussion of regression.

Regression: The Work of Balint

Balint has significantly expanded the conception of the analyst's role, especially with regard to gratification of the more disturbed patient. While Loewald writes within the context of classical psychoanalysis, Balint is rooted in British object relations theory. For Balint, a certain type of experience may be essential, in addition to interpretation, in facilitating analytic work. He gives the example of a patient who was able to hear the interpretation that she had spent her life keeping her feet planted on the ground. The patient then says that she has never been able to do a somersault, and Balint suggests that she try one then and there. The patient somersaults in his office and the treatment is advanced.

Balint (1968) terms the somersault "regression for the sake of progression," a necessary experiencing of a new insight in the transference. It is not a manipulation intended to replace interpretive work, nor is it a noninterpretive technique used to get to feelings (such as the technique of speaking to an empty chair, used in psychodrama). One might see it as an experiential symbolic summary and signature to the interpretive work already accomplished. Freedman (1985) understands it as an intervention that allowed the patient to integrate her image of herself as incompetent with her image of what she was actually able to accomplish. Freedman agrees with Balint that, for a patient at this level, the action was the form within which integration took place.

Balint contends that such experience and gratification is necessary for the treatment to move further toward insight. He understands the patient's progress from an object relations framework. He believes that the new object relationship is essential, and he writes of gratifying patients in the service of this new relationship by, for example, giving an extra session or letting a patient hold his finger. These patients were in the midst of regressions, and Balint believed that their needs for relationship should be gratified. The gratification was in tandem with interpretation, either preceding or succeeding it, and was never thought of as replacing interpretive work. Gratification was necessary because Balint (1968) believes that the analyst must provide an atmosphere "in which an individual feels that nothing in the environment is directed towards him and, at the same time, nothing harmful in him is directed towards his environment" (p. 135). This is not seen as a gratification of regression vis à vis instincts or structure; it is understood as meeting a regression in object relationship to a "primary object relationship" or to an earlier phase in which the analyst supplies an environment analogous to sand or air. The analyst "must be pliable to a very high degree; he must not offer much resistance; he certainly must be indestructible; and he must allow his patient to live with him in a sort of harmonious interpenetrating mix-up" (Balint 1986, p. 136). This conception of the analyst is similar to Bach's (1985).

Balint strives to differentiate between regressions that demand this kind of response ("benign regressions") and those that do not ("malignant regressions"). In benign regression, the patient satisfies something in the analyst's presence, in an environment that the analyst has helped to create. The focus is on the patient's act in the analyst's presence, rather than on the analyst's doing something to the patient. In malignant regression, the situation is reversed:

> In the one form the regression is aimed at a gratification of instinctual cravings; what the patient seeks is an external event, an action by his object. In the other form what the patient expects is not so much a gratification by an external action, but a tacit consent to use the external world in a way that would allow him to get on with his internal problems—described by my patient as "being able to reach himself." Although the participation of the external world, of the object, is essential, the participation is entirely different in nature; apart from not interfering with, not causing unnecessary disturbance in, the patient's internal life (two important aspects), the chief form of this expected participation is the recognition of the existence of the patient's internal life and of the patient's own unique individuality. To contrast the two types, I would propose to call the first "regression aimed at gratification" and the second "regression aimed at recognition." [Balint 1968, p. 144]

The analyst supplies this gratification largely through listening, understanding, and tolerance, but sometimes physical contact such as hand-holding is necessary.

> This contact is definitely libidinous, on occasion may even be highly charged, and is always vitally important for the progress of the treatment; with it, the patient can get on, without it he may feel abandoned, lost, despoiled of his possible changes, incapable of moving. [Balint 1986, p. 145]

Balint makes suggestions for how the analyst can gratify, assuming both the theoretical place of gratification and the clinical indications for gratification. His guiding principle is that the analyst should be unobtrusive. Thus he should not interpret everything as transference; to do so makes him a sharply contoured object, rather than part of the environment, and it makes the patient more dependent on him. There are satisfactions that excite and satisfactions that soothe. The latter are most compatible with the analytic situation.

The question of the analyst's accentuating his importance is integrally related to the issue of malignant and benign regression. The more unobtrusive and ordinary the analyst is during periods of regression, the less he excites the patient's omnipotent fantasies and stimulates malignant regression. The analyst ought to accept the patient's nonverbal communication without trying to organize the regression prematurely through interpretation. Words are confusing to regressed patients, and if the analyst is able to magically intuit the patient's meaning, he becomes more omnipotent.

The analyst must offer the patient something. It is preferable to offer the therapeutic setting because the analyst is then less omnipotent, but if the setting is not enough, the analyst offers himself.

> [T]he analyst must function during these periods as a provider of time and of milieu. This does not mean that

he is under obligation to compensate for the patient's early privations and give more care, love, affection than the patient's parents have given him originally.... What the analyst must provide—and, if at all possible, during the regular sessions only—is sufficient time free from extrinsic temptations, stimuli, and demands, including those originating from himself (the analyst). The aim is that the patient should be able to find himself, to accept himself, and to get on with himself, knowing all the time that there is a scar in himself, his basic fault, which cannot be "analyzed" out of existence; moreover, he must be allowed to discover *his* way to the world of objects—and not be shown the "right" way by some profound or correct interpretation. If this can be done, the patient will not feel that the objects impinge on, and oppress him. It is only to this extent that the analyst should provide a better, more "understanding" environment, but in no other way, in particular not in the form of more care, love, attention, gratification, or protection. Perhaps it ought to be stressed that considerations of this kind may serve as criteria for deciding whether a certain "craving" or "need" should be satisfied, or recognized but left unsatisfied. [Balint 1968, pp. 179–180]

For Balint, insight and interpretation are not the mutative factors, although he certainly gives them great importance. Rather, it seems that the patient must regress to his "basic fault" in the analyst's presence. It is recognition and acceptance of his "scar," a "basic fault" which "cannot be analyzed out of existence," in the presence of the analyst which seems necessary in order for the patient to "find his own way" to the analyst and reality and then, presumably, to analysis of object-directed transference wishes. All this occurs within a "holding environment" (Modell 1976, 1978), which has mutative qualities of its own.

Balint's differences from the more classical analysts are apparent. He believes in interpretation, but he gives experience, particularly libidinized gratifications of early object needs, a much more prominent role than do the analysts we have discussed. Further, while Loewald focuses on the organizing aspect of interpretations, Balint downplays this aspect. Interpretations at early stages are impingements, demands that the patient forsake his view of himself and his environment in favor of an external view. Provision of an adequate holding environment is most central, and interpretations tend to interfere. The patient must not feel that the analyst questions the validity of his complaints; such a questioning stance is implicit in the traditional analytic attitude, which assumes that things are not as they appear. It is only later in treatment, when analyst and patient share the same "reality," that interpretations are experienced as helpful.

Regression: The Right-Wing Emphasis

The right-wing conceptualization of regression differs from that of the left wing. These analysts focus more on structural regression, which jeopardizes continuation of a classical, unmodified analysis. The concern is less with facilitating therapeutic regression to an early stage and "meeting" it (Balint's approach) and more with helping the patient continue to benefit from insight into unconscious conflicts in the face of structural regression. For Balint, insight is less important than a new experience. Benign regression is welcomed because it is a step toward a needed new beginning. Accompanying structural regression, which makes insight difficult, is not as feared by the analyst because insight is not given as primary a role.

In contrast, analysts from the right wing maintain the primacy of insight as a mutative factor and, accordingly, see structural regression, which threatens the patient's capacity for insight, as quite threatening to the treatment. Further, while analysts of the British school are willing to go to extraordinary lengths to manage a patient's life during regressive periods, American analysts see such participation in the patient's life as violating the analyst's essential posture and as creating an unanalyzable situation. Finally, Balint seems to assume that the patient's regression is, in itself and on its own merits, developmentally necessary, while right-wing analysts see such regression as serving multiple functions and needing to be analyzed in terms of all its components rather than met (or gratified) based on its overt meaning alone.

In a symposium on regression described by Frosch (1967a,b), most of the participants spoke of maintaining the traditional analytic stance rather than breaking it. For example, in the symposium proceedings, Dickes (1967) argues against Winnicott's belief that the analyst should manage the patient through a regression. He notes that such direct action by the analyst facilitates further regression, involves "role playing" and direct gratification, and is disruptive to an analytic process that is "founded on free association and the frustration of infantile desires" (p. 526).

Dickes believes that direct interventions in the patient's actual life advocated by British analysts gratify infantile needs, and are "outside the scope of analysis" (p. 527). The interventions under consideration ". . . are perhaps commendable acts and may be essential for the continuity of treatment." They should not be "condemned" but can be considered as "aids" in a psychotherapy that prepares a patient for later analysis. The interventions, however, "preclude the usual analytic environment and should therefore be considered among the deviations rather than among the modifications of standard technique." The analyst therefore should remain within the traditional analytic posture.

Dickes is referring to analysts from the British school such as Balint and Winnicott, and he is against such concepts as the corrective emotional experience. Analysts influenced by Loewald (the left wing) would also not directly gratify patients in this overt manner, would agree that such gratification does often lead to further demands and regression, and do not understand role-playing as part of the therapeutic object relationship.

Right-wing analysts view regression as reflecting wishes for inappropriate libidinal gratification rather than for exposure to the analyst of a state of relatedness important in its own right. Atkins writes that "dependency conflicts" must be allowed full emergence in the transference, but that this does not necessarily have to lead to a psychotic transference.

> It is the analyst's responsibility to convey to the patient that it is not only permissible but necessary to reveal the sick child within himself and not to keep it hidden under a mask of pseudonormality. Yet this does not mean that we expect the sick child to take over and dominate the patient's life, including the analysis. To the contrary, correct *interpretations* of the *pathogenic conflicts and the defensive aspects of the regression* tend to diminish this possibility. [Atkins 1967, p. 597, my emphasis]

Atkins goes on to discuss the manner in which regression may involve the patient's acting out of conflict in the transference. He specifically discusses the role of envy in the regression.

Atkins differs from the left-wing analysts in many ways. These analysts focus on the patient's experience of the world as a valid field of inquiry in itself, in addition to its being a product of the patient's conflicts around libidinal and aggressive wishes. For them, the mutative factor is the patient's ability to share his private world with the analyst, as a first step toward the development of the analyst as a libidinal object in a shared world of reality. Interpretation of conflict, while possibly acceptable from one perspective, is, at that moment in treatment, disruptive to the therapeutic process. The patient is not only unable to use the interpretations, but he feels impinged upon and forced to submit to the therapist. For Atkins, the regression is viewed from the classical model of conflict and defense. It is a regression involving conflicts over dependency, rather than conflicts over whether to live in the same phenomenological world as the therapist. To the extent that it is conflictual, it must be resolved through interpretation. Interpretation, which becomes more important later in treatment for the left-wing analysts, is crucial throughout treatment for the right wing.

The patient must be helped to use interpretation, and Atkins does discuss supportive elements inherent in analysis and the possibility of meeting the patient's needs in derivative form. But Atkins (1967) is clear that "we are caring for a sick adult in a state of partial regression rather than an actual infant" (p. 602). He approves of Bion's remark that the analyst must always address himself to a "sane person and is entitled to expect some sane reception" (p. 603). No one would disagree with the first part of this statement. Everyone recognizes that the patient is an adult. However, some might comment that emphasizing the degree to which the patient must be sane is a hidden way of expecting him to conform to an experience of the world that is not yet his. They might argue that the analyst speaks to the sane patient, not by interpreting directly to him, but by silently listening to his perspective and expecting him to recognize that the analyst will accept it without necessarily abandoning his own. By expecting both analyst and patient to tolerate ambiguity, the analyst implicitly speaks to the sane patient.

Finally, for the right-wing analysts, the goal of necessary modifications in treatment is to help the patient with reality-testing; they ignore the patient's relationship with reality and his experience of reality. For example, Dickes (1967) will use the phone with a disturbed patient, not as a transitional object (Adler and Buie 1979), but to enhance reality-testing. He explains

[a]nother mode of relationship to the analyst is established for these patients enhancing his [the analyst's] reality as well as that of the analysis. Some of the isolation of the analyst in his office is thus lifted for the

patient, and the analyst as real and representative of reality becomes more significant. This strengthens the therapeutic alliance *which is basically reality oriented.* [p. 530, my emphasis]

The therapeutic alliance is bolstered by these noninterpretive means, rather than developed through the analyst-patient relationship.

As Frosch (1967b) notes in his discussion of the various papers from the panel on regression, analysts disagree on how to modify technique during periods of severe regression, but most analysts do modify their work. It is their attitude toward these modifications and the different kinds of modifications that they favor that has been our major focus here. They view these modifications as abandonment of analytic work rather than as facilitative of such work.

In our discussion of regression, we have also considered issues of abstinence and gratification. These issues will now be elaborated further.

Abstinence

Casement (1982) has discussed a patient who was severely scalded when she was 11 months old. At the age of 17 months, she required surgery, which was performed under local anesthesia. During the surgery, the patient's mother fainted. The patient had felt panic when her mother fainted and her hands slipped out of her mother's. She felt that she had been seeking the physical contact of her mother's hands since that time, and she asked to hold Casement's hand. Casement said that he would consider the request, believing that it was important for the patient to have this as a possibility in order to get through her fear in the treatment.

As he thought about it over the weekend, he decided that it would be a mistake to hold her hand for several reasons, including the idea that he would be offering to be a better mother than the mother who had fainted. He balanced the gain of supporting the patient through a period of the treatment by providing physical contact versus the loss in insight, and he decided not to hold her hand. He provided the following rationale for refusing:

> If I were to hold this patient's hand it would almost certainly not, as she assumed, help her to get through a re-experiencing of the original trauma. (A central feature of this had been the *absence* of her mother's hands.) It would instead amount to a by-passing of this aspect of the trauma, and could reinforce the patient's perception of this as something too terrible ever fully to be remembered or to be experienced. [Casement 1982, p. 280, his emphasis]

The patient developed a psychotic transference reaction in response to Casement's refusal to hold her hand. He was able to analyze this transference productively, however. He realized that by first considering the possibility of contact and then refusing it, he recapitulated the patient's experience of her mother's first holding her hand and then fainting. Yet he ultimately believed that this violation of the classical conception of abstinence (that is, even considering the possibility of physical contact) and the subsequent reliving of the trauma was useful and necessary for the patient because it made the original trauma vivid in the transference and allowed him to be the surviving and interpreting analyst, rather than the "collapsed analyst" once he had withdrawn the possibility of contact.

Fox (1984) takes Casement's case, along with others, and reviews it in an attempt to enlarge the definition of abstinence. The reader may recall Stone's remark that transference is facilitated when the patient has some, relatively neutral, sense of the analyst (Langs and Stone 1980, p. 113). Fox builds on this idea. In disagreement with Brenner, who minimizes the effect of the average expectable analyst's behavior on the transference, Fox (1984) believes that there is an interactive dimension to the therapeutic process:

> I believe this two-party interaction has a function more complicated than that of merely safeguarding the transference. It is uniquely designed to stimulate desire and to channel its expression into the form which is the transference; that is, the transference is induced by the nature of the interaction, an interaction characterized by an admixture of deprivations and gratifications. [p. 228]

Fox's conception of the analyst can be summarized using Hoffmann's (1983) phrase that the analyst is a "magnet" for transference. Fox discusses three cases as he amplifies on this view. One of these is Casement's case. Fox does not view Casement's considering to hold his patient's hand as a violation of abstinence. Rather, he believes that it is one aspect of abstinence—the positive aspect. For Casement to have held his patient's hand would, Fox agrees, have constituted an offer to be a better mother. But to have immediately refused would not have permitted the transference to develop as it did. A balance is necessary, and this balance was achieved by Casement's agreeing to the *possibility* of holding the patient's hand. Fox (1984) writes:

> [I]f he had originally not allowed the possibility by an immediate resort to the "rule" of abstinence, I believe, he would have become the unempathic surgeon—not a figure for a resolvable transference illusion but instead a figure for a persecutory delusion. In fact, one can read into his ongoing management of the transference illusion/delusion the continuing need to demonstrate his empathic understanding in order to sustain the analysable transference of the mother who failed. As this was being interpreted and worked through there was the constant threat of the reappearance of the delusion of the persecuting surgeon. The closeness–distance issue which made its initial presentation in the form of the request for

holding his hand was managed and partially gratified by the analyst's emotional closeness expressed in his empathic concern. It appeared that a too distant presence was experienced in a persecutory fashion (the surgeon transference), an aspect which was not interpreted. [p. 231]

Fox believes that there are two aspects to abstinence. The negative aspect—that of supplying optimal frustration—has been most emphasized. However, Fox believes that there is also a positive aspect—that of providing enough emotional availability so that the transference illusion becomes possible. It is that balance between frustration and emotional availability which the analyst must maintain. All of this is inherent in the classical analytic stance.

There are certain essential ingredients in the analytic situation which facilitate the patient's capacity for illusion by heightening this tension about the presence/ absence of the analyst. The position on the couch with the analyst out of sight, the relative silence of the analyst and the lack of contact between sessions, all tilt in the direction of absence, aloneness and the need to conjure up that which is needed or desired. The physical presence of the analyst, his active participation with the patient, the regularity of the sessions and the evidences of his attention, interest, and even preoccupation mitigate the fear of isolation and abandonment and raise hope for involvement—a hope that must be sustained in order to be frustrated in the classic meaning of abstinence. [Fox 1984, p. 234]

Fox is not advocating an interpersonal model, because his focus is still on unconscious distortions and analysis of transference neurosis. Nor is Fox talking about a corrective emotional experience, as his focus remains on insight and interpretation. Fox emphasizes the analyst's actively balancing frustration and object gratification in order to facilitate and sustain an illusional transference. The analyst does not simply wait for transference to be "transferred" onto him; rather, it is part of his stance, part of what Fox considers abstinence, for the analyst to facilitate an analyzable transference.[5]

Fox's conception was shared by Freud, who wrote, in a letter to Binswanger regarding countertransference, that "What is given to the patient" . . . must be "consciously allotted, and then more or less of it as the need may arise. Occasionally, a great deal . . ." Freud continues, "To give someone too little because one loves him too much is being unjust to the patient and a technical error" (Freud, quoted by Kohut 1968, p. 105).

The Role of Gratification

It becomes apparent that the role of gratification, and even the term itself, changes depending on one's conception of the analyst's role. Analysts with a right wing emphasis see no place for gratification. The term is understood as referring to gratification of transference fantasy and is thus an interference with verbal analysis of transference. Further, it is seen as an attempt to replace analysis of a fantasy with a "corrective" repair. Gratification is thus either a theoretical error or a countertransference error.

For those who have a different conception of the analyst's role, support is an integral aspect of treatment, something silent, present in the background, sustaining the work-

---

[5]While this concept may seem to involve manipulation of the transference, I do not believe that this is what Fox intends. He does not speak of the analyst's playing a role, or of the analyst's actively encouraging certain transferences rather than others. I believe he is saying that, inherent in the analytic situation, the patient must be able to find some soil in his analyst within which to grow his transference neurosis. I believe that Loewald and Stone have a similar conception of the analyst's role.

ing alliance. When clinically necessary, gratification consists of amplification of elements of the analyst's role, rather than of additions to the role. One does not gratify a patient in order to develop or build an alliance. Rather, gratification is part of the foundation of the working alliance.

It is interesting to note that for Grunes (1984), it is therapeutic permeability which sustains both a working alliance and transference, while for Tarachow (1962), it is the opposite, the "therapeutic barrier," which makes the transference and its analysis possible. The difference may result from Tarachow's focus on analysis with neurotic patients versus Grunes's concentration on analytic work with more disturbed patients. This explanation is not sufficient, however, because Grunes sees empathic permeability between analyst and patient as a direct path toward analysis, while Tarachow sees greater relationship between analyst and patient to be a form of support that leads away from analysis. One who agrees with Tarachow's conception would not tend to see therapy as evolving into analysis, at least not with the same therapist, because the relationship would have been too real, leading to problems in the later evolution and analysis of transference. Those who agree with Grunes, however, could easily see the therapy evolving into an analysis with the same analyst.

The difference between Tarachow and Grunes seems to be based on different metapsychological assumptions rather than on different clinical populations. Grunes criticizes aspects of structural theory that emphasize opposition between ego and id, and that overemphasize the role of the ego in reality adaptation. Such a conception of the ego, in metapsychological terms, and of the working alliance, which is the extension of this concept to clinical theory, leads to difficulties:

> The way in which Greenson dichotomizes the real from the transference relationship results in the assignment of the deepest intensities of analyst–patient interaction to

the pathological transference. The reality of the relationship, on the other hand, is consigned to a kind of upper-level, rational, and conscious friendly helpfulness. The result, I think, is that the transference analysis becomes overburdened by the patient's sense of an endless reductionism to the past and to pathology. I believe that Greenson's dichotomy makes the analytic work oppressive. The patient feels that his nonrational intensities are pathological errors, and he is left with a sense of dubious adaptation to an attentuated reality relationship—the isolated instances of "realness" in the treatment. [Grunes 1984, p. 138]

It is from this metapsychological distinction that we can further understand the opposition by analysts such as Brenner to the idea of a working alliance. They need to understand it as either transferential or nontransferential, and the choice is obvious, for reasons we have already discussed. However, the relationship can be *both* transferential and nontransferential. The height of psychological development does not necessarily lie in the triumph of nontransference over transference (ego over id), although that is certainly something desired. Development can be understood as also including permeability and accessibility between transference and nontransference (between ego and id). Ego and the working alliance would be understood as "strong" not only in measures of reality (such as reality-testing) but also with regard to measures of sensitivity to one's own unconscious process. In fact, this is understood by all analysts in their evaluations of patients for analysis.

Thus, for analysts such as Grunes, gratification is not as threatening to the analysis as it is for others. In the same way that some permeability between ego and id nourishes the ego and strengthens it in all of its functions—from reality-testing to regression in service of the ego—permeability between analyst and patient, in the form of implicit background object relationship, strengthens the working alliance in treatment. While this is recognized clinically by many analysts, it is only given serious theoretical consideration by analysts of the left wing. It should be emphasized that these analysts gratify *within* the traditional stance. Modell, who is one of the analysts emphasizing the mutative effects of background gratification in the traditional stance, writes of the paradoxical fact that the patient is helped most with reality-testing through analysis of transference fantasy by an abstinent and neutral analyst. Modell writes:

> This paradox is also relevant to our consideration of the "holding environment." For although there are "real" caretaking elements in the analyst's customary activity, if he does in fact assume an actual protective role . . . this will interfere with the analytic process. We wish to reiterate, therefore, that the caretaking elements we have described are implicit in the classical analytic technique itself (in Eissler's terms, without parameters). If active measures are introduced into the analytic situation, there is the paradoxical effect of weakening the analytic holding environment. [Modell 1976, p. 292]

Thus, even left-wing analysts stress implicit rather than explicit gratification—the gratification inherent in the classical stance rather than active gratification, which exceeds the traditional stance.

Factors Leading to Structural Change

Have we moved too far from traditional conceptions of analytic work? In our urge to emphasize what have been theoretically neglected (although perhaps clinically assumed) aspects of the analytic stance, have we abandoned some essential tenets of analysis? Is the analyst's role to "hold" the patient, to repair early traumata, to interpret unconscious conflicts, or all of these? Can these concepts be reconciled? Is there any way of understanding the common context of right and left wing analysts while acknowledging their differing emphases?

Freedman asks what factors account for "transformation" of mental structures in analytic work. He states that there is a dialectic between thesis, antithesis, and synthesis. The thesis is a wish; the antithesis is a contradictory wish that cannot be reconciled with the thesis; and the synthesis emerges through the reconciliation of conflict between the two.

Freedman (1985) writes that transformation of psychological structure results from expanding awareness of conflicting internal states, each with its own inner (and often contradictory) requirements. It is tolerance for and insight into these "disjunctive experiences," acquired "under the hegemony of a libidinal object relationship" (p. 335) which lead to inner change.

> I have found it increasingly useful to speak of disjunctive experiences as a way of thinking about conflict across the developmental spectrum recognizing, of course, that the nature of conflict or of disjunctions changes with increased capacities for internalization. . . . It is the experience of a disjunction which is the origin of a psychic structure and . . . it is in the symbolization of disjunctive experiences that psychoanalysis effects its cure. [p. 335]

The analyst has a dual role in this experience. Freedman cites Loewald's conception of the mother's and analyst's roles in facilitating secondary-process formation through periods of disorganization and reorganization in the context of an object relationship.

> In the transition from thesis to antithesis, we noted the dual function of the analyst's presence as the inevitable provocateur of the antithesis at the prerepresentational level, and the facilitator of the synthesis at the representational level. Thus the analyst's activity can be thought to

provide both the inhibitory structure as well as the facilitating structure. [Freedman 1985, p. 336]

Analysts from almost all therapeutic models report a sequence of the sort described by Freedman. The analyst begins
by meeting the patient in his world in an affective experience.
All speak of some kind of transitional transference experience
with the patient, be it "merged transference," "self–object
transference," or something else. Even Kernberg's accounts of
projective identification may be seen as evidence of the particular kind of transference neurosis established with the borderline patient. Whatever else it may signify, projective identification is a form of connection through which patient and analyst
enter each other's affective world. As Searles (1965) states, the
analyst may need to live through certain kinds of part-object
transferences with the patient. That experience itself, along
with its analytic resolution (instead of that experience as an
impediment to an analytic resolution, as Kernberg sees it) may
be necessary for a mutative effect.[6]

---

[6]The exception is Abend and colleagues (1983), who, in their
discussion of treating four higher-functioning borderline patients, emphasize the degree to which the analytic process was similar to that with
the neurotic patient. This emphasis tends to minimize or neglect certain
core borderline difficulties in the aim of preserving a certain metapsychological position. Perhaps one reason for Abend and co-workers' belief
that projective identification is not a unique defense is that it keeps the
analyst outside of the patient's affective system and is consistent with the
concept of insight as mutative without prerequisite affective connection
and experience, an essential belief of right-wing analysts. However, in
the concept that a transference neurosis must be established and then
analyzed in analysis with the neurotic patient, even these analysts agree
with the others to some extent. In a transference neurosis, the analyst is
affectively experienced within the patient's inner world, through object-
directed transference wishes. This transference neurosis is essential for a
successful analysis. Disagreement would come in areas such as whether
the experience of the transference neurosis itself has some mutative effect,
whether the analyst has some mutative role other than interpretation, and
whether the patient may experience the transference neurosis without
some corresponding muted noncountertransferential affective experience
by the analyst.

For Sechehaye, very active gratification is the way to reach her regressed psychotic patient, to become a part of her "reality." For others, including Searles, Bach, Grunes, Modell, and Kohut, the analyst does not become as active with the patient. Despite differences regarding degree of analyst activity (gratification), however, all see themselves becoming enmeshed in the patient's reality through certain forms of regressed preverbal transferences that must be established and lived through before they are worked out. These analysts may differ on whether the experience is curative in itself or whether it merely helps to establish an analyzable transference, but the point is that this kind of transference is necessary if analyst and patient are to be joined in the patient's internal subjective world and, simultaneously, in the analyst's external, objective world. Just as a transference neurosis must be established and then analyzed with the neurotic patient in analysis, so must a similar experience be established and then analyzed with the more severely disturbed patient.

All analysts then speak of a disjunction, at the patient's particular developmental level, in terms appropriate to that developmental level (frustration of transference wish, failure of empathy, and so on). This disjunction is then analyzed. Resolution of disjunction leads to structure formation at a higher level of psychic organization.

In analysis with the neurotic patient, the combination of abstinence and gratification implicit in the usual analytic situation is sufficient to draw the patient's unconscious object-directed wishes to the analyst and to hold the patient through frustration of these transference wishes and their subsequent analysis. Within this perspective, the difficulty with too much gratification with the neurotic patient is that it keeps the connection at a level that is too psychologically low. The gratification makes it too difficult to establish a transference neurosis, an ambiguous and paradoxical sense of connection and distance. If the analyst is unnecessarily gratifying, he removes the possibility of illusion.

With the psychotic patient, however, the therapist must move more actively toward the patient's experiential world in order to establish an illusion with him within it—that is, a transference (actually pretransference) relationship that is not autistic. In this case, for the analyst to be too abstinent—to refuse to answer a question, for example—may be a conceptual and countertransferential error because it prevents the patient from joining the therapist's world and therefore interferes with development of a necessary transferential relationship.

At each level of development, analysis depends on the patient's letting the analyst into his world at his particular developmental level; further, there must be some frustration, and finally some resolution, through insight in the context of a valued object relationship. There is always a paradox in this process. Thus, as Tarachow notes, an interpretation is a deprivation, but, simultaneously, interpretation is also a form of connection at a higher psychological level. The paradox of the analyst as simultaneously transference object and real object, as abstinent and gratifying, as in the patient's subjective world and yet in the external world of "reality," must be sustained throughout analytic work. It is the analyst's sustaining of the paradox as paradox which leads to the possibility of resolution through insight. That is, as long as wishes toward the analyst are experienced only as direct and to a current figure rather than as also directed to a transference figure, then no paradox is sustained and the patient will not tolerate interpretation; he will experience it as frustration. Only the patient's tolerance of paradox, of the continuous interplay between past and present, unconscious and conscious, and primary process and secondary process, allows for the possibility that he may use interpretation and the deprivation that it entails while still experiencing the analyst as supporting him in the deprivation.

A necessary part of the paradox is a strong affective experience, with the analyst included. How is such an experience facilitated? In classical analysis, the patient comes to the analyst with an object-directed transference neurosis. This constitutes the analyst's immersion in the patient's affective world, and this immersion is analyzed. In patients with more severe disturbances, the analyst may have to come closer to the patient in order to become part of his world. Disagreements about gratification and the analyst's stance then become disagreements about how best to become part of the patient's world in a manner that does not preclude eventual interpretation and working through of transference wishes, and then about how best to help the patient analyze these wishes.

10 _____

Clinical Applications

Difficulties in Working with the Disturbed Patient in Psychoanalytic Psychotherapy

The classical psychoanalytic situation assumes a neurotic patient—a patient with what Eissler (1953) has termed a "normal ego" (p. 121). Eissler defines this ego operationally as an ego within which symptoms are removed through interpretation alone. While Eissler recognizes that such an ego is a hypothetical construct and that no one possesses this ego in pure form, the analytic situation relies on this hypothetical normal ego so much that the propriety of analysis with patients who do not have such an ego is debated (see, for example, the symposium titled "The Widening Scope of Indications for Psychoanalysis" in the 1954 *Journal of the American Psychoanalytic Association*). Patients who do not have "normal" egos are often considered unanalyzable or, at best, as in need of a period of preparatory psychotherapy.

To have a "normal ego," to be neurotic, is a developmental achievement. The patient with such an ego has devel-

343

oped a sense of psychological separation from others and, accordingly, has what Pine (1979) terms "pathology of the relation to the differentiated other" rather than "pathology of the relation to the undifferentiated other" (p. 225). The neurotic patient has an intact ability to test reality, a demarcated tripartite internal structure, and a reasonably stable sense of identity. The borderline patient, on the other hand, has more primitive structural precursors, nonspecific ego weakness, and what Kernberg terms "identity diffusion." Reality-testing is reasonably intact for most borderline patients, although it becomes impaired often enough to be a significant issue in treatment. In addition to the borderline patient's symptoms, the psychotic patient also has impaired reality-testing and fluid self–object boundaries. For Kernberg (1980b), the type of defenses (organized around splitting rather than repression) and the identity diffusion differentiate borderline from neurotic patients, while the capacity for reality-testing differentiates borderline from psychotic patients. Adler and Buie (1979) believe that the capacity for holding introjects is most diagnostically important.

For all these analysts, the neurotic patient has achieved libidinal object constancy (Pine 1974)—the capacity to summon the internal image of the primary caretaker and soothe oneself in the caretaker's absence. This developmental step, which occurs as the child emerges from the rapprochement crisis, is fundamental. A patient who has not attained this capacity functions on the borderline, narcissistic, or psychotic level. Before libidinal object constancy is established, (1) defenses are organized around splitting, (2) anxiety leads to panic and movement toward soothing by an actual object, (3) immediate connections with objects are necessary for self-soothing and psychological equilibrium, (4) objects are experienced as part-objects, (5) relationships are stormy, and (6) there is insufficient neutralization of aggression, and primitive internal structure. As libidinal object constancy is established, the child moves from functioning primarily in the external world to functioning in a world mediated by internal psychological structure. Included in this developmental achievement are (1) greater neutralization of aggression, (2) the capacity to see others as whole objects (and thereby the capacity for ambivalence), (3) the capacity for self-soothing, (4) the organization of defenses around repression, (5) the development of a signal function for anxiety and the consequent mobilization of more adaptive defenses, (6) greater coherence of self, and (7) conflict that occurs more between internal structures (intrapsychic conflict) at the oedipal level than between inner and external world, with greater emphasis on preoedipal conflict.

These structural differences lead to difficulties in therapy with severely disturbed patients that are less likely to occur with neurotic patients. These problems include the following:

1. Difficulty establishing and maintaining a working alliance, and a focus on intense and concrete demands. These result from problems in symbolic communication, impulse control, and secondary-process functioning, along with dynamic conflicts around object relationships.

2. Intense rage, the result of either incompletely neutralized aggression and consequent splitting defenses (Kernberg) or narcissistic rage (Adler and Buie). This affect leads to psychotic transference reactions within sessions.

3. Inability to hold the therapist between sessions, leading to dangerous acting out and self-destructive behavior. Such behavior reflects intense aloneness, anger, and attempts to manage these feelings. The acting out may include sexual promiscuity, drug use, bulimia, and so on.

4. Inability to use anxiety as a signal to call in protective defenses. Instead, anxiety leads to more anxiety and panic and then to acting out and/or structural decompensation.

5. Difficulty with the therapeutic relationship because of part-object functioning. This may be manifested in a

stormy transference, emotional flooding, transitional relatedness, a narcissistic cocoon, or a demand for more
nurturance than is the norm in the therapeutic situation.

The Diagnostic Importance
of Signal and Panic Anxiety

The therapist faced with the difficulties just noted must
assess the extent to which they are the function of pathology
in relation to the undifferentiated other versus the differentiated other. As Pine (1979) writes, the therapist makes such
diagnostic distinctions not on the basis of the manifest content of the patient's statements but through evidence of
structural weakness (manifested, for example, in panic and
disorganization as a response to anxiety). Pine (1979) presents several clinical examples that illustrate this diagnostic
differentiation when the manifest content seems to indicate
problems in psychological separation but the structural diagnosis indicates that such separation has been achieved and
that the problem is more usefully conceptualized as neurotic
conflict.

One cannot simply state, however, that if there is evidence of structural weakness, then the patient is functioning
at a borderline or psychotic level, while if there is no such
evidence, then the patient is relatively neurotic. At times the
patient may not show evidence of such weakness, but the
defenses serve to cover annihilation anxiety and to protect
against decompensation. In such cases, we must infer these
patients' more disturbed level of functioning even if, at times,
they do not present obvious structural deficits. Patients with
similar symptoms may be at quite different structural levels.

One such patient suffered from severe anorexia. The
symptom served to bind his annihilation anxiety. He also
dealt with his anxiety by taking his wife with him every-
where. She even came to therapy sessions, waiting outside
for him in the reception area. While anorectic, the patient was

able to consistently deny any need and to devalue his therapist. He showed no evidence of panic, thought disorder or
other manifest ego difficulty. However, structural difficulty
and annihilation anxiety were inferred from the patient's
inability to be alone. After a good deal of therapeutic work,
he began to eat more. He was also able to spend some time
alone, and it was only then that he began to experience panic
and loosening of associations. At that point the inferred
panic anxiety became obvious, and the task of treatment
became to help maintain the patient while the therapeutic
work continued.

Evidence of structural disorganization is crucial in diagnosing a patient as borderline or psychotic because therapists
tend to overdiagnose patients in this way as soon as they
become difficult in treatment. Difficult patients are not necessarily borderline. The fact that panic anxiety must sometimes be inferred complicates diagnosis, however, and seems
to leave open the possibility of using such inferences to
overassign borderline and psychotic diagnoses. Therefore,
one must not infer recklessly. The following factors should
be taken into account when considering such inferences:

1. *The kinds of defenses.* Defenses that are more primitive
   (organized around splitting rather than repression), that
   are more gross and nonspecific (withdrawal rather than
   intellectualization), and that are more maladaptive (denial rather than isolation of affect) reflect a lower level of
   ego development.
2. *The kind of symptom presented.* Symptoms that are highly
   maladaptive also reflect more ego difficulties. Severe
   anorexia and bulimia are examples of such difficulties.
   The patient who must wash his hands 100 times a day
   and who cannot work because of this symptom has a
   more severe problem than does the patient who must
   wash his hands when he has specific thoughts, but who
   is able to continue to function.

3. *The level and kind of object relationships.* The patient who has no friends is generally more disturbed than the patient who has social relationships. The therapist must also evaluate the nature of these object relationships. Are they based on need gratification? Are they long-lasting? Do they reflect genuine love and mutuality or are they based on fantasy?

All these factors are considered, along with relevant dynamic factors, in a therapist's evaluation of a patient's ego and superego functioning. There is no attempt here to be comprehensive; the intention is merely to indicate the kinds of factors to be considered in assessing the extent, level, and nature of a patient's anxiety.[1]

Reality and the Disturbed Patient

In contrast to the neurotic patient, the more seriously disturbed patient is often chronically panicked and desperate. Others, including the therapist, are used for structural maintenance. (Jacobson [1967], Kohut [1971], Modell [1976, 1978], and many others have discussed this form of part-object relationship.) When stressed, the patient reacts with some form of structural decompensation, the defenses being inadequate to deal with the added anxiety. The patient becomes narcissistically angry, acts out, or demonstrates, in one way or another, that he is unable to contain his anxiety. He redoubles his efforts at structural maintenance through objects. There is frequent demand for therapist gratification and contact, with little impulse control, capacity for delay, or consideration of the therapist's needs. Although Kernberg is

---

[1]The reader who is interested in diagnosis is urged to consult Kernberg's (1975) classic first chapter and his other writings on diagnosis and prognosis, along with the work of Pine (1979), Meissner (1984), and Frosch (1980).

certainly correct in his discussion of the dynamic factors involved in such behavior, interpretation of such factors is often not heard or used by the patient. Even more often, the patient experiences interpretation as rejection by the therapist, which exacerbates the situation and leads to more rage and more demands for concrete manifestations of the therapist's love, caring, commitment, and availability.

Tarachow's (1962) remark that interpretation is experienced as deprivation is especially apt for this kind of patient. Interpretation both leads to perspective and implies the therapist's distance and perspective. To listen analytically and to interpret is to say to a patient, in both words and manner, that wishes will not be met directly but rather will be understood and thereby frustrated, at least at the concrete level at which they may be expressed. Gratification will be more abstract and symbolic (through the therapist's understanding the patient rather than, for example, taking him out for dinner). The patient is asked to accept a relationship that functions in a less concrete and immediate way than he might like. To a more disturbed patient, this attitude is infuriating, and the analytic attitude underlying insight-oriented treatment itself becomes something to be fought and resisted. The resistance is not only against uncovering repressed wishes; it is also against the assumption of secondary-process functioning and the frustrations inherent in accepting the reality principle.

Stone (1961, 1984), Tarachow (1962), and Loewald (1951, 1960), among others, have described the analytic process as involving the patient's acceptance of both separation from the analyst on more concrete, physical, immediate levels, and connection with the analyst on more verbal and abstract levels. This parallels a conception of development in which the child moves from close physical connection with the mother to separation from the mother made possible by internalization of her soothing and other functions. Once this separation is achieved, the child accepts the world or reality as his, rather than as something to which he must reluctantly submit. He makes this step because he feels connected to his mother at a higher level of abstraction through his increased organization of reality (Loewald 1951). Perhaps this is why Adler (1980) states that a working alliance is the product of analysis rather than the precondition for it. For the disturbed patient, to accept a working alliance and all that it implies in terms of object relationship and secondary-process functioning is to accept psychological separation, and it is this form of separation that the disturbed patient will not acknowledge. To operate on the basis of the pleasure principle is thus consistent with denial of separation.

One patient made a slip of the tongue, stating that a man she had met, who was actually half her age, was twice her age. She refused to look at this slip for most of the session, but she finally admitted that she wanted a man to look up to, to be her "savior," and that to accept his being half her age would make gratification of this wish less possible. She refused to examine the matter further, however, saying that she did not want to accept the depression that she knew she would feel if she accepted her wanting a savior as a *wish* that would be analyzed rather than as a demand she needed to have met.

Thus, while a variety of dynamic factors affect the demands that the patient makes of the therapist, there is also sometimes a more basic factor, presupposed in analytic work: the patient's willingness to accept secondary process and "real life." This acceptance is manifested in the patient's willingness to accept the "rules of the game" in the therapeutic alliance and the context of life outside the therapeutic situation. For patients who are unwilling or unable to do this, interpretation alone is often insufficient. There must be an underpinning of support, gratification, and object relationship with such patients sufficient to hold them and help them tolerate and mitigate the frustrations inherent in assuming the overall context of reality. This accomplishment is manifested in the patient's learning to accept the therapist as a symbolic transference figure and to accept interpretation and its gratifications as sufficient.

There are those who feel that such support interferes with the patient's willingness to do interpretive work. They see an opposition between analysis and gratification; it is as if the patient will not want to examine his motivations if he is gratified. Such a view is widespread in analytic work, beginning with Freud's belief that abstinence and frustration further the transference and interpretive work.

Such a view, in which gratification and frustration are counterposed, with frustration seen as leading to a higher goal, is widespread in our culture, particularly in these more conservative times. It is expressed in a *New York Times* column by William Safire (1986) discussing King Edward VIII's abdication of the British throne to marry a divorced woman. Safire presents what he sees as the conflict between love and duty. Was it right for the king to abdicate his duty to the British people in favor of his love for a woman and his personal happiness? Safire believes that the king was wrong to abdicate his throne, because duty transcends love. Safire assumes an opposition between duty and love that is psychoanalytically understood as the opposition between id and superego. It is clinically seen as the alleged opposition between frustration, which leads to the working alliance and eventually to insight, and gratification, which leads to transference satisfaction without insight. It is assumed here that there is no inherent satisfaction in insight—that insight is a secondary accommodation we make to the world as we realize that our wishes can never be met in the manner we would like.

This opposition may not be inevitable, however, as we have seen in our discussion of Loewald's work. For Loewald, one may choose to embrace reality and the world rather than reluctantly accommodate to it. From this perspective, insight is, in itself, a means of gratification, in that it allows one to maintain object connection at a higher level of abstraction and at a developmental level that takes into account both the wish for connection and the wish for developmentally appropriate separation. As we have seen in the preceding chapter, such a view leads to very different therapeutic choices. It can also lead to very different life choices. To return to Safire's example, the duty that he would have the king accept was in opposition to love only because it was experienced (rightfully or not) as one forced upon him and which required him to relinquish his libidinal wishes. It was responsibility imposed on him without his approval or acceptance. In the latter case, he would be doing his duty because it was experienced as *his* duty, as submission to a loving superego rather than a punitive one.

One can accept the demands of duty if one has internalized them as one's own demands, just as one can accept the difficulties of reality (the secondary process) if it is one's own reality. One can accept the demands of the therapeutic process, with its inherent frustrations, limitations, and lack of fulfillment of wishes to have an omnipotent other solve life's problems, if one feels that one has understood and accepted the frustrations of therapy as reasonable.

If this is so, then there is no inherent conflict in accepting duty, analytic treatment, and reality. All may be accepted and infused with a kind of love, whether it is termed neutralized energy, narcissistic cathexis, or another term. Any conflict is then between various aspects of the self, all of which the patient accepts. The patient may be caught between conflicting but equally valued goals, rather than between something he wants and something that he feels has been imposed on him. In the latter case, obeying the demands of conscience feels like submitting to a foreign internalized demand rather than doing what one feels is "right." We see this distinction when a parent gives up certain personal satisfactions for his child's needs. Although he acknowledges his own deprivation in meeting some of the child's demands, he does not resent the deprivation because he accepts the demands and restrictions (as well as the joys) of parenthood as *his*. Performance of parental duties reflects his love rather than cold, externally imposed obligation. Thus duties and realities can give meaning and purpose to life. This is the case not only in the rigors of parenting, but also in the acceptance of religious obligations.

The kind of superego we are discussing—one that reflects an internalized sense of the outer world, as opposed to one that is experienced as imposed by the external world—reflects the union of various elements of superego proper and ego ideal. This is what is meant by, in lay terms, "having one's act together." The individual in whom this union has not occurred experiences anger and frustration at reality itself and its underlying fabric (secondary process, inherent frustrations of life, and narcissistic losses). Internal and external struggle is constant, and life is experienced as comprising opposing polarities: To have one thing is to relinquish another.

We see such a difficulty in treatment when patients project their non-assimilated reality demands onto the therapist and feel that to recognize the demands of "reality," they must submit to the therapist's will, as though the therapist, if he simply wanted to, could change reality. Thus, patients may simply deny that, because of certain psychotic symptoms, they must consider the possibility of hospitalization or medication. They would rather see the choice as revolving around a power struggle between themselves and the therapist. By opposing the therapist, the patient not only resists the transferentially experienced oppressor; he also resists taking onto himself as factors worthy of his consideration the realistic dangers to which he has become exposed because of his psychopathology. The therapist often has quite a job resisting the patient's attempts at battle and projection and helping the patient take onto himself the idea that his behavior has created circumstances that he must address. In order to help the patient with this task, the therapist may have to resist taking over for the patient in trying times.

We also often see this difficulty as countertransference in the therapist's assumption of a cold, "classical" stance that is bereft and denying of the aim-inhibited lovingness which is *inherent* in that stance. To some degree, it is through this inherent loving that the patient, regardless of diagnostic category, learns to accept reality, demands, and duty, manifested in the working alliance, as compatible with feeling and love, and as *his* rather than as something imposed on him by the therapist as a condition for the therapist's love. That is, the patient learns to accept reality as his through both primary identification and secondary identification or identification with the aggressor (Loewald 1959). Many therapists seem to emphasize the latter at the expense of the former.

It is clear, then, that a true working alliance itself is not something assumed but may be, as Adler writes, the product of a successful analysis, inasmuch as it reflects the patient's capacity for mature object relationships, capacity for both work and play—reflected in free associations and subsequent reflection on those associations—and combination of narcissistic and dependent wishes with a sense of consideration for the therapist's needs and the demands and realities of the therapeutic task. While we look at the presence or absence of an alliance as a diagnostic indicator, in a more profound way it reflects an acceptance of life, reality, and duty that is not imposed on the patient but that truly belongs to him.

The Issue of Support and Gratification

In working with patients whose diagnostic category is predominantly within the realm of pathology in relation to the undifferentiated other, the therapist must reexamine the structure of the therapy. Techniques that usually work well enough because of the inherent holding structure of the classical situation and the inherent internal structure of the neurotic patient's "normal ego" are not as effective with the more disturbed patient. The question of gratification arises anew. Does the seriously disturbed patient require more support and gratification than is usual in psychoanalytic psychotherapy in order to benefit from it? If so, what kind of support and gratification is appropriate and consistent with traditional analytic concepts?

As noted in Chapter 9, the issue of support and gratification in psychoanalysis and in psychoanalytic psychotherapy has been controversial. It has seemed to threaten the very essence of analytic theory of technique: that cure is largely a function of insight via interpretation of transference. Support and gratification seem to substitute suggestion or corrective emotional experience for insight. They seem to contradict the principles of abstinence and neutrality, which both stimulate transference and safeguard the patient's autonomy. They may brush over resistance. They may meet demands that should instead be interpreted so that the patient can deal with them on a verbal and higher developmental level. Full acknowledgement of the roles of support and gratification appears to disregard the dynamic point of view and to substitute one based on deficit repair. Although these are important cautions for the analyst, Freud himself viewed support and gratification as part of the background of analysis. In an effort to emphasize what is unique to analysis— interpretation of unconscious conflict—analysts may have too severely limited their understanding of other mutative factors.

Dangers in Reliance on Support and Gratification

There are dangers to excessive reliance on support and gratification:

1. The patient will find it difficult to be angry at the analyst who has given him an abundance of support and gratification. The therapist practicing supportive psychotherapy usually attempts to be supportive and to maintain a "warm" atmosphere in sessions because he believes that expression of unneutralized aggression is not useful to the patient. Such expression is believed to gratify unneutralized drive (rather than being a cathartic

expression of repressed anger) and often leads to decompensation. Decompensation is facilitated because the patient feels that he has "killed" the therapist; he then feels the loss of his therapist's holding or he feels that the therapist will retaliate and kill him. A "warm" atmosphere is also valued as an end in itself (rather than as a means for avoiding aggression), because internalization of the therapist as a helpful, supportive, and affirming figure is more likely to occur in a positive affective climate. Such internalization is believed to be a primary mutative factor in therapy. These therapists therefore attempt to titrate frustration and the concomitant rage, or they may deal with unneutralized aggression by directly limiting its expression. The aggression must be expressed at some point, however, even if in a modulated way. Too "kind" a therapist makes such expression difficult, and lack of expression in the treatment may lead to expression outside of treatment, or to a clinging, "sticky," covertly hostile transference.

2. As Blanck and Blanck (1979) note, anger is part of a thrust toward separation from the analyst/mother. Treatment must have both periods of closeness and periods of separation, and to suppress the modulated expression of aggression may be to suppress the patient's psychological separation.

3. Excessive support and gratification may replace insight and interpretation for both analyst and patient. Those analysts who write of support and gratification and who emphasize new experience and internalization do not intend that these interventions be substituted for insight. Rather, they usually see these as counterpoints to a process that is understood from both libidinal and object relations frameworks but is never a kind of bland, vaguely supportive, manifest–content oriented treatment.

4. Excessive support and gratification may lead the analyst to emphasize only certain aspects of the therapeutic rela-

tionship at a time when the patient is ready to express other aspects of the transference. Thus the analyst may be led not only toward emphasis on a corrective emotional replacement experience, but also toward a more subtle and chronic loss of neutrality and to a treatment that becomes fixed at a certain level of transference and object relationship.

5. In all these cases, excessive support and gratification may express the analyst's countertransference—his desire to be loved and to be important, for example, or his fear of the patient's rage or disapproval.

Some of these dangers are apparent in the following clinical illustration:

> The therapist is seeing a volatile patient, an intelligent man who easily and frequently regresses and makes suicidal gestures. The patient is difficult to assess, and the therapist cannot accurately predict when the gestures will become serious atempts. The patient has a history of many hospitalizations, several minor arrests, and a number of attempts at outpatient treatment with a variety of therapists.
>
> The patient has an idealized transference to the therapist. He cannot acknowledge anger at him, although he is frequently angry at outside authorities who are easily recognized as transference displacements. However, the patient does become angry at the therapist—and expresses this feeling in suicide gestures—when the therapist suggests that the patient may be angry at him.
>
> The patient has been reading about criminals in preparation for application to law school and work as a criminal lawyer. He brings in information he has learned about criminals. His focus is always on mistreatment of the criminals, sociological factors that predispose to criminal behavior, and so forth. He never discusses anger in the criminal. At one point, he brings in several thinly concealed angry fantasies. He becomes slightly agitated.

At this juncture, the patient urgently asks the therapist whether he is similar to those who later become criminals. The therapist reassures the patient that he is not, without inquiring into the motives for the question. The therapist comes to supervision uncertain about whether he should have gratified the patient in this manner.

The therapist explains that he answered the patient's question because he felt that to interpret possible anger behind the question would increase the patient's anxiety level and perhaps overwhelm his defenses. He also answered because of his knowledge of the patient's history. This patient would witness bitter fights between his parents, become frightened, and then urgently ask his parents for an explanation of what had happened, in a quest, he said, for reassurance. His parents reacted by screaming at him, and thus he felt "unsafe." The therapist wanted to give the patient a different experience and thus believed that he should answer the question.

One argument against answering the question was that the therapist was substituting his idea of what would be a corrective emotional experience for insight. By answering the question without exploration, the therapist went along with, rather than interpreting, a possible fantasy—that if the patient's question led to a reassuring response (rather than a questioning response which provoked more anxiety) from his transferential mother/therapist, then he would, in effect, receive reassurance for all those past occasions, thus undoing all the times when his questions led to more anxiety and anger from his actual parents. The therapist thus made several questionable inferential leaps and did not interpret displacement (from past to present [parents to therapist]), from inside the sessions to outside the sessions (the patient's going to the library to learn about criminals), and from affective life to cognitive defenses [intellectualization]).

The patient's question can also be understood as an attempt at using the therapist as a source of necessary defensive strength. That is, the question might have reflected the tenuousness of the patient's defenses of displacement, intellectualization, and reaction formation. In this context, then, the request reflected an upsurge of angry (criminal) wishes and an attempt at borrowing ego and superego support from the therapist. However, even if the therapist felt this to be the case and thus believed that his answer was necessary, he could have answered the question while also acknowledging the impulses behind the question. By not acknowledging the impulses, the therapist acted to deny their existence and treated them as unmentionable. Thus, whatever his assessment of the patient's defenses and of the patient's tolerance for interpretation, his quick response reflected a defensive and countertransferential substitution of gratification for dynamic thought. The gratification substituted for, rather than supplemented, insight-oriented work.

It became apparent that the therapist feared the patient's anger. The therapist felt constrained in what he could talk about and even in what he could allow himself to feel, because broaching the subject of anger led to the patient's regression and to unpredictable suicidal impulses. The therapist became angry as he experienced this control by his patient, and he dealt with it defensively by trying to remain in control. As the therapist discussed this countertransference in supervision, he realized that the patient had been treating him as if he were the repository of all feeling (especially anger) and needed to be controlled by the patient; the defense of projective identification thus became evident.

There is a legitimate problem here, however, on which therapists of different persuasions disagree. When working with a patient who is so unstable, is it wise to confront an idealization that holds the patient, and to encourage aggression that could prove disruptive?

For Kernberg, ignoring the aggression merely leads to an artificial alliance inside therapy and to expression, in self-destructive activity, of the split-off aggression outside of treatment. Kernberg might make another, perhaps more fundamental point with regard to interpretation. He might say that this therapist is being overly simplistic in his developmental assumptions. The therapist assumes that the patient is acting on a split-off self-representation—as the fragile, fearfully questioning child—and the therapist wants to introduce a corrective experience with regard to that self-representation; that is, the therapist wants to be a new object who soothes the patient rather than further overstimulating him. Perhaps, on the other hand, the patient is acting on a split-off object representation and it is the therapist who, through projective identification, is living out the self-representation. The patient, then, would be acting out the role of the overstimulating out-of-control parents, and the therapist would be in the position of the fragile, afraid-to-question child. For the therapist to refuse to answer the patient's question, and to instead say that the denied anger exists and is being acted out (that is, for the therapist to tell the truth as he sees it) would be to face and contain the fury that the patient faced as a child. To gratify the patient, by answering the question, is to do what the *child* never did—that is, to avoid the anger.

There are many who would not focus on the aggression, however. In this case, the defenses against anger were weak, and there was a history of both legal difficulty and suicidal impulses. It is likely that focus on anger would have been disruptive to the patient and to the treatment. The therapist would want to acknowledge the patient's feelings, but in a manner that would let him control his anger. In this way, the therapist would acknowledge the impulse, but in a manner that supported defense. The therapist might do this by asking the patient about the defenses—that is, about his extreme insistence that he hasn't a trace of anger toward the therapist, and about his avoidance of an issue often associated with criminals, that of anger. The therapist would thus be able to evaluate the effect of his interventions on the patient as the defense against anger is discussed.

Uses of Support and Gratification

A shift of emphasis to support and gratification depends on the therapist's assessment that the patient's structural difficulties are great enough that exclusive reliance on interpretive work with dynamic aspects of the patient's material, in a climate of abstinence, is not possible. The emphasis does not shift solely to structural deficits, but these deficits are taken into account either in the therapist's interpretation of dynamic issues or in his decision to refrain from such interpretation at a particular moment.

As the therapist decides that interpretive work needs to be supplemented, he may decide what it is he will attempt to support or gratify, depending on the weaknesses of the particular patient. This is in accord with Schlesinger's (1969) recommendation that the therapist specify exactly what is to be supported and what is to be expressed in a given case. Such diagnostic assessment is subtle but necessary.

Planning a Supportive Psychotherapy

A beginning therapist was frustrated in his meetings with a psychotically depressed woman on an inpatient unit. He felt that he could not do insight-oriented work with the patient and that a psychoanalytically informed treatment was therefore impossible. He didn't know what purpose there was in spending time with the patient other than to provide supportive companionship.

It turned out that the patient had become depressed after her children moved out of the house. She had always thought of herself as a "giver" and had felt uncomfortable as she grew older and had to rely more on her children. In addition, she had worked as a nursery school teacher but had been forced to leave her job because of her age and various physical ailments. Her depression had worsened right after she gave up her job and her last child moved out. She was uninterested in introspection and spent most of her therapy time recounting, in a tone of suppressed anger, episodes of her giving to others. The therapist believed that it would be inappropriate for him to help her express the anger because this was a "supportive" therapy, and affect expression, by definition, was not encouraged.

As the therapist described the case, several possibilities emerged. First, the question of expression of anger was reevaluated. The analyst would avoid encouraging such expression in cases in which the anger would lead to structural regression due to loss of a holding introject. The analyst could evaluate expression of anger at both the therapist and outside figures; for some patients, expression of anger might be encouraged for some objects and not for others. In cases in which such expression of anger would not lead to structural regression, there is no reason that the analyst would need to discourage such expression; in fact, expression of anger might be indicated, even in a "supportive" psychotherapy, for certain depressed patients.

Second, for this patient, her self-representation as a helper had sustained her, and its loss was depressing her. It was this self-representation which the therapist decided to "support" in sessions. He did this by discussing with the patient her disappointments and losses, while emphasizing the fact that the manner in which one helps others changes and evolves with adult development and aging. He focused on her reluctance to shift the means of her helping, but he explicitly and implicitly agreed with her self-image as a helper. He listened to her when, at times, she began advising him on his dress and his appearance on the ward; that is, he allowed her to be a helper to him without labeling the behavior resistance and taking away from her in sessions what she was losing in her life. He encouraged her to take a helping role with other patients in ward groups. Finally, as part of her discharge plan, he encouraged her to volunteer at the nursery school.

Thus, in this overall approach, what was supported was the patient's self-representation as a helper. What was expressed was her feelings of loss, including anger about the physical, vocational, and familial changes in her life. What was interpreted was her reluctance to shift to a different way of helping. What was not addressed (but would have been addressed in analysis) was the way in which her self-representation as a helper served to defend against other wishes and self-representations, particularly her dependent longings.

This case provides an example of the way in which psychoanalytic theory can be used to diagnose areas of difficulty (structural and dynamic) and to gear a therapy toward these areas. (Another such example can be found in Knight [1953].) Broad concepts such as support and gratification take on specific meaning in the context of a particular clinical situation. For example, there are those who maintain, almost as a matter of principle, that borderline patients need firm limits and should never be gratified. This may be true for some patients, but it is more often the case that a certain amount of yielding to the patient's preferences is quite necessary.

Certain patients constantly test limits and provoke the therapist to lash back at them under the guise of "firmness." For such patients, an excessively rigid stance that attempts to question each request and maintain firm limits inevitably provokes fury, acting out, and failure to develop insight. The therapist may prefer to accommodate the patient whenever he can, and to build shared positive working capital so that he will be able to draw on some positive experience in those times when it is impossible to oblige the patient and when he believes that there is more to be understood. Thus, in order to choose the occasions when he must frustrate the patient, he must gratify at other times. The analyst must somehow balance between being *solid* but not *rigid*. He must attempt measured, disciplined, theoretically informed gratification, meeting the demands of the patient within the context of insight-oriented psychoanalytic psychotherapy.

Structural versus Dynamic Issues

One aspect of diagnosis is the assessment of the extent to which an issue is predominantly structural (that is, pertaining to deficits in internal structure) or predominantly dynamic (that is, pertaining to difficulties between formed structures, or intrapsychic conflict). Such an assessment strongly influences the overall treatment approach.

> A patient in her 30s was living at home with her mother and had a boyfriend who attended engineering school in another city. The patient was jealous of her boyfriend's friends and feared that he would leave her when he was away from her. She tended to "intrude" on him when they were together on weekends: She felt that she had to know all his thoughts all the time. She also suffered from obsessional thoughts: She would see another man's face on the street; she would imagine that she was a "piece of shit" being flushed down the toilet; she would wonder what it would be like to be a man and have women looking at her; she would wonder what it would be like to be an alien being.
> In sessions, she would leave the door open and would talk so quickly that the therapist was unable to understand what she was saying. She often remained at home, fearing that if she were to go to work, her thoughts would "paralyze" her. She described her mother as "intrusive," going through her clothes and her desk, wanting to know details of her life.

Diagnostically, this patient seems to be more disturbed than the traditional neurotic patient. Her symptoms do not serve to bind her anxiety, and reflect a sense of discontinuity. She does not appear to be someone who is sure of the continuity of her experience who is thinking unwanted thoughts; rather, the thoughts are too effective in disrupting her experience of herself and her life. She fears loss of her boundaries. She is unable to have the door closed with her therapist because she needs a concrete reminder that she can escape from her fears of an engulfing therapist. These fears are experienced as concrete imperatives. They are not symbolic, embedded in a context of reality-testing that would give her some distance and allow her to reflect on the feelings, tolerate and explore the anxiety, and leave the door closed. The anxiety is panic, rather than signal, anxiety.

Given these diagnostic considerations, the therapist's focus is less dynamic than it would be for a neurotic patient. To focus the treatment in the direction of interpreting sexualized fantasies of merger, or to talk about the initial transference to the therapist and the door which she must concretely leave open, would panic the patient at this time. The focus at this point could be toward addressing the patient's structural difficulties, such as helping her to deal with her ego difficulties in relation to her sense of reality (Frosch 1980). Thus the therapist would focus not on the patient's anger, which would lead to further panic and the possibility of further regression, but rather on her fear that her anger will rip her apart. The therapist might do this by asking about her difficulty with continuity, and by noting the points in the session when she needs to speak more quickly. The therapist might look at how the extreme variability in the patient's speech rate reflects her feeling out of control and serves to disorient both patient and therapist. The therapist's acceptance, in addition to his making the behavior an ego-alien subject of reflection by the patient in his presence, supplies a holding function which should help to stabilize the patient. The therapist's equanimity, and his message to the patient that there is insight to be gained and that one can reflect on these feelings, should lead to internalization by the patient of the therapist's perspective, his tranquility, and his continuity. If this serves to decrease the patient's anxiety, then the dynamic issues can be addressed at the patient's pace.

It should be clear, however, that the therapist has not "done" anything extraordinary, anything that would obviate a later focus on dynamic issues and on interpretation of transference. The therapist has not given advice, has not intervened in the patient's outside life, has not told the patient to go to work. He has simply been there, but in a way that attempts to focus on the patient's current area of weakness without precluding the possibility of later dynamic work that would rely more on insight than on internalization for its mutative effect. While the therapist's approach is focused on ego support, the support is part of a broader picture. Within the broader scheme, the therapist is helping his patient adjust to the beginning of a treatment that will progressively focus on dynamic issues, a treatment in which internalization will function as a basis for insight-oriented work. Seen this way, the therapist's focus on ego functions is similar to the analyst's preparatory work in analysis.

Are Conflict and Deficit Approaches Irreconcilable?

The issue of structural versus dynamic emphasis is often an either/or question; one sees things within a deficit or a conflict model. This dichotomy is exaggerated however, and leads to a controversy that is ultimately detrimental to the therapist, who may feel compelled to declare allegiance to a particular model and who thus loses clinical options as a result of this forced choice. The choice is a false one: a patient who has a deficit is probably internally conflicted as well. It is not that conflict does not exist for this patient; rather, it is that the conflict may be different for the more disturbed patient. It may be less a function of conflict between formed intrapsychic structure and more a function of conflict between developmental precursors of internal structure or between inside and outside. The anxiety may be different (annihilation anxiety, along with anxieties over loss of an object, loss of the object's love, and superego anxiety). Finally, the patient's ego structure may be such that he is less well equipped to handle the conflict.

Eagle (1984) has criticized what he believes to be a false dichotomy between conflict and deficit perspectives. He contends, first, that these perspectives are different ways of looking at complex phenomena. For Freud, the structural and dynamic perspectives were complementary. Structural deficits, such as splitting of the ego in fetishism, were dynamically determined. Dynamic conflicts reflected developmental difficulties, including strong and persisting drives and infantile wishes, psychosexual fixations, and ego failures in adaptation. The traumata that are thought to lead to structural deficits always bring with them strongly conflicted wishes and feelings so that, for example, deprived children become conflicted about taking and giving. Eagle (1984) states that ". . . we are most conflicted in the areas in which we are deprived" (p. 130). Thus the therapist's job inevitably requires more than compensating for past parental failure, even in cases of "developmental deficit." Second, Eagle states that contrary to the hypothesis that patients with deficits are primarily concerned with self-coherence while patients with conflict are concerned with drive satisfaction, the two levels are quite connected, in that both conflict and deficit interfere with what is a superordinate aim for everyone: self coherence, continuity, and integrity. Someone conflicted with regard to ego-alien wishes experiences both frustration of wishes and feelings of disunity with regard to self-coherence. While the goal of self-coherence might involve avoiding fragmentation at one developmental level and attempting to unify discordant wishes within a generally cohesive self at another developmental level, for all patients the resolution of conflicting wishes will enhance the integrity of the self.

Third, Eagle believes that to adopt an exclusively deficit point of view is to return to a static, prepsychoanalytic conception of neurosis in which constitutional or environmental deficits result in neurosis. In such a view, the role of the mind as shaping, elaborating, and transforming these factors is neglected. The patient's role in his difficulties is thus deemphasized. Further, the patient's fantasies that he is defective are confirmed, and it becomes more difficult to look at the defensive use of traumatic factors in the patient's current life and at the unconscious fantasies around the traumas and developmental arrests.

Eagle also objects to the dichotomization of treatment conceptions that results from understanding a symptom as either the result of a deficit or the result of conflict. The therapist using the conflict model focuses on interpretation of unconscious conflict, whereas the therapist focusing on a deficit model relies on the relationship itself to be a reparative experience. The idea is for the treatment to compensate for early trauma. Eagle believes, however, that in treatment of the disturbed patient, interpretation of conflict is also useful; whatever the deficit, anxiety and unresolved conflict weaken personality functioning, and interpretation of conflict strengthens functioning and improves self-cohesiveness.

Eagle argues further that deficit conceptions assume—inaccurately—that the adult patient is frozen at a child's developmental level. But adult narcissism is different from childhood narcissism. Further, there is no evidence that the child needs a certain kind of experience (mirroring, for example) if the self is to develop in a certain way. Theories based on relatively specific hypotheses of the etiology of trauma have very little evidence to support them. Eagle believes that to conceptualize adult pathology in terms of infant development is to adultomorphize the infant with analogies that are superficial and insufficiently substantiated by research. He contends that there is some similarity between adult and childhood states but that they are not identical.

Eagle argues that instead of maintaining a dichotomized view (deficit or conflict, preoedipal or oedipal, for example), the therapist must look at how these viewpoints affect each other. Psychotic and borderline patients do suffer from oedipal conflicts, but these conflicts are heavily influenced by preoedipal concerns. Deficits do not halt development. Rather, early deficits make it more difficult for the patient to negotiate further developmental steps. Healthier patients resolve oedipal conflicts in healthier ways; more disturbed patients deal with the oedipal conflicts in more maladaptive ways. Everyone must face and deal with oedipal conflicts, however, and with later developmental steps.

Preliminary Considerations in Clinical Work

The therapist working with the more seriously disturbed patient faces the difficulty of interpreting dynamic issues in a manner appropriate to a patient who may, because of structural difficulty, be unable to use only interpretation of transference in a context of abstinence. The therapist may find it helpful to consider treatment recommendations from followers of both the deficit and the conflict theories as he approaches this therapeutic task.

Integration of the varying treatment recommendations is facilitated through an overall diagnostic assessment that includes such factors as the nature of the dynamic conflict and the patient's level of ego functioning; any approach must be based on these two variables. While the therapist may choose not to interpret dynamic issues, he cannot do ego supportive work without awareness of these issues since, for example, certain dynamic constellations will lead to patients' wanting help from the therapist (thus facilitating ego support), while others will lead to wishes to defeat the therapist (hindering ego support). The latter dynamic constellations will more likely call for some early interpretive work.

The clinical recommendations to be discussed depend on expansion and amplification of the mutative factors that, as we have discussed, are inherent in the classical analytic situation. Several mutative factors have been discussed, but the two most fundamental are insight through interpretation and some form of internalization, with the two working in tandem. It is assumed that internalization supports and facilitates insight, but does not replace it. Insight may be possible for certain patients only under the condition of a certain form of experience, and it may follow rather than precede certain experiences that themselves have a major mutative effect.

The Therapeutic Relationship

The therapist–patient relationship is the focus of all analytic treatment modalities. In analysis, however, the transferential aspect of the relationship is the focus, and the working-alliance aspect is assumed, while in supportive treatment it is the working alliance that takes center stage. Working alliance is here used to refer to the manner in which the non-analyzed positive therapist–patient relationship is used to facilitate the patient's self-reflection.

Wallerstein (1986) discusses varieties of change in therapy attributable to the positive relationship between patient and therapist. We should be clear that what he is discussing is the manner in which this relationship, which is usually thought to support the frustrations and deprivations in the transference and its interpretation, is here seen as the curative factor in itself. This is the "transference cure," whereby the patient changes to please the therapist. Transference cure holds a place of value in analytic thought equivalent to that of suggestion as a mutative factor. Analysts are against both such "cures" because they are the opposite of change through insight, with corresponding growth and autonomy. In a transference cure, insight is not developed, and the relationship of subject to object is maintained at the regressed pretreatment level. Further, the transference cure is seen as fragile, dependent on a continuing relationship between patient and therapist, and subject to later vicissitudes of the internal object representation.

Wallerstein (1986), however, offers the following observation:

> That this mechanism [transference cure] operated as clearly and as pervasively as it did in so many of our cases (the putatively supportive and expressive alike) was no great surprise. What was surprising, however, was how stable and durable such changes could turn out to be. [p. 690]

These changes also depend on a "corrective emotional experience," but not one in which the therapist plays a transference role. Rather, Wallerstein says, the therapist attempts to maintain a kindly and neutral position without falling into countertransference or role-playing interactions in response to the patient's transference.

It should be emphasized that I am not advocating reliance on a transference cure. Wallerstein is also not advocating such work; he is simply reporting that in the Menninger study such a factor did prove to be a major influence. However, when we distinguish supportive therapy from analysis by noting that in supportive therapy we *use* the transference whereas in analysis we *analyze* the transference, we should understand that using the transference brings us into the realm of transference cure.[2] Wallerstein contends that the Menninger study supports the idea that, regardless of the type of

---

[2] A third alternative, put forth by left-wing analysts, is that the patient–therapist relationship first facilitates structural development and is then, itself, analyzed. Thus the relationship may be unanalyzed at the outset, but it does not remain unanalyzed. This kind of evolution was not an aspect of the treatments reported in the Menninger Study partly because those therapists were attempting to adhere to strict boundaries between psychoanalysis, expressive therapy, and supportive therapy. The mutative role of support and internalization reported by Wallerstein was not built into the therapist's stance; it operated despite the therapist's planned posture. Further, many patients were not able to use interpretation even late in therapy. They were not suitable even for an expanded definition of analytic work.

treatment, the positive transference has an important effect on our therapeutic results.

If the patient is improving largely through a transference cure, how can this improvement be maintained after termination of treatment? In other words, how can internalization of the therapist be encouraged when structural change cannot adapt to this function? (For if this is impossible, then the patient must continue in treatment interminably.) Wallerstein states that some patients in the study became "therapeutic lifers." Others were able to "transfer the transference" to another figure, such as a spouse. With other patients, the neurosis was "displaced into the transference" (Wallerstein 1986, p. 692), which means that the submissive patient submitted to his therapist instead of to others. As part of that submission, the patient became more assertive with others, as a way of transferentially pleasing the therapist. Based on the transference, the patient then attempted new behaviors. If the behaviors were successful, then the gratification achieved, along with the "transfer of the transference," helped the patient to terminate treatment without regressing to a pretreatment level of functioning.

Wallerstein also cites the opposite kind of change, the "antitransference cure," whereby the patient attempted new behaviors so that he could transferentially triumph over the therapist by succeeding in life. Wallerstein further includes the therapist's educative efforts and his helping the patient change his external circumstances (through hospitalization, for example) as examples of the manner in which the therapist supports his patient. In none of these cases was the transference analyzed.

While all of these are means through which the therapist–patient relationship is mutative, no analyst is content to rely on just this. All analysts attempt to achieve more, particularly insight, because insight aids autonomy, internalization, and generalization. Some of the means through which support and gratification are used to facilitate insight will be explored in the remainder of this chapter.

Adjustments

Most therapists find themselves adjusting the treatment to the patient. The more a patient is understood to be functioning at a borderline or psychotic level, the more adjustments the therapist will make.

> These adjustments may consist of such matters as: an initial emphasis upon object relation and ego function rather than drive; dosage of amount of silence; recognition that the more regressive patient at times needs to take some form of action because of the preverbal level of much of the pathology, and that to designate such action as acting out can only lead to a sense of defeat and feeling misunderstood; awareness on the analyst's part that exaggerated drive states are often not the result of instinctual repression, fixation, and regression, but perversion-like attempts to deal with structural impairment of ego functions and object relations; restraint and delay of interpretation of certain behaviors which these patients use to regulate the treatment relationship, such as turning to look at the analyst from the couch and lateness. There are many other ways the analyst adjusts the treatment relationship to the patient's maturational capabilities, often described very inadequately as "helping the patient to feel understood." [Grunes 1984, pp. 126–127]

For Bach (1985), one of the analyst's most important tasks is to help the patient feel that it is *his* treatment. Bach helps the patient with this through restraint, including restraint in interpretation.

> Thus, we start from the not-always-obvious assumption that it is better to have a patient who is trying to reach an analytic situation than to have a patient who refuses to begin treatment, who has left in a rage, or who is locked into an unanalyzable transference. And we begin with the attitude of permitting and encouraging the patient to treat himself in our presence, much as one might allow a child to

play in his parent's presence, or a student to paint in the artist's presence, or a musician to practice in the presence of his teacher without criticism or instruction other than the basic rule. The crucial point is that the patient can only start to reveal his inmost self, to painfully expose himself and to begin to treat himself if he feels that the treatment is *his* rather than ours. Naturally, this does not eliminate resistances magically, but it may help the patient to take responsibility for them and to talk about them rather than making the analyst primarily responsible for ferreting them out. [Bach 1985, pp. 224–225, his emphasis]

Bach does not impose himself on the patient by direct fiat, by fiat disguised as interpretation, or by premature interpretation. He prefers, like Balint (1968), to be unobtrusive. This means that the therapist must allow the patient "to call a spade by any name he wants, and to tilt at windmills until he himself is satisfied that they are not giants" (Bach 1985, p. 235). It involves keeping options open and tolerating regressive transference reactions without either gratifying the patient or prematurely interpreting the transference in an effort to pull the patient up to a higher structural level. Bach works by listening. He follows the patient in the patient's space, which is created by the structure of the analytic situation. The support is in restraint, in understanding, in allowing for the reality of the patient's private world and for its expression without squashing it in a premature attempt at direct gratification or at interpreting it as if the patient were neurotic, thus creating a pseudo-analysis.

Thus Grunes and Bach do not view every symptom manifestation as a sign of interpretable intrapsychic conflict (especially resistance), nor do they see it as a sign of ego weakness that must quickly be supported. They attempt a balance, characterized by restraint, by tolerance, by careful dosage of interpretations, and by helping the patient come to his own conception of the analyst and reality. It might seem that their approach could be understood as encompassed within clinical suggestions such as interpreting adaptive rather than defensive aspects of behavior. They might agree with such an interpretive focus at certain moments in treatment, but they are speaking of something basic and more subtle than a certain interpretive focus. They write of allowing a patient to grow into a relationship with the analyst (who may be experienced as a part-object). Through the relationship, the patient comes to have a sense of himself and then of both himself and the analyst in an evolving developmental process conducted at the patient's pace within what Grunes (1984) terms a "therapeutic object relationship." The analyst's interventions are designed to facilitate this process. While one would then certainly consider whether a given interpretation supports a fragile ego defense, one would consider this not only from the point of view of ego building or of narcissistic development but also from the point of view of the patient's construction and development of object relationships and of his acceptance of reality.

ALLOWING THE PATIENT TO FIND THE THERAPIST

A therapist has been seeing a patient for several years, during which time the patient has had a number of psychiatric hospitalizations and has functioned poorly. The therapist is unexpectedly called away for three months. The patient does not decompensate while the therapist is away, as she had on previous occasions. Rather she begins, for the first time, to take a course and to attempt part-time work. The patient also increases her contacts with friends. At the first session upon the therapist's return, the patient is quiet, hesitant, reluctant to speak openly. The therapist comments on the silence, with little response. She then says that the patient must be angry with her.

This is a questionable intervention. First, the therapist has no material from the patient to support this conclusion. She has reason to assume that the patient would be angry, but she is attempting to deal with "resistance" by interpreting based on a theoretical hypothesis rather than on what the patient has said. It is the therapist's fear, whether or not it applies to the patient. Technically, it might be preferable for the therapist to note the patient's reluctance to speak and then wait for the patient to say more about it.

The therapist's intervention has yet a second difficulty. To interpret the patient's anger so quickly, *without material from the patient*, is to abruptly and one-sidedly draw the patient back into the transference relationship that existed before the unexpected break. While it is possible that the patient's gains were motivated by her wish to deny the therapist's loss, it is also true that for the therapist to plunge in and ignore both the patient's defense and the adaptive results of this defense is at best insensitive and at worst an act that reasserts the therapist's dominance, importance, and omnipotence. It reveals what Balint (1968) has termed an "ocnophilic bias." This is not to say that the patient's steps during the therapist's absence and her reserve during the session did not serve defensive functions, including defense against anger. However, the patient is entitled to defenses and to discuss the positive moves she made in the therapist's absence. These ought not be dismissed as merely defensive. The patient may then move into feelings of anger and disappointment at her therapist, but she will do so at her own pace and under her own direction. To pull the patient into these feelings makes the patient passive, removes her control, and diminishes her attempts at autonomy in the transference; to follow the patient's lead in the session, on the other hand, implicitly supports autonomy in the transference and encourages her adaptive efforts and initiative outside the session.

Variations in Interpretive Focus

Pine has written of the "interpretive moment." For the neurotic patient, the analyst interprets at a time of affect, a time of some defensive openness. Yet this moment, for the more disturbed patient, is apt to be a moment of maximum potential for panic anxiety and associated defenses that make it difficult for the patient to use the interpretation. Pine focuses on various ways to interpret in a manner that recognizes the fragility of the patient's ego, supports the patient's defenses, and yet emphasizes the insight-oriented work of therapy. Pine (1984) suggests four ways of interpreting:

1. "Close off the implicit expectation of patient responsibility for associative response to the interpretation" (p. 58).
   In treatment with the neurotic patient, the analyst attempts to be brief in his remarks and is silent after he speaks, with the expectation that the patient will associate to what he has said. However, the more seriously disturbed patient may panic in reaction to the interpretation and may feel alone with his disturbing feelings. Thus Pine suggests making the interpretation, but in a more lengthy manner and in a way that explicitly supports the patient by saying (in the length of speech and in the content of what is said) that the therapist will not leave the patient alone to deal with the newly interpreted content but will be there with him as they look at it together.

2. "Strike while the iron is cold."
   With the neurotic patient, the analyst's timing is crucial, since he wants to interpret at a point of maximum conflict. However, the borderline or psychotic patient is likely to panic at such a point. Thus Pine (p. 60) suggests interpreting at a later time, when the patient is more defended and more likely to be able to handle the interpretation.

3. "Increase the patient's relative degree of activity vis-à-vis the interpretive content."
   The classical analytic situation puts the patient in a formally passive position (he lies on the couch, free asso-

ciates, cannot see the analyst, and so on), which encourages regression (p. 62). Yet the patient is also expected to be able to move from such passivity to psychological activity—that is, to attempt to understand, with the analyst's help, what he has said. This capacity for regression in the service of the ego is one of the qualities that determine analyzability. In the more seriously disturbed patient, the movement from experience to thought and from formal passivity to cognitive activity is difficult. Instead, the regression induced by the couch may be too much for the patient and may lead to further regression. Pine thus attempts to encourage the patient's cognitive activity and control in an effort to avoid overwhelming the patient and to increase the probability that the patient will be able to process the interpretation. He does this, with children and adults, by making statements that allow them to anticipate an interpretation so that they can ready themselves for it. He might say, for example, "I'm not sure about this idea; I'd like you to tell me what you think. It occurred to me that (and he makes his interpretation). Does that sound possible to you?" (p. 64). Such an intervention not only helps the patient anticipate an interpretation and remain in control, but it affirms his right to accept or reject the interpretation and deemphasizes the therapist's omniscience.

4. "Increase the 'holding' . . . aspects of the therapeutic environment" (p. 64).

Pine does this by increasing the amount of speech and by ensuring that his tone is supportive.

The foregoing suggestions are based on the observation that the moment of opportunity for interpretation with the neurotic patient is the moment of heightened vulnerability for the more disturbed patient. For the neurotic patient, the structuring aspects of defense are assumed, and the confining aspect of the defenses are the focus of inquiry. For the more disturbed patient, the structuring aspects are often missing or inadequate. Thus the optimal point for interpretation and the optimal method of interpretation differ for the different kinds of patients. As Pine (1984) writes, "The intent of these variations is to increase the defense and object-relational support structure while increasing the anxiety level (through the interpretation), thus supporting the patients' tolerance for strain at a higher level of demand" (p. 69). However, Pine's focus is always on interpretation.

> [T]he fact that these variations are always around *interpretation* is what, in my experience, prevents the work from ever becoming simply caretaking, in which patient pseudosafety and passivity are the outcomes. For the patient's hand is being held (figuratively, by the style of interpretive intervention) *only* and *always* so that he can take a difficult and threatening next step in the therapy. My impression is distinctly that patients who are worked with in this way feel themselves *supported in hard work* and not just "taken care of by a kindly doctor." I cannot stress this point too strongly. [Pine 1984, p. 66, his emphasis]

The therapist can also work interpretively and supportively by focusing on higher-level defenses. Whereas the analyst in Pine's examples attempts to support the patient's capacity to hear an interpretation, in this latter case it is the interpretation itself which is selected to support a tenuous defense. (The two are not mutually exclusive; while Pine discusses delivery of an interpretation and we are here discussing the interpretation's content, it is understood that delivery and content complement each other.) Such an insight has been termed a "defensive" insight (Wallerstein and Robbins 1956), used to bolster an ego threatened by the failure of repression.

By interpreting upward rather than downward, the therapist can help a patient to use insight in a manner that is both uncovering and yet primarily useful with regard to its defensive aspect. To interpret upward is to interpret the patient's associations in a way that is more socially and intrapsychically acceptable to the ego or the superego. The terms *up* or *down* in this context come from the notions of interpreting "down" and "deep" into unconscious id content, or interpreting "up" into material that is more conscious and acceptable to the ego. However, the therapist is simply varying the levels of an interpretation based on the degree to which the interpretation will be acceptable to the patient at his current level of functioning. For example, a patient's difficulties with his boss could be interpreted as social awkwardness with others, as trouble with authority figures, or as a defense against homosexual attraction, depending on the patient's ego state or on the stage of treatment. A patient's "accidentally" breaking a glass when toasting his father at an honorary dinner may be interpreted downward, as a manifestation of unconscious rage and as a means of focusing the attention from his father to himself, by smashing the symbol that represents his father's honor (the glass/penis). It may also be interpreted upward, as a manifestation of social awkwardness and anxiety stemming from, perhaps, a wish to honor his father and a fear that he won't be able to honor his father properly.

Since associations can always be understood on varying levels, the analyst is free to interpret at the level that he believes will be most acceptable and supportive to the patient. The therapist might choose to interpret upward if he felt that the patient would not only not hear an interpretation directed downward, but might also react to such an interpretation with increased symptomatology and acting out or flight from treatment. Varying the level of interpretation is especially useful when the situation demands that the analyst make some sort of intervention, either because the patient is in crisis or because the analyst wants to say something to encourage the patient to think about his problems in a reflective manner.

Some of these considerations in interpretive focus are evident in the following example.

A female therapist was in her third session with a successful college administrator who came to treatment because of difficulty with her colleagues and her inability to marry or to have an intimate relationship with a man. The patient had a strong temper. She spent some time in the military, where she fought with other people, even striking them and being severely disciplined as a result. She had difficulty acknowledging her temper and usually dealt with it by projection (she felt that others were at fault and that her friends turned against her when she most needed them), and avoidance (she would go off to a vacation home by herself for several days when she felt most stressed).

She began this session by stating that her superior had asked her to discuss her temper in therapy. She then spoke of the past weekend, when she had felt that she was being assertive but others had misunderstood her actions as excessive anger. She mentioned that she had been on a train with her brother and sister-in-law and their baby. They took seats together but another passenger, also looking for a seat, questioned the baby's having a seat. The patient told the passenger to mind his own business and told the conductor that she would pay for the baby's seat. Her brother felt that she had been too rough with the passenger, but she believed that she had been within her rights.

As she spoke, she recalled an incident years ago when her mother had come to the city for a visit. They were taking a taxi, and the driver hadn't followed her instructions as to which route to follow. The patient stopped the taxi in a deserted area and got out, with her mother, in the cold night, necessitating a walk for several blocks to find another taxi. When her mother questioned her stopping in the middle of the ride, and the discomfort and possible danger in their having to walk, the patient became furious at her mother and almost hit her. She needed to leave her mother for several hours in order to calm down.

As she described this incident in the session, she became visibly tense. Her face started to twitch and she shifted from side to side in her chair. She couldn't talk and she couldn't look at the therapist. The therapist asked several questions about how the patient was feeling and about the incident with her mother, but each question increased the patient's obvious anxiety. The therapist was impressed by the patient's anxiety and also by her seeming to be overcome by anger in the session as she recalled her anger about events outside the session. She was in visible agony. The therapist commented on her effort to retain control, in the hope that this intervention, designed to support defense, would encourage the patient's control. Instead, the patient looked more upset and began to speak of people turning against her. Fearing a paranoid episode, the therapist told her patient that they did not have to discuss the matter further at that point, since it seemed to be making the patient too uncomfortable. They could discuss these issues at the patient's own pace. She further suggested that what others saw as part of the problem—her going off by herself when she was upset—was an example of the patient's use of good judgment to control herself in a difficult situation. The patient calmed down briefly, but five minutes later she said that she wanted to leave the session early. The therapist didn't make an issue of this decision.

In the following session, both patient and therapist acknowledged the events of the previous session and agreed that the patient's reaction to stress was a major problem that would be taken up in its own time. The patient reported that she had had a difficult time in the previous session because she didn't fully agree with what seemed to her to be the therapist's assumption that she had used poor judgment and was excessively angry. She felt that the reality circumstances of these events were sufficient to explain her behavior. The therapist didn't contest the patient's assertion, and that session and the next few were spent on other problems.

Several sessions later, the patient opened the session by stating that she had had a "temper tantrum" at work when her boss had asked her to take on new duties. Her boss was disturbed by what had happened and had asked her to think about it. The patient agreed that she was nervous about taking on the additional responsibilities, and that this had contributed to her anger, but she had no idea what had made her nervous. The therapist was uncertain as to how to proceed. The patient had again brought up her anger as a therapeutic issue, but she had brought it up projectively, by stating that her boss had wanted her to discuss it. The therapist considered asking the patient to associate to what she was feeling and thinking when she had the temper tantrum. However, she was afraid that such an approach might precipitate a rerun of the previously described session. She also feared that to assume too quickly that the temper tantrum was the patient's problem might leave her too open to the patient's projection, as had occurred weeks before. She feared that the patient would have difficulty maintaining perspective as she spoke of the incident and that she might react with greater mistrust, anxiety, or flight. (She might have asked why the patient had referred to the incident as a "temper tantrum." This might have helped her to evaluate the patient's ability to discuss the anger and might have avoided projection in the process. If the patient had denied that it was her own definition, the therapist could have refrained from pursuing the issue.)

The therapist decided to focus on the patient's assuming additional responsibility, something she believed that the patient would feel comfortable discussing and "owning," rather than on the *result* of her taking on too much responsibility—the temper tantrum—which was still predominantly ego-alien and more easily projected onto the therapist. From this position, the therapist would remain on the patient's side and the anger would come up in a manner controlled by the patient. If the therapist broached the subject of the patient's anger, she would be more apt to be seen as critical and as the source of the patient's discomfort rather than as a source of comfort and understanding. The therapist would be more easily seen as putting the anger into the patient because the reality of her having brought the subject up would support the patient's projection.

The therapist asked about past situations when the patient had received additional responsibilities. The patient reported that, at such times, she had developed neck cramps and had had several angry outbursts. On further exploration, it turned out that these situations involved separations from others, including moves to graduate school, job transfers from one city to another, and changes in office locations away from colleagues she liked. The therapist suggested that these events might have idiosyncratic psychological meaning beyond that which might immediately meet the eye. In response, the patient began to speak of how she had always felt that she had to perform at an exceptional level and how she had felt that she would not be liked unless she proved herself to be always capable and in control. She then spoke of how ashamed she felt after she became angry with others for not meeting her standards. From this vantage point, she began to speak, hesitantly but a bit more directly, about her angry outbursts. The therapist was careful to stay at the patient's level and to avoid introducing any line of interpretation, specifically about anger, that had not already been mentioned by the patient. She also remained with the theme of performance anxiety and did not interpret downward to speak of separation anxiety.

Increasing the Patient's Activity and Control

The more severely disturbed patient often experiences himself as the victim of those around him, particularly with regard to separation. Separations are fraught with psychological danger; the patient has difficulty with holding introjects to begin with, and the narcissistic rage caused by separation makes maintenance of the holding introject even more difficult. The anger is projected onto the therapist, so that the patient feels angrily, deliberately, and maliciously extruded from the analyst's life. The patient often responds by turning from passive to active. He then gives back to the therapist, measure for measure, what he feels has been given to him, denying the therapist what he feels denied, acting cold to the therapist when he experiences himself as being treated coldly, and so on. We have discussed Pine's attempts to deal with the issue of activity/passivity in the realm of receiving interpretations; here we are discussing this issue with regard to the overall therapeutic approach.

When the patient feels that he is an active participant in setting the ground rules of the therapy, he has less basis for arguing with the therapist that he is the passive victim of an arbitrary structure. The issue will still come up in treatment—this kind of thing cannot be resolved solely by administrative decisions—but there will be less reality support for the patient's contentions and there is likely to be more of a working alliance as the patient's difficulties around separation are examined.

One patient was quite suicidal and vowed to kill herself if she was "pushed out" of a time-limited day treatment program. The staff decided to allow her to fix her own discharge date, within a broad time frame set by the staff in accordance with administrative rules regarding length of stay. It seemed important to her that *she* pick the discharge date, that she be allowed to remain in the program longer than she had expected, and that staff respect her need to move at her own pace rather than at the staff's pace. Once the patient picked a date, she was asked to draw up a set of predischarge activities that would help prepare her for discharge. The patient was able to feel some control over the discharge and was thus able to examine her strong feelings about it. Again, the administrative move was not a panacea, but it did make her paranoid reaction to discharge a bit easier to deal with since she knew that the reality of her circumstances did not fit her fears.

Allowing a patient to participate as fully as possible in decisions about treatment arrangements is also important in private practice, although it is more complicated because the therapist's needs are more pressing with regard to these arrangements in private practice than they are in hospital work. For example, the therapist loses money when a private patient misses a session, but he loses nothing when the patient does not attend a hospital program. It is thus important that the therapist be clear about his own needs, both to himself and to the patient, and that he not attempt to rationalize his needs as being good for the patient. Once therapists are clear about their own needs, they are more able to let the patient participate in areas that are not crucial to their capacity to work.

Bach (1985) discusses the value of letting the patient control the therapy once the therapist has established the conditions that he must have satisfied in order to work comfortably. Bach presents an example in which he allowed a patient to forbid him to speak. Bach allowed this because of his concern that the patient be permitted to create the private world he needed within the analytic hour. This is contrary to the approach advocated by Kernberg, who refuses to allow a patient to exert this sort of control because he views such control as an expression of pathological defenses. Bach's recommendation and rationale are consistent with Loewald's (1951) description of the child's construction of reality. Bach (1985) writes:

> What I have reported, of course, has often been described as an omnipotent transference, an anal-sadistic transference, or a mirroring transference. The aspect I am emphasizing here is the creativity, spontaneity, or voluntary effort involved in the construction of a personal world; it is this that stamps the personal world with the feeling of reality, with the hallmark "this is my world, made by me!" And it is only after this point has been reached, when the person owns his personal world, that

> interpretation in the classical sense becomes useful and
> not simply an interference with the construction of a
> personal reality. [p. 209]

The value of allowing a patient to participate in determining the ground rules thus extends beyond that of facilitating a working alliance, although it is certainly important in that regard as well. More fundamentally, such an attitude allows a patient to come face to face with the limitations and frustrations of reality rather than allowing him to continue to see such frustrations as the result of the therapist's rigidity. It allows the patient to come to accept the reality principle through his own experience, mediated by the therapist's support and presence, rather than to feel that he has submitted to a reality that he does not fully accept.

Certain kinds of stereotyped "empathic" responses (such as "It must feel horrible") tend to increase a sense of passivity. Here, empathy for manifest content (feeling horrible) takes precedence over empathy for preconscious content or for the patient's process of conflict and defense as it is manifest in the transference (for example, "You seem to feel most horrible when you are torn between wanting something extra from me and feeling that if I give it to you, you will have asked too much of me and you'll have to pay a steep price"). In the latter intervention, the patient experiences a sense of active involvement in inner conflict; he is not just the recipient of affect caused by unnamed internal forces.

Advice

In the more supportive psychotherapies, with psychotic patients, advice is sometimes an aspect of treatment. The patient's judgment and reality-testing may be quite poor, and the therapist can be called upon to help the patient with these ego functions.

If the therapist believes that he needs to give advice, he

can first focus on ego functions such as reality-testing and judgment. He can attempt to clarify a situation for the patient and to think it out with him without actually making decisions. That is, he can advise about the process of decision-making rather than the content of the decisions. The therapist can also give advice in a way that attempts to move the therapy along, by helping the patient with reflective awareness. The patient who asks the therapist what he can do about some symptom can be told to notice at what times it comes up or when it gets worse, or what he was feeling or thinking before it started, or what ended it; he can then be told that this will be the subject of future sessions.

Reassurance to a psychotic patient also falls within this rubric. There are times when a patient asks for reassurance and the therapist may feel that it is important to respond. He may believe that an interpretive response would not be helpful and that another form of response is preferable. He ought not reassure the patient about the future ("I'm sure you'll pass the exam," or "I'm sure the baby will be healthy"). Aside from any issues involved in the transference (such as acting like the omnipotent authority who can foresee the future), and aside from ignoring relevant dynamic issues in the patient's request (such as his possible wish for the opposite of what he wants—to fail the exam or his anger toward the baby), there is a more fundamental issue. Any patient will know that the analyst is simply posturing and empty reassurances are never helpful.

Instead, the therapist can decide to reassure the patient by confirming his experience of reality or by giving him information. In so doing, he makes the therapist–patient relationship more real (Tarachow 1962) and also confirms that the patient's judgments, assumptions, hypotheses, and thoughts about his experience are shared by another person and that these are based primarily on secondary rather than primary process. In this case, the support and reassurance is based not on empty promises, but on affirmation of reality. The therapist functions not as an omniscient object, but as a representative of secondary-process functioning in the shared real world, who is able to share the processes by which he comes to certain perceptions and conclusions.

Another way to reassure a patient is through feedback. A borderline patient, would become paranoid and strike people on the street because she thought they were calling her homosexual. At the end of a session in which she had experienced closeness with and dependency on her analyst, she began to fear that she *was* homosexual. She asked whether she appeared homosexual in her dress. The analyst felt pressured to answer the patient; interpretation of the patient's sexualization of dependency had proved inadequate, in itself, to help the patient contain herself away from sessions. The therapist believed that she had to say something or else risk another psychotic episode on the street, with potentially dangerous consequences for the patient. The therapist decided to tell her patient that she did not look homosexual in her dress, that she looked like another of the many young professionals who lived in her neighborhood. The feedback was reassuring to the patient, but it was neither empty (that is, the therapist was not relying on magic in her feedback; she was using her rational assessment) nor global (that is, she did not tell her patient that she was not homosexual, which would have skewed the therapy in an unanalyzable manner). Rather, she said that the patient *appeared unremarkable* in her dress. The remark was meant to help the patient test reality, and it was reassuring because it did just that.

However, the therapist cannot focus exclusively on ego issues (such as reality-testing) and neglect dynamic issues. (This is one of Brenner's [1979] major points.) The therapist might end up reassuring the patient rather than interpreting, but the decision ought to be based on a judgment of the dynamics at that moment.

Another patient's father was dying in the hospital. His psychotic daughter, currently hospitalized on a psychiatric unit, had always had a symbiotic relationship with him. She became convinced that her father was going to live but that she was going to die, of the same ailment that was killing her father. The therapist had allowed her to visit her father in order to come to terms with his illness and to say goodbye. At one point, though, the therapist attempted to deal with her patient's increasingly vivid belief that she too would die, by reassuring her that she and her father were separate people and that she would not die. The patient became furious and stormed out of the session.

One can argue that the reassurance was not successful because it contradicted the other aspect of the therapist's treatment plan—that of letting the patient visit her dying father. Why let her visit? To help her, through her own reality-testing, see that her father was dying and to enable her to accept it on her own, based on her own evidence. She would come to terms with reality at her own pace. The therapist's job, then, was not to force reality upon her prematurely, but to sit with her, listen to her, and, if necessary, interpret pathological defenses against her coming to terms with what she experienced through her own eyes and ears. Interpretation of gross denial would be an example of such work. When the therapist told the patient that she and her father were separate, she was imposing her own reality on the patient (rather than helping the patient see how she, the patient, was ignoring her own senses) and thereby insulting the patient by too quickly imposing the thought of psychological loss of a symbiotic object. The patient probably felt abandoned as well as angry and fled in a narcissistic rage.

Further, the therapist, by focusing exclusively on ego difficulties (such as reality-testing or judgment), did not allow the patient the opportunity to explore dynamic issues around her father's impending death, such as the guilt provoked by his dying (why him and not her?), her unconscious belief that her love for her father required her to die in his place, and her identification with him. The patient's expressed fear of dying would then be understood not only as a manifestation of symbiotic object relations, difficulty with libidinal object constancy, and annihilation anxiety (that is, ego weaknesses), but also as reflecting the unconscious fantasy that her dying would be an act of love and devotion and that to be separate from her father and to want her own life was a hostile act, a manifestation of ingratitude. The therapist's "ego support" would then be understood by the patient as temptation to separate. These dynamic issues, parenthetically, were probably active throughout the patient's life, as rapprochement crisis issues. To relinquish one's own identity was to retain the object, and to allow the anger connected with the aggressive drive and separation threatened the object.

Thus, the patient's difficulty was not with reality-testing: rather, it was with the internal conflict precipitated by her father's impending death, and its resultant symptomatology (the belief that she would die). The therapist would have done well to work as interpretively as possible with this symptom while continuing visits to the father. He might have focused his questions by discussing the factors that made it difficult for the patient to accept her father's condition. Reality-testing would thus form the context for the question. By asking the patient to focus on her idiosyncratic implications of what is evident to her, as opposed to why she fears her father's death or fantasizes about the death, the therapist assumes the eventual death; the patient, by responding to the question, accepts the assumption that her father is dying. Thus reality-testing is facilitated, but the process of insight-oriented therapy is also facilitated. This focus also allows the patient to concentrate on whichever aspect of the situation she feels most comfortable discussing. The therapist becomes more of an ally rather than one who provokes her facing conflicted feelings before she is ready.

The therapist can also give advice by telling a patient that he wants him to do something, like take medication or be admitted to a hospital. This is a delicate matter with a patient who believes that there is nothing wrong with him, and it can lead to the dissolution of treatment. The therapist must balance sensitivity to the narcissistic wound even as he helps the patient see that he is seriously and dangerously misjudging reality and needs something further (such as medication)—something that will mean to the patient that the therapist is not agreeing with his denial or delusion. This process may take time, and the therapist will have to assess the seriousness of the patient's condition and his own tolerance for stress in order to determine whether he can wait for the patient to agree to take the additional step. If possible, though, it is worth waiting for the patient's voluntary agreement (rather than demanding it of the patient as a condition for continued treatment) so that the patient can actively take responsibility for the decision and for the reality-testing prompting the decision.

The therapist can accomplish this goal by discussing the consequences of the patient's current situation and the factors that interfere with his ability to assess its reality. For example, if the therapist wants the patient to go into a hospital, he can discuss it openly as his possible response to some of the patient's symptoms. He can ask the patient whether he too has been troubled by these symptoms, how he has understood them, what he expects will occur as the situation continues, and what alternative solutions he can suggest. The attempt is to maintain an environment in which both patient and therapist are problem-solving in a mutually cooperative manner, with the therapist interpreting dynamic factors that interfere with this problem-solving. The therapist must attempt to ensure that his suggestions are phrased as possible solutions to a clearly stated problem rather than as authoritarian demands. The patient's responsibility for accepting the existence of the difficulty and for grappling with it is thus emphasized and maintained, and the therapist ensures that he is not cast in the role of ego, with the patient free to play the unrestrained id.

Epilogue

Psychoanalytic theory views unconscious conflict as the primary cause of neurosis. The therapist proceeds by analyzing expressions of, and defenses against, such unconscious conflict as they become manifest in the transference neurosis. Conflict is intrapsychic. That is, it takes place between formed internal structures: id, ego, and superego. Each of these structures, to varying degrees, has its own process of development, and mature structures reflect developmental achievements. If internal structures are not fully developed, then conflict continues. However, there are changes that reflect the lower level of structural development. The kinds of anxieties, the defenses used, the nature of object needs, and the capacities of the ego and superego are different in the more severely disturbed patient, and thus there are differences in type of anxiety, experience of conflict, tolerance of conflict, and manner of dealing with conflict.

Therapists disagree about whether the changes that take place when the patient's psychological structure is less fully developed can best be understood within the conflict model or whether they can be better understood using a deficit model. Some believe that it is a mistake to counterpose conflict models and deficit models. Some acknowledge the importance of conflict but believe that other causes of psychopathology should also be given a central focus. Therapists disagree on whether differences between neurotic patients and those who are more severely disturbed are quantitative or qualitative (for example, whether defenses organized around splitting are different from defenses organized under repression, or whether they are the same, but with a weaker ego). We have seen that different answers to these questions lead to variations in clinical approaches with more seriously disturbed patients.

The degree to which the patient has attained fully developed structure necessarily affects his response to classical analysis, which is predicated on the ability to tolerate and benefit from a transferential object relationship with a neutral and abstinent analyst, controlled regression in a transference neurosis, and analysis of the transference through interpretation. We have determined that noninterpretive factors have always been understood to be operative in analysis, but they have been relegated to the background. We have not had to move them to the foreground because the neurotic patient does not need them to be emphasized.

What happens if the patient does not meet criteria for analyzability? What if, for example, we cannot assume enough autonomous ego functioning to sustain a patient through the development of a transference neurosis and its analysis? For a great number of seriously disturbed patients, this is the case. Some patients cannot develop the illusional, symbolic, play state required for development of a transference neurosis. They remain reality-bound. Others become overwhelmed by their fantasies, fears, and wishes, and they lose contact with reality. In these cases, difficulties in the working-alliance aspect of the therapeutic relationship become prominent, and issues of abstinence, gratification, and the like take center stage. It is easy to say that these patients are not analyzable by traditional means. It is more difficult—

and also more challenging—to find a way for them to become analyzable without violating fundamental tenets of psychoanalysis. This issue has been the focus of this book.

The severely disturbed patient generally requires some modification of technique. The kinds of changes cannot be specified in advance and are not correlated with diagnostic categories. Each patient will have different capacities and difficulties, depending on his own balance of ego and superego strengths and weaknesses, kinds of object relationships, capacity for development and analysis of illusional transference, capacity for trust in the therapist, capacity for regression in the service of the ego, and other factors. One of the most important factors is the patient's motivation for therapy and his desire to change. Such motivation will often sustain a patient through powerful regressive periods. Another factor that affects treatment is the patient's particular dynamic conflict. Certain kinds of conflicts, such as severe superego conflicts leading to negative therapeutic reactions, in combination with structural difficulties, worsen the prognosis.

The therapist must carefully assess these factors. Difficult patients are not necessarily borderline or psychotic; the diagnosis, and any corresponding changes in therapeutic stance, depend on evidence of certain kinds of ego weakness. For some borderline and psychotic patients, little modification in the classical stance will be required. Most will require some therapeutic alterations, however. Changes that move background aspects of the analytic situation into the foreground and that stress the role of object relations in structural development have been stressed throughout these chapters. These changes are made in an effort to help the patient manage a controlled regression, leading to analysis and working through of conflict. Attempts at supportive psychotherapy that do not allow for such controlled regression may offer the patient a certain amount of ego building, and this should not be underemphasized. It is regression, however, and the eventual analysis of regressive transferential experience, which allows the greatest possibility for maximal structural change. The therapist does not have to foreclose work on dynamic issues in order for the ego to be strengthened; these factors may work in tandem.

In this book, I have emphasized the close connection between theory and technique. I believe that theoretical assumptions—which are often implicit and not thoroughly considered—are an important determinant of the therapist's responses to the patient. The therapist who is aware of these assumptions will be better able to be consistent with the patient and will have a broader sense of his treatment options.

Although I have chosen to focus on theory, I believe that, ultimately, the therapist's character is the most important determinant of the success of an analytic treatment. This is true in work with all patients, but it is especially true in work with those who are severely disturbed. The mesh between therapist's and patient's personalities becomes particularly important because of the intense nature of the patient's transference. Therapists differ in their capacity to allow for regressive states, in their capacity to hold the patient through such states without major modifications in the treatment situation, and in their capacity to respond therapeutically to these states.

The topic of countertransference has become a central issue of study precisely because of work with this kind of patient. Many have written sensitively about countertransference reactions (including Adler [1985] and Kernberg [1975, 1984]), but Searles (1965, 1979, 1986) has written most extensively, eloquently, and openly about such reactions.[1]

We have undertaken a comparative analysis of several psychoanalytic models. The connection between theory and technique for four broad models of work with the borderline

---

[1]Searles's short summary paper on work with schizophrenic patients in private practice (1979, Chapter 24) is one of many valuable papers. See also 1965, Chapters 3 and 18.

patient has been stressed. Each of these models provides important insights into problems with the borderline patient. Each has made a major contribution to our understanding and our work. The models lead to different clinical interventions and conceptions of the analyst's stance. They also differ in the potential they offer for further insights. The models of Kernberg, the ego-deficit, and the representational deficit/self deficit psychologists seem to have become closed systems. They lead to relatively predictable behavior by the therapist because of the close connection between their theoretical postulates as to cause of pathology and their corresponding emphases on technique. As Calef and Weinshel (1979) have noted, with respect to Kernberg, and as Reed (1987) has discussed with reference to the self psychologists, their methods of understanding tend to reconfirm their theories.

The situation is somewhat different with the fourth model, modifications of classical psychoanalytic technique. Reed (1987) has emphasized that the focus of clinical work within classical theory is on the *process* by which clinical material is disguised, rather than on *why* it is disguised. She writes that "In classical analysis, theory guides exploration, not explanation" (p. 441). Thus there is more room to be surprised by what one hears from the patient. Yet, even in the fourth model, the way in which exploration is conducted is affected by the analyst's theoretical beliefs.[2]

The connection between theoretical presuppositions and clinical work, while relevant in classical analysis with the neurotic patient, becomes even more important in therapy with the borderline patient. As the patient becomes more

---

[2]One may even argue that, despite Reed's contention, even in classical analysis, the theory strongly indicates what one will find along with how one may look. Abend and colleagues' (1983) book would support this contention, as would definitions of analysis that include postulates regarding beliefs about pathology as well as postulates regarding method.

unanalyzable by traditional means, as he has difficulty with traditional means of exploration, the way in which the analyst believes that he can appropriately respond to the patient and continue to explore—and even the question of *whether* or not he feels he can respond within an analytic framework and continue to explore—will depend on his overall Weltanshauung. The right-wing emphasis in classical analysis has either tended to stress traditional treatment of the borderline patient (Abend et al. 1983) without fully acknowledging the challenges raised by these patients to traditional concepts, or has led to modifications of technique and conceptions of supportive and expressive therapy that are limited in scope, theoretically neglected, and deprecated by most analysts.

The left wing within classical analysis seems to offer the most room for evolution. Whereas the right wing stresses the way in which all patients and analysts must be basically the same if they are to be analyzed, the left wing examines analytic adaptations to the patient's difficulties. The emphasis here is on recognizing the more disturbed patient's difficulties within the analytic framework, determining which elements of the framework are most troublesome for the patient and why, and attempting to adjust those elements to the patient's difficulties. Analysts from this model may use clinical insights from the other models without changing their entire theoretical rubric, however. This group does not turn the borderline patient's difficulties into a new theory of the patient or a new theory of technique. However, they do follow a metapsychological position that differs from that of the right wing and leads to a different conception of the analytic situation within classical analysis.

Brenner and Loewald *do* differ, and their assumptions lead to different analytic possibilities. With regard to the analyst's stance and the working alliance, we have seen that the not-yet-interpreted relationship between analyst and patient can be seen as central and as part of an analytic process, rather than as a deviation from the analytic task. What keeps this within the classical analytic framework is that the relationship functions to facilitate structure formation and analysis of conflict. A relationship that first serves to build greater capacity for interpretation is itself eventually subject to interpretation. The outcome is not a restricted one—a transference cure based on repression and selective identification—but a broad one, similar in its goals to psychoanalysis proper.

As we continue to examine concepts such as the analyst's stance, interpretation, gratification, abstinence, neutrality, transitionality, defense, and reality, we will continue to find room for expansion of theory and technique within the existing analytic framework.

References

Abend, S. M., Porder, M. S., and Willick, M. S. (1983). *Borderline Patients: Psychoanalytic Perspectives*. New York: International Universities Press.

Adler, G. (1974). Regression in psychotherapy: disruptive or therapeutic? *International Journal of Psychoanalytic Psychotherapy* 3:252-264.

——— (1980). Transference, real relationship, and alliance. *International Journal of Psycho-Analysis* 61:547-558.

——— (1985). *Borderline Psychopathology and its Treatment*. Northvale, NJ: Jason Aronson.

Adler, G., and Buie, D. H. (1973). The misuses of confrontation in the psychotherapy of borderline cases. In *Confrontation in Psychotherapy*, ed. G. Adler and P. G. Myerson, pp. 147-161. New York: Science House.

——— (1979). Aloneness and borderline psychopathology: The possible relevance of child development issues. *International Journal of Psycho-Analysis* 60:83-96.

Arlow, J. (1964). Symptom formation and character formation. *International Journal of Psycho-Analysis* 45:151-154.

Arlow, J. (1969a). Fantasy, memory, and reality testing. *Psychoanalytic Quarterly* 38:28-51.

—— (1969b). Unconscious fantasy and disturbances of conscious experience. *Psychoanalytic Quarterly* 38:1–27.

Arlow, J., and Brenner, C. (1964). *Psychoanalytic Concepts and the Structural Theory*. New York: International Universities Press.

Aronson, G. (1977). Defense and deficit models: their influence on therapy in schizophrenia. *International Journal of Psycho-Analysis* 56:11–16.

Atkins, N. B. (1967). Comments on severe and psychotic regressions in analysis. *Journal of the American Psychoanalytic Association* 15:584–607.

Bach, S. (1985). *Narcissistic States and the Therapeutic Process*. Northvale, NJ: Jason Aronson.

Balint, M. (1968). *The Basic Fault*. New York: Brunner/Mazel.

Barkin, L. (1978). The concept of the transitional object. In *Between Reality and Fantasy: Transitional Objects and Phenomena*, ed. S. A. Grolnick and L. Barkin, in collaboration with W. Muensterberger, pp. 513–535. New York: Jason Aronson.

Bellak, L., Hurvich, M., and Gediman, M. (1973). *Ego Functions in Schizophrenics, Neurotics, and Normals*. New York: Wiley.

Bibring, E. (1954). Psychoanalysis and the dynamic psychotherapies. *Journal of the American Psychoanalytic Association* 2:745–770.

Blanck, G., and Blanck, B. (1974). *Ego Psychology: Theory and Practice*. New York: Columbia University Press.

—— (1979). *Ego Psychology II*. New York: Columbia University Press.

—— (1982). Letter to the editor, G. and R. Blanck on "Modes of cure." *International Journal of Psycho-Analysis* 63:87.

Blum, H., ed. (1985). *Defense and Resistance*. New York: International Universities Press.

Brenner, C. (1976). *Psychoanalytic Technique and Psychic Conflict*. New York: International Universities Press.

—— (1979). Working alliance, therapeutic alliance, and transference. *Journal of the American Psychoanalytic Association* 27(Suppl.):137–157.

—— (1982). *The Mind in Conflict*. New York: International Universities Press.

Buie, D. H., and Adler, G. (1973). The uses of confrontation in the psychotherapy of borderline cases. In *Confrontation in Psychotherapy*, ed. G. Adler and P. G. Myerson, pp. 123–146. New York: Science House.

—— (1982). Definitive treatment of the borderline personality. In *International Journal of Psychoanalytic Psychotherapy*, ed. R. Langs, vol. 9. New York: Jason Aronson, 1982–1983.

Calef, V., and Weinshel, E. M. (1979). The new psychoanalysis and psychoanalytic revisionism. *Journal of the American Psychoanalytic Association* 48:470–491.

Casement, P. J. (1982). Some pressures on the analyst for physical contact during the re-living of an early trauma. *International Review of Psycho-Analysis* 9:279–286.

Corwin, H. S. (1973). Therapeutic confrontation from routine to heroic. In *Confrontation in Psychotherapy*, ed. G. Adler and P. G. Myerson, pp. 67–95. New York: Science House.

Curtis, H. C. (1979). The concept of therapeutic alliance: implications for the "widening scope." *Journal of the American Psychoanalytic Association* 27(Suppl.):159–192.

Dickes, R. (1967). Severe regressive disruptions of the therapeutic alliance. *Journal of the American Psychoanalytic Association* 15:508–533.

Druck, A. B. (1978). The role of didactic group psychotherapy in short-term psychiatric settings. *Group* 2:98–109.

—— (1982). The role of the psychoanalytically oriented psychotherapist within a therapeutic community. *Psychiatry* 45:45–59.

—— (1987). The psychoanalytic position. *Contemporary Psychotherapy Review* 4:80–95.

—— (1988). The classical psychoanalytic stance: what's love got to do with it. In *Love: Psychoanalytic Perspectives*, eds. J. Lasky and H. Silverman, pp. 213–227. New York: New York University Press.

Eagle, M. (1984). *Recent Developments in Psychoanalysis*. New York: McGraw-Hill.

Eissler, K. R. (1953). The effect of the structure of the ego on psychoanalytic technique. *Journal of the American Psychoanalytic Association* 1:104–143.

Fox, R. P. (1984). The principle of abstinence reconsidered. *International Review of Psycho-Analysis* 11:227–236.

Freedman, N. (1985). The concept of transformation in psychoanalysis. *Psychoanalytic Psychology* 2:317–339.

Freud, A. (1946). *The Ego and the Mechanisms of Defense.* New York: International Universities Press.

Freud, S. (1899). Screen memories. *Standard Edition* 3:303–322.

—— (1904). On psychotherapy. *Standard Edition* 7:257–268.

—— (1909). Notes upon a case of obsessional neurosis. *Standard Edition* 10:155–318.

—— (1910a). The future prospects of psychoanalytic therapy. *Standard Edition* 11:139–151.

—— (1910b). Observations on "wild" psychoanalysis. *Standard Edition* 11:219–227.

—— (1912a). The dynamics of the transference. *Standard Edition* 12:97–108.

—— (1912b). Recommendations for physicians on the psychoanalytic method of treatment. *Standard Edition* 12:109–120.

—— (1913). On beginning the treatment: further recommendations on the technique of psychoanalysis I. *Standard Edition* 12:121–144.

—— (1914). Remembering, repeating, and working through: further recommendations on the technique of psychoanalysis II. *Standard Edition* 12:145–156.

—— (1915). Further recommendations in the technique of psychoanalysis: observations on transference love. *Standard Edition* 12:157–171.

—— (1916). Introductory lectures on psychoanalysis, #23. *Standard Edition* 16:358–377.

—— (1919). Lines of advance in psychoanalytic therapy. *Standard Edition* 17:157–168.

—— (1926). Inhibitions, symptoms and anxiety. *Standard Edition* 20:87–174.

—— (1937a). Analysis terminable and interminable. *Standard Edition* 23:216–253.

—— (1937b). Constructions in analysis. *Standard Edition* 23:257–269.

Friedman, L. (1969). The therapeutic alliance. *International Journal of Psycho-Analysis* 50:139–153.

—— (1978). Trends in the psychoanalytic theory of treatment. *Psychoanalytic Quarterly* 47:524–567.

Frosch, J. (1967a). Severe regressive states during analysis: introduction. *Journal of the American Psychoanalytic Association* 15:491–507.

—— (1967b). Severe regressive states during analysis: summary. *Journal of the American Psychoanalytic Association* 15:606–625.

—— (1980). Neurosis and psychosis. In *The Course of Life, vol. 3*, eds. S. I. Greenspan and G. H. Pollock, pp. 381–407. Washington, DC: National Institute of Mental Health.

—— (1983). *The Psychotic Process.* New York: International Universities Press.

Gill, M. M. (1951). Ego psychology and psychotherapy. *Psychoanalytic Quarterly* 20:62–71.

—— (1954). Psychoanalysis and exploratory psychotherapy. *Journal of the American Psychoanalytic Association* 2:771–797.

—— (1984). Psychoanalysis and psychotherapy: a revision. *International Review of Psycho-Analysis* 11:161–179.

Giovacchini, P. L. (1982). Structural progression and vicissitudes in the treatment of severely disturbed patients. In *Technical Factors in the Treatment of the Severely Disturbed Patient*, ed. P. L. Giovacchini and L. B. Boyer, pp. 3–64. New York: Jason Aronson.

Gray, P. (1973). Psychoanalytic technique and the ego's capacity for viewing intrapsychic conflict. *Journal of the American Psychoanalytic Association* 21:474–494.

—— (1982). "Developmental lag" in the evolution of technique for psychoanalysis of neurotic conflict. *Journal of the American Psychoanalytic Association* 30:621–656.

Greenacre, P. (1971a). The fetish and the transitional object. In *Emotional Growth*, pp. 315–334. New York: International Universities Press.

—— (1971b). The transitional object and the fetish: with special reference to the role of illusion. In *Emotional Growth*, pp. 335–352. New York: International Universities Press.

Greenson, R. R. (1967). *The Technique and Practice of Psychoanalysis.* New York: International Universities Press.

Grunes, M. (1984). The therapeutic object relationship. *Psychoanalytic Review* 71:123–143.

Gutheil, T., and Havens, L. (1979). The therapeutic alliance: contemporary meanings and confusions. *International Review of Psycho-Analysis* 6:467–481.

Hartmann, H. (1950). Comments on the psychoanalytic theory of the ego. In *Essays on Ego Psychology*, pp. 113–141. New York: International Universities Press, 1964.

——— (1952). The mutual influences in the development of ego and id. In *Essays on Ego Psychology*, pp. 155–181. New York: International Universities Press, 1964.

——— (1955). Notes on the theory of sublimation. In *Essays on Ego Psychology*, pp. 215–240. New York: International Universities Press, 1964.

——— (1958). *Ego Psychology and the Problem of Adaptation.* New York: International Universities Press.

Havens, L. (1976). *Participant Observation.* New York: Jason Aronson.

Hoffman, I. Z. (1983). The patient as interpreter of the analyst's experience. *Contemporary Psychoanalysis* 19:389–422.

Hurvich, M. (1985). Traumatic moment, basic dangers, and annihilation anxiety. Paper presented to the New York Freudian Society, New York, May.

Jacobson, E. (1954). Transference problems in the psychoanalytic treatment of severely depressive patients. *Journal of the American Psychoanalytic Association* 2:595–606.

——— (1967). *Psychotic Conflict and Reality.* New York: International Universities Press.

——— (1971). *Depression.* New York: International Universities Press.

Kernberg, O. F. (1975). *Borderline Conditions and Pathological Narcissism.* New York: Jason Aronson.

——— (1976). *Object Relations Theory and Clinical Psychoanalysis.* New York: Jason Aronson.

——— (1977). Structural change and its impediments. In

Borderline Personality Disorders, ed. P. Hartocollis. New York: International Universities Press.

―――― (1980a). *Internal World and External Reality*. New York: Jason Aronson.

―――― (1980b). The development of intrapsychic structures in the light of borderline personality organization. In *The Course of Life*, vol. 3, ed. S. I. Greenspan and G. H. Pollock, pp. 349–366. Washington, DC: National Institute of Mental Health.

―――― (1984). *Severe Personality Disorders*. New Haven: Yale University Press.

―――― (1985). Object relations theory and character analysis. In *Defense and Resistance*, ed. H. Blum, pp. 247–271. New York: International Universities Press.

―――― (1986). Identification in psychosis. *International Journal of Psycho-Analysis* 67:147–159.

―――― (1987a). Projection and projective identification: developmental and clinical aspects. *Journal of the American Psychoanalytic Association* 35:795–819.

―――― (1987b). Interview. *Contemporary Psychotherapy Review* 4:1–33.

Khan, M.M.R. (1979). *Alienation in Perversions*. New York: International Universities Press.

Knight, R. P. (1953). Management and psychotherapy of the borderline schizophrenic patient. *Bulletin of the Menninger Clinic* 17:139–150.

Kohut, H. (1968). The psychoanalytic treatment of narcissistic personality disorders. *The Psychoanalytic Study of the Child*, 23:86–113.

―――― (1971). *The Analysis of the Self*. New York: International Universities Press.

―――― (1972). Thoughts on narcissism and narcissistic rage. *The Psychoanalytic Study of the Child* 27:360–400. New Haven: Yale University Press.

―――― (1984). *How Does Analysis Cure?* Chicago: University of Chicago Press.

Kohut, H., and Wolf, E. S. (1978). The disorders of the self and their treatment: an outline. *International Journal of Psycho-Analysis* 59:413–426.

Langs, R. (1981). Modes of "cure" in psychoanalysis and psychoanalytic psychotherapy. *International Journal of Psycho-Analysis* 62:199–214.

—————— (1984). Letter to the editor, G. and R. Blanck on "modes of cure." *International Journal of Psycho-Analysis* 63:87.

Langs, R., and Stone, L. (1980). *The Therapeutic Experience and Its Setting*. New York: International Universities Press.

Laplanche, J., and Pontalis, J. B. (1973). *The Language of Psychoanalysis*. New York: W. W. Norton.

Leites, N. (1977). Transference interpretations only? *International Journal of Psycho-Analysis* 58:275–287.

Levy, S. T. (1985). Empathy and psychoanalytic technique. *Journal of the American Psychoanalytic Association* 33:353–378.

Lichtenberg, J. D., ed. (1987). How theory shapes technique: perspectives on a clinical study. *Psychoanalytic Inquiry* 7:141–299.

Lichtenberg, J. D., and Slap, J. W. (1973). Notes on the concept of splitting and the defense mechanism of the splitting of representations. *Journal of the American Psychoanalytic Association* 21:772–787.

Lipton, S. (1977). The advantages of Freud's technique as shown in his analysis of the rat-man. *International Journal of Psycho-Analysis* 58:255–273.

—————— (with reply by M. Kanzer) (1983). A critique of so-called psychoanalytic technique. *Contemporary Psychoanalysis* 19:35–52.

Little, M. (1985). Winnicott working in areas where psychotic anxieties predominate. *Free Associations* 3:9–42.

Loewald, H. (1951). Ego and Reality. In *Papers on Psychoanalysis*, pp. 3–20. New Haven: Yale University Press, 1980.

—————— (1952). The problem of defense and the neurotic interpretation of reality. In *Papers on Psychoanalysis*, pp. 21–32. New Haven: Yale University Press, 1980.

—————— (1960). On the therapeutic action of psychoanalysis. In *Papers on Psychoanalysis*, pp. 221–256. New Haven: Yale University Press, 1980.

—— (1962). Internalization, separation, mourning, and the superego. In *Papers on Psychoanalysis*, pp. 257–276. New Haven: Yale University Press, 1980.

—— (1971). On motivation and instinct theory. In *Papers on Psychoanalysis*, pp. 102–137. New Haven: Yale University Press, 1980.

—— (1973a). Comments on some instinctual manifestations of superego formation. In *Papers on Psychoanalysis*, pp. 326–341. New Haven: Yale University Press, 1980.

—— (1973b). Ego organization and defense. In *Papers on Psychoanalysis*, pp. 174–177. New Haven: Yale University Press, 1980.

—— (1973c). On internalization. In *Papers on Psychoanalysis*, pp. 69–86. New Haven: Yale University Press, 1980.

—— (1978). Instinct theory, object relations, and psychic structure formation. In *Papers on Psychoanalysis*, pp. 207–218. New Haven: Yale University Press, 1980.

—— (1978). The waning of the Oedipus complex. In *Papers on Psychoanalysis*, pp. 384–404. New Haven: Yale University Press, 1980.

—— (1980). *Papers on Psychoanalysis*. New Haven: Yale University Press.

Mahler, M., Pine, F., and Bergman, A. (1975). *The Psychological Birth of the Human Infant*. New York: Basic Books.

McDougall, J. (1980). *Plea for a Measure of Abnormality*. New York: International Universities Press.

Meissner, W. W. (1984). *The Borderline Spectrum*. New York: Jason Aronson.

Modell, A. H. (1976). "The holding environment" and the therapeutic action of psychoanalysis. *Journal of the American Psychoanalytic Association* 24:285–307.

—— (1978). The conceptualization of the therapeutic action of psychoanalysis. *Bulletin of the Menninger Clinic* 42:493–504.

Myerson, P. (1973). The meanings of confrontation. In *Confrontation in Psychotherapy*, ed. G. Adler and P. G. Myerson, pp. 21–37. New York: Science House.

—— (1981). The nature of the transactions that occur in other than classical analysis. *International Review of Psycho-Analysis* 8:173–189.

Ogden, T. (1979). On projective identification. *International Journal of Psycho-Analysis* 60:357–373.

———— (1982). *Projective Identification and Psychotherapeutic Technique.* New York: Jason Aronson.

Pine, F. (1974). Libidinal object constancy. In *Psychoanalysis and Contemporary Science* 3:307–313. New York: International Universities Press.

———— (1976). On therapeutic change: perspectives from a parent–child model. In *Psychoanalysis and Contemporary Science* 5:537–569. New York: International Universities Press.

———— (1979). On the pathology of the separation-individuation process as manifested in later clinical work: an attempt at delineation. *International Journal of Psycho-Analysis* 60:225–242.

———— (1984). The interpretive moment: variations on classical themes. *Bulletin of the Menninger Clinic* 48:54–71.

———— (1985). *Developmental Theory and Clinical Process.* New Haven: Yale University Press.

Poland, W. S. (1984). On the analyst's neutrality. *Journal of the American Psychoanalytic Association* 32:269–299.

Porder, M. (1987). Projective identification: an alternative hypothesis. *Psychoanalytic Quarterly* 3:431–451.

Pruyser, P. W. (1975). What splits in "splitting"? *Bulletin of the Menninger Clinic* 39:1–46.

Reed, G. (1987). Rules of clinical understanding in classical psychoanalysis and self psychology. *Journal of the American Psychoanalytic Association* 2:421–446.

Safire, W. (1986). Lov'd I Not Honor More. *New York Times,* May 23, 1986.

Schafer, R. (1983). *The Analytic Attitude.* New York: Basic Books.

———— (1985). Wild analysis. *Journal of the American Psychoanalytic Association* 33:275–299.

Schaffer, N. D. (1986). The borderline patient and affirmative interpretation. *Bulletin of the Menninger Clinic* 50:148–162.

Schlesinger, H. J. (1969). Diagnosis and prescription for psychotherapy. *Bulletin of the Menninger Clinic* 33:269–278.

Schwaber, E. (1983). Psychoanalytic listening and psychic reality. *International Review of Psycho-Analysis* 10:379–392.

Searles, H. F. (1965). *Collected Papers on Schizophrenia and Related Subjects.* New York: International Universities Press.

—— (1979). *Countertransference and Related Subjects.* New York: International Universities Press.

—— (1986). *My Work with Borderline Patients.* Northvale, NJ: Jason Aronson.

Sechehaye, M. A. (1951). *Symbolic Realization.* New York: International Universities Press.

Shapiro, T. (1984). On neutrality. *Journal of the American Psychoanalytic Association* 32:269–282.

Silverman, D. (1986). A multi-model approach: looking at clinical data from three theoretical perspectives. *Psychoanalytic Psychology* 3:121–132.

Silverman, L. H. (1984). Beyond insight: an additional necessary step in redressing intrapsychic conflict. *Psychoanalytic Psychology* 1:215–234.

Steingart, I. (1983). *Pathological Play in Borderline and Narcissistic Personalities.* New York: Spectrum.

Stolorow, R. D., Brandchaft, B., and Atwood, G. E. (1987). *Psychoanalytic Treatment: An Intersubjective Approach.* Hillsdale, NJ: Analytic Press.

Stolorow, R. D., and Lachmann, F. M. (1980). *Psychoanalysis of Developmental Arrests.* New York: International Universities Press.

Stone, L. (1954). The widening scope of indications for psychoanalysis. *Journal of the American Psychoanalytic Association* 2:567–594.

—— (1961). *The Psychoanalytic Situation.* New York: International Universities Press.

—— (1981). Notes on the noninterpretive elements in the psychoanalytic situation and process. In *Transference and Its Context*, pp. 153–175. New York: Jason Aronson, 1984.

—— (1984). *Transference and Its Context.* New York: Jason Aronson.

Tarachow, S. (1962). Interpretation and reality in psychotherapy. *International Journal of Psycho-Analysis* 43:377–387.

——— (1963). *An Introduction to Psychotherapy*. New York: International Universities Press.

Tolpin, P. (1978). The borderline personality: its makeup and analyzability. In *Advances in Self Psychology*, ed. A. Goldberg, New York: International Universities Press.

Torrey, E. F. (1983). *Surviving Schizophrenia*. New York: Harper & Row.

Waelder, R. (1936). The principle of multiple function: observations on overdetermination. *Psychoanalytic Quarterly* 5:45–62.

Wallerstein, R. S. (1969). Introduction to panel on psychoanalysis and psychotherapy. *International Journal of Psycho-Analysis* 50: 117–126.

——— (1985). Defenses, defense mechanisms, and the structure of the mind. In *Defense and Resistance*, ed. H. Blum, pp. 201–225. New York: International Universities Press.

——— (1986). *Forty-two Lives in Treatment*. New York: Guilford.

Wallerstein, R. S., and Robbins, L. L. (1956). Concepts, Part IV. *Bulletin of the Menninger Clinic* 20:239–262.

Wexler, M. (1951). Schizophrenia: conflict and deficiency. *Psychoanalytic Quarterly* 20:62–71.

——— (1971). Schizophrenia: conflict and deficiency. *Psychoanalytic Quarterly* 40:83–99.

Willick, M. (1985). On the concept of primitive defenses. In *Defense and Resistance*, ed. H. Blum, pp. 175–200. New York: International Universities Press.

Winnicott, D. W. (1951). Transitional objects and transitional phenomena. In *Through Paediatrics to Psychoanalysis*, pp. 229–242. New York: Basic Books.

——— (1954). Metapsychological and clinical aspects of regression within the psycho-analytical set-up. In *Through Paediatrics to Psychoanalysis*, pp. 278–294. New York: Basic Books, 1975.

——— (1975). *Through Paediatrics to Psychoanalysis*. New York: Basic Books.

Zetzel, E. (1970). The analytic situation and the analytic process. In *The Capacity for Emotional Growth*, pp. 197–215. New York: International Universities Press.

Index